Industrial innovation and environmental regulation

The research in this volume originates from joint research by UNU-INTECH (now UNU-MERIT) and Canada's International Development Research Centre, (IDRC) which examined how environmental regulations interact with trade and innovation policies. Since the early 1970s a series of highly publicized environmental accidents and persistent problems such as acid rain and surface- and groundwater contamination in numerous industrialized and less industrialized countries have led to a proliferation of legislative measures to curb pollution at the business enterprise and public utility levels. The volume combines theoretical and conceptual analysis with empirical case studies of particular firms and industries in Argentina, Taiwan, Nigeria, Japan and Canada.

UNITED NATIONS
UNIVERSITY

UNU-MERIT

Industrial innovation and environmental regulation: Developing workable solutions

Edited by Saeed Parto and Brent Herbert-Copley

International Development Research Centre
Ottawa – Cairo – Dakar – Montevideo – Nairobi – New Delhi – Singapore

United Nations University Press

TOKYO · NEW YORK · PARIS

The views expressed in this publication are those of the authors and do not necessarily reflect the views of the United Nations University or IDRC.
IDRC shares non-saleable digital rights to this volume.

International Development Research Centre
PO Box 8500
Ottawa, ON, Canada K1G 3H9
E-mail: info@idrc.ca
http://www.idrc.ca/
ISBN (e-book) 978-1-55250-296-9

United Nations University Press
United Nations University, 53-70, Jingumae 5-chome,
Shibuya-ku, Tokyo 150-8925, Japan
Tel: +81-3-3499-2811   Fax: +81-3-3406-7345
E-mail: sales@hq.unu.edu   general enquiries: press@hq.unu.edu
http://www.unu.edu

United Nations University Office at the United Nations, New York
2 United Nations Plaza, Room DC2-2062, New York, NY 10017, USA
Tel: +1-212-963-6387   Fax: +1-212-371-9454
E-mail: unuona@ony.unu.edu

United Nations University Press is the publishing division of the United Nations University.

Cover design by Mea Rhee

Printed in Hong Kong

ISBN-13: 978-92-808-1127-8
ISBN-10: 92-808-1127-4

Library of Congress Cataloging-in-Publication Data

Industrial innovation and environmental regulation : developing workable solutions / edited by Saeed Parto and Brent Herbert-Copley.
    p.   cm.
  Includes index.
  ISBN-13: 978-9280811278 (pbk.)
  ISBN-10: 9280811274
  1. Environmental policy—Case studies. 2. Industries—Environmental aspects—Case studies. 3. Technological innovations—Case studies.
4. Environmental management—Case studies. I. Parto, Saeed.
II. Herbert-Copley, Brent, 1960–
GE170.I49 2007
363.7′05—dc22   2006032036

Contents

List of tables and figures

Tables

Contributors

John O. Adeoti holds a PhD in Economics from Maastricht Economic Research Institute on Innovation and Technology (MERIT), Maastricht University, the Netherlands and is a Senior Research Fellow at the Nigerian Institute of Social and Economic Research, Ibadan, Nigeria.

Jonathan R. Barton is Senior Research Associate at the School of Development Studies, University of East Anglia. He has done extensive work on industry and environmental regulation and maintains an interest in broad political geography issues, including patterns of the Twentieth Century Anglo Southern Cone trade and commerce.

Anthony Bartzokas is Professorial Fellow and PhD Programme Coordinator at UNU-MERIT and a faculty member at the Department of Economics, University of Athens, Greece. His work in recent years has focused on trajectories of technological change, with special reference to the role of financial markets, industrial organization and environmental regulation in developed and industrializing countries.

Daniel Chudnovsky holds a DPhil in Economics from Oxford University. He is Professor at the University of San Andrés and Director at the Centro de Investigaciones para la Transformación (CENIT) in Argentina. He has written extensively on trade, industrial restructuring, foreign direct investment, environmental and technology issues, mostly in relation to Latin America.

John Devlin is Assistant Professor in the International Development Studies Program of St. Mary's University where he teaches development theory, comparative development in Asia and environment and development. His research focus is on comparative environmental and agricultural policy, the state and governance.

Kevin P. Gallagher is Assistant Professor in the Department of International Relations, Boston University and Research Associate at the Global Development and Environment Institute, Tufts University. He serves as an advisor to numerous international organizations, national governments and non-governmental organizations.

Neil Gunningham is an interdisciplinary social scientist and lawyer who specializes in safety, health and environmental regulation. He currently holds Professorial Research appointments in the Regulatory Institutions Network, Research School of Social Sciences, and in the School of Resources, Environment and Society, at the Australian National University.

Brent Herbert-Copley holds a PhD in Political Science from Carleton University (Ottawa, Canada) and is Director, Social and Economic Policy at the International Development Research Centre (Ottawa, Canada). He has worked on industrial environmental management, the political economy of industrial and trade policymaking and the creation of innovative support services for SMEs.

Jan Hesselberg is Professor of Human Geography at the University of Oslo. His research includes rural production processes and levels of living (Botswana and Sri Lanka), poverty and slums in the large cities in the South, and location of

pollution-intensive industries from a North/South perspective.

Rhys Jenkins is Reader in Economics at the School of Development Studies, University of East Anglia. His research has focused on trade and economic development, the role of multinational corporations in developing countries, impact of trade liberalization on local production, and environmental regulation and trade and investment patterns.

René Kemp is Senior Fellow at UNU-MERIT (Maastricht, the Netherlands) and Senior Advisor to TNO-STB. He has published extensively on the topic of environmental innovation and policy instruments.

Hege M. Knutsen is Associate Professor at the Department of Human Geography of the University of Oslo. Her research includes economic development in Asia, industrial upgrading in global networks, informal labour and corporate social responsibility.

Ad Lansink holds a PhD in Chemistry from the University of Utrecht, the Netherlands and was a Member of the Dutch Parliament (Second Chamber) from 1977 to 1998. "Lansink's Ladder", based on prevention and re-use of waste, was adopted by the Dutch Parliament in 1979.

Derk Loorbach is a Researcher for the Dutch Research Institute on Transitions, Erasmus University, the Netherlands. His current research is focused on the development of transition management in theory and practices.

Andrés López is Principal Researcher in Centro de Investigaciones para la Transformación (CENIT) and Associate Professor, University of Buenos Aires. He has published extensively on economics of innovation and technical change, foreign direct investment and development issues.

Saeed Parto is Senior Researcher in Economic Governance at the Afghanistan Research and Evaluation Unit (Kabul, Afghanistan) and visiting Lecturer at the Faculty of Arts and Social Sciences, Maastricht University. He holds a PhD in Human Geography from the University of Waterloo.

Shanshin Ton is Associate Professor at Feng Chia University in Taichung, Taiwan. Dr Ton's research is focused on environmental engineering.

Chih Chao Wu is Associate Professor at Feng Chia University in Taichung, Taiwan. Dr Wu's research is focused on environmental engineering.

Nonita T. Yap is Professor at the School of Environmental Design and Rural Development at the University of Guelph (Canada). Her research includes the role of technology in environmentally sustainable development and the role of public policy in influencing technology choices in countries of South and South-East Asia, Central and South America and Southern Africa.

Masaru Yarime holds a PhD from the University of Maastricht, the Netherlands. Currently he is Research Associate of the Research Center for Advanced Science and Technology of the University of Tokyo.

List of acronyms

ABCSD	Argentine Business Council for Sustainable Development
AOO	Afval Overleg Orgaan (Netherlands; specialized agency set up by VROM – the Ministry of Environment)
AOX	absorbable organic halides
APEC	Asia-Pacific Economic Cooperation
APO	Asian Productivity Organization
BCPPDP	British Columbia Pollution Prevention Demonstration Project
BMBF	Bundesministerium für Bildung und Forschung (German Ministry for Education and Research)
BOD	biological oxygen demand
BOF	basic oxygen furnace
CANACEROL	Cámara Nacional de la Industria del Hierro y el Acero (Mexico's national association for the iron and steel industry.)
CAVA	Concerned Action on Voluntary Approaches
CBC	Conference Board of Canada
CED	Commission for Environmental Cooperation
CEPA	Canadian Environmental Protection Act
CFC	chlorofluorocarbon
CIP	clean in place
CLC	Canadian Labour Congress
CMRH	Dutch Environmental Advisory Board
COD	chemical oxygen demand
COMAH	Control of Major Accident Hazards (European Union)
CONACYT	El Consejo Nacional de Ciencia y Tecnología (Mexico's national council for science and technology)

CONCAMIN	Confederación de Cámaras Industriales de los Estados Unidos Mexicanos (Mexican federation of industrial associations)
CP	cleaner production (pollution prevention)
CRTK	community right to know
CSIS	Center for Strategic and International Studies (USA)
CSS	corporate synergy system
CTMP	chemo-thermo-mechanical pulping
CTOT	Canadian Trade Office in Taipei
DRI	direct reduced iron
DTO	Defensie Telematica Organisatie (Dutch sustainable technology development programme)
EAF	electric arc furnace
ECF	elemental chlorine-free
EEC	European Economic Community
EKC	environmental Kuznets curve
EMAS	European Eco-management and Audit System
EMS	environmental management system
EOP	end-of-pipe
ENGO	environmental non-governmental organization
EPA	Environmental Protection Administration (Taiwan)
EPA	Environmental Protection Agency (USA)
EU	European Union
EZ	Ministry of Economic Affairs (Netherlands)
FAO	UN Food and Agriculture Organization
FCT	Federal Capital Territory (Nigeria)
FDI	foreign direct investment
FEPA	Federal Environmental Protection Agency (Nigeria)
FIEL	Fundación de Investigaciones Latinoamericanas (fund for Latin American economic research)
FIPREV	NACEC (North American Commission for Environmental Co-operation) fund for pollution prevention projects in Mexican small- and medium-sized enterprises
FUNTEC	Fundación Mexicana para la Innovacíon y Transferencia de Tecnología en la Pequeña y Mediana Empresa (Mexican fund for technology transfer in small- and medium-sized enterprises)
GATT	General Agreements on Tariffs and Trade
GBN	Green Business Network
GDP	gross domestic product
GLPPC	Great Lakes Pollution Prevention Centre
GMP	good manufacturing practice
HACCP	hazard, analysis and critical control points
HCFC	hydrochlorofluorocarbon
HFC	hydrofluorocarbon
IDB	Industrial Develoment Bureau (Taiwan)
IDRC	International Development Research Centre (Canada)
INDEC	Instituto Nacional de Estadística y Censos (Argentinean national institute for statistics and censuses)

INEGI	National Institute for Statistics, Geography and Information Systems (Mexico)
INPO	Association of Nuclear Power Producers (USA)
ISI	Fraunhofer-Institut für Systemtechnik und Innovationsforschung (Germany)
ISTC	Industry, Science and Technology Canada
ITRI	Industrial Technology Research Institute (Taiwan)
IWM	industrial waste minimization
JEC	Joint Economic Committee (USA)
JIT	just in time
JPEC	NACEC's Joint Public Advisory Committee
LCD	liquid crystal display
LNV	Ministry of Agriculture (Netherlands)
LPFO	low pour fuel oil
MAN	Manufacturing Association of Nigeria
MITI	Ministry of International Trade and Industry (Japan)
MNC	multinational corporation
MOEA	Ministry of Economic Affairs (Taiwan)
NACEC	North American Commission for Environmental Cooperation
NAFTA	North American Free Trade Agreement
NCCP	National Centre for Cleaner Production
NGO	non-governmental organization
NIDO	Nationaal Initiatief Duurzame Ontwikkeling (Dutch national initiative for sustainable development)
NIS	National Innovation System (Mexico)
NISER	Nigerian Institute of Social and Economic Research
NMP	National Environmental Policy Plans (Netherlands)
NPI	National Pollutant Inventory (Australia)
NPCA	Norwegian Pollution Control Authority
NRL	National Reference Laboratory (Nigeria)
NSST	National Secretariat of Science and Technology
NVVP	Perspectievennota Verkeer en Vervoer (new national plan for traffic and transport in the Netherlands)
OECD	Organization for Economic Cooperation and Development
Paprican	Pulp and Paper Research Institute of Canada
PCB	polychlorinated biphenyl
PET	polyethylene terephthalate
PP	pollution prevention
PPMP	Pulp and Paper Modernization Program
PT	particulate matter
PVC	polyvinyl chloride
R&D	research and development
RIVM	Rijksinstituut voor Volksgezondheld en Milieu (Dutch national institute for public health and the environment)
SBR	sequence batch reactor
SCBL	Stichting Centraal Bureau Levensmiddelenhandel (Dutch foundation of food retailers)

SMEs	small and medium-sized enterprises
SVM	Stichting Verpakking and Milieu (Dutch foundation of packaging and the environment)
TAPs	technical assistance providers
TCF	totally chlorine-free
TCPS	Texas Center for Policy Studies
TMP	thermo-mechanical pulp
TNC	transnational corporation
TQC	total quality control
TQM	total quality management
TRI	Toxic Release Inventory (USA)
TSS	total suspended solids
UABR	upflow anaerobic sludge blanket reactor
UNEP	United Nations Environment Programme
UNIDO	United Nations Industrial Development Organization
UNU-INTECH	United Nations University Institute on New Technologies
US-AEP	United States-Asia Environmental Partnership
VAM	Vuilafvoer Maatschappij (Netherlands association for waste removal)
VROM	Netherlands Ministry of Housing, Spatial Planning and the Environment (which succeeded VoMill)
VVAV	Vereniging van Afvalverwerkers (Netherlands association of waste removal workers)
WBCSD	World Business Council for Sustainable Development
WIR	Wet Investeringsregeling (Netherlands investment regulation law)
WTO	World Trade Organization

Preface

Policy instruments to control industrial pollution are all based – implicitly or explicitly – on an assumption that public policy can alter the extent and direction of technological change in industry, either by promoting the diffusion of existing technologies, encouraging the development of new technological solutions or stimulating firms to engage in incremental improvements to products or production processes.

Yet it is only in the last few years that we have begun to amass a body of empirical evidence on the links between environmental regulation and innovation. This is true in both developing and developed countries. However, the efforts to synthesize and analyse the available empirical data have to date focused largely on issues of instrument choice, notably the debate over the relative merits of "command and control" regulations versus market-based instruments such as pollution charges and tradeable emissions permits. Policy makers in the environmental or innovation fields thus have little basis on which to assess the likely influence of regulation on the innovation process in particular firms and industries.

This volume approaches the issue from a different perspective. It examines the way in which environmental regulations interact with the characteristics of particular industrial sectors and firms in different socio-economic systems to influence the development of environmental technologies. The focus, in other words, is less on the design of optimal environmental policy measures and more on understanding how environmental regulations fit into an overall innovation system, complete with context-specific institutional landscapes. This volume explores the scope for integrating environmental and innovation policymaking processes. The view adopted in compiling this volume is that the regulation-environmental innovation nexus can be more comprehensively investigated through understanding the formal and informal institutions that govern and transform industrial activity over time.

The volume combines theoretical and conceptual analysis with empirical case studies of particular firms and industries in both industrialized and developing countries. It concludes with a discussion of implications for environmental and innovation policy, based in part on the proceedings from the workshop held during 4–5 March 2002 in Maastricht, the Netherlands. The workshop involved researchers as well as public-sector officials responsible for environmental or innovation policy in countries included in the study.

This project is a collaborative initiative between the United Nations University's Institute on New Technologies (UNU-INTECH) and the International Development Research Centre (IDRC), Canada. It draws in particular upon research supported by INTECH and by IDRC, along with contributions from other experts in the north and the south.

Brent Herbert-Copley
Saeed Parto

Introduction

Saeed Parto

Since the industrial revolution and until around the mid 1960s, the environment and environmental issues were viewed as secondary to economic development and technological progress. A polluted river or lake or ravaged countryside was a sign of progress and prosperity. The full extent of the negative impacts of industrial activity was unknown and therefore not a policy concern at any level. The environmental awareness that began in the 1960s culminated in a series of national and international forums on the links between economic development and the environment and the importance of environmental protection at a global scale. There was increasing recognition that the unprecedented environmental problems of the time had been caused by accumulated pollution from intensive industrial activity over many decades; pollution that contaminated food, fodder and water resources and endangered humans and other species.

The current focus on the environment and environmental protection has its roots in the period between 1965 and 1970. A series of highly publicized environmental accidents and persistent problems such as acid rain and surface- and groundwater contamination in numerous countries in the industrialized North led to a proliferation of environmental groups, followed by a series of legislative measures aimed at curbing pollution at the business enterprise and public utility levels. The period of politicization that ensued saw environmental non-governmental organizations (ENGOs) and business corporations pitted against each other as the main protagonists, with governments often acting in a catch-up mode initially

1

and later as the arbitrator of the conflicts. By the late 1990s these roles had evolved in many industrialized and industrializing countries. Many governments had begun a move away from introducing reactive and output-oriented regulations to deal with acute environmental problems and toward interactive regulatory regimes and process-oriented regulations. Many business enterprises employed highly sophisticated techniques to manage their environmental impacts and undertook lobbying to ensure that environmental regulations caused minimal interruption to normal business activity. In the meantime, NGOs in some industrialized countries made themselves available to work with willing government and private-sector actors toward meeting shared environmental objectives.

Although the history of environmental regulations goes back a few centuries, the modern era of environmental regulation began in the early 1970s. Since then environmental regulation (or the threats thereof) has been used with increasing intensity and sophistication as a main instrument of steering the behaviour of economic agents in industrial production. The purpose of environmental regulation has been to coerce producers of goods and services into internalizing environmental costs of production. These attempts have not gone without facing opposition on practical and ideological grounds. For example, a report by the United States' Joint Economic Committee (JEC) in 1996 argued that as far as firms were concerned, environmental regulations were no different from taxes as they were both costs to be incurred over and above the "normal" production costs. Furthermore the report argued that environmental regulations were not conducive to innovation because "the very nature of innovation is its unpredictability [and] future innovations cannot be directed by bureaucrats" (JEC, 1996: 2).

The arguments for environmental regulation are usually based on what has come to be known as the "Porter hypothesis". In addition to recognizing the need for environmental regulation to address acute and chronic environmental problems, Porter (1991, 1996) and Porter and van der Linde (1995) push the envelope further by suggesting that at least in some sectors carefully designed environmental regulation as a key feature of industrial policy can increase firm competitiveness by encouraging innovation in environmental technologies. This could be particularly the case if environmental regulations are products of interactive and systems-based policy thinking and policymaking. Whether environmental regulation leads to more or less innovative activity remains a contested issue among commentators from government, industry and academia, however.[1] There are numerous case studies in support and rejection of the Porter hypothesis.[2] Interestingly, in some cases the hypothesis is used to argue for (unregulated) environmental management through voluntary initiatives by firms since the potential economic advantages of cleaner production are viewed as providing sufficient motivation for firms to clean up and potentially innovate to protect the environment.[3] Regardless of orientation, all the arguments and counter arguments are premised on the recognition that environmental regulations represent a significant factor in shaping the environmental behaviour and economic performance of industrial firms and in setting the parameters that determine the environmental sustainability of the economic system.

As far as the interplay between environmental regulation and innovation is concerned, three overlapping features of the Porter hypothesis are worth highlighting.[4] First, the hypothesis emphasizes outcomes and not processes and thus excludes process innovation. Second, regulations may constrain "normal" profit-making activity and force firms to explore uncharted profit-making territories and to become innovative in taking advantage of new opportunities. Finally, environmental regulations could act as shocks to the normal operations of the firm, inducing it to innovate for compliance and profit maximization. The economic costs and regulatory ramifications of these outcomes have important implications for innovation policy. However, these features of the hypothesis are difficult to investigate systematically (Jaffe and Palmer 1996) due to the inadequacies of the available data and are perhaps best tested in context-specific case studies. In addition, the Porter hypothesis rather neglects the institutional context of environmental innovation since Porter, like most of his critics, views the regulations-innovation nexus in a linear fashion and as something that is singularly "good" or "bad" for innovation, competition and sustained economic growth.

A broader view of environmental regulations characterizes them as one element in a plethora of "institutions" that collectively structure social interactions and economic transactions through redefining (or steering) firm behaviour and economic activity as a whole. Some have argued that the new environmental awareness among economic actors, the proliferation of new or adapted technologies to address environmental problems, and reduced materials use combined with evolving environmental regulations constitute "ecological modernization" of industrial activity (see Mol and Sonnenfeld 2000; Murphy 2000)[5] while others have used the term "transition" (see Kemp, this volume) to conceptualize this transformation. A key point of departure for the proponents of ecological modernization theory and transitions is that improvements in environmental well-being can be achieved through technological advances and other forms of innovation leading to increased efficiency in systems of production and consumption.

The (largely) retrospective perspectives of ecological modernization and transitions are based on the transformation process to which the environmentalism of the 1970s has been subjected. The loosely organized and NGO-based environmental movement of the 1970s had become, by the late 1980s, a largely institutionalized source of information dissemination on significant environmental issues for a host of actors, including regulatory agencies. By the early 1990s it had become apparent that many of the environmental problems targeted by policymakers required more than end-of-pipe solutions and incremental innovation. Increasingly, environmental scholars and policymakers were using such terms as paradigm shift, regulatory reform, regulatory regime change, structural transformation and ecological modernization.

For the most part the new vocabulary was more reflective of the political implications of environmental protection and environmental policy-making. The move toward liberalization coupled with the continued failure of the market to protect the environment as a public good resulted in a dialogue involving the private and public interests on the role of governments in environmental protection and improvement. "Transition management", adopted as a policy style by the Dutch government, and ecological modernization, adopted by the red-green German government since 1998, are products of this dialogue in the European context. Elsewhere, numerous countries in the north and south have adopted environmental policies and issued comprehensive formal statements on their commitment to environmental protection and sustainable development.

The complexities of the environment-economy relationships disallow "one-size-fits-all" solutions to similar environmental challenges in different contexts. It would be naïve to expect that the Dutch or the German deliberative policy styles could be readily adopted by other countries since there are fundamental differences among the modes of governance and stages of economic development that characterize the different nation states. To be successful, an environmental policy has to resonate with the formal and informal institutions through which governance is exercized. The long tradition of democratic and participatory modes of governance in Nordic and western European countries is not present in many countries experiencing similar environmental challenges. For example, in Taiwan (see Yap et al., this volume) environmental policy, much like other policies, is implemented in a top-down fashion by a rather paternal state apparatus that systematically induces firms to invest in process and product innovation including environmental technologies. Historically, inducement in the case of Taiwan has employed both regulatory and non-regulatory incentives.

Regardless of how regulatory and other changes have come about in each of the cases in this volume, it is clear that in every case a transition or a significant degree of ecological modernization has taken place. The transformation in each case has been problem-driven and, in some cases, achieved through deliberate planning. For example, as Chudnovsky and Lopez illustrate in chapter 3 the structural transformation of the Argentinean industry took place in response to exogenous economic factors but yielded direct environmental benefits as various sectors needed to modernize in order to remain competitive. The need for modernization led many firms to adopt technologies with superior environmental performance. A similar point is made by Herbert-Copley (this volume) in the case of Canada's pulp and paper industry. The case studies in this volume illustrate the need to adopt a non-linear perspective on the evolution of environmental regulatory change and environmental innovation. To attend to this need we utilize the notion of transitions and draw on the institutionalist literature to provide a more encompassing view of the environment-regulation nexus.

The remainder of this introductory chapter is organized as follows. We reconceputalize the notion of transitions from systems and institutional perspectives and then proceed to provide a summary of the case studies to underline the extent to which the notions of transitions and institutional change can assist us to understand environmental regulatory change and its implications for environmental innovation. One important caveat in our conceptualization is that we adopt a wide definition of innovation to include novelty not only in products and processes but also in policymaking styles.

A systems-based view of transitions

A transition is a process of change through which society, or a subsystem of society, moves to a different stable state. A transition is induced through interplays of social, economic, ecological, technological and institutional developments (Rotmans, Kemp and van Asselt 2000). Transitions are evolutionary phenomena embodied in systemic processes that combine new and old elements to generate a new regime or state through a relatively rapid and sometimes chaotic process. The concept of transition thus articulated is firmly rooted in the development of complex systems (Nicolis and Prigogine 1989; Kay 1991), which holds that under certain conditions open systems will ultimately move away from equilibrium and will establish new stable structures. The development of complex systems is characterized by phases of rapid (re)organization leading to steady states, which after a period of relative calm tend to lose their stability and move toward rapid reorganization to constitute a new dynamic equilibrium.

The organization/disorganization/reorganization process that characterizes a given (sub)system may be continuous or catastrophic, but is in both cases evolutionary in that at no time are all total system components "stationary". In addition, each new state has elements or remnants of past states and thus there are no entirely "new" states. Some steady states may be more stable than others, however. A transition is thus said to occur when a new (significantly different) dynamic equilibrium is reached (Rotmans, Kemp and van Asselt 2001). The occurrence of a transition can be traced to a series of interrelated institutional changes in and between the stable states.

Transitions occur over relatively long periods of time (twenty to thirty years or longer) and the process of change is non-linear and analogous to the development of Kay's (1991) "thermodynamic branches" (figure I.1). To illustrate, the path in figure I.1A depicts a subsystem that develops along a thermodynamic branch toward an "optimum operating point" where the organizing and disorganizing forces neutralize one another and thus stabilize. Changes in the total system can cause a movement from the stable optimum operating point to a new optimum operating point (figure I.1B, 2). This is equivalent to moving to an earlier, less stable, "successional" stage. In figure I.1B, the (sub)system is more volatile at point 2 than at point 1. If this new balance is further disturbed, due to additional changes in the larger system, the subsystem can move away, through a bifurcation, from the original thermodynamic branch to a new branch and onto a new optimum operating point (figure I.1C, 3). Kay (1991) refers to these transitions as "flips" in the subsystem.

Using similar metaphors to Kay's (1991) conceptualization and drawing on "demographic transitions" (Davis 1945), Rotmans, Kemp and van Asselt (2001) hypothesize that transitions consist of the following stages (see figure I.2):

(1) A pre-development phase of dynamic equilibrium where the status quo does not visibly change.
(2) A take-off phase where the process of change gets under way because the state of the system begins to shift.
(3) A breakthrough phase where visible structural changes take place through an accumulation of socio-cultural, economic, ecological and institutional changes that react to each other. During the acceleration phase, there are collective learning processes, diffusion and embedding processes.
(4) A stabilization phase where the speed of social change decreases and a new dynamic equilibrium is reached.

In the predevelopment phase, clearly defined structures, routines and repetitions characterize the subsystem and provide a certain degree of predictability of events. The onset of change is evidenced through the occurrence of unprecedented events, a weakening of existing structures and decreased repetition. "Events" may be significant social, environmental

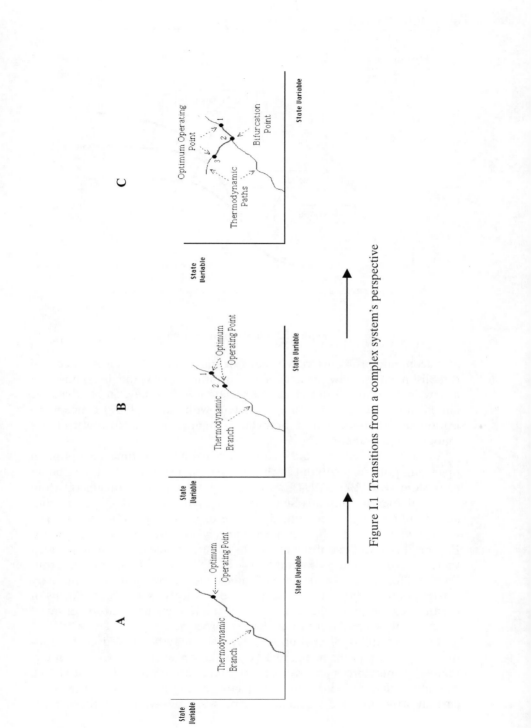

Figure I.1 Transitions from a complex system's perspective

7

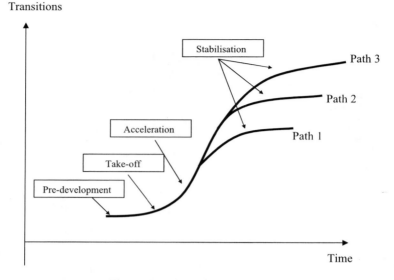

Figure I.2 Phases of transitions

and economic problems, new visions or innovation. The emergence and establishment of new structures and routines mark the beginnings of a new institutional order closely associated with a new, stable dynamic equilibrium. These phases are consistent with Kay's (1991) conceptualization of "thermodynamic branches" (figure 1) and Rostow's (1960) "modernization theory".[6]

A transition may be said to have occurred every time an optimum operating point is instituted in the subsystem. The subsystem may be an ecosystem (Kay 1991, 1994), an organization, a policy domain (Ostrom 1999; Sabatier and Jenkins-Smith 1999), a system of production and consumption, a group, a scientific discipline or a paradigm (Gersick 1991).[7] Change viewed in this light is never entirely constituted of new elements. Rather, it is a product of the processes of variation and selection in which there is heredity and recombination of technologies, ideas, practices, routines and forms. The occurrence of radical technology and its adoption by existing organizations, or the occurrence of surprises and breakdowns of existing regimes, are all events that can catalyze change and the onset of new trajectories and institutionalization processes.

Relative stability of institutional dynamics may be viewed as the optimum operating point in figure I.1C. When an event, or a set of interrelated events, forces a movement to a bifurcation point (figure I.1C, 2), stability is undermined. A new trajectory is more likely to set in when current structures are weakened. If pressure by events on the current structures persists, in all likelihood a new trajectory will result and lead to a new optimum operating point (figure I.1C, 3). In a socioeconomic context, an optimum operating point in figure I.1 is produced through a coming together of scientific knowledge, production process technologies and practices and infrastructure. The move from one optimum operating point to the next is often the product of a co-evolutionary process characterized by the interplay between endogenous and exogenous factors. Analysing transitions and the emergence of environmental innovations requires in-depth knowledge of the endogenous and exogenous factors and the institutionalization processes that they may have set in motion. Stability at the end of a process of reorganization can be traced to specific, socially embedded bodies of knowledge and technologies, habits, norms and forms, which collectively structure economic activity. These structuring phenomena are synonymous with institutions.[8] Transitions become apparent when one compares different periods of stability through historical examination and analysis of quantitative and qualitative empirical data as illustrated in the chapters by Gunningham, Herbert-Copley, Kemp and Parto et al. in this volume.

An institutional view of transitions

An evolutionary approach to innovation recognizes irreversible and continuing processes in time; long-run development rather than short-run marginal adjustments; variation and diversity as the fuel of all evolutionary processes of selection; non-equilibrium as well as equilibrium situations; and the possibility of error-making and non-optimizing behaviour as these are part and parcel of both human learning and evolution itself (Hodgson 1994: 223).[9] Elsewhere, Hodgson (1993: 258) echoes Nelson and Winter (1982) by pointing out that radical change may be a product of gradual change when the cumulative strain of gradual change leads to outbreaks of conflict or crisis in a stable system, resulting in a radical change in actions and attitudes. The cumulative effect of incremental or sudden change over time may culminate in gestalt shifts or "transitions" (Rotmans, Kemp and van Asselt 2001). A transition, or a structural change, such that the mode of production or materials' flow in the economy is fundamentally reconstituted, requires persistent external attractors and responsive internal actors over time to mould the new "instituted process" born of a combination of old and new institutions. As noted earlier, the concept of transition is firmly rooted in the development of complex systems.

Analysing transitions with the intent to identify the causal chain and thus the steering opportunities from a policy perspective requires adopting an evolutionary perspective and a focus on what the economic system "ought to" be doing. Environmental regulations have emerged as structuring phenomena to steer industrial activity away from excessive environmental damage as something that ought to be avoided or minimized. The different types of transition reported in the case studies of this volume have all taken place through "a set of connected changes, which reinforce each other but take place in several different areas, such as technology, the economy, institutions, behaviour, culture, ecology and belief systems" (Rotmans, Kemp and van Asselt 2001: 16). An institutionalist perspective on transitions attaches considerable weight to "historical contingency" that underlies the institutional functionality within a particular historical, social, political and cultural context.

An important feature of managing transitions is the development of alternative technologies and alternative ways of instituting technology.[10] It is worth pointing out that Polanyi (1957) placed great emphasis on the links between policy and technology and how policy, not process, determines alternative technology and alternative ways of instituting technology. A significant part of economic policymaking focused on innovation should thus be about determining the desirability of the technology in question, the institutionalization process(es) required to adopt the technology, and whether or not expectations of adoption and the subsequent changes are realistic – given the institutional context. The institutional context can reveal why people make the choices they do and how deeply felt beliefs or political ideology can shape choice over time. The role of ideology and other beliefs cannot be fully appreciated, however, without digging deeply into how cognitive processes evolve and how learning occurs (North 1993). Thus the frame of reference for economic actors is never a given, but created by (and for) them based on values ranging from deeply felt beliefs, e.g., religious conviction, to opinions about how best to fix a shared problem, such as air pollution. If in the assumption is one of supremacy of the market, it is likely that the ensuing analysis would focus on market "efficiency" rather than material sufficiency.

Transitions are often triggered by external events, such as macroeconomic crises, or shifts in consumer preferences. This is especially the case in the diffusion of ecologically sustainable technologies. The period preceding a transition is characterized by firms, customers, policymakers and other parties all claiming a stake while learning, adapting, negotiating and making compromises with regard to the changes that need to be made and the technologies adopted. In other words, the output characteristics of technologies are socially constructed. We might further conclude that this process is embedded, cumulative, path-dependent, based on changes in existing institutional textures and dependent on windows of opportunity to "lock-in". Each new dynamic equilibrium state has elements or remnants of past states and thus there are no entirely "new" states.

To illustrate, consider the case of the European pulp and paper industry where high levels of chlorine in wastewater discharge from pulp and paper mills acted as the main trigger for the technological transition that ensued (Reinstaller and Kemp 2000; Herbert-Copley, this volume). Two types of technology constituted the policy alternatives within the pulp and paper subsystem. These were: elemental chlorine-free (ECF), which removed only elemental chlorine and was the cheaper and less effective of the two technologies; and totally chlorine-free (TCF) which completely removed chlorine from the process of bleaching. During the 1990s the European pulp and paper industry largely opted for the TCF technology while the North American counterparts widely adopted the ECF. The European subsystem's environmentally superior technological transition may be attributed to the institutional dynamics that underpin the pulp and paper subsystem in Europe. An important characteristic of these dynamics is the central role played by associative institutions, e.g., environmental and non-governmental organizations including industrial associations, in influencing the perception of key actors such as consumers and government policymakers about the desirability of certain technologies.

In Europe, consumer preference played a key role in forcing the adoption of the "cleaner" technology, i.e., TCF, whereas the case of the United States is said to have been centrally influenced by the pulp and paper industry's vested interests resulting in the widespread adoption of the environmentally less benign ECF technology. In the case of Europe, in addition to changes in the existing and new associative institutions one could also detect changes in behavioural, cognitive, constitutive and regulative institutions (table I.1). Arguably, the deeply felt contentions surrounding the ways of doing things (behavioural institutions) in the pulp and paper production process, based on opposing value sets of environmental non-governmental organizations and industry associations (cogni-

Table I.1 Types of institution

Behavioural Institutions: Institutions as standardized (recognizable) social habits – manifest in activities of individuals and groups as reflections of social norms
Cognitive Institutions: Institutions as mental models and constructs or definitions – based on values and embedded in culture
Associative Institutions: Institutions as mechanisms facilitating prescribed or privileged interaction among different private and public interests
Regulative Institutions: Institutions as prescriptions and proscriptions
Constitutive Institutions: Institutions as the bounds of social relations

Based on Parto (2005b)

tive institutions) and initiated and fought out through civic and other channels shaped by property-rights structures (constitutive institutions), resulted in a series of legislative measures (regulative institutions) that transformed interrelations at the individual, organizational and societal levels. These developments underlined new key factors (such as the integrity of the ecological system) to be considered in economic policy-making and political discourse with significant ramifications for the socio-economic, political and cultural spheres.

A second example is provided through the evolution of waste management in the Netherlands (see Parto et al., this volume). In this case two transitions seem to have occurred since around 1900. The first transition signalled a move from unregulated handling of waste to centralized systems of collection and disposal. The stabilization period for the first transition appears to have been between the 1920s and the 1960s. The second transition began in the 1970s and was to a large extent related to widespread concerns about the state of the environment. This transition was characterized by a move from centralized disposal to central management of waste and was preceded and accompanied by significant changes in production and consumption patterns. The stabilization period for the second transition seems to have commenced in the late 1970s and ended by the mid 1990s. It may be suggested that a third transition, or a period of turbulence preceding a new transition, may have started in the early 1990s. The evidence includes new European Union (EU) directives on waste management, a significant drop in the total volume of non-separated household waste from the peak 1995 level, doubts about the health effects of incinerating waste, and the "entrepreneurial" drive to take advantage of the weak environmental regulations in the former eastern bloc countries as cost effective alternatives to managing wastes domestically.

The evolution of waste management in the Netherlands (Parto et al., this volume), the adoption of new technologies in the pulp and paper industry (Herbert-Copley, this volume) and the ecological modernization of the Japanese chlor-alkali industry (Yarime, this volume) can be understood in terms of changes in the behaviour of agents as well as changes in the structure of the political economy. One may thus underline changes in the perception of an environmental problem (behavioural institutions), emergence of mental models about how things "ought to" be done (cognitive institutions), legislation on how to deal with an environmental problem (regulative institutions), changes in the behaviour of individuals, organizations, and the society in assuming the responsibly about environmental problems (behavioural and constitutive institutions), and the stratification of public and private actors through the formation of alliances and interest groups (associative institutions) ex ante and ex post in each case.[11]

Collectively, the chapters in this volume adopt a broad perspective on innovation as follows. Innovation is viewed as a social process, based on learning and occurring at multiple levels. At the firm level innovation translates into new products, processes and organizational forms. At the policy level innovation manifests as novel ways of experimentation. Innovative policymaking draws on learning from past experiences to carry out new experiments to attain broad societal goals such as pollution prevention, facilitating a shift to new technologies or nurturing additional technologies to support predetermined and desirable development trajectories. In the next section we provide an overview of the chapters and underline some of the key issues raised based on this broader view of innovation. This book is organized as follows.

Summary of chapters

Yap et al.'s (chapter 1) opening argument is that in environmental protection, the innovation process goes beyond the firm and includes government and policy innovation and learning. This chapter's study of Taiwanese firms underlines the importance of adequate national policy, effective regulatory enforcement, and competitive pressures as catalysts for firms to move toward adopting cleaner production methods. Having placed the environment on the economic development agenda, the government of Taiwan has actively pursued the integration of industrial development and environmental protection. The Taiwanese government has managed to create the demand for environmental innovation while providing support for the industry through dissemination of research and development (R&D) findings from government-funded institutions. The government's approach to implementing environmental policy has also been innovative in its own right. One significant policy innovation is the promotion of voluntary initiatives such as ISO 14001 through regulatory and other measures, making Taiwan a country with one of the highest number of firms certified to ISO 14001.

Barton et al. (chapter 2) point out that the dynamics of environmental innovation are best understood at the sectoral level of analysis because sector studies are more likely to reveal the systemic nature of innovation and to generate generalizable findings for further research and policymaking purposes. Barton et al.'s sectoral focus is unique as it transcends national boundaries. In-depth studies of the iron and steel, leather tanning and fertilizer industries in European and several industrializing and transition economies identify industry-specific environmental problems, regulatory responses to these problems and the impact of environmental regulation on the competitiveness of each sector. The starting point in this analysis comprises the southward move of the most polluting segments of pollution-intensive industries, decreased competitiveness of those industries in industrialized European countries, and the increased competitiveness of those same industries in less industrialized countries.

The study by Chudnovsky and López (chapter 3) focuses on the institutional and organizational factors in the diffusion of pollution prevention technologies in Argentina since the early 1990s. After experiencing major pollution problems, a series of regulations were introduced to curb industrial pollution. As with many other less developed economies, environmental regulations had limited success. This was mainly due to inadequate enforcement mechanisms and a lack of "institutional responsibility for environmental management". The environmental regulations were nevertheless used in closing down some of the most polluting firms and forcing other industrial firms to consider environmental management more seriously. The new regulations – coupled with trade liberalization, significant flows of foreign direct investment, and popular sentiment for environmental protection in the mid 1990s – facilitated a move into a new phase in environmental management in the Argentinean industry.

Chudnovsky and López examine this new phase through the interplay between environmental management, innovation and technological modernization activities by Argentinean firms. The findings from two surveys conducted by the authors are combined with information from secondary sources to test Porter and van der Linde's (1995) hypothesis of higher environmental standards as a catalyst for product and process innovation offsets that reduce pollution but also improve productivity through efficiencies in resource use.

Herbert-Copley (chapter 4) examines the response by the Canadian pulp and paper industry to new, stringent environmental regulations introduced in the 1990s. The introduction of the new regulations occurred at a time when the sector was being forced, due to international competitive pressures, to modernize. Using a survey of pulp and paper firms carried out in 1997, this chapter examines how the industry responded to the new regulations and the extent to which other factors shaped the course of this response. The chapter offers two "narratives" of the events that followed the introduction of the regulations. The first narrative points to the historically reactive approach of the Canadian pulp and paper sector to regulatory compliance to underline a needs-based, end-of-pipe oriented strategy of technology adoption rather than continual innovation in environmental management. This reactive approach is also the point of departure for the second narrative, but with an emphasis on process innovation as a result of adopting environmental technologies to address compliance issues.

Gallagher's chapter (5) provides a retrospective account of the events in Mexico since the first liberalization policies were introduced in 1985 to develop a more integrated economy and boost the country's economic growth. In the 1990s Mexico signed to the North American Free Trade Agreement (NAFTA) and entered into the Organization for Economic Cooperation and Development (OECD). Since 1995 Mexico has negotiated over twenty other free trade agreements with other countries. The outcome of these developments has been a more integrated economy with manufacturing exports comprising close to 85% of all Mexican exports. However, the integration has been accompanied by lower than average GDP growth and less than 1% annual per capita income growth since 1985.

In the early days of NAFTA, an assumption by many environmentalists was that the most polluting industries from the north would move to Mexico and thereby export their pollution. Several studies have suggested that the main motivation for industrial firms to move operations from Canada or the United States to Mexico is labour cost minimization. Gallagher points out that Mexico's regulations on pollution prevention are modelled on the United States' regulatory system. The key difference in Mexico is laxness in the enforcement of environmental regulations, making pollution a "bonus" for the environmentally callous industrial firm.

The Mexican government's policy on economic integration has not resulted in technological innovation, or improvements in environmental protection, as had been hoped. In fact, like most developing countries Mexico prioritized economic integration and growth at the expense of environmental protection on the implicit assumption that once a certain level of per capita income has been reached, environmental problems could be more effectively addressed. In 1985 Mexico had a per capita income of US$5,000. With the liberalization policies that ensued from 1985 onwards, there have been only small rises in per capita income while there has been significant environmental degradation. Paradoxically, the financial costs of environmental damage and degradation are estimated at 10% of the GDP from 1988 to 1999, an amount that far exceeds the 2.5% average rate of economic growth.

Adeoti's point of departure (chapter 6) is to question the wisdom of the view held by some economists that environmental policy is the main driver for industrial innovation. Based on an analysis of case study data from Nigerian food processing and textile firms, Adeoti identifies a number of "third-party factors" as key determinants of environmental innovation, in addition to firm-level environmental policy and the regulatory framework. He also points to the importance of existing structures and the institutional context for successful environmental policy development and implementation conducive to environmental innovation. The third-party factors are the combination of influences on polluting firms from such sources as host communities, public corporations affected by private sector pollution, ENGOs, parent company requirements and environmental technology suppliers. A key insight in Adeoti's analysis is that to have maximum effect, environmental regulations have to be designed in recognition of the capacity of affected firms to adapt, economically and technologically.

The capacity for compliance to stringent regulations and to innovate in environmental protection is the main theme of Yarime's analysis (chapter 7). Yarime examines the co-evolution of the Japanese chlor-alkali industry and its regulatory arena since the 1950s. The Japanese government introduced stringent environmental regulations in the 1970s to stop the mercury contamination traced to the chlor-alkali industry. In a top-down manner, a newly appointed Countermeasures Council demanded that the industry install a closed effluent system to contain mercury by the end of 1974. The council also specified the diaphragm process – the only available technology at the time – as the technology to be adopted by the industry. Faced with strong opposition from the industry on the grounds that there were many unresolved technical and economic issues, the government agency moved the date to 1975 for the majority of operations and made a concession to the laggards to install a closed effluent system by March 1978.

Given the tight timetable for the majority of the firms in the sector, many had to imitate rather than innovate to convert their processes and meet regulatory requirements. Once adopted, the diaphragm process turned out to be expensive and produced inferior quality product. Energy consumption of the diaphragm process was significantly higher than the mercury process. At first the government attempted to compensate for the weakened competitive position of the converted firms by organizing a barter system and guaranteed product sales. Sharp rises in energy prices put additional pressures on converted plants leading to additional production costs. This prompted the government to provide compensation to the modified firms by financially penalizing the mercury process firms. The government objective of safeguarding public health and the industry's concern about costs and loss of market share due to inferior quality were clearly not being resolved adequately. A new technology was needed to bring about this resolution and a new approach to policy making had to be adopted.

Gunningham (chapter 8) recognizes the limitations of the command-and-control approach to environmental policymaking, but cautions against dismissing regulations as unnecessary obstacles to economic efficiency as argued by a large number of economists and other commentators. He also recognizes that since the beginning of the 1990s regulatory regimes in general have suffered from shrinking resources, particularly in terms of enforcement. In addition, much of the low-hanging fruit has been picked already, rendering the "first-generation regulations" blunt as tools to achieve economically viable and lasting environmental benefits. The answer according to Gunningham lies in nurturing environmental innovation through "second-generation" regulations, which still require a central but selective role for government but also draw on a range of market and non-market solutions. Gunningham then proceeds to evaluate the main instruments for second-generation regulations, including self- and co-regulation, voluntary agreements, economic incentives, informational regulation, performance- and process-based standards, and regulatory flexibility against empirical findings from a study of the pulp and paper sector in multiple national settings.

Parto et al. (chapter 9) begin with a brief overview of the evolution of the waste arena ("subsystem") in the Netherlands since the mid-nineteenth century. The notion of "transitions" is reconceptualized from a systems perspective in an attempt to represent transitions as more than just a tool for retrospective analysis of past events. Parto et al. state that through historical overviews it is often possible to point to a certain set of developments or events as having constituted a transition. However, policymaking aimed at facilitating transitions requires rather more than retrospective overviews and intuitions on what has already occurred. As well as documenting and understanding how transitions may have occurred, Parto et al. underline the importance of identifying the structural and other factors that lead to transitions. These factors include formal and informal institutions, significant events (including innovations and societal problems) and the processes of institutionalization set in motion by these events.

The authors view institutions as structuring phenomena in transitions and transition analysis. Institutions are defined as multifaceted; durable but evolving social structures made up of symbolic elements, social activities and (sometimes) material resources. Institutions weave together social, economic, environmental and political systems or "spheres". Institutions collectively shape interactions and transactions among economic agents and are manifest at different levels of interrelation and territorial scales of governance. The policy implications (for transition management) of this view of institutions is that to facilitate transitions policymakers need to know what degree of control may be exercised over specific key factors, given the institutional context. To identify and to take advantage of context-steering opportunities, a policymaking arena or subsystem needs to be viewed as a constellation of problems, policies and politics. This constellation can explain when, how and most importantly why significant changes occurred in the subsystem over time.

The chapter by Kemp (10) examines the effectiveness of innovation policies and environmental policy in bringing forth environmental innovations – innovations offering environmental gains relative to existing technologies. Kemp argues that innovation policy is insufficiently oriented toward broader sustainability goals, while environmental policy hardly acts as a pull for innovation to lead to the emergence of new products and processes with environmental benefit. The chapter makes suggestions on how to narrow this gap through "transition management", described as being concerned with altering social trajectories through innovative and interactive policy-making. In transition management the emphasis is placed on process management so as to nurture not one, but a set of preferred options leading to environmentally superior outcomes. Transition management has been adopted by the Dutch government as a steering model for working toward sustainable energy, mobility and agriculture. To make a case for transition management, Kemp examines and compares the German BMBF (Bundesministerium für Bildung und Forschung – German ministry for education and research), the Dutch DTO (Defensie Telematica Organisatie – sustainable technological development) and the Danish Clean Technology Development programmes. These programmes were funded by the three national governments to induce innovation in environmental technologies. The comparison reveals different styles of interaction between policy makers and industry. The Danish programme appears to have had the highest element of mutual learning – having yielded the highest environmental benefits – followed by the German programme. The Dutch programme was successful in yielding environmental innovation but had little impact on policy learning. Drawing on these three cases, Kemp argues that in transition management there is an integrated innovation policy for the environment, supported by programmes that go beyond providing research funding.

In most countries, environmental and innovation policies are not fully or adequately integrated. Yet, it is widely accepted that there is constant interplay between innovation, environmental protection and further innovation. Given that numerous countries, particularly in the north, have at least a formal environmental policy and an innovation policy, it is only the next logical step to attempt to integrate the objectives of the two policies. Innovation policy can be more explicitly directed toward environmental protection by providing support for R&D in the development of environmental technologies, e.g., fuel cells as an alternative to the combustion engine to power vehicles. Environmental innovations such as fuel cells could become economical and institutionalized through regulation and other incentives that steer vehicle makers and users away from gasoline and diesel toward fuel from renewable sources. In managing a transition to a more sustainable technological trajectory, innovation policy on transportation should not focus only on fuel cells but promote a series of more sustainable alternatives, leaving the choice of the fittest alternative technology to the variation/selection process as articulated under "transition management"[12] or as illustrated through the various case studies by the authors contributing to this volume.

The concluding chapter (11) provides a synthesis of the case studies followed by some broad insights into the interplay between environmental regulation, innovation as a process and a policy objective, and the implications for integrated policymaking geared toward better protection of the environment and improved economic performance.

Notes

1. See, for example, Gibson, R. B. (1999). Voluntary Initiatives: The new politics of corporate greening (Peterborough, Ont.: Broadview Press).
2. See, for example, Welford and Starkey (1996) for a selection of the arguments for and against.
3. The oft-cited case example is 3M which reportedly has saved close to $800 million since 1970 through implementing its ambitious "Pollution Prevention Pays" programme.
4. See Welford and Starkey (1996).
5. For more information on ecological modernization theory we refer the reader to Hajer (1995) Jänicke (1991), Mol (2001) and Spaargaren, Mol and Buttel (2000).
6. Rostow (1960) describes economic development as the passage of society through five evolutionary stages: traditional society, the stage of the preconditions for take-off, the take-off stage, the drive to maturity and the age of high consumption as exemplified by modern industrialized states.
7. The metaphors and examples drawn from biology and ecology are used here insofar as they deepen appreciation and understanding of socioeconomic complexities. This selective utilization of other disciplines is consistent with Nelson and Winter's (1982: 11) "Lamarchian" approach.
8. See Parto (2005a) for elaboration and further discussion.
9. This section is based on Parto (2005a).
10. Technology, defined as "the combination of tools, skills, and knowledge ... organized as the industrial arts of a society... [whose] change stimulates creation of new social relationships and thus a new society", is the most emphasized aspect of policymaking in the institutionalist literature (Hayden 1993: 291).
11. See Parto et al. (this volume) and Parto (2005b) for more elaborate discussions of waste management in the Netherlands.
12. See Kemp, this volume, and Parto et al., this volume.

REFERENCES

Davis, Kingsley (1945) "The World Demographic Transition", Annals of the American Academy of Political and Social Science 235: 1–11.

Gersick, C. J. G. (1991) "Revolutionary change theories: A multilevel exploration of the punctuated equilibrium paradigm", Academy of Management Review, 16: 10–36.

Hajer, Maarten A. (1995) The Politics of Environmental Discourse: Ecological Modernisation and the Policy Process, Oxford: Clarendon Press.

Hodgson, Geoffrey M. (1993) Economics and Institutions: Bringing Life Back into Economics, Cambridge: Polity Press.

——— (1994) "Evolution, Theories of Economics", in Hodgson, Geoffrey M., Warren J. Samuels and Marc R. Tool (eds.), The Elgar Companion to Institutional and Evolutionary Economics, Aldershot: Edward Elgar Publishing Limited, pp. 218–223.

Jaffe, Adam B. and Karen Palmer (1996) "Environmental Regulation and Innovation: A Panel Data Study", Working Paper 5545, Cambridge, Mass.: National Bureau of Economic Research.

Jänicke, M. (1991) The Political System's Capacity for Environmental Policy, Berlin: Freie Universität.

Joint Economic Committee (JEC) (1996) "Smothering Economic Growth One Regulation at a Time", Joint Economic Committee Report, available at: http://www.house.gov/jec/cost-gov/regs/cost/regulate/regulate.htm, accessed 15 October 2005.

Kay, James J. (1991) "A Nonequilibrium Thermodynamic Framework for Discussing Ecosystem Integrity", Environmental Management, 15(4): 483–495.

——— (1994) "Some notes on: The Ecosystem Approach, Ecosystem and Complex Systems and State of the Environment Reporting", Waterloo, Ont.: University of Waterloo.

Mol, Arthur P. J. (2001) Globalization and Environmental Reform: The Ecological Modernization of the Global Economy, Cambridge, Mass.: MIT Press.

Mol, Arthur P. J. and David A. Sonnenfeld (2000) "Ecological Modernization Around the World: An Introduction", Environmental Politics 9(1): 3–16.

Murphy, J. (2000) "Ecological modernisation", Geoforum 31: 1–8.

Nelson, Richard R. and Sidney G. Winter (1982) An Evolutionary Theory of Economic Change, Cambridge, Mass.: Harvard University Press.

Nicolis, Gregoire and Ilya Prigogine (1989) Exploring Complexity, New York: W.H. Freeman.

North, Douglass C. (1993) "Douglass C. North – Autobiography", available at: http://www.nobel.se/economics/laureates/1993/north-autobio.html, accessed 15 October 2005.

Ostrom, Elinor (1999) "Institutional rational choice: An assessment of the institutional analysis and development framework", in Sabatier, Paul A. (ed.), Theories of the Policy Process, Boulder, Colo.: Westview Press, pp. 35–71.

Parto, Saeed (2005a) "Economic Activity and Institutions: Taking Stock", Journal of Economic Issues, 39(1): 21–52.

——— (2005b) "'Good' Governance and Policy Analysis: What of Institutions?", MERIT/Infonomics Research Memorandum 2005-001.

Polanyi, Karl (1957) "The Economy as Instituted Process", in Polanyi, Karl, Conrad M. Arensberg and Harry W. Pearson (eds.), Trade and Market in the Early Empires, Chicago: Henry Regnery.

Porter, Michael E. (1991) The Competitive Advantage of Nations, New York: The Free Press.

—— (1996) "What Is Strategy?" Harvard Business Review 74(6): 61–78.

Porter, Michael E. and Claas van der Linde (1995) "Toward a new conception of the environment-competitiveness relationship", Journal of Economic Perspectives, 9(4): 97–118.

Reinstaller, Andreas and René Kemp (2000) "Consumption dynamics in a world of technological regimes. Consumer-driven technical change: Theoretical considerations and a case study on bleaching technology in the pulp and paper industries of Sweden and Austria", Paper presented at the Conference of the European Society for Ecological Economics (ESEE), Wirtschaftsuniversität Wien, 3–6 May 2000, Vienna, 36 pages.

Rostow, Walt (1960) The Stages of Growth: A Non-Communist Manifesto, London: Cambridge University Press.

Rotmans, Jan, René Kemp and Marjolein B. A. van Asselt (2000) "Transitions & Transition Management, the case of an emission-free energy supply", International Centre for Integrative Studies, Maastricht, The Netherlands.

—— (2001) "More evolution than revolution: Transition management in public policy", The Journal of Futures Studies, Strategic Thinking and Policy 3: 15–31.

Sabatier, Paul A. and Hank C. Jenkins-Smith (1999) "The Advocacy Coalition Framework: An Assessment", in Sabatier, Paul A. (ed.), Theories of the Policy Process, Boulder, Colo.: Westview Press, pp. 117–168.

Spaargaren, Gert, Arthur P. J. Mol and Frederick H. Buttel (eds.) (2000) Environment and Global Modernity (London: Sage Publications).

Welford, R., and R. Starkey (1996) Earthscan Reader in Business and the Environment, London: Earthscan.

1

Corporate environmental innovation and public policy: Case studies from Taiwan

Nonita T. Yap, John Devlin, Chih Chao Wu and Shanshin Ton

Technological "innovation" is frequently conceived as the transformation of an idea into a *marketable* product, process or service (See for example Palda 1993; Voyer and Ryan 1994). Indeed "the perspective of a potential market" is posited as "the starting point for the chain of innovation at the firm level" (UNIDO Secretariat 1997: 10). But environmental innovations within firms often do not meet this criterion. Environmental innovations, or "incremental technical change" (OECD 1993), are introduced primarily to reduce the environmental impacts of a manufacturing process or product and not for commercialization purposes (Beise and Rennings 2003). These innovations are therefore not always apparent to external observers. To study environmental innovation it is necessary to work within firms. This chapter analyses environmental innovation in 13 manufacturing enterprises in Taiwan. The study asked whether Taiwanese firms had engaged in environmental innovation, and if so, what form it had taken. The study also considered what factors influenced environmental innovation among these firms.

Previous international studies have suggested that regulations, or what are frequently called "command and control" approaches, have not played an effective role in stimulating environmental innovation (Baas et al. 1992; Hanks 1998; Kemp 2002; Palda 1993).[1] Others assert that the picture is mixed (Ashford 2002; Boyd 1998; Christie et al. 1995; Ecotec 2000; Halme 1995; Hassanali-Bourdeau 2004; Lebourveau 2004; Ministry of Economic Affairs [MOEA] 1999; NUTEK 2003; Tilley 1999; Yap 1988, 2000a; Yap and Heathcote 1995; Yap and Zvauya 1999).

Taiwan has gained a reputation not only as an "Asian tiger" but also as a "developmental state" (Wade 1990; White 1988) where economic growth has been achieved through persistent state policy and regulatory activity successfully undertaken by a state characterized by what is termed "embedded autonomy" by Evans (1996) or "insulation [from the private sector] but not insularity" by Weiss (1998). The study thus considered what role public policy has played in firm decision making, the policy instruments that the Taiwanese state has used to pursue its environmental goals, and whether and how public policy has encouraged environmental innovation.

Environmental innovation, cleaner production and firm behaviour

A waste generator has three options for dealing with waste. One is to dispose of the waste in the easiest and cheapest way possible, i.e., untreated release into the environment through effluent discharge, emission release and/or dumping as solid waste. A second option is to use end-of-pipe approaches to treat the waste prior to release into the environment, thereby bringing hazardous constituents to within legally acceptable levels through dilution, neutralization, solidification or incineration. Any "innocuous" waste can then be landfilled. The third option, the cleaner production option, is to analyse the sources of waste and put in place organizational, process and/or equipment changes to eliminate, minimize, or otherwise control the volume and hazard of the waste. Cleaner production (CP) is based on the simple principle of "continuous application of an integrated preventive environmental strategy to reduce risks to humans and the environment" (UNEP 1994). Applied to production processes, cleaner production is concerned with conserving raw materials and energy, eliminating toxic raw materials, and reducing the quantity and toxicity of all emissions and wastes. Applied to products, a cleaner production strategy focuses on the reduction of the environmental impacts during the entire life cycle of the product from raw materials extraction to the ultimate disposal of the product at the end of its useful life.

Cleaner production innovation among Taiwanese firms is the focus of this paper as it is the only option that provides the opportunity to reconcile economic growth with environmental protection objectives.[2] Some would argue that CP innovation improves the triple bottom line.

Cleaner production improves the financial bottom line by increasing production efficiency and productivity, reducing costs for waste disposal, and reducing liability risks. Unlike end-of-pipe expenditures which are, without exception, sunk costs, CP options are investments with potentially favourable rate of return and short payback periods (Anderson

1998; Baas et al. 1992; Boyd 1998; Cheung 1995; Christie et al. 1995; Ciambrone 1995; EPA 2000; Fischer 2002, 2003; Fresner and Engelhardt 2004; Fryzuk 2005; GLPPC 1994; Gordon and Zettler 2005; Higgins 1995; Kerr et al. 1998; NPCA 1995; Russell 2005; Sarokin et al. 1985; Yap 1988, 2000a; Yap and Heathcote 1995; Yap and Zvauya 1999). CP can also generate revenues from the sale of secondary materials. *Non-product outputs* (wastes) can constitute up to 10 to 30% of production costs depending on the technology used (Kürzinger 2004). CP improves the environmental bottom line by reducing pollution releases to all media – air, water and soil – and reducing the risk of non-compliance. What leaves the plant as a pollutant starts within as a workplace hazard. CP thus improves the social bottom line by improving workplace health and safety (Bennett 2004; Canadian Labour Congress [CLC] 1998).

As shown in table 1.1, all categories of cleaner production involve varying degrees of environmental innovation, either developed internally or acquired from outside the firm. The innovations vary in complexity and cost.

What makes a firm choose one option over the others? Existing literature suggests three somewhat overlapping explanations: self interest (profit maximization), preferences of key actors and social norms. The

Table 1.1 Categories and examples of cleaner production innovations

Good Housekeeping. On-time purchasing of raw materials, proper storage, labelling and handling of materials, eliminating leakages and spills in unit operations, reduced packaging and timely shipment of products.

Process Modification. Multiple and counter current rinsing systems in the metal plating industry; use of supercritical carbon dioxide, near-critical water and carbon dioxide in "gas-expanded" organic liquids as replacement solvents in a variety of chemical reactions and separations.

Recycling. Distillation and re-use of spent organic solvents in the electronic industry.

Resource Recovery. Chromium recovery in tannery wastewater; use of rubber tyres as a fuel supplement in cement kilns.

Materials Reformulation. Shift from organic to water-based paints; use of low toxicity, high surface-active rhamnolipids as replacement biosurfactants in the petroleum, agriculture and cosmetics industry.

Product Substitution. Replacement of PCB in transformers; replacement of heavy metals – lead, chromium and cadmium – in pigments, with calcium, strontium and barium counter ions.

Enhanced Product Durability. Changes in the design, shape or color of packaging materials and/or containers of consumer products to optimize re-use or recyclability.

"self interest" view predicts that a waste generator invariably chooses the least costly option, actual or perceived (Palda 1993; Conference Board of Canada [CBC] 1997; Voyer and Ryan 1994; Walley and Whitehead 1994). The second school posits that corporate decisions are made by specific managers, not by the firm as a unitary entity (Prakesh 2000). The ultimate decision to "green the corporation" depends on the ability of individual social agents of change within the firm to bridge the gap between cognition and action (Corral 2002) and the consensus-building ability of these key employees (Stanwick and Stanwick 1995). The "social norms" school views firm decision-making as multi-stage, and largely driven by the external environment. A firm will consider making changes only when it recognizes that there is problem, for instance because of regulations, demand from consumers, or changes in the competition. It will then seek alternatives. In evaluating its options, several factors are considered. How much investment is required? How does cost compare with the "no change" option? To other investment options? What are the implications on the quality and market acceptability of the existing product? On the level of skill of its workers? On production and delivery schedules? The interplay of these evaluation criteria can be complex, rendering the outcome difficult to predict (Ashford 2002; Boyd 1998; Christie et al. 1995; Ecotec 2000; Halme 1995; Hassanali-Bourdeau 2004; Lebourveau 2004; MOEA 1999; NUTEK 2003; Tilley 1999; Yap 1988, 2000a; Yap and Heathcote 1995; Yap and Zvauya 1999).

Figure 1.1 provides a heuristic framework of the decision-making process of the firm. Reflecting the social norms perspective, decision-making is viewed as an iterative process in five distinct internal stages: problem recognition, search for alternatives, evaluation, decision and implementation. The firm is pictured as being influenced at the different stages of its decision-making by various push, pull and drag factors – regulation, pressure from public interest groups, the media, organized labour, competition, informal systems of authority (i.e., professional, religious or industry associations) and international organizations (e.g., WTO, and in the case of developing countries, donors). The framework depicted in Figure 1.1 suggests that decision-making at the firm level can be influenced by changes in the policy and regulatory environment. The study reported in this chapter sought to determine these influences with respect to environmental innovation in Taiwanese manufacturing firms.

The study

This research covered four counties in central Taiwan with a total population of 5,010,000. The counties were chosen because of the dominance of small and medium-sized manufacturing firms. Taichung County alone

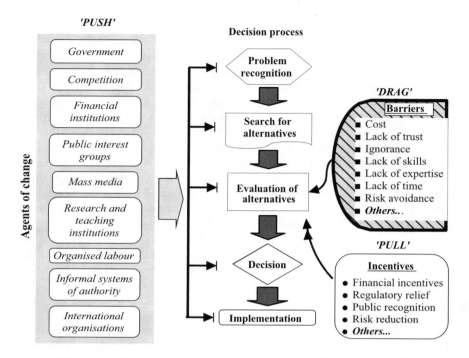

Figure 1.1 Decision-making framework (Adapted from Yap 1988)

is home to over 14,000 factories located in three industrial parks and one export-processing zone (Taichung County [TC] 1999). The case studies included three electronic firms, four textile plants, one food processor, and one electrical equipment manufacturer. Because of the significant wastes generated by the SMEs, four small- and medium-sized establishments located outside industrial parks or an export-processing zone were also included.[3]

The firms were selected based on the following criteria: economic importance, hazard or volume significance of industrial waste generated and willingness to share information with the research team. The following specific questions were examined regarding firm-level decisions: How does the firm deal with its wastes? What environmental innovations have been adopted? What drives decisions? What has been the role of public policy? And, how effective has public policy been?

A combination of primary and secondary research techniques was used. Documents obtained from different institutions – government, industry and non-governmental organizations – were reviewed, industrial establishments visited and plant management and technical personnel interviewed. Interviews were also conducted with twenty key informants drawn from universities, government departments, R&D institutions and industry associations.

Environmental innovations: What and why

All 13 firms adopted cleaner production approaches to varying degrees. Of the 13, 5 had achieved ISO 14001 certification and another 6 were preparing for certification. Table 1.2 provides a profile of the case study firms. Firms 10, 11, 12 and 13 are outside the industrial park. The analysis will focus on the major innovations introduced by these firms and the factors driving the decisions to innovate.

Firm number one, the biggest of the 13 case study firms with 2,000 workers, is a branch plant of a multinational corporation. The manager asserts that the plant has no R&D capacity and hence process changes cannot be made quickly. The firm relies on its employees for suggestions on waste reduction and provides monetary awards for winning ideas. It separates its solid wastes to facilitate recovery and recycling, has adopted a green procurement policy, and has taken measures to minimize water and energy consumption. It has replaced the Freon® spray for the mould package. The firm is certified to BS 7750 and ISO 9002 and claims to be the first company in Taiwan to get ISO 14001 certification. The management cites worker enthusiasm as among the "real benefits" of these changes. While the middle level workers see their involvement as "extra work", the lower level workers apparently welcome "the sense of order and system".

Firm two, also a branch plant of a multinational corporation, did not anticipate difficulties in obtaining ISO 14001 certification because it already has "total quality management" (TQM) and "total quality control" (TQC). Several cleaner production changes had been introduced, costing the company NT$2 million in capital equipment and NT$500,000 in maintenance. Trichloroethylene was replaced with a reusable non-chlorinated solvent; energy consumption was reduced by 13%, water consumption by 37%, gas (hydrogen) by 17% and chemicals by 63%. The changes apparently resulted in savings totaling NT$10 million; more than recovering the cost of ISO 14001 certification. The company provides CP training for its employees, oftentimes sending them to sister plants in the region. It gives monetary awards for good participation in the CP programme. The firm received the National Quality Award from the Ministry of Economic Affairs. The management asserts that they are simply conforming to corporate policy established by the parent company. Interestingly however, firm two landfills its epoxy resin wastes (10 to 15 tons a month) although the same waste is reportedly reclaimed as fuel in its parent plant. It also sends fifty to sixty units of waste fluores-

Table 1.2 Profile of case studies

Firm	Main product	Annual sales/ market	Ownership	No. of employees	Certification
1	cameras	NA/70% export	Japanese	2000	BS 7750, ISO 9002, ISO 14001
2	integrated circuit boards	NA/Export	Japanese	750	ISO 14001, TQM/ TQC
3	LCD	NA/70% for export to HK, Japan, Korea and Germany	National	600	–
4	frozen and dried food products and sauces	NT$150M*/ exclusively domestic	joint Japanese/ Taiwanese	55	HACCP, ISO 14001 planned
5	knitted fabrics	NT$1.1B/88% exported to Hong Kong, People's Republic of China and other Southeast Asian countries	National	150	ISO 9002, ISO 14001 planned
6	dyeing and printing	NT$0.9B/ exclusively domestic	National	400	ISO 9002, ISO 14001
7	textiles	NT$300M/PRC, domestic, Australia	National	184	ISO 9002, ISO 14001
8	textiles	NT$300M/ domestic, Japan and US	National	50	ISO 14001 planned
9	electrical machinery and appliances	NT$100M/ exclusively for export to the USA, the European Union, People's Republic of China and other Southeast Asian countries	National	47	ISO 9002, ISO 14001 planned

Table 1.2 (cont.)

Firm	Main product	Annual sales/ market	Ownership	No. of employees	Certification
10	solar panels	NT$42M/for export to southern Europe and northern African countries	National	14	ISO 9002, ISO 14001
11	aluminium windows	NA/90% domestic, 10% to PRC	National	20	ISO 9002, ISO 14001 planned
12	artificial leather	NT$80.4M/ domestic and PRC	National	18	–
13	plated metal pieces	NA/domestic	National	13	–

*NT$1 = US$0.031 (1999)

cent bulbs every month to the landfill, simply because they "do not have the knowledge to recycle them" (Chang, C. C., Manager, interview, 16 July 1999).

Firm number three is a Taiwanese-owned operation that went public in 1995. The plant manufactures liquid crystal displays (LCDs), 70% of which are exported to Hong Kong, Japan, Korea and Germany. Production waste such as glass is sent to a recycler. The wastes generated in significant quantities in this plant are primarily from packaging, specifically wood pallets, plastic (PET and PVC) and styrofoam. Both plastic and styrofoam wastes are sold to a recycling company. At the time of this research the firm had started to replace organic solvent with ultrasonic and aqueous cleaning agents. The change was expected to be completed in a year. The wooden pallets, generated at a rate of five to six tons a month, are landfilled. The management claimed that it could not find a way to divert this waste from the landfill.[4] It has no plans to seek ISO 14001 certification. "It is too labour-consuming; we have done okay and will do okay without it" (Ho, M. T., Manager, interview, 16 July 1999).

Firm four, on the other hand, decided to seek ISO 14001 certification after only one year of operation. This was considered achievable with little difficulty since the plant had already been certified for ISO 9002, GMP (Good Manufacturing Practice), and HACCP (Hazard, Analysis and Critical Control Points).[5] A joint venture (Taiwanese and Japanese) operation that sells exclusively for the local market, the company appears to seek ISO 14001 certification simply in a spirit of competition with its sister facilities. "We competed with our Japanese sister facility and we beat them to ISO 9002 certification" (Shu, H. T., Manager, interview, 21 July 1999). Preparation for ISO 14001 certification included the implementation of additional cleaner production changes. The facility donates its food waste (100kg/day) to a pig farm and sells its paper packaging materials (1 ton/month) to a recycler.

With firm five, a manufacturer of knitted fabrics with 150 workers, process modification changes introduced resulted in reduced use of several inputs: reaction chemicals by 80%, dye chemicals by 30%, and dispersion chemicals by 10%. The finishing process was automated, reducing resin contamination of the wastewater by 66%. Paper, cardboard, plastic and fibre wastes are sold to a recycler. The company plans to significantly reduce their water consumption (1,600 tons for a daily output of 200,000 yards of fabric) through treatment and a recirculation system. It is collaborating with a research institute to develop biotechnological treatment of its wastewater and eventually to reduce its sludge disposal cost (NT$2,500/ton). The effluent from its wastewater treatment plant has a moderate load of COD (chemical oxygen demand) and is currently discharged directly to canals and reportedly used by farmers for irrigation. It claims to have no product rejects as off-specification products are recycled back into the process. Firm five was certified under ISO 9002 in 1999 and expected ISO 14001 certification within two years. The manager, who proudly stated that he only completed high school, asserted that their ISO 14001 system will be performance- rather than conformance-based ("paper work") (Yap 2000b).

Firm six, a dyeing and printing plant, saw dramatic improvement in product quality after ISO 9002 certification. The ISO 9002 certification drive also drew the management's attention to wasteful processes in the facility. An in-house energy and waste audit identified the characteristics and the sources of its inefficiencies. They initially had to contend with "poor attitude of the workers" toward the programme. However this was overcome through a worker education and a high profile awards – and – penalties programme.[6] The environmental management and quality improvement programme is now implemented through "technical and quality circles". Changes, primarily process modification, were introduced. The switch to a non-carcinogenic dye eliminated all the costs associated with importing, managing and disposing hazardous material. A switch from continuous to batch dyeing allowed for better process control. After dyeing, the whole roll is kept rotating, allowing the dyeing process to complete at ambient temperature, thereby reducing energy consumption. The finishing process was computerized. The reject rate was reduced by 25% in two years; the chemical use was reduced by 30% and resin contamination of wastewater reduced to 2% from 6%. Because the company basically dyes for clients and therefore has a guaranteed market, it was thought that ISO 14001 would not be of any benefit to the company. The management decided to secure ISO 14001 certification nevertheless to "follow the trend" and because the savings from the cleaner production programme reportedly more than covered the cost of certification.

Firm seven, a textile factory, has two full-time and six part-time employees dedicated to R&D. Like other textile factories, the biggest environmental concern is the wastewater. Through process modification and sludge dewatering, the firm has achieved tremendous reductions in the volume as well as the COD and BOD (biological oxygen demand) load of its wastewater. The firm is introducing tertiary-level wastewater treatment and plans to reuse a significant amount of treated water. They succeeded in reducing their water consumption by 50%. Textile, plastic, and paper wastes are sold to a recycler, with the revenue being donated to the workers. The company is seeking ISO 14001 certification because of a plan to expand its export market.

Firm eight is a textile firm that had been in operation for only a month at the time of the study. The management expects to have two or three staff dedicated to R&D. It sells its nylon, plastic, cotton and polyethylene plastic packaging materials to a recycler. In spite of being highly mechanized, this facility does not have energy efficient equipment and generates massive volumes of wastewater (40 to 60 kilograms of water per kilogram of product). It is planning for ISO 14001 certification and thus is currently planning to change its suppliers and looking at wastewater treatment and recirculation.

Firm nine minimizes its hazardous-waste generation through material substitution and redesign of products and packaging materials. However, it subcontracts the cutting and finishing operations of metal components to small, family-owned satellite firms, in effect shifting the environmental burden and responsibilities of its production up the supply chain. When asked whether the satellite firms had adopted cleaner production processes, the response was "No, the firms are small, family-owned enterprises which cannot afford the expense" (Wang, B. C. H., Consulting Engineer, interview, 17 July 1999). This perception of the lack of capability of small firms is contradicted by firm ten.

With only 14 employees, firm 10 successfully achieved ISO 9002 and ISO 14001 certification. The owner-manager attributed his success to the waste minimization changes implemented with the help of a local consultant through the government's cleaner production demonstration project. Lead and cyanide were eliminated from the plant operations. A heavy metal recovery system allows the reuse of wastewater. Wooden pallets are reused for packing and shipping products. Energy consumption has been reduced by 15% through equipment redesign. Plant wastes that cannot be totally eliminated are neutralized and detoxified before disposal. The openness to innovation of firm ten, the smallest among the case-study firms, also makes for a very interesting contrast with firm one, the largest. The management of firm one asserted that its ability to introduce innovations is limited by the fact that the facility has "no R&D capacity and no authority to make decisions" (Lin, C. C., Environmental Assurance Manager, interview, 16 July 1999).

The main input of firm 11 is aluminium window panels from New Zealand. The panels are already painted and only need to be cut and framed. The aluminium shavings are sold to a local recycler. The other major waste generated is packaging materials made of polyvinyl chloride (PVC). The firm claims to have tried to get its supplier for packaging materials to change to environmentally friendlier materials but has not succeeded. It is currently landfilling this waste. The firm is confident of its technical competence, despite being small with only twenty workers. It certified for ISO 9002 using internal auditors. It is planning to register its environmental management system (EMS) under ISO 14001 through self-declaration.

Firm 12 fabricates consumer items of artificial leather, mostly for export to the Peoples' Republic of China. It appears to be a more typical small firm. The proprietor has attended waste reduction workshops run by the IDB (Industrial Development Bureau) but insists that the scale of his operation is too small to generate serious wastes. Its conservation efforts have been focused exclusively on water and solid *leather* fabric waste.

Firm 13, a primarily family-operated metal finishing and plating firm, is the least innovative of the case-study firms. Although it has a wastewater treatment and metals recovery system for compliance purposes, the owner-manager indicated that he had no intention of going beyond compliance since "my son is not interested in taking over the plant, the young people don't want to work in this kind of operation. They want to work in big factories" (Chen, K. T., owner and Manager, interview, 23 July 1999). The three most frequently cited reasons for introducing the innovations were public image, profitability and regulatory compliance. Firm one and firm nine cited the export market as the primary driver for their decision to seek certification under ISO 9002, BS7750 and ISO 14001 and for undertaking cleaner production to achieve the certification. Firm two was ordered to seek certification by its parent company in Japan, reportedly driven by its commitment to the Kyoto Protocol. In firm four the ISO 9002 certification was pursued by the management as a way of "improving the management system, to educate our workers that we want quality" (Shu, H. T., Plant Manager, interview, 21 July 1999). CP changes followed because they emerged as sensible after the certification drive revealed wasteful processes in the facility. Firm five and firm six introduced changes toward implementing quality and environmental management systems because they "seemed like a good idea". ISO 14001 certification was viewed as an opportunity for achieving further quality improvement as well as increased sales. The cleaner production changes introduced in firm six resulted in a win-win outcome. The winter quarter, traditionally a loss-making period, became profitable. The company manager explains: "ISO certification costs money, but if you do cleaner production you will make money so we put the two together." (Chen, H. Y., interview, 23 July, 1999). The owner of firm ten asserted likewise. The cost of the metal-recovery system was reclaimed in less than two years. Close quality control has reduced the reject rate to less than 1%. The rest of the 13 case-study firms cited the need for compliance as the primary motivation.

How representative are the case-study firms? Reports on other industries with good environmental performance suggest that the motivation of the environmental management choices of the thirteen case-study firms may not be all that atypical of the manufacturing sector (Chang Y. T. 1998; Hsieh and Chen 1998; MOEA 1999; Yang 1999). Respondents to an MOEA survey of 408 firms certified to ISO 14001 identified the following factors as influencing their environmental management decisions: (a) to improve public image (91%); (b) to achieve development in a sustainable manner (87%); (c) to be compatible with international trends (86%); (d) to raise worker environmental awareness (85%); (e) to ensure compliance with environmental regulations (84%); (f) to integrate/ improve environmental management systems (83%); (g) to improve manufacturing efficiency (82%); (h) to extend ISO 9000 efforts to solving environmental problems (82%); (I) to reduce investors' concerns (75%); and (j) to expand product markets (73%).

All of these objectives are widely shared corporate values, yet there is frequently a gap between corporate policy statements and actual performance. How might one explain that in Taiwan businesses appear more willing to translate policy statements into concrete and, more importantly, measurable, environmental performance?

Public policy context for environmental innovation

The external environment for Taiwanese industrial firms has been evolving rapidly over the last three decades. Taiwan's per capita income has more than quintupled from US$2,500 in 1983 to $15,200 in 1998 (Canadian Trade Office in Taipei [CTOT] 1999). This has been made possible by a rapid expansion in industrial output. Manufacturing made up 19% of the GDP in 1960, compared to 36% in 1980.

The index of manufacturing output, which stood at 100 in 1985, stood at 215 in 1999, more than double in less than 15 years. Industry now makes up 96% of total exports. Electronics are the top export commodities followed by textiles, telecommunications, plastic and rubber goods. With a GDP of US$294 billion in 1997 and a real GDP growth rate averaging over 8.6% in the last three decades, the island economy, once dubbed as the "umbrella kingdom" for its production of cheap goods, is currently the nineteenth largest in the world, its productive sectors ranked fourth in terms of competitiveness and its foreign exchange reserve of US$84 billion the third largest.

The environmental costs of this rapid industrial growth have been considerable. In the late 1980s Taiwan was considered as having one of the world's most serious cases of environmental pollution (Bello and Rosenfeld 1990; Chieh 1994; Vogel 1991). Heavy metal contamination of the soil from industrial activities around Tao Yuan County forced the government to ban agricultural activity in the region. Pollution from pulp mill operations resulted in a government freeze on construction of new pulp mills (Cheung 1995). Perhaps not surprisingly, awareness of environmental problems and pressure for improved environmental quality increased with increased incomes. Organized community opposition held up construction of two naphtha-cracking plants and several infrastructure projects in 1988, the same year that the government paid US$1.5 million in compensation for pollution of coastal land (Devlin and Yap 1994). Industrial pollution is on the top of the advocacy agenda (Lin 1998; Rock 1996). Advocates for environmental protection and resource conservation include prominent industrial leaders. In 1998 for example, the founder and chairman of Taiwan-based Chi Mei Corporation, the world's top producer and exporter of plastic resins, admitted using his influence to oppose the establishment of more petrochemical, steel and cement plants in Taiwan (Cheng 1998).

The "grow first, clean up later" industrial strategy had to change. In 1987 the government of Taiwan placed the environment on its economic development policy agenda. Several departments were given responsibilities for environmental management with the Environmental Protection Administration (EPA) as the flagship agency. The EPA sets standards for controlling air emissions, liquid effluents, and hazardous waste disposal. It also plays an active and complementary role in the Ministry of Economic Affairs (MOEA), through the Industrial Development Bureau (IDB) and its mandate for industrial development and expansion. Consistent with the pattern established in other sectors

(Wade 1990; Weiss 1998), Taiwan has pursued a publicly coordinated approach to environmental innovation. The government creates the demand for innovation but also helps develop industry-specific responses through various R&D institutions. It has set up channels for communicating, transferring and diffusing innovation to industry, has set up numerous industry outreach programmes, set goals, devised environmental legislation and, most importantly, allocated resources to enforce environmental regulations.

Creating a demand for environmental innovation

The advantages to the economy of pollution prevention over pollution control were recognized early on by the government. In 1989 the MOEA and EPA established a Joint Waste Reduction Task Force with the mandate of developing a national industrial waste minimization (IWM) strategy. An Industrial Waste Minimization Programme was formally established in 1990. This programme was integrated within a broader framework in 1995 with the creation of the National Centre for Cleaner (NCCP) by the Industrial Development Bureau (IDB). The development of cleaner production indices has been a priority of the NCCP. A waste generation index, energy consumption index and hazard index have been developed for application in different industries including specialty chemicals, bulk drugs, polyurethane synthetic leather and printed circuit boards, as well as semiconductors. Software was developed to help researchers assess the cleanness of a product or process (Su et al. n.d.a). Recyclability, resource-efficiency, and low pollution intensity became part of the criteria applied to consumer products seeking "Green Mark" certification, Taiwan's Eco-Labelling Programme (Shen 1998).

As part of its outreach programme, the National Centre for Cleaner Production launched a formal partnership programme with industry associations. Member companies of partner associations are expected to commit to compliance with environmental regulations and to apply cleaner production principles in process and product design with the NCCP providing technical assistance and audit facilities.[7]

Unlike the trend in developed economies, Taiwan has increased its environmental protection expenditures to over 1.2% of the central government budget. The EPA budget increased from NT$26.9 billion in 1992 to NT$44.03 billion in 1998. This was accompanied by an increase in staff from 29,769 to 34,272.[8] For the period 1997 to 2005, US$10 billion has been allocated for the procurement of environmental technology.

Table 3 provides a selected set of environmental legislation and regulations in Taiwan with provisions relevant to the generation, management and disposal of industrial wastes. Some regulations were introduced in

Table 1.3 ROC environmental laws and regulations

Title	Relevant provisions/features
Environmental Impact Assessment Act (1994)	Initiated at the planning stage, the Act applies to public- and private-sector activities in resource extraction, manufacturing, transport, dam building, flood control, recreation and tourism, cultural, educational and medical facilities and power generation – as well as government policies.
Toxic Chemicals Substances Act (1986/a. 1999) Implementation Rules for the Toxic Chemicals Substances Act (1989/a. 2000)	Requirements cover labelling, documentation, equipment, permitting conditions, testing, inspection, sale and the qualification of personnel. – Penalties for non-compliance include jail terms up to 3 years and fines up to 5M NTD. – Stipulates awards for those "inventing or improving pollution prevention".
Waste Disposal Act (1994/a. 2001)	Mandates the Responsible Agency with setting and enforcing standards for disposal and disposal sites, including the *prohibition* of the "manufacture, importation, sale of articles or packaging that may cause serious pollution to the environment" as well as providing incentives for recycling. – Penalties for violation include jail terms of up to 7 years and a fine of up to 10M NTD.
Soil and Groundwater Pollution Remediation Act (2000)	Requires the provision of soil pollution inspection information for any land sale, or establishment, suspension or termination of an industrial operation; established the Soil Pollution and Groundwater Remediation Fund. – Penalties for violation include life imprisonment and a fine of up to 5M NTD.
Air Pollution Control Act (1975/a. 1999) Air Pollution Control Act Implementation Rules (1975/a. 1993)	Requires industrial parks to have buffer zones and air quality monitoring facilities; local level emission limits may be more stringent than those set by central agency.
Water Pollution Control Act (1974/a. 1991)	Industries submit a Water Pollution Control Plan prior to operation.
Environmental Agents' Control Act (1997)	Aims to "prevent damage" of pesticides, pollution control chemicals and microbial preparations by controlling the conditions for their manufacture, storage, sale, use and disposal.

Table 1.3 (cont.)

Title	Relevant provisions/features
Criteria Governing Methods of and Facilities for Storage, Clearance and Treatment of Industrial Wastes (1979/a. 1999)	Designated industries must file an "industrial waste management plan" prior to commencing operations; the plan must include a "waste reduction plan" and emergency plan; requires detailed documentation of waste generating and treatment processes as well as storage and disposal sites.
Hazardous Industrial Waste Import, Export, Transit and Transhipment Management Measures (1993/a. 1997)	Permit requires extensive documentation, emergency response plan, financial guarantee or liability insurance.
Measures for Management of Environmental Inspection and Testing Institutions (1997/a. 2001)	Stipulates the academic qualifications of personnel in institutions licenced to perform environmental quality assurance and testing of facilities.
Effluent Standards (1987/a. 2000)	Standards set for heavy metals, pesticides, ammonia, fluoride apply across all sectors; effluent limits on BOD, COD and suspended solids are sector-specific.
Fundamentals for Promoting the Use of the Taiwan Ecolabel (1992/a. 1997)	Criteria for obtaining the label include "significant waste reduction", energy conservation, ISO 14001 certification and product safety.

the late 1970s and subsequently amended to respond to changed conditions within the economy. The government is paying attention to enforcement. A special police force of about two thousand was established and dedicated exclusively to cracking down on environmental violations. This "green police" unit has been granted the power and resources to arrest violators (Chang 1999). Illegal dumping of hazardous waste can result in a fine of between US$11,538 and US$38,461.

As shown in the list in table 1.3, penalties for non-compliance can include life imprisonment and fines of up to US$310,000. Since the passage of air pollution control regulations, the Environmental Protection Agency has reportedly collected US$300 million in fines. In 1993 alone the fines levied totalled US$21 million, half of which came from point sources of water and air pollution (Yap 2000a). In 2001 it amounted to US$58 million. The inspection of facilities handling toxic chemicals was increased from about 7,500 in 1992 to nearly 30,000 in 1998 (Yap

2000a). There were plant closures or suspension of operating permits, the most notable being the closure of Taiwan VCM Corporation in Kaoshiung and the Chung Hwa Pulp Corporation plant in Hualien (Rock 1996).

Voluntary programmes are made attractive to industry through incentives such as highly publicized and prestigious government awards. For example, every year awards are given to companies that demonstrate the best improvement in environmental performance through adopting cleaner techniques (Hu 1998; Yang 1999). The strategy seems to work. It was with obvious pride that one company executive told us, "The cleaner production changes significantly increased our profits as well as reduced our environmental impacts. We are getting an award for environmental performance from the Ministry of Economic Affairs" (Chen, H. Y., interview, 23 July 1999).

The progress reported on other voluntary environmental programmes suggests a similar pattern. For example, we were told that the Waste Exchange Information Center had successfully exchanged 217,216 tons of industrial wastes ranging from acid solutions to mine dregs, reportedly resulting in US$54.3 million worth of savings (Su et al. n.d.b). Within four years after the introduction of the Green Mark programme, 490 products were awarded the certification (MOEA 1999).[9] Also, eight years after the introduction of ISO 14001, just over 1,300 Taiwanese firms had been certified to ISO 14001, mostly by European certifying auditors (MOEA 1999).[10]

Helping develop innovation: R&D

Like its economic development strategy, product and process R&D, information acquisition and dissemination is at the heart of the Taiwanese government's cleaner production strategy. In the 1990s in particular, R&D and technology diffusion was given prominence in the government's industrial strategy (Weiss 1998). In 2000 US$6.2 billion, or 2% of Taiwan's GDP, was spent on R&D; 10% on basic research, 30% on applied research and the rest on experimental development of the technology (Chung 2002). In 1999 the MOEA introduced a new criterion for industrial research funding in universities. The guideline was apparently unequivocal – "no cleaner production, no R&D funding" (Su T. T., Director, interview, 29 July 1999).

Several institutions outside of universities have been created and funded to undertake R&D on more efficient manufacturing technologies and processes. Among those most prominent are the Industrial Technology Research Institute (ITRI), the Textile Research Centre, and the

China Productivity Centre. If, for example, research is needed to determine the suitability for reuse of a particular waste stream, the research is done by any one of the three. ITRI also houses the innovation- and industry-dedicated laboratories such as the Electronic Research and Services Organization and Computing and Communications Laboratory. In addition to undertaking R&D, ITRI also monitors new technologies, products and processes developed by international competitors, organizes transfer of technology, and coordinates new research projects with local firms. ITRI mediates between industry and the civil service and is, in effect, part of the policymaking process. It is worth noting that ITRI puts its technical resources to serve the needs of SMEs. As part of the government's efforts to enforce zero discharge in electroplating operations, most of which are SMEs, the ITRI developed an optimized cleaning technology, a chromium recovery technology and a new ion-exchange resin. This system was installed for demonstration purposes at a barrel electroplating factory with three workers, and a bicycle parts rack-plating factory with eleven workers. In both cases all costs were recovered in less than three years. Several hundred electroplating firms have since benefited from this technology. Such direct technical assistance to SMEs is rarely provided in other jurisdictions, despite policy statements in support of such interventions.[11]

Communicating, transferring and diffusing innovation to industry

In the last five years ITRI claims to have transferred around 350 technologies to more than 500 companies. It has signed research contracts with over 1,000 companies (Chung 2002).

As part of EPA's promotion of inter-firm waste reuse and recycling programme, a Waste Exchange Information Centre provides information on waste stream quantities and composition to potential users. It is housed at the Union Chemical Laboratories of the Industrial Technology Research Institute. The IDB regularly organizes sector-specific cleaner production training workshops for industry (Chiu 1998; Hu 1998; Lee and Lee 1998; Wu 1998). This is done alone or in collaboration with the EPA, the Asian Productivity Organization (APO) and Asia-Pacific Economic Cooperation (APEC). Since 1994 over 10,000 SMEs have participated in two- to three-day information workshops on cleaner production and ISO 14001 (MOEA 1999).

When the IDB created the National Centre for Cleaner Production, it also launched a campaign to promote ISO 14001 among industry. What is rather unique about this programme is that the IDB strongly encourages that the ISO 14001 certification be preceded by cleaner production changes. According to one key informant, the advice from the government is clear: "do waste minimization first and it will be easier to establish ISO 14001" (Hsieh, C. C., Taichung County Vice Director Industrial Development Promotion Committee, interview, 23 July, 1999). Recognizing the technical constraints faced by SMEs, the IDB is encouraging large firms to help their suppliers and distributors adopt cleaner production and then an environmental management system (EMS) based on ISO 14001 by establishing what are called corporate synergy systems (CSSs), which are essentially networks for sharing technical information.[12]

The transfer and diffusion of environmental innovation to industry is done mainly through what are called "technical assistance providers" or TAPs. The first two TAPs – the Industrial Pollution Control Technical Service and the Industrial Waste Minimization Technical Service – were created by the IDB in 1992 to assist firms to solve pollution problems. Many privately owned TAPs were established in the 1990s. Over the years the focus of the TAPs has shifted from pollution control to pollution prevention or cleaner production. The government still actively funds demonstration projects in both cleaner production and ISO 14001. Participants in a demonstration project receive between 40% (for large enterprises) to 60% (for SMEs) of the cost of the technical assistance from the government, up to a maximum of US$12,000 for each firm. Technical assistance to qualified firms is channelled through the TAPs. When a firm applies to participate in the government's demonstration projects, it has to identify a TAP to work with. The TAP assists the firm in its search for and implementation of appropriate methods and technologies. The government thus effectively reduces the technical and financial risk to industry, acknowledged to be the biggest barrier to the adoption of cleaner production (See for example Boyd 1998; CEC 1996, Yap and Heathcote 1995).

Ensuring programme coherence and integration

Many of the staff, functions and resources of the EPA and MOEA are decentralized to the county and city level. This makes industry outreach programmes in both cleaner production and EMS much easier to integrate with the mandate of the industrial promotion and investment agencies, both of which play a critical role at the county and city level. In 1998 for instance, of the 80 training workshops organized by the Taichung County Industrial Promotion and Investment Agency, fifteen to twenty were on cleaner production and ISO 14001. Over four thousand companies, mostly SMEs, reportedly participate in these workshops annually.

Influence of public policy on firm environmental innovation decisions

In the case studies, regulation was only one of several factors cited to have triggered environmental innovation in the firms. But in all cases the decision to choose and adopt cleaner production was facilitated by information on alternatives as well as cleaner production training and technical assistance, all provided by the government. With reference to the decision-making framework in figure 1.1, one might say that in Taiwan the state systematically nudges the firm from one stage of the decision-making process to the next. Key to the government's success is its ability to (a) design programmes on the basis of a strategic analysis of where public policy and private sector interests coincide; (b) establish credibility with industry; and (c) monitor and evaluate the effectiveness and continuing relevance of its programmes, and, where necessary, to make modifications. These factors are discussed next.

Strategic analysis

The government uses the profitability enhancing potential of cleaner production approaches to motivate the private sector to meet environmental protection objectives. The critical role of technology in the search for cleaner production alternatives is fully recognized. The government's approach can be characterized as a balancing of *yin* and *yang* forces which, crudely translated, means wielding both the "sticks" and the "carrots". The EPA is provided with resources to establish and enforce high environmental standards, while the IDB has the resources to assist firms to comply.

Credibility with industry

In more than thirty interviews conducted for this study, not a single complaint against the government was raised. Industry-government relationship appears remarkably cordial if not trusting.

It is our analysis that such a relationship was established by having technically competent government personnel and consultants on the "front line" of the fight to protect the environment. This is consistent with the observations by many writers on the high quality of the civil service in Taiwan, attributed to the merit-based recruitment and promotion system (Weiss 1998).[13] It is interesting to note that several of the pieces of legislation listed in table 1.3 above indicate the "training and management of ... professionals" as part of the mandate of the *responsible agency*. Almost all stipulate the academic qualification of personnel employed to perform environmental tasks.[14]

In the government's cleaner production and EMS strategy, high-quality performance of the TAPs is ensured through a government-run certification system. Only certified individuals or groups can compete for the subsidies provided by the IDB for the demonstration projects. To achieve certification, consultants are required to undergo 130 hours of training and an examination. The consultants must also have two years of work experience in the sector in which they claim to have an expertise. Beginning in 1999, all registered EMS TAPs have been required to take an IDB certified fifty-hour advanced course once every three years as a condition for renewal of registration.

Adaptive administration

The government maintains an adaptive approach to programme implementation, allowing for course corrections. Institutional mandates and programmes are evaluated for effectiveness, responsiveness to changes in the environment, mutual coherence, minimal redundancy and competition. The government's relationship with technology assistance providers (TAPs) is illustrative. Initially established to deal with pollution control, some of these agencies were then redirected and their members retrained by the government to focus on cleaner production while others were redirected and retrained for the promotion of ISO 14001 (MOEA 1999). Some provide assistance in both.

The effectiveness of the TAPs was evaluated in 1999. One of the conclusions was that the approach of having TAP professionals specialized in environmental management in relation to a particular environmental aspect, e.g., air emissions or liquid effluents, was causing some confusion and leading to inefficiency among industry managers in deciding which TAP to approach for assistance. The government decided to retrain TAP professionals to deal with sector-specific environmental problems. This would allow a firm to consult only one TAP, instead of several, to deal with its problems. The evaluation also concluded that the EMS/cleaner-production TAPs outperformed purely EMS TAPs in terms of satisfying the client's need for technical assistance in achieving continual improvement (MOEA 1999). At the time of this research, the government was reviewing its training for TAPs professionals and considering granting regulatory flexibility to firms who demonstrate measurable and significant environmental improvement.

Future challenges and opportunities

The Taiwanese state has demonstrated its capacity to analyse the demands of the economy in the different stages of industrial modernization, and to adjust its industrial strategies and reconfigure its formal institutions accordingly. There are indications of success. The air quality of Taiwan as a whole and Taipei in particular has significantly improved. The levels of ozone and sulphur dioxide for example, are comparable to OECD countries such as Canada. In 2000 the government reported that 61% of its major rivers are unpolluted, 9.7% lightly polluted, 16.4% moderately polluted, and 12.6% severely polluted (Yap 2000a). Capital investment in pollution control, which accounted for 2.8% of the total capital investment in 1987 (Chieh 1994) rose to 4.3% by 1992, with the investment of state-owned enterprises being three and a half times those in the private sector, and apparently higher than the pollution control investments made by Japanese firms at the height of Japan's pollution control effort (Rock 1996).

However, formidable environmental challenges remain for the Taiwanese government and industry. Industrial pollutants contribute 30% of river pollution load (MOEA 1999). Factories, farms, ranches, power plants, waterworks and medical establishments in the Taiwan area reportedly generate 440,000 tons of hazardous industrial waste yearly. What will happen once the "low-hanging fruits" of environmental innovation have been harvested by industry? Will industry continue to pursue cleaner production changes with longer payback periods and/or uncertain return on the investment? Such longer term investment perspectives could be encouraged by designing a set of incentives and disincentives to: (a) oblige the firm to internalize in its accounting system the medium- and long-term environmental and resource use impacts of its operations; (b) encourage advocacy groups on "brown" environmental issues; and, (c) "nudge" industries to examine and take advantage of symbiotic relationships among different manufacturing processes and facilities. These challenges present opportunities. Industrial parks are a central feature of the government's economic development strategy. The application of the principles of industrial ecology to industrial parks offers potentially significant opportunities for reaching beyond the low-hanging fruits: In closing the production loop it would be possible to eliminate certain wastes and minimize numerous others and hence increase the possibility of finding win-win solutions.

The biggest challenge however looms off-shore. Now that Taiwan has become a member of the World Trade Organization, its state-industry relations will come under close scrutiny. The government may have to review, restructure and perhaps dismantle some of the programmes that have been responsible for bringing about improved environmental management practices by industry. How will the government of Taiwan deal with the contradiction between the demands for a "level" global playing field and its well-established practice of guiding national development and environmental management? Even those who led the WTO membership drive admit that industries producing for the domestic market "will probably face a challenge" (Shapiro 2002: 33).

There are grounds for optimism that the post-WTO Taiwan will continue to seek to minimize the environmental impacts of industrial growth. At the Fourth National Industrial Development Conference in 2001, industrial leaders, scholars and government officials reached a consensus in redefining the types of emerging industries that Taiwan should promote. They recommended those industries that have "high 'value-added', generate minimal pollution, and consume relatively little energy" (Hwang 2002: 7).

The first Taiwan-born president of Taiwan, Lee Teng-hui, has been quoted as saying that "the main secret of Taiwan's development was not her ability to meet the technological requirements for increasingly productive gadgets, but her ability to meet the organizational requirements of new combinations ... of mutually helpful behaviour necessary to achieve the gadgets" (cited in Vogel 1991: 22). It bears watching whether the state in Taiwan can continue to find organizational innovations that will allow it to continue to catalyze environmental innovation in its industrial firms.

Notes

1. There are two opposing views on the role of public policy in innovation. One argues that there is no useful role for governments in encouraging technological innovation, that innovation decisions are best driven by market forces. Palda (1993) argues, "Technology policy, and in particular R&D subsidization, present a fertile opportunity for the extraction of rents from taxpayers" (p. 254). On the other hand, Voyer and Ryan (1994) assert that "Governments support the strategies of the firms ... through research and development programmes and tax incentives because ... technological innovations leads to economic activity, job creation and the socio-economic well-being of their citizenry, not to mention the taxable revenues that can be derived" (p. 3).

2. Indeed Rock (2002) asserted that an indicator of success in Taiwan's integration of environmental protection in its industrial development strategy would be "the demonstration that manufacturing plants and firms in ... reducing the energy, materials, water, and pollution intensity of production by fundamentally altering production processes rather than by simply cleaning up pollution after it has occurred ..." (p. 1451).

3. Comprehensive pollution or resource consumption data for SMEs do not exist, making it difficult to precisely determine SME contribution to environmental degradation (Ecotec 2000; OECD 2002; Tilley 1999). The estimates range from 50% (Ecotec 2000; Lebourveau 2004) to 70% (Groundwork 1995, cited in Tilley 1999: 239; Hillary 1999). All agree that because of their sheer number the collective environmental impacts of SMEs are significant (Ecotec 2000; Fischer 2003; OECD 2002; Stratos 2004). Some sectors are viewed as among the worst polluters – metals, electrical and electronic engineering facilities, food, drink, tobacco, printing, textiles and leather, woodworking and paper and certain specialty chemicals (KPMG 1997, cited in Ecotec 2000; OECD 2002).

4. These pallets could be sold to a pulp and paper mill and there was a proposal to establish one in the industrial park which had to be shelved. The ban on new pulp and paper facilities continues.

5. HACCP (Hazard, Analysis and Critical Control Points) is an internationally accredited method of analysing a food processing system to determine potential hazards to food safety. Once identified, critical control points are identified and managed.

6. Workers who are found to have violated environmental management rules are given fines. Those who excel are given both cash and material awards.

7. The importance of involving industry associations or sector networks in outreach programmes has been argued by many who have studied the lack of effectiveness of government outreach programmes in environmental management (Ecotec 2000; Kürzinger 2004; Stratos 2004).

8. The EPA started in 1987 with three hundred staff (Chieh 1994).

9. By comparison, Canada's Environmental Choice Programme, established in 1985, has currently two hundred products certified.

10. For Canada the corresponding number is 252, for the United States 710 and Japan, 2,873.

11. An indication of the high quality and practical relevance of research done in Taiwan is the fact it is currently in fourth place in terms of the number of patents obtained in the United States.

12. A "corporate synergy system" is a mechanism through which a group of manufacturing companies work together to achieve certain production of management goals. It is established among firms linked by supply chains and usually consists of a central firm and its manufacturing suppliers or satellites (Shen-yann n.d.).

13. More than 25% of the workforce in Taiwan have a college degree or higher level of education (Chiu 2000). It is interesting to note that those who have played a major role in shaping and implementing Taiwan's economic development strategies have been engineers and scientists. Ten of the fourteen ministers of economic affairs between 1949 to 1985 were trained engineers. When technical expertise on macroeconomic policies was required, the government called on Chinese-born economists in the United States for assistance (Vogel 1991).

14. The World Business Council for Sustainable Development estimates that only 5 to 10% of SMEs are reached by government SME-outreach programmes. Apart from the observation that the programmes are "too general and supply-driven, poor quality" (Young 2004), the lack of qualified and competent technical assistance providers is cited as a barrier (BCPPDP 1999; GBN 2001; Hillary 1999; Huppé 2005; Huppé et al. 2005; Johannson 2005; Lebourveau 2004).

REFERENCES

Anderson, R. C. (1998) Mid-Course Correction: Towards a Sustainable Enterprise; The INTERFACE Model. Distributed by White River Junction, Vt.: Chelsea Green Publishing Company.

Ashford, N. (2002) "An Innovation-based Strategy for a Sustainable Environment" in Hemmerlskamp, J., K. Rennings and F. Leone (eds), Innovation-oriented Environmental Regulation. Mannheim: Physica-Verlag, pp. 67–107.

Baas, L. W., M. van der Belt, D. Huisingh and F. Neumann (1992) "Cleaner Production: What some governments are doing and what all governments can do to promote sustainability", European Water Pollution Control, January 2(1): 10–25.

Beise, M. and K. Rennings (2003) Lead markets of Environmental Innovations: A Framework for Innovation and Environmental Economics, Mannheim: Centre for European Economic Research. Available from ftp://ftp.zew.de/pub/zew-docs/dp/dp0301.pdf. Retrieved November 21, 2004.

Bello, W. and S. Rosenfeld (1990) Dragons in Distress: Asia's Miracle Economies in Crisis, San Francisco, Calif.: Institute for Food Policy and Development.

Bennett, D. (2004) "Pollution Prevention Planning in Canada", paper presented at the Canadian Pollution Prevention Roundtable, Ottawa, November 24.

Boyd, J. (1998) "Searching for Profit in Pollution Prevention: Case Studies in the Corporate Evaluation of Environmental Opportunities", unpublished paper prepared for the United States EPA Office of Pollution Prevention and Toxics, Washington, D.C. April.

British Columbia Pollution Prevention Demonstration Project (BCPPDP) (1999) Final Report of the Steering Committee, 29p.

Canadian Labour Congress (CLC) (1998) National Pollution Prevention Strategy: A publication of the Health, Safety and Environment Department, February, 20p.

Canadian Trade Office in Taipei (CTOT) (1999) TAIWAN: A Briefing Book, Taipei.

Chang, L. (1999) "'Green police' unit to protect environment", Free China Journal, April, p. 4.

Chang, Y. T. (1998) "Cleaner production at Hsin-chu Mill of Cheng Loong Corporation, Taiwan, ROC", MOEA Cleaner Production Newsletter, 3(3): 19.

Cheng, J. (1998) "Industrialist speaks out on pollution", Free China Journal, May 15, p. 3.

Cheung, P. S. (1995) "Republic of China" in K. Sakurai, ed., Cleaner Production for Green Productivity: Asian Perspectives, Asian Productivity Organization, Tokyo, pp. 11–69.

Chieh, C. C. (1994) "Growth with Pollution: Unsustainable Development in Taiwan and its Consequences", Studies in Comparative International Development 29(2): 23–47.

Chiu, S. Y. (1998) "APEC Training Program on Cleaner Production for the Metal Finishing Industry", MOEA Cleaner Production Newsletter 3(3): 10–12.

Chiu, Y. W. (2000) "Technology Key to the Economy", Taipei Journal, August 18, p. 3.

Christie, I., H. Rolfe and R. Legard (1995) Cleaner Production in Industry, London: Policy Studies Institute, pp. 78–81.

Chung, O. (2002) "Where the Future Lies", Taipei Review, July, pp. 18–23.

Ciambrone, D. F. (1995) Waste Minimisation as a Strategic Weapon, New York: Lewis Publishers.

Conference Board of Canada (CBC) (1997) "The Optimal Policy Mix: Phase 1; An Initial Framework for Discussion", Draft, August 26.

Commission for Environmental Cooperation (CEC) (1996) "Status of Pollution Prevention in North America", Ottawa, June.

Corral, C. (2002) Environmental Policy and Technological Innovation: Why do firms adopt or reject new technologies? Cheltenham, England: Edward Elgar.

Devlin, J. and N. Yap (1994) "Sustainable development and the NICs: Cautionary tales for the South in the New World (Dis)Order", Third World Quarterly 15(1): 49–62.

Ecotec Research and Consulting (2000) "Report on SMEs and the Environment", prepared for the European Commission, Brussels, February 17.

Environmental Protection Agency (EPA) (2000) Profits from Cleaner Production: A Self-Help Tool for Small and Medium-Sized Businesses, Vol. 1. New South Wales Department of State and Regional Development.

Evans, P. (1996) Embedded Autonomy, Princeton: Princeton University Press.

Fischer, P. (2002) "Pollution prevention initiatives across Canada", HazMat Management, October/November, available from http://www.hazmatmag.com/issues/ISarticle.asp?id=74134&story_id=HM130092&i.

Fischer, P. (2003) "P2 for SMEs: How to advance pollution prevention in small and medium-sized organizations", HazMat Magazine, June/July.

Fresner, J. and G. Engelhardt (2004) "Experiences with integrated management systems for two small companies in Austria" in Journal of Cleaner Production, 12: 623–631.

Fryzuk, L. (2005) "P2 Measurements and Results Database", paper presented at the Canadian Pollution Prevention Roundtable, Victoria, June 1–2.

Gordon, M. and S. Zettler (2005) "Evaluation of the P2 Experience at Alcan Primary Metals – British Columbia", paper presented at the Canadian Pollution Prevention Roundtable, Victoria, June 1–2.

Great Lakes Pollution Prevention Centre (GLPPC) (1994) "Manufacturing and the Environment: Staying Competitive and within Compliance", proceedings of a teleconference, November 9.

Green Business Network (GBN) (2001) "Standardizing Excellence: Working with Smaller Businesses to Implement Environmental Management Systems", National Environmental Education & Training Foundation, Washington, DC: National Environmental Education and Training Foundation, October.

Halme, M. (1995) "Shifting Environmental Management Paradigms in Two Finish Paper Facilities", paper presented at the Greening of Industry Conference, Toronto, November 12–14.

Hanks, J. (1998) "Sharing responsibility": Co-regulatory policy instruments as a means of achieving industrial sustainable development in South Africa and other developing countries", UNEP Industry and Environment (21): 1–2, 36–41.

Hassanali-Bourdeau, M. (2004) "Pollution Prevention Practices in Small and Medium-sized Metal Finishers", paper presented at the Canadian P2 Roundtable, Ottawa, April 29.

Higgins, T. E. (1995) Pollution Prevention Handbook, Boca Raton, Fla.: Lewis Publishers, pp. 1–13.

Hillary, R. (1999) Evaluation of Study Reports on the Barriers, Opportunities and Drivers for Small and Medium Sized Enterprises in the Adoption of Environmental Management Systems. Prepared for the U.K. Department of Trade and Industry, Environment Directorate, 5 October.

Hsieh, C. S. and C. H. Chen (1998) "Role of Industrial Waste Minimization in Implementing the Environmental Management System at President Enterprises Corporation", MOEA Cleaner Production Newsletter 3(3): 17.

Hu, A. (1998) "CP Partnership Initiative in Taiwan", in MOEA Cleaner Production Newsletter 3(3): 12.

Huppé, F. (2005) "Enviroclub™: Five years of results and lessons learned", paper presented at the Canadian Pollution Prevention Roundtable, Victoria, B.C., June 1–2.

Huppé, F., R. Turgeon, T. Ryan and C. Vanasse (2005) "Fostering pollution prevention in small businesses: The Enviroclub™ Initiative", Unpublished paper.

Hwang, J. (2002) "Structural Reengineering", Taipei Review, pp. 4–11, July.

Johannson, L. (2005) "Small and Medium-sized Enterprise and Sustainability: Do we have the right equipment?" paper presented at the Canadian Pollution Prevention Roundtable, Victoria, B.C., June 1–2.

Kemp, R. (2002) "Integrating Environmental and Innovation Policies", paper prepared for UNU/UNITECH, Maastricht, the Netherlands, June.

Kerr, R., A. Cosby and R. Yachnin (1998) Beyond Regulation: Exporters and Voluntary Environmental Measures, Winnipeg, Manitoba: International Institute for Sustainable Development and the Canadian Environmental Technology Advancement Corporation-West.

KPMG Environmental Consulting (1997) The Environmental Challenge and Small and Medium Enterprises in Europe. Amsterdam.

Kürzinger, E. (2004) "Capacity building for profitable environmental management", Journal of Cleaner Production 12: 237–248.

Lebourveau, S. (2004) "Environmental Innovation in Canadian SMEs", paper written to satisfy the requirements for the completion of Semesters 9 and 10 of the Masters in Environmental Management Programme at Aalborg University, Denmark, June 28.

Lee, S. and C. Lee (1998) "Taiwan IDB-Held Training Workshop for CP Technical Assistance Providers", MOEA Cleaner Production Newsletter 3(3): 13.

Lin, D. (1998) "Environmentalism support flowering in Taiwan", Free China Journal, February 13, p. 7.

Ministry of Economic Affairs (MOEA) Industrial Development Bureau (1999) ISO 14000 in Taiwan, May.

Norwegian Pollution Control Authority (NPCA) (1995) A Study of Financial Support for Cleaner Production Assessments in Norway, 95:05E.

NUTEK (2003) "Environmental work in small enterprises – A pure gain?", The Situation and Conditions of Enterprises 2002, Stockholm, Sweden.

Organization of Economic Cooperation and Development (OECD) (1993) "Technical Co-operation, Technology Transfer and Environmentally Sustainable Development: Background Paper", prepared by the Working Party on Development Assistance and Environment, DCD/DAC/ENC (93)5.

——— (2002) Small and Medium Enterprise Outlook, Paris: OECD.

Palda, K. (1993) Innovation Policy and Canada's Competitiveness, Vancouver, B.C.: The Fraser Institute.

Prakesh, A. (2000) Greening the Firm, Cambridge: Cambridge University Press.

Rock, M. T. (1996) "Toward More Sustainable Development: The Environment and Industrial Policy in Taiwan", Development Policy Review 14: 255–272.

——— (2002) "Integrating Environmental and Economic Policy Making in China and Taiwan", American Behavioral Scientist 45(9): 1435–1455.

Russell, C. (2005) "Environmental Strategies for Industrial Development", paper prepared for the South Carolina Environment and Business Roundtable, July, available from www.ase.org/section/topic/industry/. Retrieved May 9, 2005.

Sarokin, D. J., W. R. Muir, C. G. Miller and S. R. Sperber (1985) "Cutting Chemical Wastes: What 29 Organic Chemical Plants are doing to reduce hazardous wastes", New York: INFORM.

Shapiro, D. (2002) "Entering the WTO: A Major Milestone", Taipei Review, January, pp. 32–34.

Shen, D. (1999) "Fund for SMEs expands under development plan", Free China Journal, May 29, p. 3.

Shen, J. C. H. (1998) "The Four-in-One Resource Recycling System in Taiwan", MOEA Cleaner Production Newsletter 3(3): 10–12.

Shen-yann, C. (n.d.) "The evolution of governmental incentive programs to improve environmental performance in the manufacturing sector in Taiwan", available at http://www.environet.org.tw/e-04envr05-0104.asp.

Stanwick, P. A. and S. D. Stanwick (1995) "Background Characteristics of a Chief Executive Officer: How Do They Impact the Greening of an Organisation?" paper presented at the Greening of Industry Conference, Toronto, Canada, November.

Stratos (2004) "Improving the Environmental Performance of Small and Medium-sized Enterprises in Canada", A discussion paper prepared for Environment Canada, October 29.

Su, T. T., C. H. Chen, and J. S. Hwang (n.d.a) "Qualitative and Quantitative Evaluation of Process Cleanness in R&D Stage", unpublished paper.

——— (n.d.b) "Transformation of One's Waste into Another's Resource: A Cornerstone of Industrial Ecology", unpublished paper.

Taichung County (TC) (1999) Introduction to Investment Opportunities in Taichung County, Taichung County Industrial Development & Investment Promotion Committee, Taichung.

Tilley, F. (1999) "The Gap between the Environmental Attitudes and the Environmental Behaviour of Small Firms" in Business Strategy and the Environment 8: 238–248.

UNEP I.E. (1994) "What is Cleaner Production and the Cleaner Production Program?", Industry and Environment, 17(4): 4.

UNIDO Secretariat (1997) "Technology Transfer and Development", TECH MONITOR, 14(1), January–February, pp. 8–15.

Vogel, E. (1991) "Taiwan", in The Four Little Dragons: The Spread of Industrialization in East Asia, Cambridge, Mass.: Harvard University Press, pp. 13–41.

Voyer, Roger and Patti Ryan (1994) The New Innovators, Toronto: James Lorimer & Company Ltd.

Wade, R. (1990) Governing the Market: Economic Theory and the Role of Government in East Asian Industrialization, Princeton: Princeton University Press.

Walley, N. and B. Whitehead (1994) "It's not easy being green" in Harvard Business Review, May–June, pp. 46–52.

Weiss, L. (1998) "Transformative Capacity in Evolution: East Asian Developmental States", in The Myth of the Powerless State, Ithaca, N.Y.: Cornell University Press.

White, G. (1988) Developmental States in East Asia, Basingstoke, England: Macmillan.

Wu, C. (1998) "APEC Training Program on Environmental Management and Cleaner Technology for the Printed Circuit Board Industry", MOEA Cleaner Production Newsletter 3(3): 3.

Yang, F. (1999) "1998 National Industrial Waste Minimization Outstanding Performance Awards", MOEA Cleaner Production Newsletter 4(2): 4–11.

Yap, N. T. (1988) "The Private Pursuit of Public Interest: A Framework for Low-Waste Pollution Control Policy", thesis submitted to Dalhousie University, Halifax, N.S.

Yap, N. T. (2000a) "Who says command-and-control doesn't work?" Policy Options, April 21(3): 65–70.

Yap, N. T. (2000b) "Performance-based ISO 14001: Case Studies from Taiwan" in R. Hillary, ed., ISO 14001: Case Studies and Practical Experience, London: Greenleaf Publishing, pp. 138–147.

Yap, N. and I. Heathcote (1995) "If low-waste technologies are a low-hanging fruit: why don't industries pick it?" in N. T. Yap and S. K. Awasthi, eds., Waste Management for Sustainable Development: Policy and Administrative Dimensions with Case Studies from Kanpur, New Delhi: Tata-McGraw Hill Publishing Company Limited.

Yap, N. T. and R. Zvauya (1999) "Business Decision Criteria with Respect to Waste Management: Case Studies from Southern Africa" in N. T. Yap, ed., Cleaner Production and Consumption: Challenges and Opportunities in East, Central and Southern Africa, Harare, Zimbabwe: Weaver Press.

Young, R. (2004) "Small & Medium Enterprises and Sustainable Development: Large company engagement", paper presented at the Canadian Pollution Prevention Roundtable, Ottawa, April 27.

2

Environmental regulation and industrial competitiveness in pollution-intensive industries

Jonathan R. Barton, Rhys Jenkins, Anthony Bartzokas, Jan Hesselberg and Hege M. Knutsen

The adoption of new technologies at the firm level is a result of many different factors. When it comes to addressing pollution problems, the development of environmentally conscious technologies takes place in both production processes and products. Given the diversity of industries in terms of production processes, products and hence pollution sources, the incentives structure and other considerations at the firm level are difficult to generalize. In this paper, we suggest that a better understanding of technological trends at the sectoral level is a necessary precondition for better understanding of the impact of environmental regulation on technological change.[1]

This paper synthesizes the research findings of in-depth studies of three pollution-intensive industries: iron and steel, leather tanning and fertilizers. Each of the three studies was based on fieldwork carried out in a number of European countries and in several industrializing and transition economies where it was anticipated that environmental regulation would be much less stringent than within the EU. Both in Europe and outside Europe, interviews were carried out with environmental and/or plant managers in a number of firms and with national and European trade associations, technical experts and regulators. In each industry, the aim was to understand the environmental problems of the industry, the impact of regulation and the evolving competitive position of the sector. This involved establishing where the critical environmental pressures were within each industry and understanding the corporate strategies that have been adopted. The rationale for choosing the iron and

51

steel, leather tanning and fertilizer industries is that these three industries are perceived as accounting for a significant amount of industrial pollution.

This paper is organized as follows. In the next section we briefly present the literature on environmental regulation and competitiveness in the global economy and discuss the scale at which the links between environmental regulation and competition may be studied and make an argument for adopting a sectoral approach in multiple countries.

Section 3 discusses some of the emerging challenges associated with the globalization of trade.

Section 4 discusses the factors that contribute to changes in the distribution of industrial activity, followed by a discussion of sectoral structure and competitiveness in the context of environmental regulation in the iron and steel, leather tanning and fertilizers industries. Section 4 also discusses the relationship between environmental regulation and technological change, as well as the relationship between environmental regulation and corporate strategy.

In Section 5 we discuss the factors that contribute to changes in the global distribution of industrial activity, paying particular attention to the environmental implications of industrial relocation.

Sections 6 and 7 discuss sectoral competitiveness and corporate strategy in light of industrial relocation and regulatory pressure with reference to the three sectoral case studies of iron and steel, leather tanning and fertilizers.

Section 8 explores the implications of this study for environmental improvement, while Sections 9 and 10 conclude this chapter by underlining the opportunities for environmental improvement and drawing attention to the policy implication of these opportunities.

Environmental regulation and competitiveness

A number of different hypotheses have been advanced concerning the relationship between environmental regulation, competitiveness and industrial location and it is necessary to distinguish between them and to clarify some of the terminology used. Previous studies have not always been consistent in the way in which they refer to the phenomena that are set out here. In general terms there are two sets of linkages, those running from environmental regulation to trade, investment and competitiveness, and those which run in the opposite direction, from globalization to environmental regulation. This chapter is primarily concerned with the first set of linkages.

There are a number of ways in which it has been suggested that environmental regulation may affect competitiveness and industrial location. First of all there is the *industrial flight hypothesis* that firms relocate their operations from highly regulated economies through investment in less strictly regulated jurisdictions. The emphasis here tends to be on the "push" factor of stricter environmental regulation in the North leading firms to transfer production to less regulated areas. The focus is on foreign investment by firms from the developed countries that relocate to the South. A rather broader approach revolves around the *"loss of competitiveness" hypothesis*. There is considerable literature which discusses the possibility that highly polluting industries will become less competitive in more regulated economies as regulation is increased and/or trade is liberalized. This loss of competitiveness hypothesis does not necessarily involve any relocation of production by firms from the North, but does affect the global distribution of industry as a result of differences in costs between firms located in different jurisdictions. In other words, firms that face high environmental compliance costs may lose market share to those located in less regulated jurisdictions. Whereas the last hypothesis refers to inter-industry shifts in location, the *"source-and-hide" hypothesis* refers to intra-industry shifts (Bergstø, Endresen and Knutsen 1998). As international production is increasingly organised in *commodity (or value) chains* (Gereffi 1994), new opportunities arise for firms to externalize their pollution by using less-regulated suppliers. In other words, those parts of the commodity chain that generate most pollution can be located in developing countries where environmental regulation is less stringent. All the hypotheses referred to so far are essentially pessimistic in that they assume that there is a conflict between stricter environmental regulation and competitiveness. The *Porter hypothesis* claims that, on the contrary, environmental regulation can, and often does, lead to economic benefits and hence to increased competitiveness. If that were generally the case, then the concerns raised above would be quite unfounded.

Turning to empirical validation, many recent studies reflected considerable scepticism as to the validity of the various hypotheses. It was suggested then that this was due, in part, to the high level of aggregation in most studies. It was also noted that there was a tendency to isolate environmental regulation and not consider how it interacts with other factors.[2] There are a number of reasons why the specific focus chosen for the case studies is at the level of industry. First, the theoretical and empirical literature on the interface between environmental regulation and competitiveness has shown a very mixed picture. Looking at the firm level, it has proved very difficult to establish causal links between environmental and economic performance. It is therefore necessary to take account of the interaction of environmental regulation with other factors, which influence corporate decisions. At the industry level, there is evidence of a shift of pollution-intensive industries to less regulated countries in the South. There is also evidence that competitiveness has increased in a number of these industries in developing countries while it has declined in the advanced industrialized countries. However, as with firm-level studies, it has been difficult to establish the causal linkages. A firm's behaviour, its competitive strategies, investment decisions, and locational choices need to be understood in the sectoral context where the structure of the industry and the nature and scale of competition affecting the sector determine the sector's evolution and that of the firms within it.

Second, the responses of firms to environmental regulation are critically dependent on the competitive characteristics of the industries within which they operate. Indeed, technological developments and production processes are industry specific. The environmental impact of an industry, and the way in which it changes over time, depends on the technological trajectory of the industry.

Third, in order to understand how environmental regulation leads to changes in technology and how these affect competitiveness, it is also necessary to look at specific industries. Macro-studies in the past have failed to arrive at very clear conclusions concerning the impact of environmental regulation on competitiveness, technological change and industrial location. On the other hand, examples of specific firms that have relocated production or gained competitive advantages as a result of environmental regulation can be dismissed as "anecdotal". Firm-level case studies, therefore, are unlikely to produce conclusive evidence on either the negative impact or the advantages of environmental regulation. As this chapter demonstrates, sectoral industry studies offer specific insights without overlooking the firm dynamics, an element not captured or evident in aggregate macro-studies.

Finally, it is important to look at linkages between different stages in the production process, because often these have very different implications in terms of pollution generated and the value-added created. This again leads to an industry focus and can be usefully explored through a commodity chain approach. An additional advantage of the sectoral approach is that it provides the opportunity for a closer look at environmental problems in various stages of the production process.

For all these reasons, we adopted an industry case-study approach in the central parts of this book, which would make it possible to examine the impact of environmental regulation in the context of the competitive dynamic of different industries. This chapter looks at the debates once more in the light of the evidence from our three case studies.

Emerging challenges in the global economy

It is sometimes thought that industrialization in the developing world has mainly taken the form of the growth of light industries such as garments and electronic assembly in export processing zones, and that therefore the environmental implications of industrial growth are relatively limited.[3] However, as table 2.1 shows, the increase in the South's share of world manufacturing value added has also occurred in those industries that are identified as the most pollution-intensive sectors internationally.[4]

The increasing share of less developed countries in the production from pollution-intensive industries is not simply a reflection of the general growth in their share of world manufacturing. In fact, the share of such industries in total manufacturing value added in the South has increased since 1980, while their share in the North has fallen (see table 2.2).

Table 2.2 also shows that, contrary to popular perceptions, the most polluting industries account for a greater share of manufacturing in the less developed countries and that the gap between the share of such industries in North and South has been widening over time.

Despite the fact that there is considerable debate both over the extent of globalization and its consequences, the growth of international trade, the expansion of transnational corporations and the increased interconnections of financial markets are all indicative of a *process* which has significant implications for national economies and global change. Associated with globalization has been a significant shift in the proportion of

Table 2.1 Share of LDCs in world manufacturing value added in 10 pollution-intensive industries, 1980, 1985, 1990, 1996

	1980	1985	1990	1996
Leather	23.3	24.8	26.0	29.9
Paper	9.4	9.7	10.5	11.8
Industrial Chemicals	11.4	13.4	14.8	17.9
Other Chemicals	14.7	14.1	14.4	15.8
Petroleum Refineries	30.0	36.0	39.3	43.2
Rubber Products	15.4	16.1	18.5	21.5
Other Non-metallic Products	15.0	16.8	17.8	23.1
Iron and Steel	12.1	14.3	17.0	23.3
Non-ferrous Metals	15.4	16.5	17.0	20.3
Metal Products	8.2	9.0	9.5	11.0
Manufacturing Value Added	14.4	15.3	16.8	21.7

Source: UNIDO (1999)

Table 2.2 Percentage share of 10 pollution-intensive industries in manufacturing value added, 1980, 1985, 1990, 1996

	LDCs	Developed countries
1980	36.6	33.5
1985	37.0	31.8
1990	37.8	31.3
1996	39.0	31.3

Based on UNIDO (1999)

world industrial production which is accounted for by the countries of the South. The implication of this increased share of polluting industries within the manufacturing sector in the South is that pollution loads are likely to increase, and the need to find ways of mitigating industrial pollution will become more urgent.

The current state of environmental regulation in most developing countries is not adequate to cope with increasing pollution trends, particularly in terms of enforcement. In the present context this assumes importance because, despite the existence of a number of international environmental agreements, environmental regulation continues to be predominantly nationally based and major differences exist in the strictness of environmental regulation between countries.

Casual observation suggests that the degree of regulation tends to be positively correlated with a country's income level, and this is supported by some empirical evidence (Dasgupta et al. 1995). Particularly when account is taken of the level of monitoring and enforcement of environmental standards, it is clear that major differences exist between the advanced industrial countries and the developing and transition economies. European Union countries such as Germany, the Netherlands and Denmark have some of the strictest environmental standards in the world, and although other EU countries lag behind the leaders, they still have higher standards and more stringent enforcement than apply in the South. It is these differences that give rise to much of the concern about the interaction between globalization and increased environmental regulation in the countries of the North. These are focused on the links between environmental regulation and competitiveness and fears over "industrial flight", "pollution havens" and "eco-dumping".

At the same time, the empirical evidence regarding the impact of environmental regulation on competitiveness and the effects on investment is far from clear-cut. Indeed, many economists argue that environmental factors do not play a significant role in international trade and investment, while others go even further, arguing that environmental regulation tends to increase competitiveness. The approach adopted in this paper rejects mono-causal explanations of competitiveness and environmental regulation. A major working hypothesis is that the relationship between environmental regulation and competitiveness is a complex one. This contrasts both with those studies that tend to concentrate on the national level and those based on the experience of individual firms. Mono-causal explanations, which attribute changes in competitiveness solely to differences in environmental regulation, do not adequately capture this. They cannot explain why relocation occurs in some pollution-intensive industries and not in others, or why some countries with relatively strict environmental regulation have been able to maintain their competitiveness in such industries. What is required is a framework that allows the impact of changes in regulation to be analysed in the context of other factors affecting competitiveness and the structural features of the industry concerned.

A second factor that prompted this research was the realization that the overwhelming bulk of previous work on these issues was focused on the United States. This is not surprising since the United States has been active in environmental protection for a number of years, and it has the best sources of data on which to base such studies. It has also had the most active public debate around these issues, which reached new heights in the early 1990s in connection with the negotiation of the NAFTA agreement with Mexico.

However, particularly in the 1990s, the implications of environmental regulation for competitiveness in the countries of the European Union have also moved up the political agenda. The Maastricht Treaty of 1991 made the environment one of the major concerns of the European Union and called for the integration of environmental objectives into other EU policy matters. The EU's Fifth Environmental Action Programme, *Towards Sustainable Development 1993–2000*, emphasized the precautionary principle and encouraged the introduction and adoption of cleaner production processes (Bartzokas, Demandt and Ruijters 1997). Since 1992 the European Commission has committed itself to "turning environmental concern into competitive advantage" (EC 1992: 31).

The distribution of production in the three case studies

Along with the general trend of globalization there have been significant increases in international trade in recent years in the iron and steel, leather and fertilizers industries. In the steel industry the share of production traded internationally almost doubled from 23.2% in 1975 to 43.3% in 1997. An even more dramatic change occurred in the tanning industry where the volume of light leather exported increased as a share

Table 2.3 Percentage share of developing countries in world production in three industries

	1979	1997
Steel	14.2	36.8
Leather*		
Heavy	34.1	56.2
Light	40.5	58.9
Fertilizer	20.2	45.2**

Source: IISD (2000), FAO (2002)
* Averages for 1979–1981 and 1994–1996
** 1998

of world production from 25.6% in 1979–1981 to 61.5% in 1994–1996 (FAO 1998). Despite the decline in world consumption of phosphate fertilizer between the mid-1980s and the mid-1990s, trade in processed phosphates increased by over 70%. Increased trade in iron and steel, leather and fertilizers has been accompanied by significant changes in the location of production and, in particular, an increase in the share accounted for by developing countries (table 2.3).

The share of the world's iron and steel production located in developing countries has more than doubled since the late 1970s. In tanning, the share of production located in the South increased from 26% for heavy leather and 35% for light leather in 1969–1971 to 56% for both types of leather by the mid-1990s. Fertilizer production in developing countries has also more than doubled its share of global production since the end of the 1970s.

Factors contributing to changes in distribution of industrial activity

The case studies in our project show no evidence of industrial flight from North to South to take advantage of less stringent regulations in the South. Except for fertilizers, these are not sectors where transnational corporations or direct foreign investment are very significant. In the case of the steel industry, there has been some investment in joint ventures overseas, but these have not been motivated by a desire to relocate production from the North but rather to get a foothold in rapidly growing markets in the South. In leather there has been a certain amount of foreign investment of German capital in Poland and the Czech Republic and of Italian capital in Brazil. Again this has not been a generalized pattern.

Two European firms in the fertilizer industry, Norsk Hydro and Kemira, have adopted global strategies and made important investments in developing countries, including a number of joint ventures. There is no evidence that these have been motivated by a desire to take advantage of less stringent environmental regulations in host countries. Again, as in steel, a desire to participate in rapidly growing markets has been an important factor in some instances, while in other cases, as for example in North Africa and the Middle East, the main factor has been access to raw materials.

Indeed, demand has played a significant part in the changing pattern of industrial location in all three industries. There is evidence in the three cases that the share of world consumption in the South has increased significantly. In tanning this has been caused by the relocation of the footwear industry to developing countries. Between 1979–1981 and 1994–1996 the share of the world's leather shoe production located in developing countries more than doubled, from 35% to 71% (FAO 1998: table VIII). This represented an increased demand for leather of almost 900 million square metres (FAO 1998: table IX).

It has been observed that the steel-intensity of GDP increases as countries become more industrialized. Thus, it is not surprising to find that steel consumption has increased rapidly in a number of less developed countries in recent years. In addition, at higher levels of per capita income, the growth in demand for steel tends to level off. Finally, in the fertilizer industry the intensification of agriculture in the South has led to a rapid growth in demand for artificial fertilizers, as the case studies of Turkey and China illustrated. At the same time, environmental concerns over the excessive use of agricultural chemicals and the growth in organic agriculture in the North tend to reduce the growth of demand. Thus, growth in the world fertilizer market tends to be increasingly concentrated in developing countries.

The fact that demand patterns are changing does not however rule out the possibility that other factors have also played a role in the changing pattern of industrial production in the three industries. In particular, it is important to examine the changes which have taken place in international competitiveness within these industries. In all three industries, the share of developing countries in world exports has increased significantly since the late 1970s (table 2.4). Although this lags behind their share of world production, it does indicate that developing countries have been gaining competitiveness, and that changes in the location of production are reflecting more than just shifts in demand patterns.

There is also evidence from the case studies of shifts in the location of production within each industry that is not picked up by looking at aggregate figures. The study of tanning, which explicitly adopts a commodity

Table 2.4 Percentage share of developing countries in world exports in three industries

	1979	1997
Steel	7.8	24.2
Light Leather*	44.5	57.9
Fertilizer	11.7	19.2**

Source: IISD (2000), FAO (2002)
* Averages for 1979–1981 and 1994–1996
** 1998, based on value of exports

chain approach, underlines the production of *wet blue* as the most polluting part of the tanning chain. Unfortunately, data on leather production and trade does not distinguish between different stages of production but only separates out light and heavy types of leather. Thus, apart from highlighting the location of wet blue production, it is not possible to provide detailed evidence at the global level of the shifts that are taking place within the commodity chain.

In particular it was found that tanners in Germany and Italy had entered into sourcing arrangements with wet blue producers in Eastern Europe and Brazil. This enables the European manufacturers to avoid the most polluting stages of production and to maintain the high-value-added processes at home. Both in Italy and Germany this strategy is seen as a way of coping with local environmental regulations. At the same time, as illustrated by the case study of Brazil, it appears that the tanning industry in some countries in the South has become increasingly oriented toward the more polluting parts of the production process. In the South, in addition to the increase in the share of pollution-intensive industries in manufacturing, there seems also to be an increase in the presence of the most polluting stages of production.

While the clearest evidence of this trend comes from the tanning industry, there is also some suggestion that a similar trend may have occurred in the iron and steel industry. The most polluting stages of the integrated steel-making process are the coke ovens and the sinter plant. Production of both coke and sinter have been falling in the North but have tended to increase in the South since the late 1970s. In the European Union, imports of coke-oven products increased by more than 150% between 1988 and 1998.

In the case of the fertilizer industry there have also been changes in the location of different parts of the commodity chain. Historically, the raw-material producing countries tended to export phosphate rock, and downstream processing occurred in the North. Over the past two decades, however, exports of phosphate rock have been declining and exports of phosphoric acid have increased, particularly to western Europe and to India. In the case of Europe, most of the local phosphoric acid plants were closed down for economic and environmental reasons. Thus, the outsourcing of phosphoric acid has been an important factor in the phosphate-fertilizer industry.

The processes in which the South has tended to specialize in these industries have not only been relatively pollution-intensive, but have also tended to have low value added. In the case of the leather industry, *wet blue* accounts for a relatively small share of the value added of finished leather despite being responsible for most of the pollution. In the iron and steel industry, value added per ton of steel produced is much higher in Japan, the United States of America, Germany and the United Kingdom than in developing countries. An implication of this is that geographical shifts in the share of value added toward developing countries will lag behind increases in their share of physical output.

Environmental regulation and sectoral competitiveness

The relationship between environmental regulation and sectoral competitiveness is very much dependent on the sector. In this section we discuss sectoral structure and competitiveness in the context of environmental regulation in the iron and steel, leather tanning and fertilizer industries. We also discuss the relationship between environmental regulation and technological change, as well as the relationship between environmental regulation and corporate strategy.

Sectoral structure and competitiveness

Iron and steel

Competition in bulk steel is primarily based on price. Although raw materials are not as significant a part of total costs as in tanning, access to low-cost iron ore, coke and energy can be a source of competitive advantage in the industry. Steel making is a capital-intensive activity subject to significant scale economies, and consequently competitiveness depends both on a significant volume of production and on access to capital. Moreover, continuous technological improvement in the industry also means that the vintage of a plant is an important determinant of firm competitiveness.

Because iron and steel has long been regarded as a strategic industry, there has often been extensive government involvement in the sector, including of course state ownership, although this has become less important as a result of the privatizations of recent years. However, national government policies, including trade policies, subsidies and procurement policies, continue to be an important element influencing the competitive position of firms.

The steel industry is characterized by cyclical variations in demand and has also experienced international overcapacity in recent years. As a result, profit rates overall have been low which has meant that cost reductions have been important for firms that wish to remain competitive. Substantial rationalization has taken place in the EU iron and steel industry since the 1980s, involving mergers, plant closures, joint ventures and niche-market diversification.

Leather tanning

The tanning industry produces primarily for the footwear industry, but also supplies a range of other leather product industries such as upholstery, fashion goods and clothing. Tanners compete on both quality and price. As far as quality is concerned, the key factors are the quality of the raw materials that the tanner uses, and technology, particularly tacit knowledge regarding production processes and chemical inputs. These are important at the top end of the market.

For the bulk of the leather market, price competition is a major consideration. The cost of raw materials accounts for a significant share of the finished product, usually over half in Europe (Knutsen 1999). Tanning is also a relatively labour-intensive industry so that labour costs are an important contributory factor in price competitiveness.

Many countries have placed export restrictions on exports of salted hides, and this tends to reduce the cost to local producers in those countries vis-à-vis producers elsewhere. Thus, access to competitive hides either of good quality or low price is an important competitive advantage for some tanners. Some countries, including Poland and the Czech Republic, removed such export restrictions as part of their economic liberalization in recent years, and this has tended to reduce the cost advantage enjoyed by local tanners.

Tanning is a low-profit activity within the leather-commodity chain. Environmental costs therefore, although not necessarily high relative to the value of sales, can be quite significant in relation to profit and value added at the tanning stage. This is particularly true for those firms that compete in the most price sensitive segments of the market.

Fertilizers

Price competition is also important in the fertilizer industry. Major sources of competitive advantage here are access to raw materials, particularly phosphate rock in the case of phosphates and natural gas in the case of nitrogenous fertilizers. Thus, some of the most successful

EU producers in the industry such as Kemira and Norsk Hydro base their competitive position on their raw materials. In the case of phosphate fertilizers, the high cost of transporting phosphate rock also gives a cost advantage to firms whose fertilizer production is close to rock deposits.

Like steel, and in contrast to tanning, the industry is relatively capital-intensive and large-scale so that access to capital is an important factor. Some of the major producers form part of large chemical groups while others, although specializing in fertilizers, are relatively large firms in their own right.

A further important element in the competitiveness of fertilizer manufacturers is their distribution networks. As application techniques are becoming an increasingly important element in the productivity of fertilizers from the point of view of farmers, user-producer links have become an important strategic factor for firms.

Developments in the agricultural sector are crucial to the demand for fertilizers. Although world demand for fertilizers continues to be strong, there is a shift in demand toward developing countries. In the European Union, demand is very much affected by the Common Agricultural Policy. This, together with the environmental requirements imposed on agriculture, for example through the Nitrate Directive and the Drinking Water Directive, is likely to mean a downward trend in fertilizer consumption within the EU.

The impact of environmental regulation

The impact of environmental regulation on competitiveness differs from industry to industry, and within industries between different segments.

Iron and steel

As was seen above, price competition is an important factor in the iron and steel industry. It is also estimated that environmental investments account for around 10% of total investment and of operating costs in the industry in the EU. It might seem likely therefore that environmental regulation would be a significant factor in competitiveness.

However, other factors appear to be far more important in the case of the steel industry. Differences in the cost of steel between different producers and countries are substantial, varying by as much as $100 a ton. These may derive from access to low-cost sources of iron ore, as in Brazil, or to large-scale production in modern, efficient plants as in South Korea. Modern plants also tend to be more energy efficient and therefore less polluting than older vintage plants. Pollution control is often built in to newly constructed plants wherever they are located so that although

local regulation may be less stringent than within the EU, this is not necessarily reflected in substantial cost savings where new plants are being
opened. However, there is a particular problem for older plants, as for
example in central and Eastern Europe. Retrofitting to reduce pollution
is expensive, and because of less-modern technology, operating costs tend
to be higher.

Although steel producers fear the impact of future environmental regulation, particularly carbon taxes, on their competitiveness, they have not
so far been a major factor overall. There are some areas of steel production however where there continue to be significant emissions, particularly from coke ovens and sinter plants. New direct reduced iron (DRI)
technologies are being developed which obviate the need for these processes in steel production, but so far these have not been extensively
adopted in Europe. These technologies depend crucially on access to
cheap energy and have been developed in Mexico (based on natural gas)
and South Africa (based on coal).

Leather tanning

To a much greater extent than the steel industry, tanning would appear
to be vulnerable to competition from countries where production is not
subject to the same stringent regulations that exist in Europe. This is
particularly true of those segments of the industry where competition is
largely based on price.

Estimates of pollution abatement costs in Europe put them as around
5% of total production costs. While this may seem not to be excessively
high, profit margins in the industry are only 2–3%, suggesting that the
cost of environmental regulation does significantly reduce profitability.
Other factors that contribute to low profitability have been the decline
in demand as a result of relocation of the footwear industry to developing
countries and greater use of synthetic substitutes, and increased competition from overseas manufacturers who have access to cheap raw materials as a result of local policies to increase domestic value added.

These problems have been particularly acute in Northern Europe,
which has also tended to be the area with the strictest environmental regulations within the EU. The experience of the German tanning industry,
where tighter environmental regulation in the mid-1980s came at a time
when the industry was already weakened by these other factors since
the mid-1960s, provides a good illustration. As a result, the industry was
poorly placed to deal with increased environmental costs since profits
were low and its competitive position already eroded.

In the top end of the market, however, competition is mainly on quality, and therefore firms that produce this type of leather are much less exposed to price competition. Value added in the tanning and finishing pro-

cess is also greater than in the price-competitive section of the market. It is thus much more feasible for firms to absorb or pass on the costs of environmental improvements, and they are less subject to competition from less-regulated producers who may not have the technological capacity to produce products of similar quality.

Fertilizers

The fertilizer case study illustrates how there may be considerable differences between segments of the same industry. In nitrogenous fertilizers, pollution abatement costs are relatively low so that the overall impact of nitrogen oxide regulations on firm competitiveness is not very significant. The key factor affecting the competitive position of the EU in this sector is increasing imports based on cheap natural gas from central and Eastern Europe and the former Soviet Union.

The situation is quite different in the phosphate-fertilizer industry where there are still technological and economic difficulties in removing cadmium from phosphate rock and phosphoric acid, and in disposing of phosphogypsum. As a result of the stringent regulations on phosphogypsum, there has been a significant reduction in production capacity of phosphoric acid and a fall in output in the EU since 1980. This has been associated with increased imports of phosphate fertilizers from integrated plants near deposits in the United States, Africa and the Middle East.

Technological change

The view that environmental regulation can lead to increased competitiveness is based very much on the argument that it will lead to technological changes that are not only environmentally beneficial but also reduce costs or lead to an improved product.

A recent review of the literature on technological change and the environment concluded that there was general agreement that environmental regulation is likely to stimulate innovation and technology adoption, which will facilitate environmental compliance. It was also agreed that external pressures can sometimes stimulate innovation that leaves the firm better off, and that where domestic regulation correctly anticipates worldwide trends, first-mover advantages may arise. However, there was considerable disagreement over the extent to which "innovation offsets" exist in practice. There is also controversy, when they do exist, over whether or not they are sufficiently large, relative to R&D and management costs, to give rise to true "win-win" situations (Jaffe et al. 2000).

Innovation offsets can arise in a number of ways. The most significant are where resources are used more efficiently and/or waste is reduced;

by-products are recycled or converted into a form that can be sold, thus generating additional revenues; or new technologies reduce production costs. In general, end-of-pipe measures to reduce pollution are unlikely to generate innovation offsets since they do not change the production process. As a result they are likely to increase total costs.

To what extent have any of these occurred in the three industries studied? In the steel industry two major technological changes have had significant environmental implications in recent years. The first of these is the growth of electric arc furnaces, which are particularly significant in many new producing countries. Although these are dependent on the existence of scrap, where this is available, it is a less polluting route to steel production than the integrated route. The second is continuous casting, which considerably reduces the amount of energy required in production. Although the introduction of both of these processes has reduced environmental damage caused by the steel industry, in neither case was the technology a response to environmental regulation. The environmental benefits were rather incidental to the economic advantages, which motivated the introduction of these technologies.[5]

Most of the other steps that have been taken in the steel industry to reduce pollution have involved end-of-pipe treatment. These include electrostatic precipitation to treat flue gas, and wastewater treatment. The rising cost of landfill in many countries has also led firms to increase recycling and to seek ways of reusing or disposing of their waste. Where landfill is not a problem however there is less interest in such measures since they also require new investments. It is not surprising therefore that steel companies tend to regard environmental improvements as involving additional costs and not to perceive them in win-win terms.

In the leather tanning industry, suppliers of machinery and chemicals are the main innovators rather than the tanners themselves. Moreover, technological change in the industry has been incremental and there have been no significant reductions in the costs of production. Indeed, as the third section of this chapter shows, the industry has currently reached a technological ceiling.

The main technological responses to environmental regulation have been to utilize less-polluting chemicals and end-of-pipe measures, particularly wastewater treatment. Not surprisingly therefore the leather manufacturers in Germany and Italy are clear that the cost of complying with environmental regulations are not compensated through innovation offsets. The new chemicals that are used do not produce such good leather as the traditional ones and "ecological leather" is both more expensive and of lower quality than that produced by traditional methods.

Production technology in the fertilizer industry has remained essentially unchanged since the late 1960s with most subsequent innovation being focused on reducing energy use and intermediate inputs. Increased energy efficiency does of course have beneficial environmental impacts through reductions in emissions such as nitrogen oxide and carbon dioxide. However, the main motivation behind energy saving is economic rather than environmental. Measures specifically designed to reduce environmental damage by the fertilizer industry are mainly end-of-pipe technologies, including gas scrubbers and dust collectors, and the reuse and recycling of process waters (Bartzokas and Yarime 1999: 42). Other examples of additional investments required to deal with effluents are specialized equipment to reduce nitric oxide emissions in the production of nitric acid, and units designed to remove fluoride compounds in phosphoric acid plants. Reuse and recycling measures usually involve concentration of process streams prior to recycling and also involve additional costs.

A major environmental problem in the phosphate-fertilizer industry is cadmium. The use of magmatic phosphate rock with a low cadmium content is one solution but world reserves are very limited so that this would lead to increased input costs, while measures to reduce the cadmium content by calcination are also very costly (Bartzokas and Yarime 1999: 44). As in the iron and steel industry therefore, environmental improvements in the fertilizer industry have either been an incidental benefit from technological changes introduced primarily for cost reasons, or have involved additional investments or production costs.

In summary therefore none of the three industries studied here provide any significant examples of innovation offsets that would suggest that environmental regulation led to increased competitiveness.

Corporate responses to environmental regulation

Given that all three industries are technologically mature and that significant segments are characterized by price competition, it is particularly interesting to discover the strategies that have been used by firms in the industry to maintain their competitive position in the face of more stringent environmental regulation and intensified international competition.

One strategy is to concentrate on the less price-sensitive segments of the market, usually by moving into production of high-quality products and/or those that incorporate more value added. This has clearly been an important strategy in tanning where firms, particularly in northern Europe, have focused their production on the quality market, and there has been a growing emphasis on upholstery leather. By emphasizing quality these firms seek to insulate themselves against competition from lower cost overseas sources. This is not easy to achieve and price remains an important consideration even among high-quality producers. Those firms that have successfully adopted this type of strategy have been able to do so despite the fact that there is little demand in Europe for environmentally friendly leather so that there is no product offset to be gained.

It is possible to detect a similar strategy in the steel industry where EU firms are concentrating more on high-value-added steel, rather than on primary steel. This is not so much driven by environmental regulation as in the case of tanning, but is a means of trying to avoid direct competition with firms that have lower costs of production often, as indicated above, for non-environmental reasons. Nevertheless, a similar outcome is likely since the most polluting processes in steel production are at the early phases of production.

A second strategy is to outsource the most polluting stages of the production process and to concentrate on producing the end product. The tendency for the tanning industry to import wet blue is an example of this, since it is this part that is the most pollution-intensive stage of the production process. By concentrating on finishing and using imported wet blue, some firms have been able to retain a position in the European market despite increasing environmental costs. The case study illustrated particularly clearly the effects of increasing demand for wet blue in the case of Brazil where environmental regulation was much less strictly enforced than within the EU, and a similar pattern was evident in Poland and the Czech Republic.

The tanning industry provides the clearest example of a competitive strategy of outsourcing amongst the three case studies. However, as was indicated above, some changes in the other two industries can be interpreted in a similar light. Coke ovens are one of the most polluting processes in the steel industry and there has been a tendency in recent years to make increasing use of imported coke within the EU while local production has declined. Germany for instance has relied increasingly on imports of Polish coke. Similarly, in the phosphate-fertilizer industry European regulations of cadmium content has led to the outsourcing of phosphoric acid and the closure of European plants.

Another important source of competitive advantage can derive from close producer-user relations. This was found to be particularly important in the fertilizer industry where some firms, faced with competition from the former Soviet Union and Eastern Europe and from North Africa, pursued a strategy of securing their own local market within Europe. A close relationship with local farmers is seen as a key part of this regional strategy.

There are also some tanning firms, especially those producing for the top end of the market, who have developed close relationships with customers. Several of the Scandinavian tanners studied by Gjerdåker (1999) emphasized the importance of developing loyal and long-lasting relationships with their clients as an important part of their competitive strategy.

Although traditionally the steel industry has not been thought of as a customer-focused industry, there is some indication that this is beginning to change and that some companies are trying to improve their profitability by paying more attention to customer service. This seems to be becoming more significant as a result of changes taking place in major downstream industries such as automobiles, which have become highly globalized and have increased their demand for uniformity of standards worldwide and reliability of supply.[6]

All these strategies that have enabled firms to maintain their competitiveness in highly polluting industries have usually involved focusing production within the EU on higher-value-added products or processes. In some cases, most clearly tanning, these processes or products tend to be less environmentally damaging. In others, specialization in high-value-added products, often incorporating a strong element of service, makes them less subject to price competition and therefore it is easier to pass on higher environmental costs.

Corporate strategy and environmental regulation

Corporate strategies are not only about adapting to external conditions, but also involve trying to shape those external conditions. There is therefore a system of feedbacks between competitiveness and environmental regulation. Our sectoral case studies have not directly examined the ways in which the three industries have influenced environmental regulation, either within the EU or in the developing and transition economies, since the main focus of the study has been the impacts of regulation on competitiveness and location. However, there is anecdotal evidence to indicate that firms do not simply take environmental regulations as a given.

In Europe, energy-intensive industries lobbied strongly against the introduction of a carbon tax arguing that it would undermine the competitiveness of European industry. Simulations of the impact of a carbon or energy tax on different sectors show that the iron and steel industry is likely to suffer major adverse impacts (Ekins and Speck 1998). It is not surprising therefore that the industry has been vocal in its opposition to any form of carbon tax. Because of its size and strategic importance, the iron and steel industry is in a stronger position to influence environmental regulation than many other sectors. In Brazil the steel industry association, IBS, is the only industry group that is represented on the Federal Environment Committee. This obviously gives it considerable influence over the evolution of government environmental policy.

The tanning industry probably suffers from the fact that it is a relatively small and fragmented industry, with a large number of small firms. This feature is particularly significant in Germany where, in the 1980s, the industry was unable to convince the authorities of the problems that new environmental regulations would cause. In contrast, in Italy where the industry is nationally more significant and also highly concentrated in a few major towns, the industry was successful in persuading the government to revise the Merli Law on wastewater discharges in 1979.

The fragmentary evidence from the iron and steel and leather industries suggests that where an industry is significant and therefore has some political clout, as in the case of European iron and steel and Italian leather tanning, it will use its influence to delay or water down environmental regulations which are expected to increase costs. Where the industry is insignificant, however, governments are able to introduce tighter controls despite the negative impact on a particular sector. Since the argument is often put in terms of the impact of regulation on the competitive position of the industry, it seems plausible that there is a "chilling" effect on environmental standards, although none of the case studies were characterized by reduced environmental standards as the *race-to-the-bottom hypothesis* implies.

Environmental implications of industrial relocation

Independently of whether environmental factors are a prime cause for the growth of pollution-intensive industries in developing and transition economies, the fact that they are growing significantly in these areas has major implications for the local environment. In this section we discuss the environmental impact due to the growth of pollution-intensive industries in the host countries of our sectoral case studies.

Environmental regulation in host countries

Weak environmental regulation is a major problem in all the developing and transition economies in which research was carried out. The case studies of industries in countries outside the EU revealed that environmental regulations were, as expected, considerably less stringent than within Europe. Often this was not so obvious in terms of environmental regulations because the key differences were at the level of inspection, monitoring and enforcement.

In central and Eastern Europe there is a considerable gap between compliance levels and those found in the EU. The steel industry continues to have some technologically obsolete plants with very high pollution levels, although these are now declining in significance due to loss of markets and closures. The leather and tanning industries in the Czech Republic and Poland continue to be high polluters, due mainly to weak environmental regulatory regimes.

In Latin America, Brazil and Mexico also lag behind EU standards. In Brazil there are differences between the various states with some in the South having more effective regulation, but in much of the country regulators are under-resourced and inspection and enforcement are limited. In Mexico, although the water discharge standards for the tanning industry were not significantly less stringent than those in the North, there was little enforcement and a lack of disposal sites for solid waste.

In Turkey the environmental agency is new, politically weak and poorly funded, and there are problems of enforcement with firms able to use their political influence and/or financial resources to avoid regulatory compliance. Moreover, in the fertilizer industry, although Turkey has similar regulations and standards to those of the EU for wastewater discharge and air emissions, there are no special regulations to cover solid waste, primarily phosphogypsum, which as was seen above was one of the major environmental problem areas for the industry. Environmental protection was also found to be extremely weak in Morocco where there are no specific Moroccan environmental norms and regulation is in an embryonic state.

In China, although there are numerous environmental laws, regulations and standards, again enforcement was found to be a key problem. Most of the firms in the fertilizer industry showed an inadequate environmental performance and this was attributable primarily to the weak enforcement of regulations. The case study of leather in India highlighted the problems of environmental regulation in that country too. Water and air pollution levels exceed the norms set by the pollution control board, suggesting that inspection and enforcement are not effective.

Although environmental regulations outside the EU were generally not as stringent as inside, the studies showed that this did not mean that firms overseas always chose the lowest possible environmental standards that they could get away with. Although lax regulation meant that many firms did not meet local norms, there were also examples of firms that exceeded such norms and had a proactive environmental policy. In the steel industry for instance, POSCO in South Korea and USIMINAS in Brazil were amongst the best environmental performers, ahead of some producers in the EU.

Environmental impacts in host countries

The combination of rapid growth of production by pollution-intensive industries and inadequate enforcement of environmental standards has led to substantial environmental stress in the countries where research for the case studies was carried out.

Poland and the Czech Republic are partial exceptions to this generalization. In common with other countries from the former Soviet bloc, they underwent major restructuring in the 1990s and a significant decline in industrial production. As a result there was a general reduction in industrial pollution in the two countries simply as a result of industrial contraction. As the case study of iron and steel shows, this meant the closure of older plants and these tended to be the most polluting. Thus it is quite possible that the drop in pollution was even greater than the decline in industrial production would indicate.

On the other hand, some of the structural changes associated with closer integration with the world economy, which were identified in the case studies, tended to increase the level of pollution locally. Thus, the location of wet blue production in Poland and the Czech Republic to supply the German leather industry, and increased German imports of Polish coke, both increased demand for products produced by particularly polluting processes.

China and South Korea have both experienced exceptionally rapid industrial growth in recent years. In China, the evidence from the chemical industry suggests that most firms do not have any facilities to treat wastewater or atmospheric emissions and that this is a particularly acute problem amongst small and medium-sized enterprises. In South Korea, too, there was a clear difference between the environmental performance of the largest steel producer, POSCO, and the other smaller companies studied. In both countries the sheer speed of industrial growth means that controlling pollution presents a major challenge.

In India, despite lower growth than in the East Asian economies, industrial pollution is also on the increase. The leather industry case study illustrates the impact that this has had on rivers and groundwater and hence on crop yields in neighbouring areas. Where attempts have been made to regulate the industry more strictly, firms have responded by shifting the most polluting processes to more remote areas in the interior of the country. This illustrates the difficulties of tackling industrial pollution in a country the size of India.

In the two Latin American countries in which case studies were carried out, Brazil and Mexico, the economic context in recent years has been dominated by trade liberalization and privatization. In Brazil the tanning case study shows that this has had a negative environmental impact because of the increased emphasis on exports of wet blue. In the iron and steel industry however, the privatization of the major state firms has been accompanied by a significant increase in the level of environmental investments, and there does not appear to have been a major structural shift toward more polluting segments of the industry.

Mexico has undergone an even more dramatic liberalization than Brazil, particularly since 1994 as a result of the creation of NAFTA. There is some evidence that in the tanning industry this has led to reductions in pollution as a result of access to more advanced chemicals. Some Mexican tanners have also used wet blue imported from Brazil, which while reducing environmental stress in Mexico tends to intensify the problem in Brazil. Even though Mexico has not specialized increasingly in pollution-intensive industries as a result of its increased integration with the United States, rapid industrial growth, particularly in the north of the country, has contributed to environmental stress (Barkin 1999).

The other two countries discussed in the case studies, Turkey and Morocco, also provide evidence of the considerable environmental impacts of industrial development. Even though there have been some attempts at regulation, these have not prevented serious environmental problems, particularly in terms of the disposal of phosphogypsum.

Potential for environmental improvement

Despite the problems associated with the growth of pollution-intensive industries in developing and transition economies, the case studies show that some advances have been made, and there are examples of good practice among the firms in our study.

In the steel industry, USIMINAS in Brazil and POSCO in South Korea have been environmental leaders and have introduced environmental measures and management systems comparable to, and sometimes even better than, those in the North. There are clear opportunities in the steel industry, where new investments are being made, to introduce equipment that incorporates the latest environmental technologies. Because retrofitting is relatively costly and may not reduce emissions to the same level as can be achieved in modern plants, the industry can achieve lower emissions per ton of steel in countries where production is growing rapidly.

A second important factor identified in the steel case study is the commitment of top management to improving environmental performance. This was clearly an important factor at USIMINAS, where the CEO emphasized the importance of environmental issues and the firm's status as the first in Brazil to obtain ISO 14001 certification. In Korea, POSCO created an environment and technology team in 1983. POSCO was also recently certified for ISO 14001.

Although tanning is a very different industry from steel, as it is made up of much smaller firms and has not generally adopted environmental management systems, there are also some positive experiences that illustrate what can be achieved in the right circumstances. In India, the United Nations Industrial Development Organization (UNIDO) has been involved in upgrading technology to reduce pollution in the leather industry. In Mexico too, the UNIDO Clean Technology Centre has provided technical support to clean up the activities of some of the León tanneries. This shows that where there is a will, and structural support is available, there are technological solutions that can lead to substantial reductions in pollution levels.

Political debates and implications for policy

The discussion of the relationship between environmental regulation, competitiveness and the location of industry has given rise to heated debate. This paper has tried to throw some light on these debates through detailed case studies of specific pollution-intensive industries. In this section we summarize our conclusions in relation to these debates and draw out the policy implications of the study.

First of all, our case studies lead us to reject the view that environmental regulation does not affect competitiveness and the global distribution of industrial activity. They suggest that in certain industries, for certain parts of the value chain, environmental regulation, in combination with other factors, has led to significant shifts. However, outcomes were found to be highly context-specific, both in terms of the industries and countries involved. It is not surprising therefore that general studies of environment-competitiveness linkages have often failed to find any specific impacts.

The case studies also show that in these industries environmental regulation does not lead to win-win situations *a la* Porter. There are cases where new technologies have led to both economic benefits and environmental improvements, as for example in the case of continuous casting of steel, but as this example illustrates, these are technologies that are adopted for economic reasons which have incidental environmental benefits. None of the case studies found significant examples of either product or process innovation offsets arising from changes motivated by environmental regulation, which are at the heart of the Porter hypothesis. There is only limited evidence, in the case of the steel industry specifically, of European firms that have been able to achieve first-mover advantage in the field of environmental technology.

A third debate concerns the impact of globalization or increased international competition on the ability of governments to protect the environment. The arguments over whether or not there is a "race-to-the-bottom" or a "regulatory chill" that affects environmental policy was not a focus of the research on which this paper was based. Nevertheless, the case studies did provide some evidence to suggest that where producers are strong and well organized they can successfully deploy competitiveness arguments against government efforts to raise environmental standards.

The findings of the study have a number of implications for the policy debates on trade and environment. As far as trade policy is concerned, one of the findings of the research is that it is often firms and industries that are under considerable competitive pressures for other reasons that find it most difficult to deal with stricter environmental regulation. There is therefore a real danger that, as many developing countries fear, measures against alleged "eco-dumping" would become an additional weapon in the North's protectionist arsenal. In other words, firms who find themselves under competitive pressure will take advantage of environmental clauses to remove potential competitors from the market. The use of protectionist measures on environmental grounds should therefore be resisted.

An alternative approach is to use eco-labelling as a means of identifying products produced under environmentally sound conditions. This is of limited applicability to the industries that were studied because they produce intermediate goods that are rather removed from the final producer. Even in the case of leather, which at least can be associated with clearly identifiable final products and would therefore appear to have the greatest potential for eco-labelling, it has not been developed on a significant scale. A certain scepticism concerning the scope for eco-labelling is therefore indicated.

Turning to environmental policies, arguments about competitiveness should not be used to block improvements in environmental standards in the North. The case studies show that successful firms are able to develop corporate strategies in response to such increased standards. The most desirable outcome is for firms to successfully upgrade, moving out of the most price-competitive markets into those where high environmental standards can be combined with competitiveness. There is evidence of this happening even within an industry such as leather tanning where the basic conditions of technological maturity and relatively labour-intensive production, are not particularly conducive to such a strategy.

The three case studies showed that there is a clear problem in the South resulting from the growth of pollution-intensive industries (partly in response to growth in demand and partly to changes in international competitiveness). This is taking place in a context where environmental regulation is weak and lags behind the growth of the problem. As a result, the environmental damage caused by these industries is likely to be even greater than in the North.

However, these industries provide important sources of employment, income and foreign exchange so that preventing their growth is not a desirable (or feasible) solution. Efforts therefore need to be concentrated on strengthening environmental regulation and encouraging the transfer of cleaner technologies at reasonable prices and without preconditions. Measures could include financial support and technical assistance to regulators in the South and credit for cleaner technologies.

It should also be pointed out that the purpose of environmental regulation is to prevent excessive environmental damage. Thus, reduced competitiveness in a particular industry leading to a reduction in the output of that industry may not be necessarily bad, all things considered. It may indeed be desirable to reduce the output of an industry that causes considerable environmental damage, since this can raise overall welfare when negative external effects are taken into account. This conclusion is reinforced when it is recognized that reduction in output in one industry as a result of environmental regulation leading to reduced competitiveness may, in a general equilibrium context, lead to increased output from other industries that cause less environmental damage. There is a danger in focusing on the effects of regulation on competitiveness in particular industries: the negative impacts at the macro level may be exaggerated.

Appendix 2.I: Definitions and terminology

Two phrases recur during the course of this paper, and it is necessary to clarify at the outset the sense in which they are used and the way in which they have been defined. These are *pollution-intensive industry* and *environmental regulation*.

The industries on which we wish to focus in this paper are among those: (a) that cause considerable environmental degradation, and (b) where the costs of reducing pollution are substantial.

It is in these industries that the impact of environmental regulation on investment decisions and competitiveness are likely to be marked. It is also these industries that are most likely to have substantial environmental impacts on the areas where they are sited and therefore where location decisions are likely to be most critical. Generally throughout the paper, we use the term *pollution-intensive industries* to describe these industries. Some authors prefer to use the terms "environmentally sensitive" rather than "pollution-intensive". The term pollution-intensive is preferred here since it captures certain parallels between the debates on environmental regulation and trade, and other areas of trade theory where industries are classified as capital-intensive, labour-intensive or skill-intensive.

There are two ways in which industries have been identified as pollution-intensive in the literature on trade, competitiveness and environment. The most common approach identifies those industries that have a relatively high share of pollution abatement costs in total costs, or relative to their turnover, as pollution-intensive.[7] The second approach considers the volume of pollution generated by an industry per dollar of output or value added, or per person employed.[8] Usually this approach relies on one indicator of pollution, often some weighted value of toxic releases.

Conceptually these two approaches could lead to the identification of very different industries as pollution-intensive. If, in the absence of any expenditure on pollution abatement, all industries generated the same volume of pollution relative to, say, output, and the marginal cost of pollution abatement were the same in each industry, then those industries with the highest pollution abatement costs would tend to rank lowest in terms of pollution per unit of output, while those with no expenditure on pollution abatement would rank highest in terms of emissions. Thus the choice of indicator would lead to totally different industries being identified as pollution-intensive.

In practice this is not generally the case since the assumptions that were made are patently not valid. Industries differ substantially in the amount of pollution that they generate per dollar of output, and the costs of abatement also differ considerably between industries. Thus, whether pollution-abatement costs or emission-based indicators are used to identify industries as pollution-intensive, the same group of sectors tend to emerge as the most problematic. As a result, there is a strong correlation between the ranking of industries by share of pollution abatement costs and by measures of toxic pollution intensity (Lucas, Wheeler and Hettige 1992: table A.1; Eskeland and Harrison 1997: table 2).[9]

A second potential problem in identifying pollution-intensive industries would arise if the ranking of industries differed significantly from country to country. Again however this is a theoretical problem rather than a practical one. Although the levels of both pollution per dollar of output and the share of pollution abatement costs may differ absolutely between countries as a result of differences in environmental regulation, the ranking of industries is broadly similar (Lucas, Wheeler and Hettige 1992: Appendix).

Because of the far greater availability of data for the United States, virtually all empirical studies use United States data as the basis for classifying industries, and this study is no exception. Industries were considered as pollution-intensive if they were ranked in the leading ten industries in terms of emissions per dollar of output for at least two key pollutants in the United States of America in 1987, or if they were amongst the ten top industries in terms of pollution abatement costs as a share of output.

These are therefore the industries that are environmentally most problematic in northern countries and where tighter environmental regulation is most likely to affect investment, location of production and technology.

Although it is generally the case that pollution-intensive industries tend to have both high emissions levels and high abatement costs, there may be firms within such industries that have relatively low levels of emissions and effluents as a result of significant investments in pollution control. Within industries, at the firm level, the assumptions set out above are more likely to apply than between industries. In other words, where basic processes are similar, firms with high abatement costs will tend to have lower emissions per unit of output and firms that do not invest in pollution abatement will tend to have high emissions, so that the inverse relation between the two criteria will hold. In practice again the picture is complicated by the fact that firms in the same industry will operate with different vintages of capital and that older equipment may involve both higher pollution abatement costs and higher emissions than more modern plants. There may also be differences where firms specialize in different stages of the production processes, so that a situation similar to that described across industries can arise.

The second term running through the paper is *environmental regulation*. The point that needs to be emphasized is that this is used in a broad sense. In other words, it refers not only to the legal and institutional framework of environmental norms and standards, but also to other environmental policies that can influence a firm's costs or the incentives that it faces. Clearly, regulation is not applied just to "command and control" type environmental measures but also includes market-based instruments.

The second way in which environmental regulation is broadly defined is that it includes not only the legal framework but also its implementation on the ground. This is particularly important to bear in mind when considering the impact in transition and newly industrializing economies. Environmental standards often appear to be quite high on paper, but the key issue is the degree of enforcement. This study found numerous examples of regulators who, because of lack of resources and/or lack of political will and the priority given to other considerations such as employment and exports, were unable to effectively enforce the standards that were legally required. Thus, when referring to "environmental regulation" this should be taken to encompass enforcement aspects.

Notes

1. For a presentation of the terminology (and what that implies) used in this study, see Appendix 2.I.

2. See, for example, the literature review in Grether and de Melo (2003).
3. In fact of course the electronic industry itself has important environmental impacts, for example, through the use of toxic materials and solvents.
4. These are identified as the ten most pollution-intensive industries overall among ISIC three-digit industries by Mani and Wheeler (1999: table 8.1).
5. As Johnstone (1997: 22) points out, this is not an uncommon pattern: "Since technological change is only partially driven by efforts to save on environmental factors, many of the resulting environmental benefits (and costs) arise almost incidentally out of efforts to save on the use of other factors of production."
6. An example is the collaboration between British Steel (now Corus) and Toyota.
7. Studies that classify industries on the basis of pollution abatement costs include Low and Yeats (1992), Sorsa (1994), Xu (1999).
8. Studies that classify industries on the basis of emissions data include Mani and Wheeler (1999) and Ferrantino and Linkins (1999).
9. Eskeland and Harrison however find that there is no correlation between pollution abatement and either suspended particulate or BOD emission intensity.

REFERENCES

Barkin, D. (1999) "The Greening of Business in Mexico", Geneva: UNRISD Discussion Paper 110.

Bartzokas, A., I. Demandt and Y. Ruijters (1997) "Environmental Legislation on Pollution Control in the European Union", Maastricht: UNU/INTECH, mimeo.

Bartzokas, A. and Masaru Yarime (1999) "Environmental Regulation and Corporate Strategies in the European Fertiliser Industry", Maastricht: UNU/INTECH Background Report No. 21, June.

Bergstø, B., S. Endresen and H. Knutsen (1998) "Source and hide pollution: Industrial organisation, location and the environment: Sourcing as a firm strategy" in H. Knutsen, ed., Internationalisation of Capital and the Opportunity to Pollute, Oslo, Norway: University of Oslo, FIL Working Papers, No. 14.

Dasgupta, Susmita, David Wheeler and Ashoka Mody (1995) "Environmental Regulation and Development: A Cross-Country Empirical Analysis", Washington: World Bank Policy Research Working Paper 1448.

Ekins, P. and S. Speck (1998) "The impacts of environmental policy on competitiveness: theory and evidence" in T. Barker and J. Köhler, eds., International Competitiveness and Environmental Policy, Cheltenham, England and Northampton, Mass.: Edward Elgar, pp. 33–70.

Eskeland, G. and A. Harrison (1997) "Moving to Greener Pastures? Multinationals and the Pollution-haven Hypothesis", Washington: World Bank Policy Research Working Paper 1744.

European Community (EC) (1992) "Towards Sustainability: A European Community programme of Policy and Action in relation to the Environment and Sustainable Development", Brussels: Commission of the European Communities.

Ferrantino, M. and L. Linkins (1999) "The Effect of Global Trade Liberalization on Toxic Emissions in Industry", Weltwirtschaftliches Archiv 135(1): 129–155.

Food and Agriculture Organization of the United Nations (FAO) (1998) World statistical compendium for raw hides and skins, leather and leather footwear 1979–1997, FAO: Rome.

Gereffi, G. (1994) "Capitalism, Development and Global Commodity Chains" in L. Sklair, ed., Capitalism and Development, London: Routledge, pp. 211–231.

Gjerdåker, A. (1999) Leather Tanning in Scandinavia, Oslo: University of Oslo, FIL Working Papers, No. 18.

Grether, J.-M. and J. de Melo (2003) "Globalisation and dirty industries: Do pollution havens matter?" CEPR Discussion Paper No. 3932, available at http://ssrn.com/abstract=432620

International Institute for Sustainable Development (IISD) (2000) International perspectives on clean coal technology transfer to China, final report to the Working Group on Trade and Environment, Winnipeg, Manitoba, August.

Jaffe, A., R. Newell and R. Stavins (2000) "Technological change and the Environment", Cambridge, Mass.: National Bureau of Economic Research, Working Paper 7970.

Johnstone, N. (1997) "Globalisation, Technology and Environment" in Globalisation and the Environment: Preliminary Perspectives, OECD Proceedings Paris: OECD, pp. 227–267.

Knutsen, H. (1999) "Leather tanning, environmental regulations and competitiveness in Europe: A comparative study of Germany, Italy and Portugal", Oslo: University of Oslo, FIL Working Papers, No. 17.

Low, P. and A. Yeats (1992) "Do 'Dirty' Industries Migrate?" in P. Low, ed., International Trade and the Environment, Washington: World Bank Discussion Paper 159.

Lucas, R., D. Wheeler and H. Hettige (1992) "Economic Development, Environmental Regulation and the International Migration of Toxic Industrial Pollution: 1960–88" in P. Low, ed., International Trade and the Environment, Washington: World Bank Discussion Paper 159, pp. 67–86.

Mani, M. and D. Wheeler (1999) "In Search of Pollution Havens? Dirty Industry in the World Economy, 1960–1995", in P. Frederiksson, ed., Trade, Global Policy and the Environment, Washington: World Bank, pp. 115–128.

Sorsa, P. (1994) Competitiveness and Environmental Standards: Some Exploratory Results, Washington: World Bank, Policy Research Working Paper 1249.

UNIDO (1999) Yearbook of Industrial Statistics, New York: United Nations.

Xu, X. (1999) "Do Stringent Environmental Regulations Reduce the International competitiveness of Environmentally Sensitive Goods? A Global Perspective", World Development 27(7): 1215–26.

3

Environmental management and innovative capabilities in Argentine industry

Daniel Chudnovsky and Andrés López

In recent years the focus in environmental management has shifted from the treatment of pollution at the end of the process, the so-called end-of-pipe (EOF)[1] reactive approach, to a more holistic and proactive approach that addresses environmental impact over a wider range of production activities including product design, procurement practices, and production processes (OECD 2001).

This new approach towards environmental management is usually referred to as "pollution prevention" or "eco-efficiency". The key idea is to shift from a "corrective" approach to a "preventive" one, as well as to try to transform what has traditionally been seen as a source of additional private costs – to meet environmental regulations – into a source of potential benefits, through environmentally friendly products or production processes.

This pollution prevention approach may not only contribute to a more efficient treatment of the environmental problems but, according to some of its promoters, may also reconcile environmental compliance with competitiveness – the so-called "win-win" scenario. This hypothesis, which was first advanced by Michael Porter (Porter 1991; Porter and van der Linde 1995a, b), is at odds with the traditional viewpoint on the relationship between environmental protection and competitiveness, where environmental regulations can only be met with additional investments and higher operative costs, hence reducing firms' profitability. While in the end-of-pipe approach a trade-off between environmental protection and private competitiveness – and hence national competitiveness – may arise, it is argued that pollution prevention or eco-efficient technologies may not only be less costly than EOP treatment but also, in some cases, may generate additional monetary benefits. Furthermore, firms may find ways to transform environmental actions into opportunities by responding to the changing demands placed on them by society in an integrated and anticipatory manner (OECD 2001).

Win-win solutions could be available for a wide range of industries and firms through what Porter defines as "innovation offsets"; i.e., process or product innovations which at the same time generate less pollution and improve firms' competitiveness, through higher productivity, decreasing costs or improved quality (Porter and van der Linde 1995a, b). This hypothesis has been rejected on the basis of conceptual and empirical objections by mainstream economists (see Palmer, Oates and Portney 1995). Nonetheless, some aspects of Porter's hypothesis may find support in another conceptual framework, namely, the evolutionary approach toward technical change. (see López 1996; and Bartzokas and Yarime 1997). Furthermore, several studies find that pollution prevention technologies are applied in many industries, but highlight the institutional and organizational obstacles to their diffusion, as well as the bias of regulations in favor of end-of-pipe solutions, confirming arguments already advanced by Porter in his papers (Hanrahan 1995).[2]

These new approaches may be of special interest in developing countries where social problems such as poverty or unemployment can only be mitigated in a context of sustained and sustainable economic growth. However, a number of obstacles, such as weak innovatory capabilities in manufacturing enterprises, lack of enforcement of environmental regulations, low priority of environmental issues in public policies and public opinion and/or the insufficient development of environmental NGOs, may constrain the adoption of a pollution prevention approach in those countries.

This paper is focused on the first of these obstacles, namely the need of manufacturing enterprises to build technological and organizational capabilities aimed at adopting pollution prevention or eco-efficient measures. These capabilities – which are usually acquired through lengthy "in house" learning processes – are required to select, adopt and master imported technologies. Moreover, since environmental problems are highly location- or firm-specific, there may also be a need to develop an endogenous innovatory capability to find solutions for pollution problems for which there are no "on the shelf" technologies available. As it is widely known, firms from developing countries seldom have such capabilities, thus constraining the diffusion of pollution-prevention measures.

In this connection, the Argentine experience since the early 1990s is an interesting case to be analysed. The levels of pollution are more serious than one would expect in a country of middle levels of income per capita and where industrial discharges are a major source of pollution (World Bank 1995). Despite this background, little progress has been made in the environmental front where regulations are mostly of the command-and-control type and their enforcement is limited. According to the World Bank (1995), Argentina's weakness in environmental management is due to an absence of clear institutional responsibility and a failure to enforce existing regulations. This situation still holds true over a decade later.

Nevertheless, the environmental situation has slowly and unevenly started to improve. In spite of their weaknesses, regulations are a source of pressures for firms to improve their environmental performance. Other factors that have induced better environmental behaviour include trade liberalization, the arrival of significant inflows of foreign direct investment (FDI) and the greater environmental concerns in some segments of the population. The fact that some industrial plants have been temporarily closed by judicial initiatives due to pollution problems has also forced many firms to consider environmental management more seriously.

Trade liberalization provided a powerful force to induce firms to reduce costs and upgrade their technologies in order to become more competitive. These processes have had favourable environmental consequences in some cases, through reductions in the consumption of energy and raw materials, waste minimization, etc. However, the available evidence shows that trade liberalization without complementary policies has often had negative effects. The difficulties faced by many firms (especially SMEs) for upgrading their technological capabilities and the poor development of endogenous innovatory capabilities were some of the key factors that contributed to the uneven impact of trade liberalization.

The main purpose of this paper is to gain a deeper knowledge of Argentine manufacturing firms' environmental management (EM) and especially to learn about the interactions between EM and innovation and technological modernization activities. With this objective, two surveys were carried out between the end of 1996 and mid-1997. One of them comprised 32 large firms and the other involved 120 SMEs. Their findings are the main source of information for this paper. Whenever possible those findings are compared with other information on the Argentine firms' industry environmental performance. Data from a survey made in 2002, which aimed at gathering information on technological issues but also contained some questions on environmental management in the manufacturing industry, were also employed.

Our previous expectation was that a more active environmental management and a wider adoption of pollution prevention or eco-efficient measures would take place in larger, export oriented, foreign owned and/or more innovative firms. Most of the findings are in line with these expectations.

In the following section we discuss the main aspects of the pollution prevention approach for firms in developing countries. In section 2 we summarize some key facts regarding environmental management and technological and innovative activities in the manufacturing industry during the trade liberalization process in Argentina. Section 3 addresses more systematically the relationship between both variables on the basis of the above-mentioned information sources. The concluding remarks, further-research suggestions and policy implications are dealt with in the final section.

Pollution prevention, innovation and learning

According to the proponents of the pollution prevention or eco-efficient approach, the traditional viewpoint on the relationship between environmental protection and private costs is based on a static way of thinking in which technology and customer needs are all considered as given, information is perfect, and profitable opportunities for innovation have already been discovered. Instead, the actual process of dynamic competition is characterized by changing technological opportunities coupled with highly incomplete information and organizational inertia. In this context, properly designed environmental standards can trigger innovation that may partially or fully offset the compliance costs. Such "innovation offsets", broadly divided into product and process offsets,[3] as Porter and van der Linde (1995a) call them, would not only reduce pollution but also improve the productivity with which resources are used.

Pollution prevention measures normally include (a) good housekeeping, maintenance and operating practices, (b) product reformulation and raw material substitution, (c) relatively simple process modifications employing currently available technologies, (d) more fundamental process modifications, mainly requiring technological innovation, and (e) external recycling. The design of "green products" is also part of the eco-efficient approach toward EM.

Pollution prevention actions can be distinguished according to their level of complexity. Some are "simple", with small investment requirements, low technological complexity and short implementation periods, such as water, energy and input savings. At the other end of the scale are more "complex" measures, generally involving greater investments, longer lead times and higher technological complexity and uncertainty; for example, the development of new, cleaner technologies. At the same time, it has been stated that there are many similarities between pollution prevention and total quality management, a key instrument for competing in open economies (OTA 1994).

Although the most exaggerated claims made by Porter on this approach are hardly supported by the available evidence, the advantages of pollution prevention or eco-efficient measures vis-à-vis conventional solutions, such as end-of-pipe,[4,5] are unanimously underlined. Compared with the conventional treatment, pollution prevention and recycling investments are often more cost-effective. Pollution prevention may produce significant environmental benefits as well, including reduced cross-media transfers and reduced environmental impacts from avoided energy and materials usage. The development of an innovatory capability to find new solutions for pollution problems in the productive sector becomes a key element to make this fundamental change possible.

As the pollution prevention approach has been encouraged in several developed countries, manufacturing firms in these countries have been adopting it, motivated by the idea of finding cheaper solutions to undertake their environmental management activities. However, these measures (especially the more "complex" ones) have not yet been widely diffused. According to Hanrahan (1995), both "exogenous" and "endogenous" factors may account for such a situation. An appropriate regulatory framework appears as a prerequisite for a wider diffusion of pollution prevention programmes. The internal dynamics, the managerial, productive and innovative capabilities and the sector of operation are some of the factors accounting for the uneven adoption of pollution prevention approaches within firms. Moreover, the lack of information on specific pollution levels in each firm may mean that PP opportunities are sometimes foregone. In addition, the lack of appropriate information on the availability and costs of pollution prevention options constrain the diffusion of such measures, especially among SMEs (OTA 1994). Supply restraints, such as the absence of the necessary technologies or the presence of an environmental lock-in situation where the equipment producers are biased to end-of-pipe solutions, could also explain the so-far limited diffusion of the pollution prevention approach.

In the case of developing countries these restrictions are still stronger. Most firms, and especially SMEs, seldom have the required endogenous capabilities to absorb and adapt modern environmental technologies and the capacity to develop innovative solutions within a context of weak public technological infrastructure and research capabilities. Those few developing countries that have made significant inroads into the manufacturing sector usually face severe industrial pollution problems. This situation is often the result of a lack of appropriate environmental regulations and/or the weakness in the enforcement of the existing norms. In turn, the deficiencies in the environmental regulatory scheme reflect both the fact that local communities are not much concerned about the protection of the environment as well as the fear that if more stringent regulations were passed, the industrialization process would be hindered.

However, this situation might have slowly begun to change. Trade liberalization, pressures from clients in developed countries, the increasing attention that transnational corporations (TNCs) are paying to environmental issues – both in the parent companies as well as in their affiliates – and the growing concern of their citizens with the protection of the environment would be drivers to stimulate the improvement of environmental performance within the industrial sector through the adoption of new practices and/or technologies.[6] This changing reality has been captured in recent econometric research.

Dasgupta, Hettige and Wheeler (2000) studied the determinants of environmental management in a large sample of Mexican factories. They found that environmental performance is mainly determined by regulatory pressures, implementation of ISO 14000 standards and provision of general environmental education for plant employees.

In Venezuela, Otero, Peterson Zwane and Panayotou (2002), using survey data from a sample of manufacturing firms, investigated the determinants of private environmental investments. They found that despite relatively weak formal regulation, past penalties and environmental permit status were strongly correlated with environmental investments and that firms that exported to rich countries choose to invest more in that area.

Ferraz et al. (2002), using survey data from a sample of manufacturing firms in Brazil, found that a past history of inspections and formal sanctions, market pressures – having received publicity about their environmental performance – and being publicly traded in international equity markets were strongly correlated with present environmental investments. Since it holds the promise of improving the environmental performance with little extra costs (or even generating additional benefits), firms in developing countries should be very interested in the pollution prevention or eco-efficient approach.

Nonetheless, the fact that many firms in developing countries have limited technological and organizational capabilities may cause them to choose end-of-pipe solutions once the environmental challenges appear. This tendency may be reinforced by the above-mentioned biases in the regulations, technology providers, etc., in favour of EOP technologies. At the same time, more complex pollution prevention measures are harder to implement: they demand planning, design, production and marketing activities redefinition, as well as the corporate management reorganization, in order to include environmental concerns in each one of these stages.

Hence, in view of organizational inertia, uncertainty about innovations and limited learning skills, it may be expected that the process of adoption of pollution prevention measures, with the exception of the "simpler" options, would be slow and gradual.

At the same time, not all firms react in the same manner and with similar technological responses to the new stimuli. The different paths available to them depend on the nature of their accumulated capabilities and learning skills. In other words, their trajectory is strongly predetermined by the nature of their specific assets (it is path-dependent). Their size, ownership structure and form of corporate governance may also influence firms' decisions, strategies and performance.

Firms with the resources and capacity to innovate and to harness technological and organizational change may be those more apt to face the new challenges. Those firms that have strong technological capabilities would be in a better position to absorb and adapt pollution prevention technologies available at international level through different channels. Furthermore, they would also have more chances to find *ad hoc* technological solutions to those pollution problems that are location specific.

In fact, those conditions are to a great extent the same as may allow developing countries' firms to successfully face the competitive pressures arising from trade liberalization in their domestic economies. Hence, it can be expected that the firms that manage to survive and expand in this context are in a better position for "greening" their operations. Furthermore, as previously stated, the pro-efficiency and quality-enhancing measures taken by firms as part of their restructuring process often have positive environmental consequences in terms of reductions in the consumption of energy and raw materials, waste minimization, recycling, etc.

In this connection, Barton (2002) studied environmental management in the iron and steel sector in Spain, the United Kingdom, Belgium, South Korea, Brazil, the Czech Republic and Poland. He found that management standards in developed countries, such as those with ISO 14000 series certification who have adopted proactive environmental management, do not always ensure that the use of clean technologies are maximized and the estimated performances of applied technologies are realized. However, for developing nations, demands of environmental compliance and innovation seem to go together.

In Brazil, for example, where the post-privatization transition period has brought environmental protection in line with firms in the European Union, production technology advances have had positive environmental benefits in the sense that there has been a shift toward pollution prevention and not solely end-of-pipe systems. Also in Brazil, Borger and Kruglianskas (2004) undertook case studies of three Brazilian enterprises (Daimler-Chrysler, De Nadai and Natura) to analyse the impact of the adoption of an integrated "corporate social responsibility" strategy on the technological innovation capacity and the environmental management of the firms. They found evidence of a strong relationship between such strategy and effective environmental and innovative performance.

In a previous study, Lustosa (2001) had examined the environmental and innovative behaviour of Brazilian industrial firms using data from a large-scale innovation survey from the State of Sao Paulo. Her main finding had been that companies with the highest efforts in R&D were the most likely to adopt environmental innovations. Moreover, she found that the consideration of environmental conservation as incentive for innovation was more clearly present in companies that attributed more importance to their internal R&D departments.

Last but not least, transnational corporations may play a key role in these processes, mostly in those developing countries that received significant foreign direct investment inflows in the 1990s. Transnational corporation affiliates are supposedly in a better position than local firms to face trade liberalization and environmental pressures since they have access to the modern technologies and management methods employed by their parent companies. Furthermore, these firms may exert a positive influence on the environmental performance of their suppliers, competitors and/or customers, both by "demonstration effect" as well as by the introduction of their own environmental standards. Local staff training on pollution control technologies, waste minimization and dangerous waste handling may also be provided by the parent companies (O'Connor and Turnham 1992; UNCTAD 1993).

It is also relevant to evaluate to what extent environmental technologies possessed by transnational corporations are diffused to domestic firms through spillovers. Environmental spillovers can occur when domestic firms are stimulated or obligated to undertake environmental management (or upgrade quality) by the parent TNC. Spillovers may also result from human capital mobility. Recent research has suggested that for spillovers to arise, local firms need to have significant absorption capabilities that allow them to reap benefits from the knowledge possessed by TNC affiliates.

While as far as we know no studies have been carried out on environmental spillovers from foreign direct investment, the environmental practices of foreign firms are analysed in recent research. Kaiser and Schulze (2003) studied the decision of Indonesian manufacturing firms to engage in reported environmental abatement expenditure using a data set of 22,000 large- and medium-scale manufacturing establishments. They found that exporting and foreign-owned firms were significantly more likely to incur environmental expenses. Ruud (2001) studied local environmental practices of transnational corporations on the basis of an evaluation of 53 affiliated Indian units and detailed case studies, finding evidence that environmental management in TNC-affiliated units in the country was strongly influenced by their parent policies and standards. However, he also found that local contextual factors counted with regard to the content and nature of the environmental measures adopted by TNC affiliates, and that local performance did not necessarily replicate headquarters' practices.

Borregaard and Dufey (2002) analysed the environmental management practices undertaken in the mining sector in Chile and Peru, based on interviews with selected experts in the respective countries and a survey applied to 50 mining companies in Chile. They found that environmental regulations regarding foreign investment (or, more often, production in general), consumer requirements, local image, international financial markets, competitor pressures, national and international NGOs pressures and environmental guidelines by the headquarters or parent companies located abroad influenced firms' environmental practices. They concluded that pressures for improved environmental performance derived primarily from international factors.

Economic restructuring, innovation activities and environmental concerns in Argentina. The evidence for the 1990s

Argentina went through a process of deep change in its economic policy regime in a very short time period, from the late 1980s to the early 1990s. During that period, a far-reaching programme of structural reforms was implemented in a quick way, including the liberalization of the trade and capital accounts, the privatization of almost all state-owned firms and the deregulation of different activities such as banking, oil, etc. The foreign direct investment regime, already one of the most deregulated among developing countries, was further liberalized. Price stabilization was achieved through a currency board scheme that pegged the Argentine peso to the US dollar from 1991.

As a result of this shift in the economic policy regime, import competition became a significant threat for firms operating in the domestic market. Argentine manufacturing firms, which had been highly protected during the import substitution industrialization stage, were expected to rapidly restructure in order to gain efficiency and thus be able to compete with imported goods in the domestic market. As public authorities put their thrust in market forces, almost no specific policies were adopted to assist the enterprises in their restructuring processes.

With the reforms, Argentina's economic performance substantially improved as inflation drastically fell and growth resumed after the so-called "lost decade" which had been marked by stagnation and hyperinflation. Even if in 1995 the "tequila" crisis had a severe impact on the GDP, growth restarted in 1996. However, from the end of 1998 until 2001 the economy was steadily contracting. At the end of 2001 a major financial and institutional crisis exploded, followed by the default of huge foreign debt and, at the beginning of 2002, the elimination of the currency board and the peso devaluation.

To cope with trade liberalization and increased competition within the domestic market, most manufacturing enterprises operating in Argentina implemented rationalization strategies to reduce costs and increase efficiency (Chudnovsky and Chidiak 1996). At the same time, as part of a technological modernization strategy, capital goods imports by manufacturing enterprises increased from an annual average of US$470 million in 1990/91 to US$2.6 billion in 1997/98. The introduction of new organizational technologies, such as "just in time" (JIT), total quality systems, work teams, etc., was also a significant feature of the restructuring process of the manufacturing industry, especially among large firms (Kosacoff 1998).

As a result of these trends, labour productivity in industry increased 52% between 1990 and 1997 (Alvaredo et al. 1998). By the end of 2000, hourly labour productivity was 50% above that of 1993. The industrial productivity gap between Argentina and the world leader, the United States, diminished as domestic productivity rose from 55% of the US levels in 1990 to 67% in 1996 (Katz 1999).

Regarding quality improvements, the number of ISO 9000 certificates granted to local firms or institutions passed from only two in 1993 to 2,275 by the end of 2001. In their search for higher productivity, many local firms reduced their personnel, as well as the local content of their products, weakening the domestic value chain and reducing the demand for labour. According to data from INDEC (Instituto Nacional de Estadística y Censos – National Institute for Statistics and Censuses), employment in the manufacturing industry decreased by 6% between 1990 and 1997; in 2000, the number of industrial workers was 25% below that of 1993.

On the other hand, not all firms could cope with trade liberalization and structural reforms. Many domestic enterprises, especially SMEs, lacked the technical and productive capabilities as well as the human resources needed to survive in the new economic environment. In turn, the absence of domestic policies aimed at facilitating the transition to the new economic policy regime and at alleviating or removing market failures (notably in the financial market) were obviously harmful for SMEs. Even some large domestic firms faced similar problems. In this scenario, while many firms went bust, others were bought by domestic enterprises and, most often, by transnational corporations.

The expansion of TNC affiliates has been one of the key features of Argentina's economic restructuring process. Foreign direct investment inflows amounted to US$80 billion between 1990 and 2000; two-thirds had materialized through mergers and acquisitions (including privatizations). As a consequence, the sales share for transnational corporations within the top one thousand Argentine firms increased from 35% in 1990 to nearly 70% in 2000 (see Chudnovsky and López 2002).

What were the sources of technological upgrading and productivity improvements within the Argentinean industry during this period? As said previously, capital goods imports were a main channel of technology acquisition during the 1990s. Foreign direct investment also played a key role, insofar as transnational corporations updated the process, product and organizational technologies employed in their already established affiliates as well as in the formerly domestic firms acquired in the 1990s. Other sources of technology imports were licences, patents, know-how agreements, etc., whose amounts also increased in the 1990s.

It is quite clear that foreign technology sources overcame domestic sources in the 1990s. Even if this had been the norm within the Argentinean economy for many decades, the dominance of technology imports was strengthened in the 1990s. Foreign firms not only displaced local companies in the domestic market, but the expenditure of industrial firms in foreign technology acquisitions saw greater growth than domestic innovation expenses. While in-house innovation expenditure by Argentine industrial firms grew by 47% between 1992 and 1996, expenditure on foreign intangible technologies (licences, patents, etc.) increased by 74% and capital goods imports by 100% during the same period (INDEC 1998). The bulk of intangible technology transfers also came from abroad during the last decade.

It should be noted that, according to data from the National Secretariat of Science and Technology, local resources for science and technology (S&T) also increased from 0.33 in 1990 to 0.52 in 1999 as a percentage of the GDP, and then fell to 0.44% in 2001 as a consequence of the macroeconomic crisis. In any case, the gap with other countries is still very significant. Spending by the business sector as a share of total expenditure in R&D is also very low in international terms, at 22%.

During the 1990s, SMEs had a higher level of innovation expenditure relative to their sales as compared with large firms. However, large firms are more prone to generating innovation expenditures than small firms: while 99 and 95% of large and medium firms, respectively, incurred innovation expenditures in 1998–2001, only 77% of small firms did likewise. (INDEC 2003).

It is certainly encouraging to find a significant group of firms that has undertaken innovation activities in response to the new rules of the game. However, besides the actual low size of the innovation outlays, it is important to bear in mind that the private sector efforts are generally of a short-term nature, do not include systematic scientific and technological research activities, are not linked up with public science and technology institutions and are not carried out in networks with active participation of suppliers, users and clients.

What has happened to the environmental performance of the Argentine industry since the early 1990s? Very little information is available on this issue, since no official statistics exist on either the resources devoted to environmental protection or on the pollution levels generated by the manufacturing industry.[7] Hence, it is not possible to examine the environmental performance of the Argentine industrial firms as such.

While the local environmental regulations[8] are quite stringent, there is a wide consensus that their enforcement is weak due to the lack of political will and/or resources to adequately monitor the environmental performance of local producers. This fact is aggravated because of the existence of multiple regulations for the same resource, since even if the provinces retain all the power over their natural resources and their environment, national environmental regulations have also been put in place.

Nonetheless, as previously mentioned, and due both to the need to meet local regulations – even if their enforcement is weak – as well as to pressures from consumers and local communities, foreign customers' requirements, etc., the environmental performance, or at least the environmental management methods in place in the Argentine industry, have improved during the last years, especially in large firms. The fact that the number of ISO 14000 certifications rose, from 9 in 1997 to 343 by April 2004, is a reflection of this trend.

In turn, the available data on private environmental expenditure suggests that the resources devoted to environmental protection by industrial firms increased in the last decade. Table 3.1 shows the environmental expenditure incurred by the Argentine Business Council for Sustainable Development (ABCSD) members between 1994 and 2001.[9] Such expenditure slowly grew from US$40 million to US$55 million from 1994 to 1998 and abruptly increased in 1999 and 2000, reaching US$120 million. In 2001 there was a fall in private environmental expenditure, which was mainly the result of the serious economic crisis that affected Argentina's economy. Since the crisis was further aggravated in 2002, it may be assumed that an additional reduction in private expenditure took place that year.

Our estimates for the private sector as a whole[10] are shown in column two of Table 3.1. In 2000, the environmental expenditure of private firms

Table 3.1 Private environmental expenditures in Argentina 1994–2001
(US$ current million and %)

Year	Environmental expenditures by ABCSD members	Estimated private environmental expenditures	Private environmental expenditures as % of GDP
1994	40	160	0.06
1995	42	168	0.07
1996	45	180	0.07
1997	50	200	0.07
1998	55	220	0.07
1999	110	440	0.15
2000	120	480	0.17
2001	102	408	0.15
Average 94–01	70	282	0.10

Source: Argentine Business Council for Sustainable Development and own estimates.

in Argentina was around US$480 million, accounting for 0.17% of the country's GDP. Given the fact that private environmental expenditures in the OECD area oscillate between 1% (in countries such as the United States, the United Kingdom, Austria and Switzerland) and 0.4% (in Australia and France), it does not seem unreasonable to assume that such expenditures reach nearly 0.17% in a country such as Argentina. In any case, even if some overestimation may exist in this figure, it is clear from ABCSD data that private environmental expenditure in Argentina grew not only in absolute terms, but also relative to the GDP (see Chudnovsky and López 2001).

No information is available on the breakdown and objectives of these environmental expenditures. Nonetheless, the information collected in previous research suggests that the increase in environmental expenditure is not only associated with the need to comply with domestic regulations but also with other factors, such as the need to meet stringent environmental standards in export markets. In the case of transnational corporation affiliates, global environmental corporate policies may entail some exigencies that could be stricter than those in force in Argentina, including the need to improve the environmental "reputation" of the firms, the possibility of obtaining cost reductions through measures such as waste recovery, energy or raw material savings, etc. (Chudnovsky et al. 1996).

In some highly polluting sectors such as pulp and paper, steel, petrochemicals and leather tanning, it was found that firms started to improve their environmental management in parallel with their restructuring efforts in a context of greater competition through trade liberalization, regional integration within Mercosur and growing inflows of foreign direct investment (Chudnovsky and Chidiak 1996; Chudnovsky et al. 1996). Export-oriented firms were especially prone to improving their environmental performance due to the requirements they found in foreign markets. Similar improvements in environmental management had been reported in other studies conducted in the pharmaceutical and food processing industries, though the motivations differed in each sector (FIEL 1996).

The above-mentioned studies found that firms had started to improve their environmental management in parallel with their restructuring efforts, and better environmental performance was often achieved as a byproduct of the efforts made to reduce costs and increase production efficiency to face the growing competition in domestic and export markets. Those studies also found that while end-of-pipe treatment was unevenly incorporated in many facilities, there was limited evidence of pollution prevention and waste-minimization activities. While several firms undertook process optimization and waste-reuse activities as part of their efforts to reduce costs and save energy, few firms adopted pollution prevention technologies (Chudnovsky et al. 1996; Chudnovsky and Chidiak 1996).

A study made by the World Bank also highlighted the positive role of economic restructuring on the environmental performance of the Argentine industry. This positive role stemmed not only from measures aimed at improving the productive efficiency and enhancing product quality, but also from the fact that "liberalization of trade and capital flows has opened up new horizons for many businesses, which are beginning to recognize that they will have to improve both their economic and their environmental performance. The crucial lesson which is gradually being learnt is that with modern technologies there may be no significant trade-off between these two dimensions of industrial performance" (World Bank 1995: 58).

The same study pointed out other trends that were judged as positive in terms of the environmental performance of the Argentine industry: (a) the massive inflows of foreign direct investment may have positive impacts since transnational corporations impose the same environmental standards that are in force in their home countries; (b) the fact that many Argentine firms had begun to take credits from foreign institutions was another source of pressure for improving their environmental performance, since many loans – notably those from multilateral agencies – include environmental clauses (environmental impact studies, audits, etc.); (c) the imports of capital goods and the deregulation of intangible technology transfers may have allowed the access to modern "greener" technologies (World Bank 1995). However, no quantitative estimates on the magnitude of those effects were presented. At the same time, the World Bank study acknowledged that SMEs were less likely to regard the new economic regime as positive and less well placed in terms of access to capital, technology and markets to take advantage of the new opportunities.

Chudnovsky and Chidiak (1996) warned that advances in environmental management were dissimilar not only among different types of firms, but also among sectors. For instance, those sectors that were more export-oriented seemed to be more prone to adopt modern environmental management systems. In turn, key variables explaining the differences in terms of EM and the rate of adoption of pollution-prevention measures were not only the size of the firms, but also other elements such as the origin of their capital (transnational corporation affiliates were seemingly more advanced than local firms), as well as the age of their facilities (modern plants were generally "greener" than older ones). Another issue highlighted by Chudnovsky and Chidiak was that "environmental spillovers" from large firms toward their small- and medium-scale suppliers and customers seemed to be very weak. It was also clear that environmental practices leading to a positive economic return were first adopted.

Even though the relationships between innovation and environmental management were not systematically explored in that study, Chudnovsky and Chidiak (1996) suggested that although the adoption of measures aimed at saving energy and raw materials, or at minimizing wastes, had implied some kind of minor technology improvements mostly based on endogenous capabilities, the weak domestic innovation capabilities could pose a limit to the adoption of more ambitious "eco-efficient" measures which often require finding ad-hoc solutions to highly specific problems.

The next section discusses the results of a survey made in 1996/97 of a group of large private firms in Argentina and, whenever possible, compares them with information regarding the environmental activities of SMEs – which comes from another survey undertaken during the same years – and with more recent information for a representative sample of manufacturing firms covering the period 1998–2001. The focus of this section is on learning and analyzing more systematically the relationship among innovation, environmental management and the adoption of pollution prevention or eco-efficient measures.

Environmental management, innovation and pollution prevention in Argentina

The first survey was prepared and distributed jointly with the ABCSD to 50 large companies (38 from ABCSD and 12 belonging to the pulp and

Table 3.2 Surveyed firms' sectoral distribution

Sector:	Firms	
	Quantity	Percentage
Chemicals and petrochemicals	7	21.9
Pulp, paper & paper products	6	18.9
Automotive	3	9.4
Petroleum	3	9.4
Food & beverages	2	6.2
Telecommunication equipment	2	6.2
Glass	1	3.1
Telephone services	1	3.1
Steel	1	3.1
Natural gas transport	1	3.1
Cement	1	3.1
Pharmaceuticals	1	3.1
Textiles	1	3.1
Tobacco	1	3.1
Electrical apparatus	1	3.1
Total	**32**	**100**

paper, steel and petrochemical sectors).[11] Answers from 32 firms were obtained (see tables 3.2 and 3.3).

The surveyed firms represented nearly 16% of the total turnover of the largest 1,000 Argentinean firms. The sales of the surveyed firms were, in turn, about 5% of the GDP, and their exports amounted to more than 10% of the country's exports. Surveyed firms' sales were, on average, US$440 million per year, and the average level of employment was 2,600 people.

To analyse the main research issues three indicators were defined to reflect, respectively, the environmental management level, the adoption of pollution prevention practices and the firms' quality and innovation capabilities. The following variables were included in the environmental management indicator: the existence of a formal EM department; the number of people involved in environmental protection activities; monitoring of environmental indicators and goals; environmental targets; an environmental accounting system; environmental investments registration; percentage of R&D expenditure geared to environmental issues; the implementation of studies on environmental impacts of product/process and on raw materials recycling; analysis of possibilities of using environmentally friendly raw materials and/or technologies; interactions with customers and/or suppliers; adoption of pollution prevention measures; and environmental certifications.

The pollution prevention indicator was estimated taking into account the importance given to the following measures: maintenance and operating practices, staff training, customer/supplier cooperation schemes, energy, water and input savings, product and/or process reformulation, raw material substitution, changes of existing processes, adoption of clean technologies and external recycling.[12]

Finally, the quality and innovative capabilities indicator was estimated through the following variables: R&D expenditure as a percentage of sales, number of engineers, professionals and scientists as a percentage of total employment and the quality certifications already[13] obtained or in-progress.

Environmental management, market orientation and origin of the firms

More than 90% of surveyed large firms had an environmental department. In addition, they defined their own environmental policies and also established targets for their environmental performance. Moreover, all these firms had staff exclusively assigned to environmental management, even if they were not full-time personnel.

These enterprises were aware of local and international environmental regulations and in several cases they were members of business associations created for the purpose of disseminating new environmental management standards. All of them had adopted primary and secondary treatment facilities, or similar end-of-pipe facilities. Of the surveyed firms, 92% carried out environmental training of their staff (even though the time devoted to environmental training activities and the number of persons involved were not yet very significant). Almost 13% of the surveyed firms had achieved one environmental certification (ISO 14000), whereas another 40% had at least one in progress.

Regarding environmental investments, the survey revealed a growing trend between 1993 and 1997, except in 1996. Moreover, the share of environmental investments in total investments had been increasing since 1993 (table 3.3).

Pollution prevention practices had been adopted by surveyed firms as part of their environmental management and were, predictably, the "simpler" measures such as energy, water and input savings, followed by good housekeeping, maintenance and operating practices and staff training. More "complex" measures – such as process modifications, cleaner new technology, raw material substitution and product reformulation – were less important adoptions.

The relevance given to pollution prevention measures within the environmental management of the surveyed large firms was also illustrated

Table 3.3 Surveyed firms' sizes

	Firms	
Firms with:	Quantity	Percentage
100 to 500 employees	8	25.0
From 500 to 1000 employees	9	28.2
From 1000 to 2000 employees	5	15.6
From 2000 to 10000 employees	5	15.6
More than 10000 employees	5	15.6

by the available information regarding the share of PP investments in the large firms' overall environmental investments: they accounted for 50 to 60% in the period 1994–1997.

Environmental management was stronger in export-oriented firms than in those geared to the domestic market (table 3.4). Most exporting firms surveyed had already obtained an ISO 9000 certification while only 25% of the firms selling to the domestic market had achieved that same level of certification. The same trend was also visible with ISO 14000 certifications, though dissemination of the latter was still incipient.

Regarding the dissemination of pollution prevention measures, a weak PP management was more often found in firms mostly selling to the domestic market than in those oriented towards the export market (table 3.5).

As expected, there was also a difference in environmental management between foreign and domestic enterprises. Broadly speaking, active EM was more frequent in foreign than in domestic firms. Nevertheless, there were also a greater percentage of foreign firms with weak environmental management (table 3.6). In the specific case of transnational corporations with a weaker EM, it is not likely that they were behaving as "environ-

Table 3.4 Environmental investments 1993–1997 (US$ thousands and percentages)

	1993	1994	1995	1996	1997 (estimated)
Environmental investments (on average)	1877	2163	2209	1504	3054
Environmental investments/total investments (on average)	10.0	11.9	8.3	18.7	19.0

Table 3.5 Firms' environmental management according to market orientation (percentages)

	Weak EM	Medium EM	Active EM	Total
Export oriented (17 firms)	12	35	53	100
Internal market oriented (15 firms)	27	53	20	100

Table 3.6 Adoption of PP practices according to market destination (percentages)

	Weak PP management	Medium PP management	Active PP management	Total
Export oriented (17 firms)	18	47	35	100
Internal market oriented (15 firms)	40	13	47	100

Table 3.7 Environmental management according to the origin of the firm (percentages)

	Weak EM	Medium EM	Active EM	Total
Domestic (15 firms)	14	57	29	100
Foreign (17 firms)	18	35	47	100

mental refugees". In fact, they were firms that had recently been purchased by foreign investors and where environmental practices had been inherited from preceding local owners. Meanwhile, most foreign enterprises with active environmental management were applying the global policies defined by their headquarters even though, in some cases, the subsidiaries retained some autonomy to react to specific local circumstances. Furthermore, on average, pollution prevention measures had been adopted more by transnational corporation subsidiaries than by domestic firms (table 3.7).

Technology sources and innovation intensity

With regard to obstacles against the adoption of pollution-prevention measures, access to cleaner technologies was the main one firms faced. Although this barrier was more frequent among domestic enterprises, it was also significant among transnational corporation subsidiaries. Furthermore, the lack of monetary and/or human resources also constrained the adoption of pollution-prevention measures, especially among domestic firms.

Table 3.8 Adoption of PP practices according to the origin of the firm (percentages)

	Weak PP management	Medium PP management	Active PP management	Total
Domestic (15 firms)	29	50	21	100
Foreign (17 firms)	23.5	17.5	59	100

Table 3.9 Environmental management according to firms' innovative capabilities (percentages)

Innovative capabilities:	Weak EM	Medium EM	Active EM	Total
Low (10 firms)	30	60	10	100
Medium (10 firms)	20	30	50	100
High (12 firms)	8	42	50	100

In-house activities were the main source for the technologies required to adopt pollution prevention measures, basically for those that could be easily implemented and/or where the problems were firm specific. Not surprisingly, other sources were as important as in-house activities when product reformulation or the adoption of a cleaner technology is required.

Expectedly, headquarters appeared as a substantial source of technology for foreign enterprises. Besides that key source, transnational corporation affiliates also relied for their technological inputs on specialized local enterprises (instead of foreign firms) and to some extent on local universities and/or research institutes. In contrast, besides the role of in-house activities as the main source of technology, domestic firms also relied on specialized foreign enterprises (instead of domestic assistance) and they had few links with local universities and/or research institutes.

A positive relationship between innovatory capabilities/quality management and environmental management and the adoption of pollution prevention measures was found (tables 3.8 and 3.9). This finding is a clear reflection of the importance of endogenous technological capabilities in the development of proper environmental management.

Firms operating in medium-high- and high-technological-content branches[14] displayed better environmental management and had made more progress in the adoption of pollution prevention practices (tables 3.10 and 3.11). These branches are the most dynamic and innovative at the international level, hence they have more possibilities of developing resourceful environmental solutions from which local firms may also benefit.

Table 3.10 PP management according to firms' innovative capabilities (percentages)

Innovative capabilities:	Weak PP management	Medium PP management	Active PP management	Total
Low (10 firms)	50	30	20	100
Medium (10 firms)	20	30	50	100
High (12 firms)	17	33	50	100

Table 3.11 Firms' environmental management according to sectoral technological contents (percentages)

Sectors according to their technological contents:	Weak EM	Medium EM	Active EM	Total
Low (11 firms)	27	62	11	100
Medium-low (7 firms)	28.5	28.5	43	100
Medium-high (7 firms)	0	14	86	100
High (3 firms)	0	67	33	100

Benefits from the adoption of pollution prevention measures

An interesting finding was that the adoption of pollution prevention measures, which in general did not eliminate the need for keeping end-of-pipe facilities, resulted in economic advantages with respect to more traditional control methods. In fact, seventy important pollution prevention projects carried out between 1992 and 1997 were identified from among the large firms surveyed. In only 17% of the projects did the expenditure for adopting pollution prevention measures indicate a non-recovered cost. Expenditures had at least been partially recovered in the remaining projects. In more than 20% of the projects additional monetary benefits had been achieved.

Most pollution prevention projects – especially those that were most profitable – were developed by firms with better environmental management, more advanced adoption of PP practices and higher innovatory and quality capabilities (tables 3.12 to 3.15). Take note that none of the pollution prevention projects with totally recovered costs or with net benefits were developed by firms with weak environmental management. Meanwhile, most of these types of projects were generated by enterprises with medium/high innovatory and quality capabilities and a higher level of progress with regard to pollution prevention methods.

An unexpected finding was the weak relationship between the origin of a firm and the project results. Since foreign firms have advantages in accessing new technologies and innovations concerning pollution preven-

Table 3.12 PP management according to sectoral technological contents (percentages)

Sectors according to their technological contents:	Weak PP management	Medium PP management	Active PP management	Total
Low (11 firms)	27	55	18	100
Medium-low (7 firms)	43	43	14	100
Medium-high (7 firms)	0	0	100	100
High (3 firms)	33	0	67	100

Table 3.13 "Preventive projects" results according to firms' environmental management level

	Expenditures for adopting PP measures have meant:							
	NRC[a]		CPR[b]		CTR[c]		Total of projects	N° of projects per firm
Firms' EM:	N°	%	N°	%	N°	%	N°	%	(on average)
Weak	4	33	5	18	0	0	9	13	1.5
Medium	6	50	12	43	12	40	30	43	2.1
Active	2	17	11	39	18	60	31	44	2.6
Total of projects	**12**	**100**	**28**	**100**	**30**	**100**	**70**	**100**	**2.2**

a. No recovered cost.
b. Partially recovered cost.
c. Totally recovered cost in some cases jointly with additional benefits with a similar or lower rate of return than other non-environmental investments.

Table 3.14 "Preventive projects" results according to firms' PP management level

	Expenditures for adopting PP measures have meant:							
	NRC		CPR		CTR		Total of projects	N° of projects per firm
Firms' PP management:	N°	%	N°	%	N°	%	N°	%	(on average)
Weak	4	33.3	8	28.5	5	17	17	24	1.9
Medium	4	33.3	8	28.5	11	36	23	33	2.3
Active	4	33.3	12	43	14	47	30	43	2.3
Total of projects	**12**	**100**	**28**	**100**	**30**	**100**	**70**	**100**	**2.2**

Table 3.15 "Preventive projects" results according to firms' innovative capabilities

| Firms' innovative capabilities: | Expenditures for adopting PP measures have meant: | | | | | | | | N° of projects per firm (on average) |
| | NRC | | CPR | | CTR | | Total of projects | | |
	N°	%	N°	%	N°	%	N°	%	
Low	3	25	11	39	2	6.6	16	23	1.6
Medium	4	33	6	22	14	46.6	24	34	2.4
High	5	42	11	39	14	46.6	30	43	2.4
Total of projects	**12**	**100**	**28**	**100**	**30**	**100**	**70**	**100**	**2.2**

tion measures, they should be in a better position to develop projects with greater economic and environmental results. However, this does not seem to be the case in our sample.

Environmental management in SMEs

A survey made of 120 manufacturing SMEs in Gran Buenos Aires in 1997 sheds light on some aspects of environmental management in that group of firms. The surveyed firms were chosen as a representative sample from a universe of 668 companies operating in an important industrial district of Gran Buenos Aires. Tables 3.16 and 3.17 include information on the sectors and size of the firms surveyed.

Expectedly, the SMEs surveyed showed strong deficiencies in their environmental management. For instance, only 20% of them had end-of-pipe facilities. Likewise, 60% did not have environmental performance targets and in several cases had no knowledge of the current national and provincial environmental regulations. Hence, it comes as no surprise to find that environmental management among SMEs was much weaker

Table 3.16 "Preventive projects" results according to the origin of the firm

| Firms: | Expenditures for adopting PP measures have meant: | | | | | | | |
| | NRC | | CPR | | CTR | | Total of projects | |
	N°	%	N°	%	N°	%	N°	%
Domestic	5	42	12	43	15	43	32	46
Foreign	7	58	16	57	15	57	38	54
Total of projects	**12**	**100**	**28**	**100**	**30**	**100**	**70**	**100**

Table 3.17 Surveyed SMEs' sectoral distribution

	Firms	
Sector:	Quantity	Percentage
Autoparts	31	25.8
Metal products, except machinery	23	19.2
Rubber & plastic	11	9.2
Machinery & equipment	11	9.2
Textiles	9	7.5
Electrical machinery & apparatus	8	6.7
Steel & aluminium	5	4.2
Wood products, except furniture	4	3.3
Publishing & printing	4	3.3
Chemicals	4	3.3
Paper products	3	2.5
Food & beverages	2	1.7
Furniture	2	1.7
Clothing	2	1.7
Leather manufactures	1	0.8

Table 3.18 Surveyed SMEs' sizes

	Firms	
Firms with:	Quantity	Percentage
Fewer than 6 employees	10	8.3
From 6 to 10	41	34.2
From 11 to 25	37	30.8
From 26 to 50	18	15.0
More than 50 employees	14	11.7

Table 3.19 Environmental management in SMEs and large firms (percentages)

	SMEs	Large firms
Absent	20	–
Very weak	31	–
Weak	21	19
Medium	16	44
Active	12	37

than in large firms,[15] and that the dissemination of pollution prevention measures was much more limited (tables 3.18 and 3.19).

According to the survey, the lack of access to modern technologies was the principal restraint to adopting pollution-prevention measures among SMEs. In addition, the lack of information was also an important obstacle

Table 3.20 Diffusion of PP practices in SMEs and large firms (percentages)

	SMEs	Large firms
Preventive maintenance	41	84
Energy, water and inputs savings	32	91
Workforce training	26	81
Process modifications through cleaner technologies	22	59
Process modifications through existent technologies	21	66
Substitution of inputs and raw materials	20	56
External recycling	16	66
Product reformulation	14	41

for many of them. Another key finding was that more than 25% of SMEs were not able to identify the difficulties they faced in order to be able to improve their environmental management.

A recent survey made with the purpose of obtaining information on the innovation activities and technological behaviour of Argentinean manufacturing firms also sheds light on some aspects of the SMEs' environmental performance. The survey covered the period 1998–2001 and included 1,688 firms, from which 1,489 were SMEs (INDEC 2003). Employment in surveyed firms amounted to 26% of total employment in the manufacturing sector in 2001.

Expectedly, environmental management activities are less diffused among SMEs than in large firms. However, the survey showed that 26% of surveyed SMEs had some kind of end-of-pipe system (table 3.20), while 50% had undertaken at least one type of environmental management activity. Furthermore, 5% of SMEs had an environmental certification. Interestingly, this survey shows that "cleaner technologies" or "pollution prevention" methods are more diffused than end-of-pipe systems among SMEs.

Technology seems to be the main obstacle for improving the level of environmental management among SMEs (table 3.21). This includes: (a) the high costs of some technologies, (b) the lack of information about feasible technical alternatives, and (c) the lack of adequacy of the technology supply to the specific needs of SMEs.

Finally, Chudnovsky and Pupato (2005) have been able to carry out an econometric analysis of micro data available for a representative sample of 716 enterprises from the previously mentioned innovation survey (INDEC 2003).

With the purpose of analysing the determinants of the quality of the environmental management in the manufacturing industry, the available information was used to group the firms into four mutually exclusive categories, according to the quality of the environmental management they

Table 3.21 Environmental management activities, 1998–2001 (percentages)

Activities:	SMEs	Large
1) Improvement of the efficiency in the use of water, inputs and energy	34	79
2) Systems for treatment of effluents and waste	26	83
3) Internal or external recycling	23	69
4) Replacement or modification of polluting processes	17	40
5) Replacement of polluting inputs or raw materials	15	40
6) Remediation actions	15	30
7) Development of "environment-friendly" products	9	32
8) Environmental management certifications	5	32
9) Others	4	9

SMEs: total panel of SMEs, conformed by 1,489 enterprises.
Large: total panel of large enterprises, conformed by 109 enterprises.
Source: INDEC (2003).

Table 3.22 Obstacles to improving firms' environmental management, 1998–2001 (percentages)

Obstacles:	SMEs	Large
High cost of the available technologies	39	54
Others	24	16
Lack of information about the available sources of technology	9	5
Lack of certain environmental technologies in the local market	7	21
The available technologies are not adequate to the needs of the firm	7	11
Lack of certain environmental technologies in the international market	2	3
The available technologies are protected by patents or other means	1	1

SMEs: total panel of SMEs, conformed by 1,489 enterprises.
Large: total panel of large enterprises, conformed by 109 enterprises.
Source: INDEC (2003).

undertook during 1998–2001 (following Chidiak and Gutman 2004): complex clean production (CP) management; simple clean production management; end-of-pipe; and firms without environmental management.[16]

Briefly, Chudnovsky and Pupato find that the size of a firm and its technology acquisition expenditure[17] (though not R&D expenditure) increased both the probability of undertaking environmental management activities as well as the quality of EM itself. In addition, they record a positive impact of environmental regulatory pressure on innovative behaviour, though such regulatory pressure induced end-of-pipe at the expense of simple clean production management. Foreign firms were more prone to undertake environmental management activities and generated positive environmental spillovers, by inducing simple clean production management in domestic firms with high absorption capabilities.[18]

While these findings are certainly more robust than those based in the descriptive statistics that we have used so far, the reported results should be read with due caution. As stated by Chudnovsky and Pupato (2005), although they have measured the explanatory variables at the beginning of the period covered by the data set and included sector-fixed effects in their regressions in order to obtain more robust estimations, endogeneity problems still remain. Hence, they prefer to view their findings as indicating conditional correlations between variables, rather than proper causal relationships.

Concluding remarks, research issues and policy implications

The surveys undertaken in the second part of the 1990s, which provided information for one point in time, showed that, as expected, pollution prevention approaches were more diffused among large firms, particularly those with higher export orientation and/or foreign controlled. Adopted pollution prevention measures were those demanding small investments and/or costs and requiring relatively "simple" technological actions.

Another important finding was a positive relationship between innovatory/quality capabilities and environmental management and the adoption of pollution prevention practices. In-house activities had been the main source of technology for the adoption of pollution prevention measures, even among transnational corporation subsidiaries, which anyway depended on technology flows from their headquarters. This finding was related to the fact that the more diffused measures were generally firm-specific. Hence, internal staff was able to develop appropriate solutions linked to their own experience and learning (i.e., it was a tacit and specific knowledge). However, endogenous efforts were also important, though with less intensity, when more technological "complex" measures such as the adoption of cleaner technologies and/or product reformulation were undertaken.

Nevertheless, since mostly "simple" pollution prevention practices had been adopted, the virtuous connection between innovatory capability and environmental management, particularly the adoption of "complex" PP measures, seemed to take place within narrow boundaries. These early findings are partially confirmed by more recent evidence and analysis. Size and technology acquisition activities are key variables explaining both the probability of undertaking environmental management activities as well as the quality of EM when a large sample of firms with information for 1998–2001 is analysed on the basis of econometric techniques. Foreign ownership is also a relevant variable in this analysis. The fact that R&D expenditures were not a significant variable deserves further research. In this connection it is important to learn to what extent R&D and/or management, design and engineering expenditures related to innovation activities have been a complement or a substitute for technology acquisition.

In any case, the access to more "complex" technologies appears as the main obstacle to making more progress in the adoption of pollution prevention practices. It may reflect that insufficient resources have been allocated to the adoption or development of environmental technologies. This is quite understandable given the risks involved in making long-term investments in an uncertain and volatile country like Argentina.

Economic reasons (environmental management cost reduction) seem to be the leading motivating factors for adopting pollution prevention practices. It has been common for PP measures to appear as by-products of actions aimed at reducing the operative costs of the firm. National regulations did not play a significant role in this connection.

As suggested in the received literature, the adoption of pollution prevention measures has meant economic advantages with respect to more traditional control methods and in many cases it also resulted in net economic benefits. The importance of local innovative and quality capabilities is also shown here: most pollution prevention projects have been developed by firms with such assets; also this type of enterprise has been responsible for the bulk of the more profitable PP projects. However, most of these projects have been based on "simple" measures, in which productive and environmental efficiency seem to be synonymous.

Summing up, the progress made in the 1990s in the adoption of more advanced environmental practices within Argentine industry seems undeniable. However, such progress was concentrated within a small group of firms, especially large, export-oriented firms or transnational corporation subsidiaries. Most Argentine manufacturing firms made little if any progress in this field. Even among those firms that apparently made greater efforts, the adopted measures were mainly of the "simpler" kind. Since good environmental management would increasingly become a crucial condition to compete in the marketplace, this situation is serious not only for environmental but also for economic reasons. This perception has not yet been incorporated among local businessmen, and particularly among SMEs (although improvements in the environmental behaviour of this group of firms has taken place in recent years).

Moreover, even among large, export-oriented and/or foreign firms, the advances do not cover the whole spectrum of environmental management. Whereas in several cases accumulated problems have to be solved, on other occasions measures involving higher costs and/or investments have to be implemented. Likewise, for greater and quicker diffusion of environmental management based on product life-cycle criteria, customer and/or supplier interactions need to be expanded.

Several issues should receive priority on the research agenda. First, information on the environmental behaviour of Argentine firms needs to be collected on a regular basis and complemented with data on key economic and technological variables in order to be able to carry out descriptive and econometric research.

Second, access to technology as a key obstacle to the adoption of pollution-prevention measures should be investigated. It would be important to learn whether the main constrains are due to supply restrictions, lack of information, cost problems or insufficient in-house resources, among others. Furthermore, the relationship between environmental management, the adoption of pollution-prevention measures and innovation capabilities in each firm should be studied with far more detail.

Taking into account the importance of transnational corporations to the Argentine economy, both their environmental management and innovation activities should be studied in depth, paying special attention to their spillovers on domestic firms.

The specific causes of environmental management and innovation weaknesses among SMEs, as well as the main obstacles to facing such problems, should be studied, considering different sectors and regions and the linkages between SMEs and large firms.

Given Argentina's situation, it is difficult to think that any of the problems discussed in this paper would receive priority in the short term. However, the improvement and preservation of the environment should become an integral part of a development strategy. Hence, instead of confronting productive activities, environmental policies should be gradually designed and implemented by introducing mechanisms to facilitate a negotiating process among the state, private firms, non-governmental organizations and other social groups. Likewise, the regulatory framework should provide incentives to induce firms to improve their environmental performance through innovative activities.

In this connection, current environmental regulations, which have been defined mostly in isolation, should be integrated with other policies in related areas. For example, it is pretty clear that firms' environmental management strongly depends on their innovative and quality management; hence, the improvement of innovatory and quality capabilities should be considered as a key component within any global environmental policy. At the same time, innovative public policies should explicitly take into account the environmental dimension.

The search for and adoption of cost-effective technologies (following a preventive approach) should become a priority in environmental policy. For example, OECD guidelines may be followed to examine which current policies constrain or facilitate this kind of approach. Moreover, since firms and sectors do differ in their environmental management, performance and problems, the policies in question should clearly differentiate between the appropriate standards and actions for each case. In particular, SMEs' environmental problems should become a priority for policymakers.

Finally, there is practically no public information on firms' and sectors' environmental performances and contamination. Since the availability of such information is a basic condition to examine the weak and strong points in environmental management and innovation within the manufacturing sector, environmental and technology authorities should make serious efforts to bridge the information gap.

Notes

1. The end-of-pipe approach is based on the identification, processing and disposal of discharges or waste. It is thus a corrective approach that tries to control the pollution after it has occurred.
2. See Bartzokas and Yarime (1997) for a review of pollution-prevention technologies in pollution-intensive industries, and Albrecht (1998) for a test on Porter's hypothesis. See also Jaffe et al. (1995) and Jenkins (1998).
3. Product offsets occur when environmental regulation produces not only less pollution, but also creates better-performing or higher-quality products, safer products, lower product costs and products with higher resale or scrap value or lower costs of product disposal for users. Process offsets occur when environmental regulation not only leads to reduced pollution, but also results in higher resource productivity such as higher process yields, less downtime through more careful monitoring and maintenance, material savings, better utilization of by-products, lower energy consumption, reduced material storage and handling costs, etc.
4. Pollution control technologies, which transform dangerous substances into harmless ones before being emitted to the environment, and cleanup technologies, which render innocuous those dangerous substances that have already penetrated into the environment and/or improve degraded ecosystems, are included in the EOP measures classification (NSTC 1994).
5. However, in many cases, the limits between pollution prevention and end-of-pipe are imprecise; for example, sometimes substances of positive economic value are recuperated by adopting EOP treatments. In addition, end-of-pipe treatment is seldom totally eliminated by the adoption of pollution prevention measures.
6. It is not always true that better environmental management represents superior environmental performance. For example, a study on a number of transnational corporation subsidiaries in the United States concludes that there was no correlation between environmental practices and pollutant emissions in each firm (Levy 1995). However, in general one can assume that firms with more active environmental management have the

conditions to control their pollutant emissions in a more efficient way than those with poor EM. Certainly, a firm with active environmental management would probably achieve a better environmental performance per product unit than their competitors in the same sector with weaker EM. At the same time, after adopting active EM the environmental performance of the firm should improve.

7. Some estimates may be found for the mid-1990s in a study made by the World Bank (1995).

8. Most environmental regulations in Argentina are of the command and control type. There are rules for air and water that set environmental quality and emission standards, as well as legislation on hazardous waste. There are some "shy" cases of environmental taxes and subsidies (see Conte Grand 2000), but they play only a marginal role in local environmental policy. In turn, no official deposit/refund scheme exists, and new policy instruments such as voluntary agreements to reduce pollution have not been introduced.

9. The Argentine Business Council for Sustainable Development (ABCSD) is an organization that gathers 38 business conglomerates – local as well as foreign-owned – that jointly represent 25% of the sales of the largest 1,000 Argentine firms. In turn, the sales of these 1,000 firms are about 50% of the domestic GDP.

10. To estimate the total environmental expenditure by Argentina's private firms the figures from the ABCSD member were increased by four. The fact that ABCSD firms are the most environmentally conscious in Argentina is compensated by the fact that the environmental expenditure for the remainder of the Argentine firms are not taken into account and probably decrease proportional to the size of the firms.

11. For a more detailed analysis of the methodology and the results of this survey, see Chudnovsky, López and Freylejer (1997).

12. Firms were classified in three groups in terms of their environmental management and pollution prevention levels (weak, medium and active). The groups were constructed in the following way. For each firm we assigned a value in each variable on the basis of its relative performance in the respective field. Then we summed up all the values assigned to each firm, which allowed us to rank the surveyed firms according to their environmental management and pollution-prevention levels. We added up the minimum and the maximum values observed in each indicator and divided this result by three. On this basis, we defined the three above-mentioned groups.

13. Three groups were constructed for this indicator, following the same procedure described in the preceding endnote.

14. The classification of branches according to their technological intensity is based on OECD methodology. Broadly speaking, such methodology takes into account, among other elements, the significance of R&D expenditures on total output.

15. For SMEs, the environmental management indicator was built considering the following variables: knowledge of environmental regulations, targets for environmental performance and measures implemented to reduce pollution levels (such as end-of-pipe treatment, maintenance and operating practices, staff training, customer/supplier cooperation schemes, energy, water and input savings, product and/or process reformulation, raw material substitution, adoption of new clean technologies and external recycling). The indicator (ISME) took values from zero to one (which resulted from the addition of the weighted values assigned to each firm in each of the variables considered). The groups were defined in the following way: (a) $ISME = 0$; (b) $0 < ISME > 0.2$; (c) $0.2 < ISME > 0.4$; (d) $0.4 < ISME > 0.6$; (e) $ISME > 0.6$.

16. Based on the activities enumerated in table 3.20, firms with complex "cleaner production" management were those that undertook at least one of the activities numbered four, five, seven and eight. Firms with simple cleaner production management were those engaged in at least one of the activities numbered one and three that did not

undertake complex CP management activities. End-of-pipe management was firms engaged in at least one of the activities numbered two, six and nine.

17. Technology acquisition includes expenditure in capital goods (related to innovation activities within the firm) and technology transfer (patent rights, licences, trademarks and designs) acquired domestically or abroad in 1998.

18. In order to measure absorption capabilities, the authors elaborated an index that includes different factors, as follows:

1) quantitative variables: the ratio of R&D employees relative to total employment, the ratio between expenditures in consultancy and sales, the payments for technology licences relative to sales, the expenditures in capital goods related to new processes or new products relative to sales and the ratio between innovation activities (including not only expenditures in formal R&D but also in adaptive and incremental innovation activities, project engineering, etc.) and sales;

2) qualitative variables: the degree of formalization of R&D activities (i.e., whether the firm has an R&D department or not), the use of modern organizational techniques, the importance assigned to product innovation in firms' strategies, the use of information technology in the relationships with customers and suppliers and the importance of tacit and codified sources of technological information;

3) qualitative-quantitative variables: whether the firm undertook training activities and, if so, the expenditures in training relative to sales.

REFERENCES

Albrecht, J. (1998) "Environmental costs and competitiveness: A product specific test of the Porter hypothesis", Working Paper 98/50, University of Ghent, the Netherlands.

Alvaredo, J., H. Cepeda, O. Kacef, J. Robbio and M. Forge (1998) La industria argentina en los noventa, Buenos Aires: UIA.

Barton, J. (2002) "The iron and steel sector", in R. Jenkins, J. Barton, A. Bartzokas, J. Hesselberg and H. Knutsen, Environmental regulation in the new global economy: The impact on industry and competitiveness, Cheltenham, England: Edward Elgar.

Bartzokas, A. and M. Yarime (1997) "Technology trends in pollution-intensive industries: A review of sectoral trends", Discussion Paper Series No. 9706, Maastricht: United Nations University, Institute for New Technologies.

Borger, G. and I. Kruglianskas (2004) "Corporate social responsibility and environmental and technological innovation performance: Case studies of Brazilian companies", International Journal of Technology, Policy and Management: Special Issue on Systems and Policies Fostering.

Borregaard, N. and A. Dufey (2002) "Environmental effects of foreign investment versus domestic investment in the mining sector in Latin America", document presented at the OECD Global Forum on International Investment, Conference on "Foreign Direct Investment and the Environment: Lessons to be Learned from the Mining Sector", Paris, February 7–8.

Chidiak M. and V. Gutman (2004) "Características, motivaciones y obstáculos a la gestión ambiental en la industria argentina: Resultados de la Segunda Encuesta de Innovación y Conducta Tecnológica", mimeo, Buenos Aires: ECLAC.

Chudnovsky, D. and M. Chidiak (1996) "Competitividad y medio ambiente: Claros y oscuros en la industria argentina", Boletín Informativo Techint 286, April–June.

Chudnovsky, D. and A. López (2001) "Gasto, inversión y financiamiento para el desarrollo sostenible en la Argentina", ECLAC/UNDP, Conferencia Regional de América Latina y el Caribe preparatoria de la Cumbre Mundial sobre Desarrollo Sostenible, Río de Janeiro, October.

———— (2002) "Integración regional e inversión extranjera directa: El caso del MERCOSUR", Serie REDINT, INTAL, Buenos Aires: Inter-American Development Bank.

Chudnovsky, D., A. López and V. Freylejer (1997) "La prevención de la contaminación en la gestión ambiental de la industria argentina", Working Paper No. 24, Buenos Aires: CENIT.

Chudnovsky, D. and G. Pupato (2005) "Environmental management and innovation in Argentine industry: Determinants and policy implications", Buenos Aires: CENIT, mimeo.

Chudnovsky, D., F. Porta and M. Chidiak (1996) "Los límites de la apertura. Liberalización, reestructuración productiva y medio ambiente", Buenos Aires: Alianza/CENIT.

Conte Grand, Mariana (2000) "Public environmental expenditures in Argentina during the 90s", Working Paper No. 169, Buenos Aires: Universidad del CEMA, October.

Dasgupta, S., H. Hettige and D. Wheeler (2000) "What improves environmental compliance? Evidence from Mexican industry", Journal of Environmental Economics and Management 39: 39–66.

Ferraz, C., A. P. Zwane, R. S. da Motta and T. Panayotou (2002) "How do firms make environmental investment decisions? Evidence from Brazil", Center for International Development, Harvard University Publications, mimeo, available from http://www.cid.harvard.edu/esd/Publications/publicationsurbanmgt.html.

Fundación de Investigaciones Latinoamericanas (FIEL) (1996) Medio ambiente en la Argentina. Prioridades y regulaciones, Buenos Aires.

Hanrahan, D. (1995) "Putting cleaner production to work", discussion draft, Washington, DC: World Bank.

Instituto Nacional de Estadísticas y Censos (INDEC) (1998) Encuesta sobre la conducta tecnológica de las empresas industriales argentinas, Buenos Aires.

———— (2003) Segunda encuesta nacional de innovación y conducta tecnológica de las empresas argentinas, Serie Estudios No. 38, Buenos Aires.

Jaffe, A. S. R. Peterson, P. R. Portney and R. N. Stavins (1995) "Environmental regulation and the competitiveness of US manufacturing: What does the evidence tell us?", Journal of Economic Literature 33.

Jenkins, R. (1998) "Environmental regulation and international competitiveness: A review of literature and some European evidence", Discussion Paper Series No. 9801, Maastricht: United Nations University, Institute for New Technologies.

Kaiser, K. and G. Schulze (2003) "International Competition and Environmental Expenditures: Empirical Evidence from Indonesian Manufacturing Plants", HWWA Discussion Paper 222, Hamburg Institute of International Economics.

Katz, J. (1999) "Cambios estructurales y evolución en la productividad laboral en la industria latinoamericana en el período 1970–1996", draft, Santiago de Chile: ECLAC.

Kosacoff, Bernardo, ed. (1998) Estrategias empresariales en tiempos de cambio, Buenos Aires, Argentina: ECLAC/UNQUI.

Levy, D. L. (1995) "The environmental practices and performance of transnational corporations", Transnational Corporations 1(4).

López, A. (1996) "Competitividad, innovación y desarrollo sustentable", Working Paper No. 22, Buenos Aires, Argentina: CENIT.

Lustosa, M. (2001) "Innovation and environment under an evolutionary perspective: Evidence from Brazilian firms", electronic paper BoA-237, Danish Research Unit for Industrial Dynamics (DRUID), prepared for the "Nelson and Winter Conference", Aalborg, June.

National Science and Technology Council (NSTC) (1994) Technology for a sustainable future, Office of Science and Technology Policy, Washington DC.

O'Connor, D. and D. Turnham (1992) "Managing the environment in developing countries", Policy Brief No. 2, Paris: OECD Development Centre.

Organization for Economic Cooperation and Development (OECD) (2001) Encouraging environmental management in industry, Business and Industry Policy Forum Series, Science, Technology and Industry Directorate, Paris.

Office of Technology Assessment (OTA) (1994) Industry, technology and the environment: Competitive challenges and business opportunities, Washington, DC: United States Congress.

Otero, I., A. Peterson Zwane and T. Panayotou (2002) "How do firms make environmental investment decisions? Evidence from Venezuela", Center for International Development, Harvard University Publications, mimeo.

Palmer, K., W. Oates and P. Portney (1995) "Tightening environmental standards: The benefit-cost or the no-cost paradigm?", Journal of Economics Perspectives 4(9).

Porter, M. (1991) "America's green strategy", Scientific American 186(264).

Porter, M. and C. van der Linde (1995a) "Toward a new conception of the environment-competitiveness relationship", Journal of Economics Perspectives 4(9).

——— (1995b) "Green and competitive", Harvard Business Review, September–October.

Ruud, A. (2001) "Environmental Management of Transnational Corporations in India: Are TNC's Creating Islands of Environmental Excellence in a Sea of Dirt?" Working Paper No. 1/01, University of Oslo, Centre for Development and the Environment.

United Nations Conference on Trade and Development (UNCTAD) (1993) Environmental management in transnational corporations, Programme on Transnational Corporations, Environment Series No. 4, New York.

World Bank (1995) Argentina: Managing environmental pollution; Issues and options, Environmental and Urban Development Division, Washington DC.

4

To the limits ... and beyond? Environmental regulation and innovation in the Canadian pulp and paper industry

Brent Herbert-Copley

In the mid-1990s, new regulations entered into force in Canada that significantly tightened limits on effluents from pulp and paper mills. Whereas earlier regulations had been relatively weak and ineffective, the new federal regulations on traditional pollutants (combined with provincial standards dealing with chlorine use) resulted in a situation where Canadian firms faced regulatory limits at least as stringent as competitor countries – and in some respects more stringent.

In the wake of the new regulations, environment-related investment by the industry expanded rapidly, and average effluent levels fell in equally dramatic fashion. By 1996 (the deadline for compliance with new regulations) only one Canadian pulp mill was consistently out of compliance with the new federal regulations.

Based on a survey of pulp and paper firms carried out in 1997, this paper examines in detail the nature of industry's response to the new regulations. In particular, it discusses the way in which regulations interacted with other structural features of the Canadian pulp and paper industry to promote innovation and diffusion of environmental technologies. The paper argues that we can "read" the story of industry's adaptation to regulatory pressures in at least two different ways. A first narrative emphasizes the compliance-oriented nature of most investment by Canadian pulp and paper firms, which focused on the adoption of proven control technologies rather than actively searching for innovative solutions to environmental challenges. A second narrative, however, takes a slightly more nuanced view of industry's response to new regulations. While "end-of-pipe" controls dominated investment programmes, many firms also introduced a series of internal process changes, resulting in levels of environmental performance well beyond mandated limits. The choice of which narrative to emphasize has important implications for our thinking on the links between environmental and innovation policy.

Regulatory influences on Canadian pulp and paper firms

Pulp and paper manufacturing is characterized by a series of environmental impacts, ranging from upstream forest management practices to downstream issues concerning recycling and disposal of solid wastes. Most regulatory attention, however, has tended to focus on direct contamination from the pulping process – and in particular on liquid effluents. Effluent quality is generally assessed along two sets of parameters:

Organic material in liquid effluents

Levels of organic matter are generally measured in terms of biochemical oxygen demand (BOD) or chemical oxygen demand (COD), which reflect the impact of biodegradeable wastes on dissolved oxygen in water – and thus indirectly on the ability of a body of water to support aquatic life. Also important are levels of total suspended solids (TSS). Levels of organic pollutants depend on a number of factors, in particular the type of process technology employed (mechanical pulping, chemical or kraft pulping or chemo-thermo-mechanical pulping, CTMP).

Toxic compounds in liquid effluents, resulting primarily from chlorine used in order to improve the colour of pulp

Levels of contamination are generally measured by levels of overall organochlorines (absorbable organic halides, or AOX) by the presence of specific toxins like dioxin and furans, or in terms of the extent of use of elemental chlorine.[1] The bleaching issue is a particularly controversial one, and over the course of the 1990s most new producers of kraft pulp switched to either elemental chlorine-free (ECF) bleaching processes, or to totally chlorine-free (TCF) processes. Prior to the 1990s, effluent regulations facing Canadian pulp and paper mills were relatively weak and ineffective. The principal legislation at the federal level was a set of 1971 amendments to the Fisheries Act, which set standards for total suspended solids, biochemical oxygen demand, and acute lethality based on the type of process technology employed at individual mills. Standards were set on a Canada-wide basis, and were meant to apply to all direct-discharge mills – although older mills were to be provided with time to adapt to the requirements of the legislation, by negotiating with authorities regarding timetables for compliance.

In practice, the Act suffered from a number of weaknesses (see Bonsor 1990; Sinclair 1991; and Stanbury 1993 for reviews). In the first place, standards were in fact not uniform across the country. Regulation of industrial pollution in Canada is shared between federal and provincial governments, and overlapping mandates have been a source of confusion and concern. Most provinces issue permits for mill operations: provincial standards are typically set on a mill-by-mill basis, and in many cases regulate additional parameters (pH, colour, and more recently AOX) beyond those covered by federal regulations.[2] Moreover, enforcement of regulations was and continues to be primarily the responsibility of provincial officials. Thus, actual regulatory limits facing mills varied widely across the country: data compiled by Sinclair (1991: 88–89) showed that of 122 direct discharge mills in operation in 1985, approximately 45% were subject to provincial limits more stringent than federal requirements, 31% faced less stringent requirements and 16% faced provincial limits equal to those required under federal law (in the remaining 7% of cases, information was not available).

Even more critically, in practice regulations were only applied to mills constructed after 1971 (or which expanded production by more than 10% after 1971); for older mills, regulations were used only as guidelines, and company officials negotiated timetables for compliance with regulatory authorities. Given the imbalance in technical and economic knowledge about mill operations between company and regulatory officials – and the potential economic impact of mill closings on what are frequently remote, single-industry communities – regulatory officials tended to be sensitive to claims about the negative economic consequences of regulations on older mills (Sinclair 1991: 98–99). As a result, most older mills were exempted from the regulations: Bonsor (1990: 169) claims that as of 1990 only 10% of all pulp and paper mills in the country were subject to the regulations. Data for 1985 indicate that a large number of mills fell below federal guidelines for environmental performance: 79% met BOD limits, 61% were in compliance with TSS limits, and only 32% met acute lethality standards (Sinclair 1991: 90). Prosecutions of violators were relatively rare, and fines levied were insufficient to act as a deterrent (Bonsor 1990: 170; see also Nemetz 1986).

By the late 1980s, pressures had mounted for changes in regulatory policy vis-à-vis the industry. In part, changes were motivated by the evident failure of existing regulations and accompanying investment subsidies to promote environmental improvements across the industry. A 1988 study commissioned by the federal environment department (Sinclair 1988) noted the failure of the guidelines approach to promoting improvements at older mills. Meanwhile, widespread media attention in 1987 and 1988 following the discovery of significant concentrations of potentially carcinogenic dioxins in kraft pulp mill effluents in Ontario raised the pressures on both government and industry to take action.

The main result was a series of amendments to the Fisheries Act and the Canadian Environmental Protection Act (CEPA), which came into effect in July 1992 – as well as a number of changes to provincial regulations announced at about the same time (or in some cases somewhat earlier). The 1992 regulations introduced new, more stringent regulations on BOD and TSS, based on performance standards that could be reached with the installation of up-to-date primary- and secondary-treatment facilities. They also maintained acute lethality standards, and added new regulations governing dioxin and furan emissions. Even more importantly, the regulations were designed to apply to all mills (not just new ones) and to dramatically restrict the scope for exemptions from regulation. In the case of dioxin and furan limits (which applied only to mills using chlorine bleaching), mills in operation prior to 1990 were given until January 1994 to ensure compliance; all mills also had to immediately cease using woodchips contaminated with pentachlorophenol, and to reformulate defoamers to remove dioxins and furans – thus removing the two major sources of dioxin/furan emissions. In the case of BOD and TSS limits, mills that needed time to install treatment facilities or alter production processes could apply for an authorization to delay compliance until December 31, 1993, and a further extension of the time limit to December 31, 1995 under exceptional circumstances.[3] In practice, extensions were widely used: of the 157 mills subject to the new BOD/TSS limits, 97 were granted extensions to the end of 1995 (Environment Canada 1998). Even so, the timetable for compliance with regulations was extremely tight by earlier standards, and there was no scope for exception beyond the December 1995 deadline.

As a result of the 1992 regulations and accompanying provincial restrictions, Canadian pulp and paper producers face effluent standards that are at least as stringent as those prevailing in competitor countries, and in many respects more stringent. Table 4.1 provides an overview of Canadian federal and provincial guidelines prevailing in the late 1990s, as well as comparable limits in the United States, and a composite measure of international "good practice" based on a review of performance in a number of countries. One point that needs to be kept in mind is that regulatory requirements vary among pulp-producing regions in Canada. In particular, the Atlantic provinces are the only major pulp-producing region which has not set provincial regulations; as a result, pulp mills in Atlantic Canada generally face lower BOD and TSS limits than mills in other provinces, and no limits whatsoever on AOX.

Strict numerical comparisons may understate the stringency of Cana-

Table 4.1 Regulatory standards in Canadian and other jurisdictions, ca. 1996 (1)

	Biochemical oxygen demand, BOD$_5$ (kg/adt)	Total suspended solids, TSS (kg/adt)	Adsorbable organic halides, AOX (kg/adt)
Federal Government	7.5	11.25	No limits set
Alberta (2)	1.5–5.5	3.0–9.5	0.54–1.5
British Columbia (2)	5.0–7.5	11.25	2.5 (various dates) 1.5 (by 31/12/95) 0.0 (by 31/12/02)
Ontario (2)	3.35–5.0	5.0–7.87	2.5 (by 25/11/93) 1.5 (by 31/12/95) 0.8 (by 31/12/99)
Quebec (3)	5.0	8.0	1.5/2.5 (by 31/12/93) 1.0/2.0 (by 31/12/95) 0.8 (by 31/12/00)
International "Good Practice" Levels (4)	Bleached Kraft 15.0 (4.0) Mechanical 10.0 (4.0)	Bleached Kraft 7.0 (5.0) Mechanical 7.0 (3.0)	2.0 (0.8)
United States (5)	5.5–8.05	11.9–16.4	0.623

(1) Canadian data are taken from Simons Consulting Group (1994: Appendix 2). Canadian regulations at federal and provincial levels set standards for both daily maximum and monthly average discharge levels; monthly figures have been used in this chart since most other jurisdictions do not set daily maximum levels. Federal regulations also set limits for pH, acute lethality and dioxins/furans, which are not included in this chart.
(2) Alberta, British Columbia and Ontario set mill-by-mill discharge limits; figures are range of permit levels.
(3) Quebec has set two AOX levels – one for predominantly softwood-based pulp mills, and one for those using primarily hardwoods. By the end of 2000, a single limit of 0.8 kg/adt will apply to all producers.
(4) International data are based on a survey of good practice in mills world-wide; numbers in brackets represent levels possible for new mills with primary and secondary treatment of effluents. See IIED (1996) Toward a Sustainable Paper Cycle. London: International Institute for Environment and Development, 1996: 119.
(5) United States figures are EPA "cluster rules" discharge guidelines for existing mills, which were approved by the EPA in November 1997. See McCubbin (1997: 193).

dian regulations, given the fact that federal regulations provide few opportunities for exemption from regulations (whereas other jurisdictions frequently set permit levels on a mill-by-mill basis, providing greater opportunities for firms to lobby for lower limits). Moreover, at least one analysis claims that the use in Canada of daily maximum limits on effluents – in addition to the kind of monthly or yearly averages applied in most other countries – increases the effective regulatory burden on mills. Monthly or annual average limits allow for "peaks" and "troughs" in mill effluents, whereas daily maximums provide much less margin for error. As a result, Canadian mills have a higher probability of exceeding limits than do their competitors in other jurisdictions, and may have to operate below permitted levels in order to ensure compliance (Simons Consulting Group 1994: 3–4). Partly as a result of these kinds of factors, a competitive cost analysis showed quite high costs to Canadian firms of meeting the new standards, at least in the case of older, smaller mills (Simons Consulting Group 1994: 10–12).

At the same time, it is important not to overstate the implications of the new regulations for Canadian mills. Federal standards in particular were based on levels of performance which could be achieved with the installation of "best available technologies" for primary and secondary treatment of effluents: while mills might choose to pursue other options for compliance, regulations were not structured to require them to search for novel means of improving environmental performance. Provincial regulations on AOX levels were somewhat more "technology forcing" in nature, since these could only be met by shifting bleaching processes to ECF or TCF methods – and/or by moving toward "closed loop" technologies in which all mill effluents are recycled. Even here, however, the main implication of the new standards was the need to move toward proven technologies for chlorine dioxide substitution – particularly since the industry effectively lobbied against the more extreme standards (notably British Columbia's proposed "0 AOX" limit for 2002, which as of the late 1990s was being quietly ignored by industry and regulatory officials alike).

Other structural influences on firm behaviour

In order to understand firms' responses to this new regulatory climate, it is also necessary to consider some of the broader structural features of the industry. Three such factors are of particular importance: the strong export-orientation of Canadian pulp and paper manufacturing; the average size and age of Canadian mills relative to those in competitor countries; and the relatively weak innovative capabilities of the industry.

Export orientation

The Canadian pulp and paper industry is highly export-oriented, with over 80% of total shipments destined for export markets. As a result, producers are extremely susceptible to shifts in environmental demands in key export markets. This is backed up by the findings of a survey of 76 Canadian forest product firms carried out by the Conference Board of Canada in 1992 (Krajewksi 1992: 39–56). Sixty-five per cent of exporting firms in the sample reported that foreign environmental measures affected their ability to access export markets. Of the foreign-market environmental measures mentioned as a barrier to market access, the most important were regulations concerning wastepaper recycling (23%), bans on harvesting of old-growth forests (21%), and chlorine bleaching/AOX regulations (14%).

Pulp and paper exports are concentrated in the United States, which accounts for approximately 60% of total exports, and 50% of total shipments. For the most part, environmental standards in the United States during the 1990s were not significantly more demanding than Canadian standards, and in many respects were less demanding – the exception being regulations on wastepaper recycling, where United States standards for recycled content placed Canadian firms at a competitive disadvantage due to the greater reliance of Canadian newsprint producers on virgin fibre, and the greater proximity of United States producers to major urban centres which are the source for recycled fibre.

However, it is likely that the key constraint regarding United States market access has not been actual regulations, but expectations of future regulatory limits. There was considerable uncertainty about the direction of United States regulatory policy in the mid-1990s, in particular concern within the Canadian industry that regulations would stipulate stringent limits on AOX levels that would be difficult for Canadian producers to meet without converting bleached kraft pulp operations to TCF production. In the end, the new guidelines announced by the Environmental Protection Agency (EPA) in November 1997 included BOD, TSS and AOX limits comparable to (or less stringent than) those in most Canadian jurisdictions (see the data presented in table 4.1 above). More stringent limits on AOX were included only as part of a voluntary incentives programme. Nonetheless, there is no doubt that uncertainty about future United States limits exerted an important influence on Canadian producers, since Canadian regulations required them to make critical investment decisions at a time when United States regulations were still under discussion.

European markets make up approximately 16% of total exports, or 13% of total shipments. Environmental demands are generally highest in European markets, due to strong consumer demand and a number of well-established eco-labelling programmes. While these market pressures are not significant for the industry as a whole, they are a considerable issue for firms producing market pulp. Whereas newsprint exports are concentrated in the United States and Asian markets (with less than 10% destined for western Europe) western Europe accounts for approximately 30% of market pulp exports. Thus, environmental standards in European markets – notably restrictions on chlorine-based bleaching – are likely to exert considerable influence on investments by Canadian bleached kraft pulp producers, but will be less of a factor for newsprint and other paper producers without bleaching operations.

Competitive position

A second major issue affecting firms' responses to regulation has been the competitive position of Canadian producers vis-à-vis foreign competitors, which is critically affected by the age and size of Canadian mills. The Canadian industry has grown based on the availability of relatively low-cost, high-quality fibre. But overall productivity rates have been relatively stagnant since the 1960s, reflecting relatively low rates of new investment and continued pressure on input and labour costs (Statistics Canada, 1996b).

While printing- and writing-paper production and exports increased significantly in the 1980s and 1990s, the industry is still dominated by commodity exports which are vulnerable to competition from new paper-producing regions with lower fibre costs. In addition, the greater average age and smaller average scale of Canadian pulp and paper mills vis-à-vis competitor countries has long been a source of concern. Given the general trend in pulp and paper production to a greater scale of new mills, new entrants generally enjoy a significant advantage in scale economies compared to established Canadian mills. Competitiveness has also been limited by the smaller average size of Canadian pulp and paper firms compared to rivals. Despite Canada's leading position as a pulp and paper producer, until recently few Canadian firms have ranked among the largest in the industry worldwide – although this has changed somewhat in recent years due to a number of high-profile mergers and acquisitions.

Competitive pressures have been particularly significant for newsprint producers, who in addition to smaller average mill size have also been affected by changes in patterns of input supply: increases in the recycled content in newsprint puts Canadian producers at a competitive disadvantage vis-à-vis American producers, who are generally located closer to major urban markets, which constitute the principal source of recycled fibre. Partly as a result of this, newsprint production and exports have stagnated over the past two decades. Market pulp and other paper products, on the other hand, have been more dynamic. Table 4.2 shows the evolution of Canada's competitive position in the three principal product groups. As can be seen, share of pulp exports remained largely steady at 30 to 35% over three decades, but newsprint exports as a share of world exports fell significantly in the same period. While still much smaller in

Table 4.2 Canada's share of world exports, by volume (percentages)

	1965–1974	1975–1984	1985–1994
Wood pulp	31	34.2	32.3
Newsprint	70	64.6	55.7
Printing and writing paper	7.2	8.6	13.3

Source: Globerman et al (1998: S30).

volume terms, Canada's share of printing and writing paper exports almost doubled (Globerman et al. 1998: S30).

Overall capacity in the industry grew relatively slowly during the 1970s and early 1980s, as a number of producers closed older, less productive mills in the face of increased competitive pressures. Capacity has grown somewhat more rapidly since the mid-1980s, at least for pulp and printing and writing papers; newsprint capacity has continued to stagnate in the face of strong competitive pressures. Even during the most recent period, however, new investment has been oriented primarily to upgrading and expansion of existing plants, rather than to new, greenfield investments. Only a very small number of new mills have been built over the past decades. Canadian government (federal and to a lesser degree provincial) grant programmes have played some role in helping firms adjust to the structural hurdles facing them – notably the age/size problems noted above. The best-known of the programmes was the Pulp and Paper Modernization Program (PPMP), a joint federal-provincial programme which operated between 1979 and the mid-1980s (and until 1991 in Newfoundland) and offered capital subsidies to firms for modernization, rationalization of production, pollution abatement, energy efficiency and development of higher value-added products.

There has been considerable criticism of the programme in terms of its overall cost-effectiveness, but there is little doubt that the PPMP helped lay the foundations for compliance with environmental regulations introduced in the early 1990s – at least among mills in Eastern Canada which faced the greatest competitive and environmental threats due to their age and size. It is unlikely that adjustment to the new regulations would have been so widespread and rapid without the upgrading investments carried out under the PPMP in the 1980s. Overall, weaknesses in terms of age and the scale of mills has affected environment-related spending in two ways. First, the cost pressures on Canadian firms (particularly newsprint producers) have meant that they are unlikely to shoulder expensive environmental measures unless forced to do so. As a result, the emphasis is on relatively minor process improvements and housekeeping measures that can produce cost savings as well as improvements in environmental performance. Second, more far-reaching environmental improvements are usually linked to broader modernization programmes that increase the scale of production. Given the large capital costs associated with pollution control measures, firms have typically financed such investments by adding capacity.

Weak innovative capabilities

Pulp and paper manufacturing is a mature industrial sector, characterized by relatively slow advances in core process technology. Moreover, much of the technical advance in the industry comes from outside sources of technology and expertise – both consulting engineering firms who design plants, and equipment manufacturers who supply specialized equipment. These factors strongly condition the ways in which producers react to environmental regulations. This situation is particularly acute in Canada. Most observers agree that the level of innovation in the Canadian pulp and paper industry is low compared to that in many competitor countries: levels of intramural R&D spending (averaging 0.4% of sales) are low by international standards; Canadians hold few patents registered in the paper products and paper-making fields in Canada or the United States; employment of R&D personnel is lower than in comparable United States or Scandinavian firms; and rates of adoption of new technologies have been slower than in competitor countries, or other industries in Canada (Globerman et al. 1998: S33–37; see also Science Council of Canada 1992).

Globerman and colleagues (1998, S35) argue that Canadian forest-product firms "have simply built their competitive success on access to high-quality fibre and an engineering focus on being cost-efficient in the production of 'commodity' products". Levels of innovation are low, and innovative effort is geared largely to improving product quality and costs, rather than promoting product innovation and differentiation. The ability of the Canadian pulp and paper industry to innovate in response to environmental pressures is also limited by the relative weakness of the domestic equipment manufacturing industry. This industry is relatively small in comparison to the United States and Scandinavian countries, and is dominated by branch offices of foreign-controlled firms. Partly as a result of this, there has been little development of the strong supplier-user linkages witnessed in countries like Finland.

The pulp and paper equipment industry grew significantly during the 1980s, but remains small in global terms (approximately 50 firms and C$250 million in sales in 1990). Most of the growth during the 1980s came as a result of increased exports from a small number of specialized suppliers – there is no evidence that linkages with Canadian pulp and paper firms have improved over the period, and there are no intercorporate holdings or alliances for technology development between equipment suppliers and pulp and paper firms. At the same time, however, the Canadian industry does have strengths on which to draw in its efforts to adapt to environmental pressures. While the domestic manufacturing base is weak, the service sector (consulting engineering companies, monitoring services) is much better developed. Canadian consulting engineering companies are strong, and in a number of cases are among the world leaders in pulp and paper mill design and engineering – including in the environmental field. Even more importantly, a well-developed structure of collaborative research provides a strong basis for adaptation. The principal institution in this regard is the Pulp and Paper Research Institute of Canada (Paprican), a collaborative research body linked to the Canadian Pulp and Paper Association. The institute, which has a current budget of approximately C$40 million annually, is funded primarily by contributions from member companies (about 75% of total revenue, with contributions levied on a per-ton of output basis).

Paprican is generally seen as an example of a successful industry-led research consortium. Its success is due in part to the highly export-oriented nature of the Canadian industry, which means that member companies view foreign producers as their principal rivals; this, plus the relatively standardized nature of pulp and paper technology, mean that the scope for collaboration in pre-competitive research is relatively large (Potworowski 1994: A-13). Paprican accounts for a significant share of total R&D activity in the industry, with active programmes in the areas of product quality and value, cost-competitiveness issues, and environmental performance. The institute has played a key role in research in the environmental field, supporting research to identify toxins in pulp mill effluents, and (more recently) on process closure for bleached kraft pulp plants. Despite the important role of Paprican, it appears likely that the primary direction of innovation in the Canadian industry in response to environmental pressures will be continued application of imported abatement and control technologies, coupled with incremental improvements in the efficiency of existing operations – what one report refers to as an "adopt and adapt" strategy (Science Council 1992: 17). More ambitious programmes, like Paprican's work on closed-cycle technologies are promising, but had not yet resulted in commercial applications at the time of this research, and were not a factor in adjustment by industry to new regulatory pressures. There have been some more major technical breakthroughs in the industry – notably pioneering work on closed-cycle processes for thermo-mechanical pulp (TMP) production by Millar Western and others, and Repap's work on solvent-based pulping processes – but these are exceptions to the general pattern of innovation in the industry.

Environmental regulation and innovation: Two narratives

How then did Canadian firms adapt to the new regulations announced in the mid-1990s? How successful were the regulations in spurring environmental improvements in pulp and paper mills? And to what extent did the regulations result in innovations by the industry? In order to respond to these questions, data were assembled from a variety of sources. First, secondary data from industry sources and regulatory agencies provided an overall picture of environment-related investments by the industry, and trends in environmental performance. Second, a mail questionnaire was administered to senior executives of pulp and paper firms in the fall of 1997, soliciting a mixture of firm- and mill-level data on environmental performance and investments. A total of 34 firms, representing 56 mills, responded to the survey – which represents approximately 48% of the mills subject to the 1992 federal regulations. Finally, questionnaire responses were coded to ensure anonymity of respondents, and then matched with additional mill-level data on the environmental performance of mills circa 1987 (prior to the entry into force of the new regulations), on the estimated costs of compliance with regulations (as calculated in background studies commissioned as part of the process of developing the new regulations), and on environmental performance of mills circa 1996 (the deadline for compliance with the new regulations).

The result is an extremely rich base on which to assess the influence of regulatory and non-regulatory factors on mill-level decision-making. Most existing studies focus on a single parameter to assess the environmental performance of firms (either pollution abatement expenditures or, less frequently, data on effluent levels themselves). In this case, the mix of survey and other data allow us to assess not only patterns of environmental investment, but also absolute levels of environmental performance, and relative changes in environmental performance of mills compared to pre-regulatory levels. Moreover, data on the anticipated costs of compliance permit a more sophisticated analysis of the regulatory burden facing individual mills than is the case in most existing studies, which generally either assume uniform regulatory pressures on firms across the industry, or use other variables (such as age of mills) as proxies for regulatory burden. There are some gaps in the availability of information – notably the lack of data on AOX levels at individual mills (since AOX data is not monitored by federal regulatory officials). Similarly, there are slight biases in the sample of reporting firms (over-representation of firms from Western versus Eastern Canada) but these are not sufficient to call into question the overall analysis.[4] Given the nature of the data used, the analysis focuses on the main period of adjustment to new regulations, up to 1996, but does not deal with more recent changes by firms.

Narrative 1: Compliance and limited innovation

A first reading of the industry's response to new regulatory pressures squares easily with existing theoretical and empirical literature. Regulations spurred a significant wave of investment by pulp and paper firms, and resulted in rapid decreases in effluent levels. But investments were heavily weighted toward end-of-pipe controls, and there is little evidence that regulatory pressures resulted in increased R&D spending, development of new technologies, or strengthening of intra-firm technological capabilities.

The first and most obvious aspect of the industry's response to new regulations was a significant increase in levels of investment. Pollution abatement expenditures – which had been below C$100 million during the mid-1980s – rose rapidly beginning in the late 1980s, and averaged more than C$700 million annually between 1990 and 1996. Spending peaked in 1996 at over C$1 billion, but declined thereafter, presumably reflecting the fact that deadlines for compliance with new federal regulations had passed. Statistics Canada figures show that the pulp and paper industry accounted for almost 40% of total capital expenditures on pollution abatement and control by all Canadian industry in 1995 (Statistics Canada 1998), compared to an average of approximately 20% during the latter half of the 1980s (Gagnon 1996: 13). Moroever, pollution abatement and control expenditures absorbed an increasing percentage of overall capital spending by the pulp and paper industry, rising from 1 to 3% annually during the mid- to late 1980s to 10 to 15% annually during the 1990s (Gagnon 1996: 14). As a result of these investments, average effluent levels also fell sharply, as table 4.3 shows. Reductions in dioxin and furan emissions were particularly striking, with overall emissions being essentially eliminated over a 10-year period; the main drop occurred at the beginning of the decade as mills took action to meet expected regulatory requirements by reformulating defoamers and ceasing the use of treated woodchips. AOX levels fell dramatically as well, reflecting the speed at which bleached kraft pulp producers have phased out the use of chlorine in favour of chlorine dioxide (see also Parsons and Luthe 1995). Biological oxygen demand and TSS levels fell less rapidly, although BOD levels dropped markedly in 1996 as a number of new secondary-treatment facilities came on stream due to the requirement for all mills to meet federal regulations by 31 December 1995. As of 1996, average BOD and TSS levels were well below federal regulatory guidelines. The drops in effluent levels between 1988 and 1996 were particularly striking given that there was relatively little greenfield investment in new pulp mills during this period; reductions thus primarily reflect efforts to improve the performance of existing mills, rather than changes in the average age of plants due to the entry into production of new mills.[5]

Table 4.3 Trends in effluent levels of Canadian pulp and paper mills

	Biochemical oxygen demand, BOD$_5$ (kg/adt)	Total suspended solids, TSS (kg/adt)	Adsorbable organic halides, AOX (kg/adt)	Dioxins and furans (g/year)
1988	26.3	10.0	4.8	360
1989	25.4	10.0	3.9	190
1990	22.9	9.0	3.4	120
1991	20.0	8.0	2.4	17
1992	16.5	7.0	1.8	12
1993	15.2	6.0	1.3	6
1994	13.3	6.0	1.0	2
1995	11.0	5.0	0.9	n.m.
1996	2.6	4.0	0.6	n.m.

Source: Canadian Pulp and Paper Association, *Reference Tables*, various years.

Equally importantly, improvements in effluent levels appear to be generalized across the industry. Environment Canada data on compliance with 1992 CEPA regulations during the 1992–1994 period show a 99% compliance rate for traditional pollutants (BOD, TSS and acute lethality), and a 93 to 99% compliance rate for dioxins and furans (Environment Canada 1998).[6] Compliance data for 1996 show similarly high levels of compliance across most firms.[7] Questionnaire responses also suggest that regulations had a considerable impact on patterns of investment and environmental performance in respondent firms. "Domestic regulations" were rated as by far the most important determinant of environment-related investments by firms, far in excess of other factors such as export market demand, pressures from parent or partner firms, expected cost savings, or corporate image.

Of the 34 respondent firms, 21 (61.8%) introduced new investment plans specifically in response to the new regulations announced in the mid-1990s, and a further 11 firms (32.4%) changed existing investment plans to respond to the new regulations. Only a minority of firms stated that regulations had no impact on their operations (seven responses) or could be met through previously planned investment programmes (six responses). Perhaps more importantly, there is little evidence of "defensive" reaction to the regulations: only two firms noted that mills were closed as a result of the regulations, and one respondent noted that production levels at one of its mills had been decreased in order to comply with regulatory limits on effluents. (Note that respondents in some cases indicated more than one response, such that totals exceed 100%.)

Analysis of levels of environmental spending and performance at individual mills provides further evidence of the impact of regulations. Levels of environmental spending are strongly correlated with the degree of regulatory burden facing individual mills (i.e., the estimated costs of compliance with federal regulations); the only other factor that strongly explains abatement expenditures is the export orientation of mills (percentage of output destined for western European markets). Meanwhile, levels of environmental performance (BOD and TSS levels in 1996) are strongly correlated with the stringency of (provincial) regulations facing mills, but largely unrelated to estimated costs of compliance. This suggests that mills geared their investment programmes to meet varying regulatory limits in different jurisdictions; it further suggests that regulations worked to reduce the gaps between "leading" and "laggard" firms, rather than promoting ongoing improvements by leading firms. (Somewhat surprisingly, while export orientation is correlated with levels of abatement expenditure, it is not correlated with levels of environmental performance. This is presumably due to the fact that mills exporting to western Europe concentrated on changes to bleaching sequences to reduce AOX levels, which are not monitored by federal regulatory officials). On the other hand, both secondary-source and questionnaire data confirm that the primary impact of regulations was to spur the adoption of end-of-pipe control technologies. Abatement expenditures focused in particular on the installation of primary and secondary-treatment facilities for liquid effluents, with end-of-pipe expenditures accounting for over 80% of all investments in 1995 (Statistics Canada 1998: 20).

A similar picture emerges from questionnaire data. Over 75% of respondents indicate installation of new or upgraded secondary treatment systems for liquid effluents; 40% new or upgraded primary treatment systems; and over 60% reported investments to improve the handling or disposal of solid wastes. In contrast, no internal process changes were reported by a majority of respondents, other than relatively simple housekeeping measures and improvements in process control. Finally, there is little evidence that regulations had an impact on the process of innovation within respondent firms and mills. As noted above, only a minority of firms introduced new product or process technology in response to environmental demands, and almost none reported that regulations resulted in improvements to in-house R&D or engineering capabilities. Even where firms introduced innovations, these have primarily been relatively simple changes in product technology (recycled paper products) rather than more complicated process innovations which hold out the promise of longer-term improvements in environmental performance. Only 21 firms (62%) reported carrying out any environment-related R&D: of this group, only slightly more than half indicated that this had increased as a percentage of total R&D spending over the previous five years. Again, this reflects the weak innovative capacities of the industry discussed earlier.

Overall intramural R&D spending by the industry was stagnant during the first half of the 1990s (Statistics Canada 1996c) and leading firms closed in-house R&D facilities. To the extent that environmental regulations spur innovation, this is likely to occur not because of breakthroughs by individual firms, but instead as a result of incremental improvements at the mill level, and because of indirect impacts on suppliers. Unfortunately, solid data on this last point is not available. This reading, therefore, suggests that regulations primarily worked by stimulating the adoption of proven "best practice" control technologies. They significantly narrowed the gap between leading and laggard firms, and in so doing dramatically changed the overall environmental performance of the industry. But regulations were not sufficient to overcome some of the structural weaknesses of the Canadian industry with regard to innovation.

Narrative 2: Moving beyond compliance?

A slightly different reading emerges, however, when we focus attention on those firms that went beyond strict regulatory limits. While the dollar value of investments has been dominated by end-of-pipe treatment technologies, most firms also introduced at least some (minor) internal process changes, with a significant minority undertaking more significant process changes. Moreover, many firms went well beyond compliance in terms of their environmental performance, with effluent levels well below limits mandated by the new regulations. This reading thus takes a slightly different outlook on the nature of changes introduced by Canadian pulp and paper firms, and on the way in which regulatory factors have interacted with other, structural influences of firms' behaviour.

As noted earlier, secondary data indicate that abatement expenditures by the industry were heavily weighted toward end-of-pipe. In part, however, this reflects the tremendous capital investment involved in secondary-treatment facilities, and may thus understate the extent to which firms have also sought out solutions through internal process changes or better "housekeeping": in their responses to a Statistics Canada survey, 61.9% of pulp and paper firms indicated investing in end-of-pipe controls – but almost as many reported investments in integrated process changes (50.9%), and a significant number mentioned improved control of operations (42.1%). Frequency of investments in integrated process changes was highest out of the 13 industrial sectors surveyed (Statistics Canada 1998: 34). Again, questionnaire data shows a similar picture. While investments were weighted toward end-of-pipe control measures, a significant minority of respondents did undertake various types of in-plant changes with, in each case, 30 to 40% of respondents reporting increases in the use of recycled fibre, improvements in the energy efficiency of machinery, improved fibre and/or chemical recovery or changes to bleaching sequences. Even if we set aside the relatively simple improvements in housekeeping and process control, the vast majority (87.5%) of respondent mills did report undertaking at least one type of internal process change between 1990 and 1996. Rather than opting for internal or end-of-pipe solutions alone, most mills appear to have combined both types of investments, as they struggle not only to ensure compliance with regulations, but also to control production costs and ensure market access.

As noted earlier, firms in most cases had to finance the costs of end-of-pipe controls by adding productive capacity – which in turn meant modernizing equipment and phasing out older, less competitive pulping lines. Thus, while there is little evidence of radical innovations by the industry in response to regulatory pressures, neither is it entirely accurate to state that firms' responses were limited to end-of-pipe compliance measures. In some cases, process changes were significant – such as the widespread shift by bleached kraft producers to ECF or TCF methods, and the large number of newsprint producers who phased out older mechanical pulping lines in favour of new TMP or CTMP processes. Even in these cases, however, firms chose to adopt relatively standard, proven technologies. This second reading also provides a somewhat different picture of the interplay between regulatory and non-regulatory factors influencing firms' behaviour.

Two factors are particularly important here: first, the competitive position of individual mills; and, second, the in-house resources and capabilities available to firms in terms of R&D capabilities and previous experience with environmental management systems. The nature of process changes undertaken was critically affected by the overall competitive challenges facing firms. Thus, bleached kraft pulp manufacturers, facing new restrictions on access to European and other markets, overwhelmingly invested in chlorine dioxide substitution to produce elemental chlorine-free pulp. Of the 21 kraft producing mills in the sample, 19 had opted to produce ECF pulp, with three mills also investing in TCF technology.

For newsprint manufacturers, on the other hand, the main competitive pressure was production costs, with smaller, older Canadian mills at a disadvantage vis-à-vis their United States competitors. Environmental regulations – and hence the need to shoulder the costs of effluent treatment – merely added to this competitive pressure, with the result that a significant number of firms chose to convert older, smaller facilities by introducing newer, larger and more efficient pulping technology. This underlines the close links between the environmental and competitive pressures facing firms: environmental regulations have worked not simply by placing new demands on firms, but also by accentuating some of the underlying competitive challenges facing them. The high rates of compliance for the industry lend support to arguments by Sinclair (1991) and others that earlier estimates of the negative impact of regulations on the economic viability of firms may in fact have been over-stated. Despite industry's claims in the run-up to the new regulations, few if any mills have shut down as a direct impact of the regulations.

The relatively strong industry response was no doubt aided by some of the broader conditions prevailing in the industry. In the first place, a number of the oldest and least competitive mills (particularly in the newsprint subsector) were shut down in the period before the entry into force of the new regulations, due in particular to low pulp prices in the 1980s and increased competition from lower-cost de-inking operations producing newsprint from recycled fibre – which had in turn been given a boost by regulations stipulating minimum recycling rates (Tremblay 1994: 83). Given that pollution loads are generally strongly correlated with age and the production efficiency of mills, this presumably eased the overall burden of compliance for the industry. Moreover, high pulp and newsprint prices in the 1993–1995 period facilitated financing of new environment-related investments. Neither regulatory nor competitive pressures alone, however, appear sufficient to entirely explain the process of adaptation by individual firms. Prior investments in R&D by the industry appear to have also played an important role. Thus, for example, collaborative research on bleached kraft effluent by Paprican set the stage for changes introduced in the 1990s, and helped stave off pressures for complete elimination of chlorine.

Also important were the in-house resources and capabilities available to individual firms. Analysis of questionnaire data shows that in addition to being linked to the stringency of (provincial) regulations, levels of environmental performance by respondent mills in the wake of regulations are also correlated with two other factors: firms' overall commitment to and experience with environmental management (as indicated by the nature of environmental reporting by the firm); and the extent to which the firm reported in-house R&D spending. Even when other factors like firm and mill size and ownership are taken into account, these correlations remain relatively strong. (See tables 4A.1 and 4A.2 for presentations of bivariate and partial correlation coefficients.) This result suggests that the ability of firms to respond efficiently to regulatory and market pressures is critically dependent on the in-house resources available to them, and the capabilities acquired by the firm in its past activities. Even in a case like the Canadian pulp and paper industry, where innovation has been slow and dependent on outside sources of technology, the gradual build-up of innovative skills and abilities is a key factor in smoothing the adaptation to environmental pressures.

Conclusions and policy implications

Ultimately, of course, these two narratives are complementary rather than contradictory. Together, they suggest that regulations did not result in the development of innovative new solutions by Canadian pulp and paper firms or domestic equipment suppliers, but were successful in spurring the diffusion of proven technologies.

The ability of firms to adapt to new environmental pressures, meanwhile, was critically affected by two factors. First, the competitive situation of the industry (notably high pulp prices and a prior phasing out of uncompetitive mills) eased the investment burden facing firms, with the result that firms were less likely to follow defensive strategies, and more likely to pursue far-reaching investment programmes. Second, the ability of firms to achieve superior levels of environmental performance appears to be linked to prior investments in environmental management and in R&D, both within individual firms and in industry-financed R&D consortia. Overall, then, this case suggests that environmental regulations can be remarkably effective in promoting diffusion of proven technologies – particularly where market conditions are supportive of new investments, and where there is a base of in-house technological capability to ease the process of adaptation.

Would an alternative approach to environmental policy that provided firms with more flexibility in the nature and timing of responses (emissions taxes, negotiated compliance schedules or "covenants") have resulted in a greater degree of innovation by the industry? In at least one case, a firm did shelve plans for innovative process changes because of the need to comply with regulatory timetables. Overall, however, there is little reason to expect radical innovation in response to alternative policy measures, given the weakness of the Canadian pulp equipment manufacturing base, and the previous response of the industry to "negotiated" compliance schedules. Rather than looking for a "better" environment to promote innovation, this case suggests that it may be more productive to examine the ways in which innovation policy can increase the effectiveness of environmental regulations. In other words, rather than expecting environmental policy to "do the heavy lifting" of promoting innovation, the opposite may be true. At least in this case, adaptive R&D investments by the industry – stimulated in part by deliberate public policy – were a critical factor permitting firms to adjust to new environmental regulations.

Table 4A.1 Determinants of environmental behaviour and performance
(Bivariate correlation coefficients)

Independent variables	Dependent variables		
	Pollution abatement and control expenditures per ton of output	Percentage reduction in combined BOD and TSS levels between 1987 and 1996	Environmental performance, ca. 1996 (based on combined BOD and TSS levels)
Regulatory stringency (Stringency of provincial regulations)	.1539 (52) P = .276	.3712 (51) P = .007	.4219 (56) P = .001
Regulatory burden I (Estimated control costs to meet BOD and TSS limits)	.2656 (51) P = .060	.2961 (51) P = .035	.0002 (55) P = .999
Regulatory burden II (Estimated control costs to meet BOD, TSS and dioxin/furan limits)	.3239 (51) P = .020	.2288 (51) P = .106	−.0619 (55) P = .653
Export orientation (Percent of 1996 output exported to western Europe)	.3264 (42) P = .035	−.0513 (42) P = .747	.0028 (46) P = .985
Foreign ownership	−.0792 (49) P = .589	−.1855 (49) P = .202	−.0633 (53) P = .652
Firm size (Log of total employment, 1996)	−.1575 (49) P = .280	.2434 (48) P = .096	.3545 (53) P = .009
Mill size (Total production capacity ca. 1990, t/day)	.0292 (52) P = .837	−.1188 (51) P = .406	−.1980 (56) P = .143
R&D expenditures ca. 1996	−.2826 (52) P = .042	.0571 (51) P = .691	.2957 (56) P = .027
Commitment to environmental management (Environmental reporting by firm)	.1196 (51) P = .398	.1121 (51) P = .433	.3012 (56) P = .024

Table 4A.2 Determinants of environmental behaviour and performance
(Partial correlation coefficients, controlling for all other independent variables)

Independent variables	Dependent variables		
	Pollution abatement and control expenditures per ton of output	Percentage reduction in combined BOD and TSS levels between 1987 and 1996	Environmental performance, ca. 1996 (based on combined BOD and TSS levels)
Regulatory stringency (Stringency of provincial regulations)	.2798 (26) P = .149	.3518 (26) P = .066	.6417 (26) P = .000
Regulatory burden I (Estimated control costs to meet BOD and TSS limits)	.3084 (26) P = .110	.2053 (26) P = .295	.0449 (26) P = .821
Export orientation (Percent of 1996 output exported to western Europe)	.3904 (26) P = .040	−.0622 (26) P = .753	−.2969 (26) P = .125
Foreign ownership	−.1654 (26) P = .400	−.0298 (26) P = .880	.1034 (26) P = .601
Firm Size (Log of total employment, 1996)	−.4221 (26) P = .025	.1801 (26) P = .359	−.2256 (26) P = .248
R&D expenditures ca. 1996	.0251 (26) P = .899	−.0734 (26) P = .711	.3452 (26) P = .072
Commitment to environmental management (Environmental reporting by firm)	.2792 (26) P = .150	.0288 (26) P = .884	.3942 (26) P = .038

Notes

1. The acute lethality parameter is peculiar to Canada as a measure of toxicity. It involves a test in which rainbow trout fingerling are exposed to effluent, and survival rates over a 96-hour period are measured. The test is still used in the latest 1992 regulations, although

there has been criticism that its relevance as a measure of the toxicity of effluents is limited (Stanbury 1993: 8–9).

2. The relevant provincial regulations are as follows:

   Alberta: Environmental Protection and Enhancement Act, June 1992 (Alberta has not issued specific regulations specifying characteristics of pulp mill effluents; instead, these are established on a mill-by-mill basis and regulated through licenses to operate.)

   British Columbia: Environmental Protection Act, 1994; and Pulp Mill and Pulp and Paper Mill Liquid Effluent Control Regulations, December 1990

   Ontario: Environmental Protection Act, 1990. Control orders for all bleached kraft mills were issued in 1989, setting limits on BOD, TSS and AOX; limits were revised and extended to all pulp and paper mills in November 1993.

   Quebec: Regulations Respecting Pulp and Paper Mills, October 1992, issued under the Environmental Quality Act

   Remaining provinces have not set limits independent of federal regulations. For an overview, see Simons Consulting Group 1994: Appendix 1.

3. The somewhat tighter timetable for compliance with dioxin and furan regulations (in comparison with limits on traditional pollutants) reflected the fact that many pulp mills had already undertaken early action to reduce chlorine use, reformulate defoamers and cut use of contaminated woodchips. At the time of promulgation of the new regulations, approximately 60% of affected mills were in compliance with the dioxin/furan limits, compared to perhaps one-quarter of mills that complied with new BOD/TSS limits.

4. One point to consider is that the sample may be weighted toward stronger environmental performers and/or to firms facing lower levels of regulatory burden, who might presumably be more willing to respond than those facing higher costs of complying with regulations. Estimates of costs of compliance do show some variation between the sample mills and the industry as a whole. However, this is largely explained by the presence in the sample of four new mills constructed since the 1980s (for which compliance costs were estimated to be zero). Once this is controlled for, differences are not significant.

5. Biological oxygen demand and TSS levels also fell dramatically during the 1960s and 1970s. In this case, however, much of the reduction occurred as a result of the entry into production of new mills and the resulting drop in the average age of mills.

6. These compliance rates are based on the number of exceedances as a percentage of all tests performed. They somewhat overstate the compliance rate for the acute lethality test, since this parameter is measured only once per month, as opposed to three weekly measurements of TSS and BOD levels. Even in 1996, a sizeable number of mills still failed to pass all acute lethality tests.

7. Two mills in British Columbia had short-term problems with their effluent treatment systems (since remedied) which caused them to exceed limits temporarily. Two other mills were out of compliance because of delays in installing treatment systems, but have since undertaken necessary investments (one of the mills was late in installing treatment equipment, and was fined under the terms of CEPA; the other mill experimented unsuccessfully with zero discharge process but abandoned this because of scaling problems and installed a secondary-treatment facility). Only one mill was consistently out of compliance with federal regulations.

REFERENCES

Bonsor, Norman C. (1990) "Water Pollution and the Canadian Pulp and Paper Industry" in G. Bruce Doern, ed., Getting It Green: Case Studies in Canadian Environmental Regulation, Policy Study 12, Toronto: C.D. Howe Institute.

Canadian Pulp and Paper Association (CPPA) (various years). Reference Tables, Montreal: CPPA.

Environment Canada (1998) "Compliance and Enforcement Report: Volume I", Ottawa: Environment Canada, June, available from http://www.doe.ca/enforce/english.htm.

Gagnon, Pierre (1996) "Private Sector Investments in Pollution Abatement and Control", in Environmental Perspectives: Studies and Statistics, vol. 3. Ottawa: Statistics Canada, June. Catalogue No. 11-528-XPE, No. 3.

Globerman, Steve, Masao Nakamura, Karen Ruckman and Ilan Vertinsky (1998) "Innovation, Strategy and Canada's Forest Products Industry", Canadian Public Policy 24: Supplement 2, S27–S40.

Krajewski, Stephen (1992) "Industrial Competitiveness, Trade and the Environment: Report on Phase II", Ottawa: The Conference Board of Canada.

McCubbin, Neil (1997) "What Does the Cluster Rule Mean for Canada?", Pulp and Paper Canada, 98: 12, 193–194.

Nemetz, Peter N. (1986) "Federal Environmental Regulation in Canada", Natural Resources Journal 26 (summer): 551–608.

Parsons, K. and C. E. Luthe (1995) "Progress in Reducing Dioxins and AOX: 1988–1994", miscellaneous report MR 308, Pointe Claire: Pulp and Paper Research Institute of Canada, May.

Potworowski, Andre (1994) "Best Practices in Cooperative Industrial R&D and Technology Transfer", report prepared for Natural Resources Canada, CANMET, November, mimeo.

Science Council of Canada (1992) "The Canadian Forest-Products Sector", Sectoral Technology Strategy Series, No. 9, Ottawa: Science Council.

Simons Consulting Group (1994) "Forest Sector Benchmarking Initiative: A Case Study in Environmental Regulation", report prepared for the Canadian Forest Service and Industry Canada, November.

Sinclair, William F. (1988) "Controlling Pollution from Canadian Pulp and Paper Manufacturers: A Federal Perspective", Ottawa: Department of the Environment, Environmental Protection Branch, July.

——— (1991) "Controlling Effluent Discharges from Canadian Pulp and Paper Manufacturers", Canadian Public Policy 17: 1, 86–105.

Stanbury, William (1993) "Regulating Water Pollution by the Pulp and Paper Industry in Canada", unpublished manuscript.

Statistics Canada (1996a) "1994 Waste Management Industry Survey: Business Sector", Ottawa: Statistics Canada, December. Catalogue No. 16F0003-XNE.

——— (1996b) "Aggregate Productivity Measures, 1994", Ottawa: Statistics Canada, March. Catalogue No. 15-204-XPE.

——— (1996c) "Industrial Research and Development: 1995 Intentions", Ottawa: Statistics Canada, January. Catalogue No. 88-202-XPB.

Tremblay, Pierre (1994) "Comparative Analysis of Technological Capability and Productivity Growth in the Pulp and Paper Industry in Industrialized and Industrializing Countries", Ph.D Thesis, Science Policy Research Unit, University of Sussex, April.

——— (1998) "Environmental Protection Expenditures in the Business Sector", Ottawa: Statistics Canada, August. Catalogue No. 16F0006-XIE.

5

Toward a theory of innovation and industrial pollution: Evidence from Mexican manufacturing

Kevin P. Gallagher

This chapter discusses how environmental conditions in Mexico are worsening in part because of a lack of capacities for linking Mexico's National Innovation System (NIS) with environmental policymaking and for a lack of innovation-based environmental policy in general. Interestingly however, this chapter will show that by no design of government policy, a few exceptional cases have occurred whereby new investment in Mexico has resulted in the deployment of less-pollution-intensive technology. Indeed, in some sectors Mexico is less pollution intensive than its counterparts in the United States. Based on these observations in Mexican industry, a theoretical framework is put forth that draws on Nelson's (1981) observations on technological change. Implications for innovation and environmental policy are then discussed for Mexico and other developing countries.

Integration, growth and innovation in Mexico

The case of Mexico offers many lessons for current discussions regarding economic integration and sustainable development because Mexico has a very long history of economic integration. Whereas many nations are just now considering a deep level of integration into the world economy through regional or bilateral arrangements, or through agreements of the World Trade Organization (WTO), Mexico began liberalizing its economy in 1985 and is now one of the more open economies in the world. This transformation has had a profound effect on Mexico's National Innovation System. Mexico's transformation to openness occurred through four rather dramatic policy changes.

First, in response to deep macroeconomic crises and pressure from international monetary institutions, in 1985 Mexico embarked on what it called its "apertura" (openness in English) policy where it began lowering tariffs for the first time in many years. Second, in 1986 Mexico joined the General Agreement on Tariffs and Trade (GATT) and became actively engaged in the Uruguay Round negotiations. Third, Mexico established its "El Pacto" policy in 1988 – an economic pact between the government, private industry and some labor organizations to stabilize prices and to further liberalize trade and investment. The capstone of these efforts came in 1994 with the passage of the North American Free Trade Agreement (NAFTA). Fourth, Mexico entered into the Organization of Economic Cooperation and Development (OECD) in 1995 and since then has negotiated over 20 other free trade agreements with other countries. In the minds of Mexico's policymakers, economic integration would attract foreign direct investment and increase exports, which would translate into economic growth and rising standards of living. Mexico's strategy of economic integration has performed remarkably well in terms of controlling inflation and increased foreign investment and exports. Mexico's export profile was radically transformed as these policies were being implemented.

During the 1970s and early 1980s the engine of growth in the Mexican economy was crude oil exports, which were as high as 80% of total exports in the early 1980s. By the year 2000, oil exports had fallen to less than 10% of total exports – oil exports were being replaced with manufactured exports. Today, manufactured exports comprise close to 85% of all Mexican exports (Gallagher and Zarsky 2004). However, this transformation is yet to translate into rising incomes. Between 1994 and 2002, GDP grew at an average rate of 2.7% per year. Gross domestic product growth in the 1990s was less than half the 6.7% average growth rate under the policies of the 1970s. In per capita terms, Mexico has grown less then 1% per annum since 1985 (World Bank 2003).

What accounts for this poor performance? Economists point to a variety of factors, such as continued macroeconomic instability due to growing deficits in both foreign and domestic accounts. One of the most cited reasons is the contraction of domestic investment or *gross fixed capital formation*. (Mattar, Moreno-Brid and Wilson 2002). Between 1994 and 2002, total annual investment as a percentage of GDP averaged 19.4%, down from almost 22% in the 1970s. However, the share of foreign direct investment (FDI) in total investment more than doubled, rising from 5.4% between 1981 and 1993, to 12.6% between 1994 and 2002 (Gallagher and Zarsky 2004; Gallagher 2004).

Secondly, Mexico's low-wage competitiveness has begun to slide. According to the *World Competitiveness Yearbook*, Mexico fell from thirty-fourth place in 1998 to forty-first in 2002. Another index, from the World Economic Forum, shows that Mexico slipped from forty-second to forty-fifth place from 2000 to 2002. Similarly, the *Microeconomic Competitiveness Index* reports a fall in Mexico's position from number forty-two in 1998 and 55 in 2002. Falling competitiveness has been attributed to three factors: the economic slowdown in the United States, the relative strength of the peso, and other factors such as the emergence of China's entry in the WTO (CSIS 2003; Gerber and Carillo 2003).

In line with the current focus in numerous countries to view growth as being a product of the national innovation system (NIS), Mexico's National Council for Science and Technology (CONACYT) recently commissioned an assessment of the state of Mexico's NIS in the context of the nation's new economic model (Cimoli 2000). Nelson (1992) defines an NIS as "a set of institutions whose interactions determine the innovative performance of national firms". CONACYT draws on an extension of Nelson's concept by Metcalfe (1995) whereby an NIS is defined as "a set of institutions which jointly and individually contribute to the development and diffusion of new technologies and which provide the framework within which governments form and implement policies to influence the innovation process". The Mexican assessment finds that the following five factors have caused Mexico's NIS to perform quite poorly:

a) Macroeconomic instability in the form of exchange rate and inflationary volatility has affected Mexico's NIS at every level. This has forced many small and medium-sized enterprises to adopt an extremely cautious and short-term investment agenda that gives little room for innovation.

b) Low technological opportunities have arisen from the fact that Mexico's static comparative advantage has been in a level of specialization that is an assembly-oriented production system.

c) Poor R&D efforts. Spending on R&D in Mexico is a mere 0.58% of manufacturing value added, compared to over 3% in the United States.

d) Globalization of production and low contribution to local R&D. Economic integration has resulted in Mexico importing the vast majority of its technology and inputs. In addition, reforms have resulted in a dominance of foreign firms that make little contribution to local R&D efforts.

e) Low interaction of science sectors with local institutions such as universities and sector-level associations.

The authors of the study fault government policymakers for assuming that technological innovation would automatically arise from integration policies. Mexico's more protectionist period resulted in a very high degree of local domestic linkages but also a fairly low level of international competitiveness and production capacity. Under integration, Mexico's local linkages have been all but lost. In return, Mexico has gained international competitiveness and is home to numerous exporting firms with large production capacities. As for increasing Mexico's innovative capacities, the challenge for the policymakers is to maintain competitiveness and production capabilities while building the technological capabilities of local firms (Cimoli 2000).

Economic integration and environment in Mexico

The context set by the members of the innovation assessment is also the context under which Mexico has developed its environmental policy. As in the case of technology policy, during the NAFTA negotiations proponents of the agreement argued that free trade would lead to seemingly automatic improvements in environmental conditions in countries like Mexico. Opponents of NAFTA said that the environment would automatically worsen in Mexico because Mexico's lower standards would attract highly polluting firms from the United States to locate there, providing, in effect, a pollution haven for US industry. The proponents were generalizing from the so-called "environmental Kuznets curve" (EKC) hypothesis. The name derives from an analogy to the original Kuznets curve – the theory that growth in per capita income over time first increases inequality, then later decreases it.

Studies in the early 1990s reported a similar relationship between environmental degradation and levels of income: environmental degradation may sharply increase in the early stages of economic development, but the rise in per capita income past a certain "turning point" seemed to gradually reduce environmental damage. Economists hypothesized that environmental improvement beyond the turning point happened for three reasons. First, multinational corporations that invest in developing countries bring more advanced, environment-friendly technologies to the developing world. Second, development itself causes structural shifts toward services and other less pollution-intensive economic activities. Finally, increasing income would eventually lead to higher levels of environmental awareness, which would translate into more stringent environmental policies as the growing middle class demanded a cleaner environment (Grossman and Krueger 1993). Early EKC studies suggested the turning point at which economies would begin to get more environmentally benign was a per capita income of approximately US$5,000. This led to the policy prescription now prevalent in many negotiating rooms: the environment can wait, since economic growth will eventually (and naturally) result in environmental improvement. More recent studies, however, have called into question both the specific findings and the broad generalizations from these early EKC studies (Stern 1998).

Mexico reached US$5,000 GDP per capita in 1985, precisely the year it began opening its economy. The analysis in this chapter, however, shows that subsequent rises in income have been small and environmental degradation has been large. Statistics from Mexico's National Institute for Statistics, Geography and Information Systems (INEGI) document how environmental degradation has taken a big bite out of the benefits of trade-led economic growth in Mexico. First, since 1985 real incomes in Mexico have grown at less than 1% annually. Second, according to INEGI, every major environmental problem has worsened since trade liberalization began in Mexico. Despite the fact that Mexico reached levels of income beyond the range of a predicted EKC turning point, national levels of soil erosion, municipal solid waste and urban air and water pollution rose quite dramatically from 1985 to 1999. According to these data, rural soil erosion grew by 89%, municipal solid waste by 108%, water pollution by 29% and urban air pollution by 97%. Regression analyses have shown that there is no sign of a turning point for these environmental indicators in Mexico (Gallagher 2004). These results have been costly to Mexico's prospects for development. The INEGI studies estimate the financial costs of environmental degradation at 10% of GDP from 1988 to 1999, an average of US$36 billion of damage each year ($47 billion for 1999). The destruction overwhelms the value of economic growth, which has been just 2.5% annually over the same period, or US$14 billion per year (INEGI 2000).

Is the Mexican environment worsening because Mexico is serving as a pollution haven for highly polluting industries in the United States? Numerous studies have tested for pollution havens in Mexico but none have found evidence. If one were to find Mexico to be a pollution haven, one would expect that the amount of pollution-intensive industry would decrease in the United States and increase in Mexico after NAFTA. Gallagher (2004) finds that the amount of dirty industry decreased more in Mexico than in the United States. A number of other studies have attempted to empirically test whether the evidence of pollution havens in Mexico has become widespread and have come to similar conclusions. Grossman and Krueger (1993) performed the only such study during the NAFTA debates.

In a cross-industry comparison of data in one year, 1987, the authors tested whether pollution abatement costs in United States' industries affected imports from Mexico, as one would expect if Mexico was a pollution haven relative to the United States. They found the impact of cross-industry differences in pollution abatement costs on United States imports from Mexico to be positive, but small and statistically insignificant. Indeed, traditional economic determinants of trade and investment, such as factor prices and tariffs, were found to be far more significant. A more recent study examined whether pollution abatement costs affected patterns of United States foreign investment into Mexico and three other countries. Also a cross-industry comparison of data in 1990 found similar results to those of Grossman and Krueger (1993). Eskeland and Harrison (1997) found a statistically insignificant, though positive, relationship between pollution abatement costs and levels of FDI.

Kahn (2001) is the only study to examine this question over time. Rather than looking at the costs of pollution abatement like the previous two studies, Kahn examined pollution intensity of United States trade with Mexico and other countries. Using United States Toxic Release Inventory data for 1972, 1982 and 1992, he found the pollution content of US imports from Mexico slightly declined during the period. The reason why this analysis and so many others like it fail to find evidence for pollution havens in developing countries is that the economic costs of environmental degradation are relatively much smaller than many other factors of production – especially those that determine comparative advantage. Mexico is factor-abundant in unskilled labour that takes the form of manufacturing assembly plants. On average, such manufacturing activity is relatively less pollution intensive than more capital-laden manufacturing activities such as cement, pulp and paper and base metals production. The latter sectors have been contracting in the Mexican case. In terms of costs, even at the margin, the costs of pollution are too small to significantly factor into the average firm's location decisions. In addition, many firms are simply too large and cumbersome to move to another location, and they need to stay close to their product markets. The marginal abatement costs are small relative to the transaction costs of decommissioning and actually moving to another country (Gallagher 2004).

Although the evidence suggests that the majority of the firms that move to Mexico do not move there because of low environmental standards, such a finding does not imply that when firms move to Mexico they are model environmental corporations. In fact, the World Bank conducted a survey of over 200 firms in Mexico and found that whether a company was a foreign firm or not had no correlation with the degree to which a company complied with Mexican environmental law (Dasgupta et al. 2000).

If the Mexican environment is worsening, but not because it is a pollution haven, what is driving environmental degradation? The answer is similar to the one which indicates why technological capabilities have not arisen from Mexico's development strategy. Costly degradation is occurring because the proper mechanisms were not put in place to help Mexico manage its economic growth in an environmentally sustainable manner. In a comprehensive evaluation of Mexican environmental conditions, the OECD applauds Mexico for establishing a number of key environmental laws and institutions, but cites Mexico's "implementation gap," as "the complex and sometimes unclear distribution of environmental competency across levels of government and limited local authority to raise revenues from taxes or charges" (OECD 2003).

Indeed, spending on environmental protection doubled in the late 1980s and Mexico started a much-needed industrial environmental inspection programme. However, shortly after NAFTA was signed and fiscal and financial woes set in, attention to the environment fell sharply (Gallagher 2004; CEPAL 2004). According to INEGI, since 1994 real spending on environmental protection has declined by 45%. Even at their highest levels, allocations for environmental protection were paltry in comparison to Mexico's counterparts in the OECD. As a percentage of GDP, expenditure on environmental protection was only one-fifth the size of other OECD nations (OECD 1998). Tellingly, the number of environmental inspections has also decreased by 45% over the same period (Merino and Tovar 2002; Stromberg 2002; Gallagher 2004).

In the meantime, the environmental "side" institutions created by NAFTA set some important precedents, but were not equipped to fill the implementation gap left by the Mexican government. At most, Mexico receives only one-third of the $9 million annual budget of the North American Commission for Environmental Cooperation. NACEC has been effective in carrying out its limited mandate, enabling citizens groups to monitor environmental progress and convening cross-national information sharing and research efforts in North America. But its $3 million budget is dwarfed by Mexico's budget shortfalls and buried by the $36 billion price tag of environmental degradation.

Investment and the deployment of environmentally sound technology

The overall trends in the Mexican environment mask some interesting exceptions that have occurred in the manufacturing sector. New investment in the manufacturing sector (both foreign and domestic) spurred the deployment of cleaner technologies where pollution is a function of plant vintage (or core technology). However, when pollution was a function of end-of-pipe technologies, new investment was not accompanied

Table 5.1 Pollution intensity for SO_x in Mexico and the United States
(Tons per US$ million)

	US	Mexico	US/Mex
Food and beverages	0.50	1.71	0.29
Textiles and apparel	0.35	1.56	0.22
Wood and wood products	0.36	0.68	0.53
Paper, printing, and publishing	2.33	5.67	0.41
Chemicals and petroleum products	3.16	2.80	1.13
Non-metallic mineral products	6.19	1.96	3.16
Iron and steel, non-ferrous metals	11.89	1.12	10.62
Fabricated metals and machinery	0.15	0.08	1.88

Source: Calculated from World Bank data[1]
[1] "New Ideas and Pollution Regulation", available from http://www.worldbank.org/ni, accessed July 2004.

by environmental improvements because of Mexico's implementation gap.

Table 5.1 shows air pollution intensities (and the ratio between the two) for sulfur oxides in the United States and Mexico. The overall result is that Mexican industry is fourteen times more pollution-intensive than is the United States. However, in some cases such as iron and steel and non-ferrous metals, Mexico is actually less pollution-intensive than the United States. Earlier work has shown that in industries where pollution is largely a function of core technologies and cleaner fuels, Mexico is cleaner than the United States. Industries using older technologies burn dirtier fuels, are more apt to need end-of-pipe technologies for pollution abatement and are dirtier in Mexico when compared to the United States (Gallagher 2004).

The United Nations Institute for New Technologies has published a useful summary of technology and pollution intensity in manufacturing (Bartzokas and Yarime 1997). According to this study, which surveys production processes throughout the world economy, the environmental impacts of manufacturing have two sources: energy combustion emissions and byproducts of the production process itself.

Energy combustion is of course essential to various parts of the production process. As a result, air pollutants such as sulfur oxides (SO_x), nitrous oxides (NO_x) and particulate matter (PT) are emitted at various levels depending upon the amount of energy used and the type of fuel used for combustion. Some of the more energy-intensive industries are more capital-intensive in that they transform matter from one form into another: iron ore and coke into steel, wood into paper products, bauxite into aluminum and so forth. To reduce emissions from this part of

Table 5.2 Energy and fuel intensity in North American manufacturing

Sector	Mexico Energy (MJ/US$)	Dirty fuel	United States Energy (MJ/US$)	Dirty fuel
Iron and steel	101.48	10%	118.79	49%
Chemicals	19.63	38%	23.77	5%
Cement	85.86	77%	160.88	64%
Pulp and paper	37.45	39%	40.36	21%
Beer and malt	6.41	41%	5.36	38%
Automotive	0.89	4%	1.24	5%
Rubber	7.38	27%	4.47	8%
Aluminium	31.36	0%	169.98	1%

Source: Personal Communication, INEGI (2002); Environmental Protection Agency, AP-42 (2002)

the production process, newer combustion technologies are being developed that are more energy efficient and thus reduce the total amount of energy used. In addition, fuel-switching away from fuels like coal, diesel and residual fuel oil and toward fuels like natural gas generally lowers emissions. Table 5.2 shows the percentage of "dirty" fuels in Mexican and United States manufacturing industries.

Although new technologies and changes in the fuel mix can reduce air pollution from energy in manufacturing, the main product and basic chemical reactions can remain unchanged. Chemical processes like the bleaching of paper, the mixing of paint for automobiles and the dyeing of wool are examples of production processes that create byproduct pollutants. To abate byproduct pollution there are two strategies. First are end-of-pipe technologies, which are devices added to the final stage of production to remove waste. Second are "process-integrated technologies" that reduce or eliminate the creation of wastes themselves by making the production process more efficient through such activities as reuse and recycling, implementing environmental management systems or redesigning basic processes (Bartzokas and Yarime 1997). The following cases provide further illustration.

Iron and steel

The iron and steel sector is the clearest example of the relatively cleaner effects of plant vintage. During the years of economic integration, the Mexican steel industry was completely transformed. Beginning in the early 1990s, large new private investments, mostly domestic in origin, began to flow into the Mexican steel industry. Compared to the United States steel industry's notoriously slow growth (less than 1% annually), Mexican steel grew 3.7% annually in the 1990s. With such investment came newer, cleaner technologies. In addition, case study evidence has shown that some firms in the Mexican steel sector have begun to employ environmental management systems (Mercado Garcia 1999).

In the late 1980s, Mexico began to integrate its steel sector into the world economy by selling its state-owned enterprises and by freeing the sector from government price controls. Adding momentum to this effort, in 1988 the World Bank gave the Mexican government a US$400 million loan to restructure the sector. Close to $170 million of the loan went to the modernization of technology and equipment at various steel facilities. In some cases, environmental clean-up and compliance were part of privatization agreements between government and private buyers (Gentry and Fernandez 1998).

A recent study on the diffusion of electric arc furnaces (EAFs) in the global economy included a variable as to whether each nation was considered "open" to foreign competition. Mexico, which has seen a surge in EAF production, was included in this study as an open nation – lending force to the article's conclusion that openness was correlated with the spread of cleaner energy technology in the world steel sector (Reppelin-Hill 1999). Electric arc furnaces were a newer and more attractive technology choice for the steel industry when Mexico was privatizing (Mercado Garcia 1999). In addition to being less capital-intensive and therefore less costly, EAFs are significantly less air pollution-intensive than basic oxygen furnaces (BOFs). In BOFs, coke, molten iron, scrap and oxygen are used. Not all of these steps are used in EAFs, which primarily rely on scrap steel and electricity. EAFs use substantially less energy than conventional steel making.

According to Mexico's National Association of Iron and Steel Industries, between 1990 and 1995 the average share of EAF in total Mexican production was 60% (La Cámara Nacional de la Industria del Hierro y el Acero [CANACERO] 2002). In addition, a number of dirtier blast furnaces were taken out of production. Indeed, 200 (relatively small) steel plants were taken out of production in Mexico between 1988 and 1998 (INEGI 2000). In the United States, EAFs were used in only 33%[1] of steel production (Crompton 2001). This observation makes it very clear that the vintage of Mexico's steel sector is an important factor explaining why Mexican steel is relatively less air pollution-intensive than United States steel.

The fuel mix in Mexican steel is also much less air pollution-intensive than in the United States. Only 10% of Mexican steel's fuel use could be classified as "dirty", whereas almost 50% of the fuel in the United States steel industry is dirty (mostly coal) (CANACERO 2002). Moreover, many United States steel plants have been "grandfathered" into major air legislation in the U.S. because they are so old.[2] Of course, this comparison does not count electricity sector emissions, which makes the EAF look cleaner. Mexico's electricity sector is dirtier than in the United States. However, if the calculations included indirect emissions in electricity generation, this gap would narrow.

Cement

The Mexican cement industry is another example of an industry that is more competitive than its United States counterpart, has newer technologies and has aggressive environmental management. Mexico's cement manufacturers own more cement plants than their counterparts in any other country.[3] Mexican companies own 15 of the 51 major cement plants in the world. The Mexican-owned plants produce 34% of world cement production. United States firms own 12 of the major cement plants and produce only 16% of global production capacity (CEMEX 2002). Between 1988 and 1994, years that coincide with the Mexico air pollution data, cement grew 4.6% annually in Mexico, compared to 3% growth in the United States (INEGI 2000).

Growth and competitiveness has allowed the Mexican cement industry to upgrade its technology. The Mexican cement industry is almost twice as energy efficient as cement manufacturing in the United States. This is consistent with other studies that have shown Mexican cement to be more energy efficient. According to the World Bank, between 1960 and 1980, Japan, Germany and the United Kingdom's cement industries were more energy efficient than Mexico's, but Mexican cement was one and one-third times more efficient than the United States (Fog and Nadkarni 1983). In a more recent study using plant-level data for 60 cement kilns in Mexico, it was found that the reduction in energy use per unit of output was due to new investment in capital equipment (Sterner 1990).

The Mexican cement industry has also taken a number of steps toward environmental management. Not all have been successful. In the 1990s the Mexican cement industry worked with international consultants to certify its plants with internationally recognized environmental management systems (Lexington Group 1998). For these efforts and others like it, Mexico's largest cement company, CEMEX, was awarded the 2002 World Environment Center Gold Medal for International Corporate Environmental Achievement (CEMEX 2002). However, in some cases such good intentions have displaced environmental problems rather than solve them. The Mexican cement industry has been involved in burning its hazardous waste as "alternative fuel" in an attempt to save money and emit less criteria air pollutants. However, as the emission of criteria air pollutants has decreased, the amount of toxic emissions has been shown to increase from the burning of hazardous wastes (TCPS 1997).

Promising policies

Though very small in scale, two innovative initiatives in Mexico toward a more comprehensive environmental policy are noteworthy: the clean industry programme and a pilot project of the North American Commission for Environmental Cooperation (NACEC).

A fairly recent development that could prove positive in the future is Mexico's "industria limpia" (clean industry) programme, which acts as a "carrot" to encourage innovative approaches to environmental compliance. The carrot is complemented by the "stick" of inspections and fines. Firms enter the clean industry programme voluntarily. Firms then choose from a list of certified auditors who conduct a formal environmental audit of the firm. After the audit is done, negotiations take place between the firm and the government concerning an action plan for environmental improvements with quantifiable targets and timetables. When the firm signs the agreement, it is granted a grace period on inspections and regulations. However, the firm must show concrete improvements on an annual basis and must meet action plan targets. In case of failure the firm is subjected to normal inspection and fined for regulatory non-compliance. This carrot-and-stick approach is intended to encourage firms to innovate toward environmental improvements. There is a risk, however, of becoming an easy target for regulators.

NACEC's Fund for Pollution Prevention Projects in Mexican Small and Medium Sized Enterprises (FIPREV) is a new source of funds for industry and communities. Although these funds are not sufficient to significantly reduce the environmental costs of industrial growth in Mexico, they serve as models for Mexico and for mechanisms that could be established in the context of the Free Trade Area of the Americas and other agreements.

Created in 1996, FIPREV is a pilot fund for pollution prevention projects in small- and medium-sized enterprises in Mexico. After an initial period of assessment, the fund now has over $2 million, and has given over 25 loans amounting to $610,000. Not only did NACEC provide funds for FIPREV itself, but was able to leverage funds from other sources. FIPREV was established through collaboration with the Mexican Fund for Technology Transfer in Small and Medium Sized Enterprises. FUNTEC is a non-governmental organization linked to the Mexican Federation of Industrial Associations (CONCAMIN). FIPREV was founded to "promote the use of pollution prevention techniques and technologies among small and medium sized Mexican industrial establishments and support them in the development of their environmental management capacities," and to "facilitate the application of pollution prevention measures in industry through the timely and appropriate offering of technical assistance, information, and financing for projects of this nature". (NACEC 2001). The administration of FIPREV brings together members of business, academia and government, and representatives of NACEC's Joint Public Advisory Committee (JPAC).

The majority of FIPREV's projects are in the leather tanning industry. However, other loans have been granted to firms in the food, metalworking, electroplating, chemicals, foundry, dry cleaning and other sectors. FIPREV's low-interest loans can amount to $30,000 or 80% of an investment project. They are most often offered in Mexican pesos but can come in the form of US dollars if the firm is exporting its goods or services. To date, most of these loans have come in the form of technical assistance to firms to make process-based technological changes to reduce water and raw materials usage. Impressively, of the 25 loans thus far granted by FIPREV, all firms have repaid both the credit and interest according to schedule. Based on the annual savings of approximately 1,465 tons of chemical substances, FIPREV estimates that the economic benefits of these environmental programmes have amounted to $646,000 each year since their inception (Dominguez 2003).

Implications for theory

Nelson (1981) has shown that technological change can occur from improving on plant vintage and from more tacit forms of incremental change that occur during the production process. He stresses that such a choice is not simply one of management. Indeed, much of technological change must be a function of labour-management bargaining. Nelson's framework for technological change can also apply to industrial pollution. Indeed, vintage effects have been shown to have been essential to the deployment of new steel and cement technologies in Mexico. However, the evidence from Mexican manufacturing suggests that a third element must be introduced for the case of innovation and industrial pollution: that of a bargain between state (or civil society) and management over end-of-pipe technologies.

The evidence from Mexican manufacturing also suggests that when pollution is in large part a function of energy-intensive technology, new investment from the integration process could bring environmental gains. On the other hand, when pollution is more a function of by-product waste that requires end-of-pipe technologies, and such technologies are

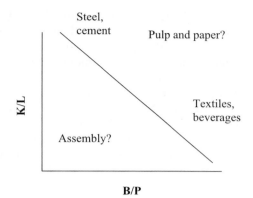

Figure 5.1 Economics of pollution intensity

not required, new investment can be relatively detrimental to the environment. Moreover, when the integration process forces firms to meet new requirements, private funds do not exist for end-of-pipe and other environmental technologies. Such a framework can be sketched as follows.

In figure 5.1, the Y-axis is the capital-labor ratio (K/L), and the X-axis is the ratio of by-product emissions to total emissions (B/P). If Nelson's notion were depicted graphically, it could be represented with K/L on the Y-axis, representing the vintage effect (as it does in figure 5.1), and with incremental technical change on the X-axis, representing the outcome of a labour-management bargain – reflecting the notion that technical change is a combination of the two. In figure 5.1, the labour-management bargain is replaced with by-product emissions, which are a function of a state–civil society (which includes the private sector) bargain whose outcome is the use of end-of-pipe technologies.

The hypothesis in this graph is that in industries where pollution is a function of energy-combustion technology, new investment will yield cleaner production; in industries where pollution is a function of end-of-pipe technologies, the effects of new investment are more ambiguous. The question is, if the data to adequately test the hypothesis were available, would sectors like pulp and paper, or even apparel, fit the pattern suggested in this graph? Pulp and paper production is highly energy-intensive and creates a significant amount of by-product waste. A related question would be how sectors like apparel fit this pattern, given their relatively low energy consumption and pollution potential.

If the hypothesis is correct, end-of-pipe technology innovation and transfer are a special case. In the absence of environmental regulations that require end-of-pipe technologies, or in cases where regulations are not enforced, such technologies will not automatically be deployed because they are not part of the core vintage of the technology. This implies a third dimension to Nelson's theories as applied to industrial pollution. For innovation or deployment for environment, change must be a function of vintage labour-management relations and firm-state (or civil society) relations. Some evidence exists of this beyond Mexico. In the case of China, it was found that United States car manufactures transferred basic car models to China but did not transfer catalytic converters that were used in the same models in the US and Europe because air pollution standards and legislation were not as stringent, making the installation of catalytic converter on cars unnecessary and uneconomical (Sims and Gallagher 2004).

This conclusion and the hypothesis presented in figure 5.1 point to the importance of upgrading environmental regulations in cases where pollution is a function of end-of-pipe technologies. Upgrading is likely to have an accelerating effect; a subject discussed in the next section.

Implications for policy

Contemporary trade policy debates suggest that environmental improvements "automatically" occur through trade and investment liberalization because developed-country firms will bring new, cleaner technologies to the developing world. This chapter indeed shows that to a certain extent such a statement is true. Perhaps more gravely, however, this chapter shows that there are a large number of cases – where pollution is a function of end-of-pipe technology – that this is not true. Such a finding makes a strong argument for making stronger commitment to environmental protection at the policy level and developing more stringent environmental regulations in the developing world. The good news is that for the foreseeable future such efforts will not seem to deter foreign investment from coming in the first place.

The case of Mexico shows that technological change and environmental improvements will not automatically come with economic integration. Indeed, both the innovation and environmental cases show that without the proper policies and structures in place, economic integration can worsen the prospects for technological change and environmental improvement. The fact that there is increasingly little evidence of pollution havens in Mexico and other developing countries is good news. One important implication is that policy-driven environmental protection and spending do not scare away the foreign and direct investment that Mexico and other developing countries desperately seek through their development process (Gallagher 2004).

The problem is, however, that without economic growth and macro-economic stability, policies for environmental protection – let alone policies for environmental innovation – will continue to be a low priority for Mexico and countries in a similar situation. Without growth, and with an economic-development strategy based on economic integration, nations like Mexico have to rely on importing technology or receiving it through foreign direct investment. This chapter has shown that such a reliance on foreign technology is no substitute for a National Innovation System or environmental innovation. In the meantime, programmes such as Clean Industry and FIPREV show promise because they attempt to spur innovation from both vintage and end-of-pipe perspectives.

Notes

1. Averaging 1982 to 1987 to correspond with the IPPS data.
2. "Grandfathering" means that they are held to much less stringent standards than newer plants.
3. Not all Mexican-owned plants are in Mexico, some are in Spain, Egypt, Colombia, Thailand and elsewhere.

REFERENCES

Bartzokas, A. and M. Yarime (1997) "Technology Trends in Pollution Intensive Industries: A Review of Sectoral Trends", Maastricht: the United Nations University.

[La] Cámara Nacional de la Industria del Hierro y el Acero (CANACERO) (2002) "1991–2000, Ten Years of Steelmaking Statistics", Col. del Valle, Mexico: CANACERO.

CEMEX (2002) http://www.cemex.com.

Center for Strategic and International Studies (CSIS) (2003) "Economic Competitiveness in Mexico", Washington D.C.: Center for Strategic and International Studies.

Cimoli, M., ed. (2000) Developing Innovation Systems: Mexico in a Global Context, London: Continuum.

Comisión Económica para America Latina (CEPAL) (2004). Anuario Estadistico de America Latina y el Caribe 2003 (New York: United Nations).

Crompton, P. (2001) "The Diffusion of New Steelmaking Technology", Resources Policy 27: 87–95.

Dasgupta, S., H. Hettige and D. Wheeler (2000) "What Improves Environmental Compliance? Evidence from Mexican Industry", Journal of Environmental Economics and Management 38: 39–66.

Dominguez, L. (2003) Necesidades de bienes y servicios ambientales en las micro y pequenas empresas: El case de Mexico, Santiago, Chile: Economic Commission for Latin America and the Caribbean.

Eskeland, G. S. and A. E. Harrison (1997) "Moving to Greener Pastures? Multinationals and the Pollution Haven Hypothesis", World Bank Policy Research Working Paper No. 1744. Available at http://ssrn.com/abstract=604985.

Fog, M. H. and K. L. Nadkarni (1983) "Energy efficiency and fuel substitution in the cement industry with emphasis on developing countries", World Bank Technical Paper, Washington, D.C.: World Bank.

Gallagher, K. (2004) Free Trade and the Environment: Mexico, NAFTA, and Beyond, Palo Alto, Calif.: Stanford University Press.

Gallagher, K. P. and Lyuba Zarsky (2004) Sustainable Industrial Development? The Performance of Mexico's FDI-led Development Strategy, Medford, Mass.: Tufts University.

Gentry, Bradford and L. Fernandez (1998) "Mexican Steel", in Bradford Gentry, ed., Private Capital Flows and the Environment: Lessons from Latin America, Cheltenham, England: Edward Elgar.

Gerber, J. and J. Carrillo (2003) "¿Las Maquiladoras de Baja California son Competitivas?", Comercio Exterior 53(3): 284–293.

Grossman, Gene M. and Alan B. Krueger (1993) "Environmental Impacts of a North American Free Trade Agreement", in P. Garber, The Mexico-US Free Trade Agreement, Cambridge, Mass.: MIT Press.

Instituto Nacional de Estadística Geografía e Informática (INEGI) (2000). XII Censo General de Poblaciœn y Vivienda. Resultados Preliminares.

Kahn, Matthew E. (2001) "United States Pollution Intensive Trade Trends From 1972 to 1992", Medford, Mass.: Tufts University, available from http://ssrn.com/abstract=214268.

Mattar, Jorge, Juan Carlos Moreno-Brid and Wilson Peres (2002) "Foreign Investment in Mexico after Economic Reform", in E. Z. Kevin Middlebrook, ed., Confronting Development, Cambridge, Mass.: Stanford University Press, pp. 1–45.

Mercado Garcia, A., ed. (1999) Instrumentos Economicos Para Un Comportamiento Empresarial Favorable Al Amiente En Mexico, Camino al Ajusco, Mexico: El Colegio de Mexico.

Merino, Gustavo T. and Ramiro Tovar (2002) Gasto, Inversion y financiamiento para el desarrollo sostenible en Mexico, Santiago, Chile: Economic Commission for Latin America and the Caribbean.

Metcalf, S. (1995) "Economic Foundations of Technology Policy", in P. Stoneman, ed., Handbook on the Economics of Innovation and Technical Change, Oxford: Oxford University Press.

North American Commission for Environmental Cooperation (NACEC). "North American Pollutant Release and Transfer Register: Project Details." Available online at: http://www.nacec.org.

Nelson, R. (1981) "Research on Productivity Growth and Productivity Differences: Dead Ends and New Departures", Journal of Economic Literature (September): 1029–1064.

———— (1992) "National Innovation Systems: A Retrospective on a Study", Industrial and Corporate Change: 347–374.

Organization of Economic Cooperation and Development (OECD) (1998). Open

Markets Matter: The Benefits of Trade and Investment Liberalisation, Paris: OECD.

——— (OECD) (2003) Environmental Performance Review of Mexico, Paris: OECD.

Reppelin-Hill, V. (1999) "Trade and Environment: An Empirical Analysis of the Technology Effect in the Steel Industry", Journal of Environmental Economics and Management 38: 283–301.

Sims, Kelly and Kevin Gallagher (2004) "Limits to Leapfrogging: Big Three Automakers and Energy Technology Transfer in China", Energy Policy, forthcoming.

Stern, D. (1998) "Progress on the Environmental Kuznets Curve?", Environment and Development Economics 3: 173–196.

Sterner, T. (1990) "Energy Efficiency and Capital Embodied Technical Change: The Case of Mexican Cement Maufacturing", Energy Journal 11(2): 155–167.

Stromberg, Per (2002) "The Mexican Maquila Industry and the Environment: An Overview of the Issues", New York: United Nations CEPAL/ECLAC: 1–56.

World Bank (2003) World Bank Development Indicators, World Bank.

6

Environmental policy, innovation and third-party factors in the Nigerian manufacturing industry

John O. Adeoti

Environmental policy is regarded by some economists as the main driver for industrial innovations that reduce external diseconomies of industrial production (Baumol and Oates 1988; Siebert 1987) in both developed and developing countries. However, recent research on the links between pollution regulation and environmental innovation suggests that environmental policy may not sufficiently explain the recently observed trends in environmentally beneficial technological innovation.[1] It is becoming apparent that a complex web of additional interacting factors determines pollution control innovations at the firm level.

This paper examines the role of third-party factors that form part of the complex web that works along with environmental regulation to generate innovations aimed at curbing industrial pollution. A case-study approach was used in analysing the empirical data obtained from six Nigerian food-processing and textiles firms. Case-study data were collected between November 1999 and April 2000. In addition, Nigerian environmental regulators were interviewed to complement the case-study findings. Particular attention was paid to how third-party factors affected the firms in their decision to adopt wastewater treatment technology.

This chapter is organized as follows. The next section provides an overview of the environmental regulatory regime in Nigeria, followed by a discussioin of the limits of environmental policy as a stimulus for environmental innovation. Using findings from the case studies, the next section illustrates the role of regulatory pressure and third-party factors as stimuli for environmental technological innovation in industrial wastewater treatment. The chapter concludes with a discussion of the policy implications of the findings.

An overview of the environmental regulatory regime in Nigeria

Generally speaking, environmental regulation in Africa remains relatively weak while there is insufficient institutional capacity to deal with industrial pollution problems. Even South Africa with relatively advanced manufacturing had not established a comprehensive programme of industrial pollution control until the second half of the 1990s (DEAT 1996). However, Nigeria appears to be an exception to the general African situation.

In 1988, the government of Nigeria established a Federal Environmental Protection Agency (FEPA)[2] to oversee and manage environmental regulatory processes in Nigeria. Industrial pollution control, which had previously been carried out on a rather ad hoc basis, came under the purview of FEPA – which has a network of zonal offices[3] and pollution control laboratories[4] for the purpose of pollution monitoring and control. In addition to the establishment of FEPA, each of the Nigerian state governments also established a State Environmental Protection Agency (SEPA)[5] in the mid-1990s. Before the advent of SEPAs, FEPA was solely responsible for industrial pollution control in Nigeria. Since SEPAs were established, FEPA and SEPAs have worked together to monitor and control industrial effluents. It should however be pointed out that SEPAs are statutorily directly responsible for industrial pollution monitoring and control in their respective states, while FEPA is expected to provide institutional support and a regulatory framework for pollution control. The institutional support provided by FEPA has included the development of standards and guidelines for pollution control in Nigeria; training programmes for state environmental regulators and officers in charge of environmental issues in industry; and effluent and emission limits.

Policy approach in dealing with industrial pollution in Nigeria has been mainly "command and control" in nature. Market-related policy instruments such as effluent taxes and tradeable permits are still alien concepts and little understood, especially among local stakeholders in industry. A composite law was enacted in August 1991, coming into full application in January 1995. The industrial pollution control law is termed "National Effluent Limitation Regulation" (S.I.8) and "Pollution Abatement and Facilities Generating Wastes Regulation" (S.I.9) (FEPA 1991a). The full implementation of this law was delayed till January 1995 to allow for a three-year moratorium during which firms were expected to have made necessary technological changes to comply with the S.I.8/S.I.9 regulation. The S.I.8/S.I.9 law specifies the maximum permissible limits for various industrial emission parameters in Nigeria. These effluent limits are binding in every Nigerian state, though states are allowed to enact stricter emission limits. For example, Lagos State, which has the largest concentration of industry in Nigeria, has recently enacted stricter effluents limits.[6] At this juncture, it is necessary to point out that the level of environmental awareness and efforts to protect the environment appear to be on the increase in Nigeria. This was further demonstrated by the upgrading of FEPA into a full-fledged government department with a cabinet minister in January 2000. With this institutional reform FEPA became the Federal Ministry of Environment (FME).[7]

Limits to environmental policy as the stimulus for green innovation in developing countries

While environmental policy is necessary to make firms appreciate and perhaps accept responsibility for the external diseconomies of their production activities, the factors determining the implementation of environmentally benign technical change largely transcend the traditional notion of environmental policy as the stimulus for innovation in pollution control. Theoretical models linking environmental policy and environmentally benign technological innovation (e.g., Downing and White 1986; Milliman and Prince 1989) are limited in their empirical applications. Such models adopt the neo-classical view of environmental policy as being the stimulus for environmentally benign technical change, and in the process assume off other pertinent factors that have been demonstrated from empirical studies as playing important roles in stimulating environment-friendly innovations.

The focus in these theoretical viewpoints is not on the kind of technical change induced by policy, but rather the kind of policy or optimal mix of policies that could achieve a predetermined level of environmental quality or pollution reduction. For developing countries still in search of relevant paths and appropriate strategy for industrialization, these theoretical ideas that focus on environmental policy may appear more of a luxury. Many developing countries lack the appropriate institutional context for developing and managing elaborate environmental policy instruments such as pollution taxes and tradeable emission permits. Most developing countries are thus forced to adopt command and control strategies and resort to regulatory means that may not go beyond specifying emission limits and technology standards to be adopted to ensure compliance.

Moreover, based largely on studies of industrial economies, the last few years have witnessed the development of theoretical and empirically tested propositions that emphasize that environmental policy does not provide sufficient impetus for green innovation in many instances. Among such propositions, Michael Porter's hypothesis that environmental regulation can create technological offsets, yielding economic benefits that write off the cost of compliance with environmental policy, is of particular importance.[8] These propositions have been extended to suggest "win-win" solutions yielding double dividends that benefit both private and social parties (see Howes et al. 1997). Some have even suggested a triple dividend that includes increased employment. Thus, the notions of double-triple-dividend suggest that the incentive to adopt green innovation may arise from a desire to attend to socioeconomic benefits rather than the compelling force of the environmental policy.

More recently, Ashford (2000: 68) has questioned the effectiveness of environmental policy alone as the stimulus to green innovation, and underlined the importance of other factors needed to generate firm-level technological change. He lists among these factors regulatory requirements (including environmental policy); possible cost savings or additions to profits; public demand for a less polluting and safer industry; and worker demands and pressures arising from industrial relation concerns.

Additionally, studies on environmental regulation and industrial pollution control in developing countries rarely focus on the impact of environmental policy on technology responses of firms.[9] Rather, the focus is usually on the impact of policy on emission reduction or pollution abatement expenditures (e.g., Aden, Kyu-hong and Rock 1999; Dasgupta 2000; Hettige et al. 1996). Though emission reduction would be impossible without technological application or change in production practices aimed at pollution abatement, the neglect of direct analysis of the technological or innovation impact of policy limits our understanding of all the factors that determine the actual emission reduction achieved. Technology is the medium through which emission reduction effects are accomplished. When the searchlight is focused on this medium, we may gain a more comprehensive perspective on the interplay of factors that interact with technology to generate the emission reduction effects.

Having argued that environmental policy alone cannot explain green innovation among industrial firms in developing countries, we need to ask what other factors, in addition to environmental policy, are needed to provide the full range of benefits from emission reduction effects. While there may be striking similarities between innovation behaviour of developed and developing-country firms with respect to pollution control, it is pertinent to note that the divergence of the north-south perception of the challenges of environmentally sustainable development would affect the level of stringency in environmental policy and its enforcement process.

Environmental policy in the South has never been, and may not in the near future be expected to be, as stringent as in the industrial countries of the North. Hence, when environmental technologies are observed among firms in the countries of the South, it is plausible to suggest that there may be other "third party" factors (apart from environmental policy) that drive firms' green innovation behaviour. Decoupling these factors from environmental policy is, however, difficult since environmental policy provides the basic guidelines for the firms' technological responses. Third party factors include, but are not limited to, community pressure on firms to reduce emission; influence of public corporations that may be affected by polluting activities; advocacy by environmental non-governmental organizations; influences of parent companies on affiliates of multinational corporations; and the influence of environmental technology suppliers.

Based on empirical case studies from the Nigerian food-processing and textile sectors, the remainder of this paper will discuss the relationship of third-party factors with firms' technological responses. First, however, a concise description of the two sectors in Nigeria and their respective pollution problems.

Pollution problems of the food-processing and textile industries

As typical of countries in the early stages of industrial development, resource-based manufacturing activities are an important feature of the Nigerian economy. Data on the structure of Nigerian manufacturing indicates that the food-processing and textile sectors contribute 29.4% of the total manufacturing output and 32.4% of the manufacturing value-added in 1994. The two sectors employ 38.7% of the Nigerian manufacturing workforce (UNIDO 2001).[10] Manufacturing activity in Nigeria is concentrated in a few large cities,[11] and its pollution effects are the subject of much concern, particularly to the city dwellers.

The food-processing and textile sectors both consume high volumes of water and have significant water-pollution potential associated with their activities. For example, from the data provided by the World Bank (2001) on industry's share of organic emissions, the two sectors accounted for nearly half (47.9%) of total polluted wastewater discharges from the Nigerian industry in 1994. Public health concerns are high with respect to the pollution effects of industrial wastewater since the majority of

Nigerians still lack access to safe drinking water.[12] Perhaps not surprisingly, Nigeria has relatively well-articulated pollution-control regulation with respect to industrial wastewater. The more specific pollution problems of the two sectors are briefly described below.

Food processing

Food processing in Nigeria may be broadly classified into seven subsectors or divisions. These subsectors are grain milling; soft drink and fruit juices; brewing; distilleries and wine; dairy products; vegetable oil and fat products; and confectionery and sugar products. Apart from grain milling, which is essentially a dry process, all other sub-sectors are water-pollution intensive, discharging wastewater largely laden with organic wastes.

The organic pollutants are mainly present in process wastewater, container/vessels washwater, clean in place (CIP)[13] rinse water and floor-wash water. In many factories visited for this research, fugitive oil emission or the dripping of other organic pollutants due to old equipment further compounded the wastewater problem. Virtually all firms in this sector have oil traps to capture the fugitive oil as much as possible, and thus limit additional pollution of the wastewater. Among the firms visited, some burned oil in boilers to generate energy, a practice that could lead to air pollution, while others sold it on the open market and mainly to the informal sector where the oil is often used as fuel. This recycling of waste oil is not peculiar to the food processing industry. Similar practices were noted among the textile plants visited.

Textiles

According to Mbendi (2000), traditional textiles have been produced in Nigeria for many years, but real industrial activity in textile production began in 1956 with the establishment of Kaduna Textile Mills Limited in northern Nigeria. The first set of Nigerian textile firms were vertically integrated mills that convert locally available raw materials (mainly cotton) to intermediate and finished textile goods. Spinning processes churn out yarn, weaving produced grey cloth, while dyeing, printing and finishing turn out finished textiles. From the account of Mbendi, the Nigerian textile industry has over the years developed to incorporate fibre production, spinning, weaving, knitting, lace and embroidery making, carpet production, dyeing, printing and finishing. In spite of the problem of importation of relatively cheap textiles through unofficial channels (BBC News, 1 September 2003), the sector produces a variety of fabrics annually, ranging from African prints, shirtings, embroideries, etc., to guinea brocades, wax prints, jute and other textile-related products. The Central Bank of Nigeria Annual Report of 2001 showed that the textile industry in Nigeria accounts for a significant proportion of the overall growth of Nigeria's manufacturing production. About two-thirds (68%) of the raw materials used in the industry are sourced locally, the main exceptions being high-quality cotton and synthetic materials. It is important to note that foreign investment in Nigeria's textile industry is limited and is mainly by Chinese and Indian investors. There is also representation from Europe, the United States, Japan and Syria. Through privatization, most of the equity investments held by government have been transferred to private hands, and foreign investors played significant roles in the ensuing acquisition of government shares and merger processes. Mbendi reported that the performance of the industry has improved significantly as a result of the implementation of the privatization programme.

The pollution problems of the textile industry in developing countries have long been a concern.[14] For textile plants in Nigeria, the handling of the wastewater effluents constitutes the most important problem. For example, 89% of the textile firms in our survey sample indicated wastewater as the most serious pollution problem they have confronted (see table 6.1). The equivalent figure of 78% for the food-processing industry suggests a relatively less difficult view of the perception of the problem of industrial wastewater by plant managers.

Moreover, our interview and survey of environmental regulators revealed that they particularly view textile firms as the worst culprits of wastewater pollution when compared with the food-processing sector. For example, while 50% of the surveyed regulators rated the compliance of the Nigerian food processing sector with the Nigerian effluent limitation regulation from "good" to "very good" on a five-step scale ranging from "very poor" to "very good", none of our respondent regulators consider the textile sector's compliance status as "very good", and only 22% consider the textile industry's compliance level as being "good".

Table 6.1 Rating of most important pollution issues

	Waste-water %	Air pollution %	Solid waste %	Noise %	Total number of responses
Food processing	78	5.5	11	5.5	91
Textiles	89	7	–	4	27
Combined	81	6	8	5	118

Third-party factors and innovation in pollution control processes

The cases discussed in this section include two breweries, two confectionery plants and two textile plants. Table 6.2 presents the summary of the background and basic characteristics of the case-study firms. For reasons of confidentiality, the case studies are designated FP1, FP2, FP3 and FP4 for the food processing plants, and TT1 and TT2 for the textile plants.

Environmentally benign technology implemented by the case-study firms can be classified as end-of-pipe, e.g., firms with industrial waste-water treatment plants, or preventive, e.g., innovative measures or technologies that reduce the generation of industrial wastewater at the source. Pollution prevention technical change was classified under four groups: wastewater reduction/recycling, raw material reuse/recycling, materials substitution, and process-integrated techniques that reduce wastewater. A firm could adopt one or more of these wastewater pollution prevention innovations. Table 6.3 shows the sectoral distribution of the adoption of these pollution prevention innovations, according to the time of adoption, among our survey sample.

Water or wastewater reuse/recycling and integrated physical devices in the production line are relatively common among the food and beverages plants. Integrated physical devices observed in the course of the field-work included improved bottle-washing devices, metering devices/equipment, re-engineering of aspects of process lines which resulted in leakage prevention or minimization, improved CIP procedure with introduction of pressurized nozzle points at strategic locations that enhance efficiency of water use during CIP, caustic soda recovery/recycling tanks/process, replacement of high-waste-producing machines with low liquor dyeing equipment in the textile sector, mixing of spent oil with LPFO (low pour fuel oil) for reuse in boilers, etc. As shown in table 6.3, most adoption of

Table 6.2 Case study profiles

Case study	Approximate age of firm	No. of persons employed	MNC* affiliate?	Capacity utilization	Manufacturing subsector	Per cent Nigerian ownership
FP1	20 years	800	yes	60%	Brewery	60%
FP2	20 years	300	no	30%	Brewery	0%
FP3	10 years	210	yes	85%	Confectionery	15%
FP4	40 years	1,131	yes	62%	Confectionery	43%
TT1	37 years	700	yes	65%	Textile	40%
TT2	23 years	376	no	20%	Textile	30%

*Multinational corporation

Table 6.3 Adoption of pollution prevention innovation according to time and sectoral distribution of adoption

	When adopted			
	Before 1995		After 1995	
Pollution prevention innovation	F&B*	Textiles	F&B	Textiles
Water/wastewater recycling	11	0	19	1
Raw material reuse/recycling	7	9	9	3
Materials substitution	4	7	2	1
Integrated physical device	8	1	12	1

*Food & beverages

wastewater pollution prevention innovation among the textile plants took place before January 1995, prior to the establishment of the State Environmental Protection Agency (SEPA). It thus appears that the textile plants might not have taken full advantage of the pollution prevention opportunities after January 1995, but focused rather on end-of-pipe wastewater treatment processes in part as a response to new, stricter regulatory requirements by SEPA.

The option of materials substitution appears relatively less common compared to other wastewater pollution-prevention innovations in food processing, perhaps due to the stringent public control of the food and beverages industry. In the case of the textiles, the raw material re-use/recycling appears relatively more common than other types of wastewater pollution-prevention innovations. This may be due to the introduction of the wax-recovery process in some textile plants. Wax recovery seemed to have been introduced as a cost-saving rather than an environmental protection measure.[15]

It is not clear from the above analysis what role third parties played in influencing the adoption of wastewater prevention innovations. However, cross-tabulation of the adoption of wastewater treatment by the adoption of wastewater prevention innovations reveals that 39 (85%) of the 46 adopters of wastewater treatment technology are also adopters of one or more forms of wastewater prevention innovation. The adoption of wastewater prevention innovations thus appear to be closely associated with the adoption of wastewater treatment technology. It is accordingly plausible to expect that the factors driving the adoption of wastewater treatment technology also play significant roles as rationales for the adoption of wastewater prevention measures. This paper nonetheless pays more attention to the adoption of industrial wastewater treatment technology because the case-study firms give clear and vivid illustrations of the role of third parties in the implementation of the adoption of wastewater treatment plants in the Nigerian food and beverages and textiles sectors.

Case Study FP1

An affiliate of a multinational company based in a west European country, FP1 is a large-scale brewing plant employing about 800 people and located in an industrial estate on the outskirts of a large city in Nigeria. When it was established in the early 1980s it was only equipped with a primary wastewater treatment plant. Over the years, the community where the plant is located began to complain of environmental damage attributable to wastewater discharges from FP1. Actions by the host community intensified, and in 1997 a community association was founded with a mandate to address industrial pollution. This non-governmental organization has instigated a court action (against FP1), which is presently one of the few high-profile environmental lawsuits in Nigeria. According to the Nigerian environmental regulators and FP1's environmental consultants interviewed as part of this research, the environmental damage reported by the community included the poisoning of groundwater, thereby rendering well water undrinkable; the nearby stream into which the discharge from the primary wastewater treatment plant flows has lost all aquatic life, especially fish; and palm and other trees of economic value are severely threatened, signalling the possibility that farmland productivity may also be threatened.

In spite of the fact that the claims of the communal association were not accepted by FP1, the firm appears not to have appropriately responded to the environmental regulatory demand of installing effective industrial wastewater treatment technology until after the community pressure became intense. According to FP1, the plant was built before the community settled in its current location, and other manufacturing plants producing wastewater (though on a much smaller scale) are also located in the same industrial layout.

In the mid-1990s, prior to community complaints becoming an issue, FP1 extended the primary wastewater treatment plant to include more oil schemers from where oil and grease are collected regularly. In addition, an aquatic weed (water hyacinth) was introduced as macrophytes to enhance the purification of wastewater in the plant's lagoon. According to FP1, the adoption of these pollution control measures was due to regulatory pressure and the desire to improve their environmental image. These measures were, however, considered unsatisfactory by both the community association and environmental regulators. Taking advantage of an expansion programme financed by the parent company, FP1 has decided to adopt modern industrial wastewater treatment technology. The company's new wastewater management system is termed "cost-effective wastewater treatment". The technology adopted incorporates an "upflow anaerobic sludge blanket reactor" (UABR) and a "sequence batch reactor" (SBR).

Case Study FP2

A medium-sized local brewing plant, FP2 employs 300 people and was established in the early 1980s. At the time of the fieldwork for this research the plant had significant under-capacity (capacity utilization was only 30% in 2000) which it hoped to eliminate with improved, and more stable, political conditions. One expected result of democratic governance in Nigeria was the positive impact of the transfer of ownership to some Asians. The plant had been built with no facility for wastewater treatment. According to FP2, regulatory-compliance monitoring had not been of much effect on the company until the establishment of SEPA in 1995 and the more stringent monitoring programme that ensued. However, FP2 interviewees stated that even after the establishment of SEPA, compliance monitoring was not carried out regularly until there was an environmental incident, which led to the shutdown of the plant in 1996.

The environmental incident arose due to a complaint from a public water corporation: FP2 was releasing its untreated wastewater into a perennial stream, which is dammed downstream and purified for public consumption. The public water corporation discovered that the cost of water purification was excessively higher than expected. On examination of the raw water, the cause was traced to the wastewater discharged by FP2. Since the water corporation had no statutory power to compel FP2 to stop the release of contaminated discharges, the problem was reported to SEPA, who acted promptly by sealing off the plant until appropriate industrial wastewater treatment was installed by FP2. The wastewater treatment method adopted was a locally built secondary wastewater treatment technology. Although the wastewater treatment succeeded in improving the effluent quality to an acceptable level for the third party (public water corporation), it was however observed that the effluent quality did not meet the statutory requirement of the effluent limitation regulation. The State Environmental Protection Agency insisted on improvement of the wastewater treatment technology while allowing more time for the firm to meet this requirement.

Case Study FP3

A large-scale manufacturing plant, FP3 is an affiliate of an American multinational company. The firm was established in the early 1990s and produces candies. It is ISO 9001 certified, employs about 200 people and operates 85% of its full capacity at the time of this research. The firm's environmental management is directed from the parent company's environmental department headquarters located in western Europe. The parent company also engages in annual environmental performance ratings of its subsidiaries. Any subsidiary that does not obtain eight-point rating out of 10 points for five consecutive years is liable to being closed down. According to sources at FP3, this challenge has largely encouraged the plant's commitment to environmental management. The firm boasts that its environmental management standard is better than that of many local plants.

It was also observed that though regulators have been visiting this plant, they have not succeeded in making the plant adopt wastewater treatment technology. Rather, under a contract with a local environmental management consultant, the plant regularly transfers its wastewater effluent to a distant stream for dilution by means of a tanker service. The parent company of FP3 appears to have ignored this aspect until regulatory pressure became more intense in recent years. However, FP3 ascribes non-adoption of industrial wastewater treatment to the high cost of the technology. It is also likely that prior relatively weak environmental policy enforcement provided little incentive for FP3 to install wastewater treatment.

When the firm finally agreed to implement wastewater treatment, there was a sharp disagreement between the regulators and FP3. While FP3 wanted to adopt an anaerobic digester, regulators recommended an aerated activated sludge system because it would be more effective in bringing the effluent quality to the statutorily required level. However, regulators had to allow FP3 to make its free choice since the effluent limitation regulation is silent on the specific technology to be employed for waste treatment.[16] FP3 later consented to installing the aerated activated sludge system after a visit by the head of the environmental management of the parent company who advised FP3 on the preference of the aerated activated sludge technology for efficiency reasons, and because methane and other gaseous products of the anaerobic system could create new sources of pollutants emission.

Case Study FP4

An affiliate of a European multinational company, FP4 is one of the oldest manufacturing enterprises in Nigeria, established in the early 1960s. It is a very large plant employing about 1,100 people at the time of this research. The plant is ISO 9001 certified and has undertaken to implement an environmental management system in compliance with the ISO 14001 standards. The plant is located in a large, privately owned industrial estate that has a centralized wastewater treatment plant. This centralized wastewater treatment facility serves about 17 plants in the food-processing and pharmaceutical sectors.

The estate's wastewater treatment plant is a large aerated lagoon. It is directly managed by the authorities of the industrial estate. The regulators who were interviewed disclosed that the wastewater treatment plant is inefficient in meeting the effluent quality standard specified by the effluent limitation regulation. They could not, however, apply the relevant sanctions because of the network of sociopolitical and economic interests represented in the industrial estate. Interviewees from FP4 acknowledged that the centralized wastewater treatment facility was inadequate but could not unilaterally adopt a new treatment technology since other plants were involved. To demonstrate goodwill, FP4 helps the operators of the wastewater treatment plant in effluent quality analysis as a voluntary contribution to signify FP4's commitment to improved environmental performance.

To minimize effluent discharges to the centralized wastewater treatment plant, the companies on the estate collectively took a decision to each adopt a primary wastewater treatment technology. FP4 adopted a primary wastewater treatment to reduce the organic contents of its effluents. The constraints of joint responsibility introduced by the centralized wastewater treatment appeared to provide a disincentive for FP4 to adopt the best available technology in wastewater treatment.

Case Study TT1

A large-scale textile plant, TT1 was established in the mid-1960s and employs about 700 people. It is located in the heart of one of Nigeria's major cities and is an affiliate of an Asia-based multinational company. For some time TT1 had problems with the environmental impacts of its wastewater, a source of much concern for people living near the plant. In response to the tightening of regulatory enforcement after the establishment of SEPA in 1995, TT1 commissioned its first environmental audit whose findings recommended the adoption of a wastewater treatment technology as required by the effluent limitation regulation.

An advanced wastewater treatment technology was subsequently adopted by TT1. According to TT1 interviewees, the motivations for the decision to implement wastewater treatment technology included environmental regulation, parent company norms of environmental management, prevention of environmental incidents and improvement of the firm's environmental image. In the opinion of the plant manager, it was difficult to ascribe adoption to any singular factor. However, he claimed that the prevention of environmental incidents was the firm's most important reason for adoption, followed by the parent company's norms.

Case Study TT2

A medium-sized local textile firm employing 376 people, TT2 was established in the late 1970s and is located on the outskirts of one of Nigeria's mid-sized towns. Unlike TT1, the plant appears not to be seriously committed to environmental management. In spite of the increased environmental awareness in Nigeria in the last decade, TT2 did not adopt a wastewater treatment plant until it was partially sealed off by SEPA in 1996. The partial forced closure was due to community pressure based on concerns about the seepage of textile effluents into drinking water wells. The risks of groundwater contamination are particularly high because this textile plant is sited on a higher elevation than the surrounding community.

The community demanded that TT2 pipe away its wastewater and compensate the community for the polluted wells. In response to TT2's refusal to address their concerns, the community complained to SEPA. The partial shutdown of the plant was decreed by SEPA, and intended to close down the dyeing section of the plant responsible for most of the plant's wastewater contamination. The dyeing section was reopened after TT2 had implemented the adoption of a locally built secondary wastewater treatment plant.

Conclusion: Third-party factors as complements to environmental regulation

The above case studies illustrate the impact of third party factors in advancement of environmentally benign technical change in two sectors. These case studies demonstrate that environmental policy, though necessary, is not sufficient in effecting environmentally responsible behaviour by firms. Table 6.4 presents the summary of the third-party factors that seem to have played important roles in the adoption of industrial wastewater treatment technologies in the two sectors.

In developing countries where environmental regulation is weak, third party factors can and do provide additional influence on how firms manage environmental impacts. However, it has to be recognized that third-party factors are incapable of acting on their own without the backing of an environmental regulatory regime. For example, in each of the case studies, third parties were not able to influence companies to implement environmentally benign technologies without the intervention of environ-

Table 6.4 Summary of third-party factors

Sector	Case study	Third-party factors
Food processing	FP1	Community NGO, parent company's environmental norms
	FP2	Public water corporation
	FP3	Parent company's environmental norms
	FP4	Other manufacturing firms, parent company's environmental norms
Textiles	TT1	Local community, parent company's environmental norms, environmental technology supplier
	TT2	Local community pressure

mental regulators, who had formal authority and supporting legislation. Even where third parties are parent companies of multinational corporations with high environmental performance norms, a decision to adopt wastewater treatment plants was not taken until regulatory demands were enforced.

It appears from the Nigerian experience that it is possible for third-party factors to catalyse processes that result in superior environmental performance by firms that lack commitment to environmental protection in the first instance. This is illustrated by case study FP4. The challenge posed by the findings of this research is how to expand the scope of environmental regulation to utilize input from third-party factors that have specific interest in industry's environmental performance.

Third parties may serve as important sources of information on the actual environmental performance of firms. Information asymmetries between regulators and industrial firms may thus be reduced. As the case studies demonstrate, information received by regulators from third parties could form the basis for sanctions that may force firms to embark on environmental innovation. Information based on third-party factors could increase the returns on investments in compliance-monitoring resources. Such information can also be used to prioritize the severity of problems and reduce the potential for environmental incidents.

In the case of parent companies as a third party, it is plausible to expect a poor environmental performer to cover up non-compliance where compliance monitoring is weak. It is possible for regulators to isolate such cases for more regular inspection visits, which may stimulate the parent company to intervene and make the necessary operational adjustments to bring the affiliate firm into compliance. From the Nigerian experience, however, affiliates of multinational corporations appear to be generally more committed to environmental management when compared to local firms, and this is reflected in the adoption of the wastewater treatment technology. Sixty-eight per cent of the affiliates of multinational corporations in the research sample had adopted wastewater treatment, whereas only 27% of the locally owned plants had adopted wastewater treatment.[17]

It is also important to note that only one out of the wastewater treatment technologies adopted by the case study firms performed satisfactorily in meeting the regulatory requirement for effluent quality (see case study TT1). There may be a case of regulatory standard being higher than the majority of firms in Nigeria could comply with, given the existing local conditions under which they operate. Since it is difficult to conclude that the case of TT1 is typical of Nigerian industrial firms, it is expedient for the regulatory authorities to re-examine the effluent standards to ensure that they are adequate and achievable.

Notes

1. See, for example, Porter and van der Linde (1995) and Hart and Ahuja (1996) on developed countries, and Adeoti (2002) on developing countries.
2. FEPA was merged with some environment-related departments to form the Federal Ministry of Environment in January 2001. The use of FEPA is retained in this paper for clarity.
3. As at the time of this research, these zonal offices were located at Ibadan, Kaduna, Kano, Lagos, Maiduguri, Owerri and Port Harcourt. The Lagos office also serves as the headquarters of the industrial compliance monitoring and enforcement department of FEPA.
4. As of 1999, these laboratories included the National Reference Laboratory (NRL) located in Lagos, and two zonal FEPA laboratories located in Port Harcourt and Kano. Other pollution control laboratories also exist in some state environmental protection agencies. While some of these laboratories have existed for almost as long as their parent institutions, they were not adequately equipped until a World Bank-assisted programme on environmental management was implemented in 1998 (see *Daily Monitor*, 16 October 1998: 16). It is nonetheless yet to be seen whether the Nigerian environmental regulatory authorities can maintain and further equip these laboratories for effective industrial pollution control.
5. Nigeria has 36 states and a Federal Capital Territory (FCT). Each state (and the FCT) has a SEPA or an environmental protection board.
6. Lagos State has at least 10% of the Nigerian population and some estimates indicated that the state has 60 to 70% of industry in Nigeria (see Lubeck 1992: 17 and LASEPA 1999).
7. For further details on the environmental regulatory regime in Nigeria with respect to industrial pollution control, see FEPA (1991b) and Adeoti (2002).
8. See Porter and van der Linde (1995) on "innovation offsets".
9. Adeoti (2002) presents a major deviation from this trend by analysing the technological impact of the Nigerian industrial pollution control policies.
10. These data are computed from UNIDO industrial statistics database 2001 CD-ROM. The data are based on the available information for 1994. Since there has been no ex-

traordinary development that would have a drastic impact on Nigerian manufacturing, these statistics are not expected to be significantly different from what could have been obtained at the time of this research. In 1994, the food-processing and textiles sectors respectively contributed 16.1% and 13.3% of total manufacturing output; 22.1% and 10.3% of total manufacturing value added; and 14.7% and 14.0% of total manufacturing employment.

11. Manufacturing in Nigeria is concentrated in the Lagos-Otta-Agbara industrial cluster, the Kano-Kaduna axis and Port Harcourt-Aba industrial zone.

12. According to UNDP (2001), only 57% of Nigerians have access to improved water sources, which includes household connections, public standpipes, boreholes with hand pumps, protected dug wells, protected springs and rainwater collection. Many of these improved sources may not guarantee the provision of safe drinking water because of the high risk of contamination during transportation from fetching point to point of use.

13. "Clean in place" operation for periodic washing of process lines and equipment.

14. According to UNEP (1993: 17–18), pollutants arise from the dirt and grease that is removed from raw natural fibres, as well as from process chemicals and dyestuffs that are lost during operations. The extensive use of synthetic chemicals in particular can lead to serious environmental and occupational impacts if proper precautions are not taken. Air pollution can arise from dyeing and finishing agents, and in the form of oil mists from machinery. Land pollution may occur from the uncontrolled dumping of chemical residues and treatment plant sludges.... Even with more-efficient processes and better handling, there will generally remain some effluent, and some waste residues. Adequate treatment processes exist for the most common pollutants, with only colour removal sometimes presenting any real difficulty.

15. Textile firms producing African wax prints import wax. The recovery of wax from wastewater effluent streams is a very dirty and difficult process. However, because of the high costs of wax, textile plants are being compelled to introduce wax recovery processes.

16. The effluent limitation regulation only recommends "best available technology" or "best practicable technology" or "technology that limits emission to the uniform effluent standards".

17. The research sample of 122 firms had 91 local firms and 31 affiliates of multinational corporations.

REFERENCES

Aden, Jean, A. Kyu-hong and M. T. Rock (1999) "What is Driving the Pollution Abatement Expenditure Behaviour of Manufacturing Plants in Korea?" World Development 27(7): 1203–1214.

Adeoti, John O. (2002) Technology and the Environment in Sub-Saharan Africa: Emerging Trends in the Nigerian Manufacturing Industry, Aldershot, England: Ashgate Publishing.

Ashford, Nicholas (2000) "An Innovation-based Strategy for a Sustainable Environment", in Jens Hemmelskamp, Klaus Rennings and Fabio Leone, eds., Innovation-oriented Environmental Regulation: Theoretical Approaches and Empirical Analysis, Zew Economic Studies 10, Mannheim, Germany: Centre for European Economic Research; Heidelberg, Germany: Physica-Verlag.

Baumol, William J. and W. E. Oates (1988) The Theory of Environmental Policy, New York: Cambridge University Press.

Dasgupta, Nandini (2000) "Environmental Enforcement and Small Industries in India: Reworking the Problem in Poverty Context", World Development 28(5): 945–967.

DEAT (1996) "An Environmental Policy for South Africa", Green Paper for public discussion, Pretoria, South Africa: Department of Environmental Affairs and Tourism (DEAT).

Downing, Paul B. and L. J. White (1986) "Innovation in Pollution Control", Journal of Environmental Economics and Management 13: 18–29.

FEPA (1991a) "National Effluent Limitation Regulation", Lagos, Nigeria: Federal Government Press.

FEPA (1991b) "National Guidelines and Standards for Environmental Pollution Control in Nigeria", Lagos, Nigeria: Federal Government Press.

Hart, Stuart L. and G. Ahuja (1996) "Does It Pay to Be Green? An Empirical Examination of the Relationship Between Emission Reduction and Firm Performance", Business Strategy and the Environment 5: 30–37.

Hettige, Hemamala, Mainul Huq, Sheoli Pargal and David Wheeler (1996) "Determinants of Pollution Abatement in Developing Countries: Evidence from South and Southeast Asia", World Development 24(12): 1891–1904.

Howes, R., J. Skea and B. Whelan (1997) Clean and Competitive? Motivating Environmental Performance in Industry, London, England: Earthscan Publications.

Lagos State Environmental Protection Agency (LASEPA) (1999) "Lagos State Government Policy on the Environment", Lagos Environment 1(1): 16–17.

Lubeck, Paul M. (1992) "Restructuring Nigeria's Urban-Industrial Sector Within the West African Region: The Interplay of Crisis, Linkages and Popular Resistance", International Journal of Urban and Regional Research 16(1): 6–23.

Mbendi (2000) Mbendi Africa Business Information Service, available from http://www.MBendi.com.

Milliman, Scott R. and R. Prince (1989) "Firm Incentive to Promote Technological Change in Pollution Control", Journal of Environmental Economics and Management 17: 247–265.

Porter, M. E. and C. van der Linde (1995) "Towards a New Conception of the Environment-Competitiveness Relationship", Journal of Economic Perspectives 9(4): 97–118.

Siebert, Horst (1987) Economics of the Environment: Theory and Policy, Berlin, Germany: Springer Verlag.

UNDP (2001) "Making New Technologies Work for Human Development", Human Development Report 2001, New York: United Nations Development Programme.

UNEP (1993) "The Textile Industry and the Environment", Technical Report No. 16, Paris: United Nations Environment Programme, Industry and Environment.

UNIDO (2001) Industrial Statistics Database, CD-ROM.

World Bank (2001) "World Development Indicators: Water Pollution", World Bank: CD-ROM.

7

Innovation on clean technology through environmental policy: Emergence of the ion exchange membrane process in the Japanese chlor-alkali industry

Masaru Yarime

Responding to the serious concern with regard to the contamination of air, water and soil with pollutants such as non-degradable toxic metals, policymakers around the world have been introducing regulations with the aim of reducing emissions from industrial activity. While there has been a decline in emission rates of pollutants in recent years, reflecting the efforts devoted to pollution abatement in most industrialized countries, there is also a growing concern about the negative impacts of increasingly tightened environmental regulations on industry (Jaffe et al. 1995). It is argued that stringent environmental regulations force firms to invest in compliance at the expense of competitiveness against countries where regulations are lax. Environmental restrictions impose significant costs and slow productivity, and thereby hinder the ability of companies to compete in international markets (Palmer, Oates and Portney 1995). Theoretical analysis is often employed to show that environmental regulations reduce productivity by requiring firms to invest additional resources on pollution abatement and control without increasing production output.

From a different perspective, an increasing number of people claim that stringent environmental regulations actually enhance the competitive position of firms. They argue that the ever-increasing stringency of environmental regulations encourages firms to conduct more research and development (R&D) activities and, consequently, become more innovative in the long run (Porter and van der Linde 1995a). That is, the necessity to comply with environmental policy prompts companies to re-examine their products and production processes. This re-examination often leads to technological improvements and innovation. Spurred by stringent environmental regulations, companies will go beyond mere compliance with regulations and may succeed in creating radically new technologies. Successful cases from the United States are cited to claim that stringent environmental regulations actually encourage innovation in industry (Porter and van der Linde 1995b).

The opposing views on the costs and benefits of regulations remain far from reconciled, and the debate continues. This chapter contributes to this debate by examining how environmental regulations affect the course and character of technological change through innovative activities in industry. As it is very difficult to measure the stringency of environmental regulations and their effects on subsequent innovations at aggregate levels, a detailed case study is conducted at a micro-level for the Japanese chlor-alkali industry. The analysis is intended to shed complementary light on the question of how environmental regulations influence firms' activities with regard to the development and adoption of new technologies. It does so by conducting interviews with companies and policy makers as well as analysing detailed data on patents and technological processes. While previous empirical studies mainly dealt with the effects of environmental regulation either on the invention or the diffusion of new technologies, this chapter examines the whole process of innovation, which covers the technological situation prior to the introduction of environmental regulations, the development of new technologies by innovators and their adoption by the innovating and other firms.

Three production technologies in the chlor-alkali industry

The chlor-alkali industry basically produces chlorine and caustic soda through electrolysis. An aqueous solution of sodium chloride (salt) is decomposed with direct current to produce chlorine, hydrogen and sodium hydroxide, that is, caustic soda. Since the electrolytic production of chlorine and caustic soda depends on a large amount of electricity, the chlor-alkali industry is a major user of electric power, and indeed its unit consumption of electricity is the one of the largest, following the aluminium, carbide and ferro-alloy industries. The Japanese chlor-alkali industry, for instance, consumed approximately 10.7 billion kWh of electricity in 1996, accounting for 3% of the total industry consumption and 18% of the total chemical industry consumption (Japan Soda Industry Association 1998). As energy accounts for a significant part of the total manufacturing cost, one of the major targets of innovative activities in the chlor-alkali industry has been to develop technologies to reduce energy consumption.

Currently, there are three types of electrolytic processes in use for the commercial manufacturing of chlorine and caustic soda in the world: the mercury process, the diaphragm process and the ion exchange membrane process. Each process represents a different method of keeping the chlorine produced at the anode separate from the caustic soda and hydrogen produced, directly or indirectly, at the cathode. Naturally, mercury is used in the mercury process, whereas the diaphragm process and the ion exchange membrane process do not involve any use of mercury. Figure 7.1 shows the shares of the three processes in the chlor-alkali industry in western Europe, the United States and Japan. As figure 7.1 illustrates, different production processes are dominant in the three regions. In western Europe, approximately 60% of the chlor-alkali plants are based on the mercury process. In the United States, more than 70% of the chlor-alkali plants are using the diaphragm process. In Japan, while there are no chlor-alkali plants based on the mercury process, the ion exchange membrane process has been adopted by more than 90% of the chlor-alkali plants. In western Europe and the United States the diffusion of the ion exchange membrane process is limited to approximately 10%.

The mercury process and the diaphragm process for chlor-alkali production were invented almost in the same period, at the end of the nine-

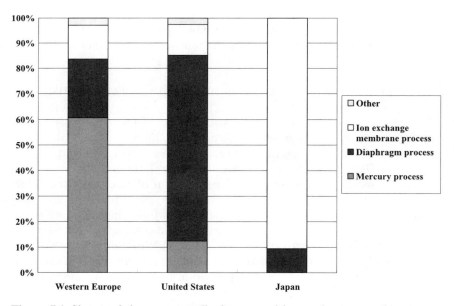

Figure 7.1 Shares of the mercury, diaphragm and ion exchange membrane processes in western Europe, the United States and Japan in 1998

teenth century. Since then, technologies for the mercury process have been mainly developed in western Europe whereas United States companies have been involved in improving technologies for the diaphragm process. The Japanese chlor-alkali industry initially introduced both processes from western Europe and the United States at the beginning of the twentieth century. After the end of the Second World War, technological progress in the United States was pursued on the diaphragm process and has remained the dominant technology in that country. In contrast, research and development efforts were devoted to improving the mercury process in western Europe and Japan. Through learning and knowledge accumulation, based on the increased adoption in the chlor-alkali industry, technologies for the mercury process were improved further, and more chlor-alkali producers adopted the mercury process in these two regions. By the late 1960s, the mercury process had come to dominate the chlor-alkali industry in Japan as well as in western Europe. Since regulations were introduced on the emission of mercury to the environment, divergent courses of technological change have been observed in the chlor-alkali industry between western Europe and Japan.

Regulatory decision on the phase-out of the mercury process

In May 1956, four cases of an unknown disease with nervous symptoms were reported in Minamata in the southern part of Japan. Further investigations revealed that more patients were suffering from the same symptoms among inhabitants in the Minamata Bay area. Although heavy metals such as selenium, manganese and thallium were initially suspected as the agent causing the disease, it proved to be methyl mercury poisoning caused by ingestion of seafood caught in Minamata Bay and the neighbouring seas; hence it came to be called the Minamata disease (Tsubaki and Irukayama 1977). While it later became clear that the methyl mercury which caused the Minamata disease was emitted from an acetaldehyde plant nearby, at that time there was no scientific explanation as to why methyl mercury, a form of organic mercury, was formed in the acetaldehyde plant where acetaldehyde was synthesized from acetylene with the use of inorganic mercury as a catalyst.

Having seen the misery of the Minamata disease in at least 700 patients, recognized by the government by the end of 1972, the general public started to raise grave concerns about seawater pollution. The Basic Law for Environmental Pollution Control had been enacted in August 1967, establishing environmental quality standards based on the designation of pollutants' target ranges, the liability of polluters and the responsibilities of the national as well as local governments. Subsequent regulations set limits to control the levels of mercury released to the environment. The chlor-alkali industry, which was using a large amount of mercury in the 1960s, particularly received public attention, although emissions from the industry did not include any trace of methyl mercury, the organic mercury that caused the Minamata disease. Without any organic substances involved in the relevant chemical reactions, there was no possibility for the formation of organic mercury within chlor-alkali plants. Nevertheless, in the presence of a significant degree of uncertainty in the scientific mechanism of the transformation of mercury in the environment, the Ministry of International Trade and Industry (MITI) started to investigate mercury uses in chlor-alkali plants in June 1968. In February 1969, all the waters linked to chlor-alkali plants based on the mercury process became subject to the Law for the Conservation of Water Quality in Public Areas (Japan Soda Industry Association 1982). At this point the emphasis of the regulatory measures was on how to reduce, but not necessarily eliminate, mercury emissions into the environment.

In May 1973 a newspaper article suggested that a case of Minamata disease was discovered in the Ariake Sea area in Kyushu (*Asahi Shinbun* 1973a). Just one month later the same newspaper reported a similar incident, which happened near Tokuyama Bay in the western part of Japan (*Asahi Shinbun* 1973b). As both cases were linked to industrial complexes with chlor-alkali operations, pressure was mounting on the government to stop mercury emissions from these plants, although there was no scientific evidence to support these allegations. Many fishermen went on demonstrations against mercury-based chlor-alkali plants in coastal areas throughout Japan, and some of the plants were actually forced to halt operation. The Environmental Agency, which had been established just two years earlier, organized the Health Examination Committee and conducted medical examination of inhabitants of nine marine areas, including the Ariake Sea and Tokuyama Bay areas. The conclusion was that no case of the Minamata disease or methyl mercury poisoning was found in any area other than Minamata Bay and its neighboring seas (Irukayama 1977). However, the public pressure for immediate action was so fierce that the Japanese government was prompted to take measures to cut mercury emissions.

In the wake of the controversies triggered by the newspaper reports, the government established the Council for the Promotion of Countermeasures against Mercury Pollution (Countermeasures Council) in the Environmental Agency in June 1973. It was chaired by the minister of state for environment, assisted by the administrative vice-minister and the state secretary for environment, and consisted of members from twelve ministries and agencies in the government (Japanese Ministry of International Trade and Industry 1979). At its first meeting the Counter-measures Council decided that the installation of the closed system for effluents containing mercury should be completed by the end of September 1974. To meet this objective, chlor-alkali producers were required to commit to converting as many mercury plants as possible to the diaphragm process by the end of September 1975.

Criticizing the decision, the chlor-alkali industry association argued that there were many technical as well as economic difficulties in the conversion of the existing mercury plants to the diaphragm process and that the conversion would take a long period of time (Japan Soda Industry Association 1973a). The request of the industry was also handed over to the minister of the Environmental Agency when the representatives of the industry visited the agency to discuss the issue (Japan Soda Industry Association 1973b). With industry's request not accepted by the minister, however, the Countermeasures Council agreed at its third meeting in November 1973 that two-thirds of the existing mercury plants were to be converted to the diaphragm process by September 1975 and the remaining one-third by March 1978 (Council for the Promotion of Counter-measures against Mercury Pollution 1973). This decision meant an immediate undertaking by many of the existing mercury plants to convert from the mercury process to the non-mercury, diaphragm process.

With a mandate to implement the Countermeasures Council's decision, the Committee for the Promotion of Process Conversion in the Soda Industry (Conversion Committee) was established in September 1973 as a private consulting body to the director-general of MITI's Basic Industries Bureau. The members of the Conversion Committee were selected from banks, academics, journalists and industry to reflect the multiplicity of issues and diversity of stakeholder interests (Japan Soda Industry Association 1974). Along with a subcommittee, three expert groups were organized on finance and tax, technology and regulation and supply and demand coordination to have more detailed and informed discussions on the schedule and criteria for the process conversion programme and the financial and tax incentives to support it. The criteria for the conversion of mercury plants set a limit for mercury consumption by the soda industry. The plants that exceeded the limit were to convert by September 1975 while those that did not exceed the limit had to convert by March 1978 (Japanese Ministry of International Trade and Industry 1973). To support newly converted production facilities, tax reductions were also introduced (Japan Soda Industry Association 1985). Initially the diaphragm process was the target of the tax reduction scheme, but was subsequently expanded to include the ion exchange membrane process.

The official decision to phase-out of the mercury process was made at a time when this process was the dominant technology for chlor-alkali production in Japan, accounting for 95% of the total capacity (Japan Soda Industry Association 1982). In replacing the mercury process, the only alternative technology available at that time was the diaphragm process, which was used for only 5% of the industry. As the regulatory schedule for process conversion required that two-thirds of the mercury process plants must be converted to the diaphragm process in just two years, the affected firms had to imitate, rather than innovate, to convert their processes. Consequently, technologies necessary for the diaphragm process had to be adopted mostly from foreign companies. Reflecting the most advanced development of the diaphragm process in the United States at that time, many of the technologies adopted for the diaphragm process were provided by American suppliers; Diamond Shamrock based in the US accounted for 32% of the total capacity, while Hooker and PPG accounted for 27% and 26% respectively (Chlorine Engineers Corp. 1999b; *European Chemical News* 1974). Only 15% of the total production capacity relied on technologies provided by Japanese companies. While Nippon Soda, Tsurumi Soda and Showa Denko had previous technical experiences on the diaphragm process, the technology developed by Kureha Chemical Industry was the first to be introduced for commercial purposes in the chlor-alkali industry (Japan Soda Industry Association 1982; Kanto Denka Kogyo 1998; *Nikkei Sangyo Shinbun* 1975a, 1975b; Shibata, Kokubu and Okazaki 1977; Showa Chemical 2001; Takeshita 1990; Tsurumi Soda 2001). Under the policy schemes, the first diaphragm plant that converted from the mercury process started to operate in March 1974, and other conversions followed in the subsequent period up to 1976.

As many mercury-based plants were converted to the diaphragm process, however, the concerns about the high production cost of the diaphragm process coupled with lower quality caustic soda came to affect the industry significantly. Many users who had previously purchased caustic soda produced by the mercury process demanded the same level of high quality for caustic soda. For about 25% of all the applications, caustic soda produced by the diaphragm process was considered not to be suitable, especially for the manufacture of rayon, a thin fibre with a diameter in the order of micrometres which was said to be weaker and more susceptible to breaking when produced using low-quality caustic soda (Japan Soda Industry Association 1982). As the demand for the poor-quality caustic soda was low, manufacturers who had already converted their plants to the diaphragm process had difficulties in selling their products to customers. They demanded a level playing field, which meant that diaphragm and mercury plant operators should consume and sell caustic soda produced by the diaphragm and mercury processes in the same proportion by making barter trades between themselves. In response to these concerns, in June 1975, MITI issued an administrative guidance according to which caustic soda producers were to submit their production plans every three months to the ministry, which in turn revised the production plans based on its demand projection for the quarter and mediated the barter trades (Japanese Ministry of International Trade and Industry 1975).

Furthermore, the diaphragm process was at a disadvantage in terms of energy consumption, which occupies a major part of the chlor-alkali production. At that time, the energy consumption of the diaphragm process was approximately 3,400 kWh per ton of caustic soda, well above 3,200 kWh per ton of caustic soda for the mercury process (Japan Soda Industry Association 1975). This difficulty was aggravated by the oil crisis of the early 1970s. The price of electricity used for chlor-alkali production almost tripled after the first phase of the energy crisis, from 3.10 yen/kWh in 1970 to 9.10 yen/kWh in 1977 (Japan Soda Industry Association 1988). By the early 1980s, the electricity price for chlor-alkali producers had reached 14.80 yen/kWh, a level more than four times larger than the price at the beginning of the 1970s. As the cost of caustic soda produced at newly constructed diaphragm plants became significantly larger than that at the existing mercury plants, the barter trading system was modified in October 1976 to include financial compensations reflecting the cost difference. Under this arrangement mercury process operators compensated their counterparts using the diaphragm process (Japan Soda Industry Association 1980a).

The first phase of the conversion programme was completed in April 1976, half a year behind schedule, due to the technical as well as economic problems. By that time, the share of the diaphragm process had increased significantly to about 60% from less than 5% prior to the commencement of the conversion programme. Chlor-alkali producers who were still operating mercury-based plants insisted that they did not have sufficient financial resources to conduct more process conversions and lobbied the ruling Liberal Democratic Party as well as MITI for postponing the implementation of the second phase of the process conversion programme (Japan Soda Industry Association 1979a). At the fourth meeting of the Countermeasures Council in May 1977, while the members were informed that the caustic soda produced by the diaphragm process had a low quality and thus was very difficult to use, it was reported that a newly developed process, the ion exchange membrane process, was in a process of rapid progress and that it was expected to be able to produce high-quality caustic soda. Taking into account the emergence of a new, promising technology, the Countermeasures Council made a decision that the implementation of the second phase of the conversion programme should be suspended until an appropriate evaluation could be made on the feasibility of the ion exchange membrane process for the whole industry (Council for the Promotion of Countermeasures against Mercury Pollution 1977).

Emergence of the ion exchange membrane process

The ion exchange membrane process operates in a similar way to the diaphragm process, with basically the same chemical reactions involving no use of mercury throughout the whole production process. However, the ion exchange membrane process, unlike the diaphragm processes, also produces the same high-quality caustic soda as the mercury process. In contrast to the end-of-pipe technology, which is installed to reduce emissions of pollutants like mercury at the end of the production process, the ion exchange membrane process is a prime example of clean technology, eliminating inputs that generate pollutants at the end of the process. The critical component for the well functioning of the ion exchange membrane process is ion exchange membranes. While ion exchange membranes determine the performance of electrolytic cells, including the current efficiency and cell voltage and hence energy consumption, they also need to have sufficient strength to withstand severe exposure to chlorine on one side and strong caustic soda on the other in electrolytic cells. Although the idea of the ion exchange membrane process for the production of chlorine and caustic soda had been known for many years, earlier work failed as a result of non-availability of suitable ion exchange membranes that could resist the very demanding conditions within chlor-alkali cells. A significant amount of research and development effort was required to invent ion exchange membranes that would be suitable for chlor-alkali production.

To investigate the extent of innovative activities conducted by Japanese firms, the research for this chapter analysed data on patent applications on the ion exchange membrane process, along with those on the mercury and diaphragm processes. Figure 7.2 shows the trends in successful applications for Japanese patents by firms based in Japan from the late 1960s to the late 1980s. Patent data on technologies related to the mercury process were obtained from the data assembled by the Japan Soda Industry Association (1982). The data set covers patents granted up to the end of the 1970s. Patents on technologies related to the diaphragm process and the ion exchange membrane process were selected by using the data set constructed by the industry association and shared by its member companies (Japan Soda Industry Association 1976, 1977, 1978a, 1978b, 1979b, 1991a, 1991b, 1992a, 1992b). The data set contains both granted patents and unexamined patent applications that were pub-

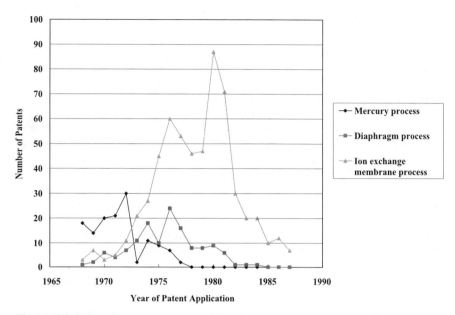

Figure 7.2 Japanese patents successfully applied for by Japanese companies on the mercury, diaphragm and ion exchange membrane processes

lished before 1988. Successful (granted) patent applications were selected and classified according to the three processes (mercury, diaphragm and ion exchange membrane). The selected patents are arranged by the year of application, rather than by the year of publication. As information on the date of patent applications is not included in the data on the mercury process, a two-year lag was assumed between patent application and granting.

As figure 7.2 demonstrates, most of the patents granted in the late 1960s were related to the mercury process. The number of successful patents on the mercury process rose at the beginning of the 1970s, as the general public's concern on mercury pollution increased. It then decreased subsequently, coinciding with the government decision that the mercury-based plants in the Japanese chlor-alkali industry were to be phased out rather quickly. Patents successfully applied on technologies related to the diaphragm process were few in the later 1960s and the early 1970s. They increased to some extent in the middle of the 1970s, as patent applications on the mercury process declined. Then, successful patent applications on the diaphragm process started to drop in the late 1970s, and had almost stopped by the middle of the 1980s. With regard to the ion exchange membrane process, although several patent applications had already been made in the late 1960s, most of the patents granted were on ion exchange membranes based on hydrocarbon polymers. These patented technologies were intended mainly for producing salt from seawater, and the application of ion exchange membranes for use in chlor-alkali electrolytic cells was very limited. In the early 1970s, at the time of the government's decision to phase out the mercury process in Japan, applications for patents on ion exchange membranes started to rise. After a patent application was filed on a new type of ion exchange membrane based on fluorocarbon polymers, on which there had been only one previous patent application, other patent applications continued for this type of membrane. Then, successful patent applications on the ion exchange membrane process increased rapidly until 1980 and declined in the 1980s, although they remained large, compared with those on the mercury or diaphragm process, throughout that decade.

The analysis in this study focused on the Japanese firms that had been innovative in the mercury process, namely, Mitsui Engineering and Shipbuilding, Osaka Soda, Kureha Chemical Industry, Asahi Glass, Toyo Soda, Tokuyama Soda and Asahi Chemical Industry, and those companies that had been innovative in the diaphragm process, namely, Nippon Soda, Tsurumi Soda and Showa Denko (Yarime 2003). Detailed analysis of patents shows that Asahi Chemical Industry, Asahi Glass and Tokuyama Soda applied successfully for many patents on the ion exchange membrane process. The three companies had earlier experiences of developing and utilizing ion exchange membranes. Traditionally, salt was produced in solar fields in Japan, where natural rock salt has not been available, and that was labour-intensive and constantly subject to adverse weather, with little prospect of significant improvement. In trying to develop a new efficient process for salt production from seawater, the three Japanese companies started to conduct R&D activities on ion exchange membranes in the 1960s. As ion exchange membranes were initially based on hydrocarbons however, they could not maintain their chemical stability in a strong alkaline environment and hence were not readily usable for chlor-alkali production. Although the idea of using ion exchange membranes for electrolytic chlor-alkali production had existed since the 1950s, a complete lack of suitable ion exchange membranes prevented industrial realization of the ion exchange membrane process.

Then, a new type of ion exchange membrane, Nafion, released by Du Pont, was made available to the Japanese chlor-alkali industry in the early 1970s. The availability of Nafion provided a fertile technological springboard for innovation on ion exchange membranes to be applied for chlor-alkali production. Almost in the same period, the government made the decision to phase out all the mercury-based plants in Japan. This policy created a demand for clean technologies with which to replace the mercury process, and in particular provided a significant impetus for those companies that had expertise with ion exchange membranes to intensify research efforts to develop the ion exchange membrane process for chlor-alkali production. While the government did not directly give any financial aid to support their R&D activities on the ion exchange membrane process, the policy worked to assure the innovative companies that the demand for alternative processes would be large, and they were thus encouraged to invigorate R&D efforts for developing the ion exchange membrane process.

The patent analysis also revealed that Mitsui Engineering and Shipbuilding, Kureha Chemical Industry and Osaka Soda, which had been innovative on the mercury process as well, did not make successful patent applications on technologies related to the ion exchange membrane process. Mitsui Engineering and Shipbuilding, through establishing an engineering company, Chlorine Engineers Corp. (CEC), immediately after the phase-out decision focused on cleaning techniques to eliminate mercury from the production process. With insufficient experience in the ion exchange membrane process, CEC chose the diaphragm process for their technological target and decided to introduce technologies from foreign companies, particularly those in the United States. Similarly, Kureha Chemical Industry chose the diaphragm process as its R&D target, following the government decision on the phase out of the mercury process. The company succeeded in developing a diaphragm-based electrolytic cell, used later to convert one of its own mercury-based plants. Although the patent data suggests that R&D activities were conducted later in the 1970s, Kureha Chemical Industry did not develop its own technologies for the ion exchange membrane process until much later. Osaka Soda focused R&D efforts on the diaphragm process, following the earlier government policy.

As discussed earlier, the diaphragm process turned out to be inappropriate for producing high-quality caustic soda. In the meantime, having seen rapid progress in developing new types of ion exchange membranes by Asahi Chemical Industry, Asahi Glass, Tokuyama Soda and Asahi Chemical Industry took advantage of the government decision to phase out the mercury process by cooperating with several chlor-alkali producers in R&D activities on electrolytic cells designed for use in the ion exchange membrane process.

Regulatory change and diffusion of the ion exchange membrane process

The rapid progress in the technological performance of the ion exchange membrane process prompted the government to establish an expert group for a technical evaluation of the emerging process. The Expert

Committee for Technical Evaluation of the Ion Exchange Membrane Process (Evaluation Committee) embarked upon its assigned task in June 1977, with all of its four members coming from academic institutes (Expert Committee for Technical Evaluation of the Ion Exchange Membrane Process 1977). This selection of academic members was intended to help the committee conduct the technological evaluation from a neutral position, avoiding the intervention of particular industrial or corporate interests. The Evaluation Committee made a thorough examination of several technologies which were being developed at that time by chloralkali companies, domestic as well as foreign, through documents, interviews, and in some cases, visits to plant sites. Various aspects were scrutinized, ranging from technical performance, such as power consumption and product quality, durability and stability, to environmental and safety measures and construction and operational costs. In October 1977, the Evaluation Committee acknowledged that the ion exchange membrane process technology had reached a level appropriate for industrialization, but called for a more cautious approach to the evaluation of the new process, taking into full account the importance of caustic soda and chlorine as basic chemical materials and thus their impact on other industries. The committee stated that the viability of the new technology must be demonstrated through the durability of various materials and the operational performance of plants. Since there was insufficient data on these aspects at the time, the committee members thought it necessary to continue their observations and to obtain more data on the operation of commercial plants for at least two years (Expert Committee for Technical Evaluation of the Ion Exchange Membrane Process 1977).

Based on these findings, the government decided to interrupt the implementation of the process conversion programme for two years. In September 1978, almost one year after the publication of the first report, the members of the Evaluation Committee resumed their activities to consider the technological progress made during the past year. Their investigation revealed that, as several companies had assiduously conducted R&D activities, considerable progress had been made on the ion exchange membrane process. Asahi Chemical Industry's first commercial plant and Asahi Glass's demonstration plant had already experienced stable operation for several years. Another commercial plant constructed by Asahi Chemical Industry, and the first commercial plant of Asahi Glass, had been functioning reliably since the beginning of their operations, though for shorter periods. Tokuyama Soda had also started to operate commercial plants, and both had been running without any serious problems since the replacement of the original ion exchange membranes with those currently in use. These examples of stable and reliable plant operation convinced the members of the Evaluation Committee that the ion exchange membrane process not only eliminated mercury emissions into the environment, but had also surpassed the mercury process in the efficiency of energy consumption while producing caustic soda with the same quality. Taking into account the operating experiences of various plants overall, the Evaluation Committee concluded that the ion exchange membrane process in Japan had reached a level that could be regarded as an established industrial technology (Expert Committee for Technical Evaluation of the Ion Exchange Membrane Process 1979).

Prompted by this conclusion, the Countermeasures Council started to review the regulatory schedule that had been initially fixed in a rigid, short-term framework. At its fifth meeting held in September 1979, the Countermeasures Council reached an agreement that the remaining mercury process plants were to be converted by the end of 1984 (Council for the Promotion of Countermeasures against Mercury Pollution 1979). This extension of the deadline for process conversion was intended to enable the operators of mercury-based plants to adopt the more efficient ion exchange membrane process, instead of the diaphragm process, in the second phase of the process conversion programme. Although some manufacturers who had heavily depended on the mercury process argued that they would need more time to see whether the newly developed ion exchange membrane process could be really reliable at the industrial level (Japan Soda Industry Association 1980b; Katsumura 1979), the Countermeasures Council did not change its revised schedule for the completion of process conversions at subsequent meetings (Council for the Promotion of Countermeasures against Mercury Pollution 1980, 1981, 1982).

Following the regulatory revision, the ion exchange membrane process technologies developed by the innovating companies came to be provided to other chlor-alkali producers in Japan. Figure 7.3 shows the trends in the supply of the diaphragm process and the ion exchange membrane process by the Japanese companies.

Immediately following the decision to phase out the mercury process, the supply of the diaphragm process increased rapidly and reached its peak in the middle of the 1970s. While the provision of the diaphragm process then declined quickly and ceased in 1980, the ion exchange membrane process started to be supplied in the middle of the 1970s and showed a large increase in the 1980s. After the supply of the ion exchange membrane process declined in the late 1980s, following the completion of the process conversion programme in Japan, it picked up again in the 1990s. In particular, Asahi Chemical Industry, Asahi Glass and Tokuyama Soda, who had accumulated experiences of utilizing their technologies at their own chlor-alkali production plants during the second half of the 1970s, started to provide their technologies to other chlor-alkali producers in Japan in the 1980s (Asahi Chemical Industry 1998;

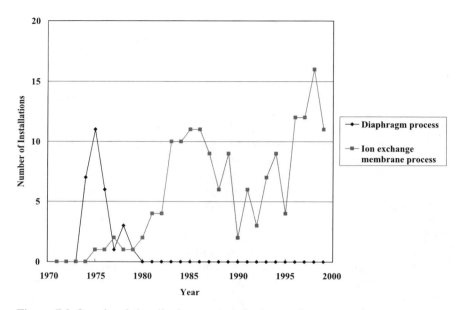

Figure 7.3 Supply of the diaphragm and the ion exchange membrane processes by Japanese firms

Asahi Glass 1999; Tokuyama 2002). The Chlorine Engineers Corp., on the other hand, introduced technologies for the diaphragm process from abroad and began to supply them to chlor-alkali producers in Japan, immediately after the introduction of the government policy for the phase out of the mercury process (Chlorine Engineers Corp. 1999b). By 1977, when the initial schedule of the conversion programme was reviewed, CEC's diaphragm process had been adopted by many chlor-alkali producers in Japan. As the diaphragm process subsequently turned out to be an inappropriate technology, CEC started to supply its ion exchange membrane process technologies to chlor-alkali producers at the beginning of the 1980s (Chlorine Engineers Corp. 1999a, 1999c, 2000). In the middle of the 1980s, as the deadline for the complete abolishment of the mercury process approached, these four companies provided their technologies to many Japanese chlor-alkali producers who had to convert their mercury-based plants. In the late 1980s, having finished supplying domestic chlor-alkali producers with their ion exchange membrane process technologies, these companies started to actively seek foreign customers, particularly those in other Asian countries such as Taiwan, South Korea and China.

The overall trends in Japanese production capacities based on the mer-

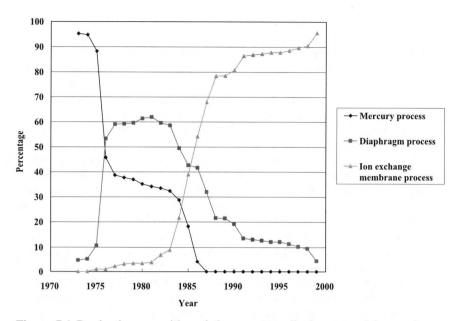

Figure 7.4 Production capacities of the mercury, diaphragm and ion exchange membrane processes in the Japanese chlor-alkali industry

cury process, the diaphragm process, and the ion exchange membrane process from the early 1970s are shown in figure 7.4.

In 1973, immediately preceding the phase-out regulation, the mercury process accounted for more than 95% of the total production capacities, whereas the share of the diaphragm process was negligible. Following the rigid schedule of the mandate, most of the mercury process plants were converted to the diaphragm process because its energy consumption was much lower than that of the infant ion exchange membrane process at that time, making it the only alternative clean technology that was feasible for industrial applications. The share of the diaphragm process jumped to more than 60% in just seven years, while the mercury process share quickly decreased during the 1970s. In that same period, the production cost of the diaphragm process was increasing due to the rapid rise in energy prices following the oil crisis, and serious concern was growing about the low product quality among chlor-alkali producers who had already finished converting their plants to the diaphragm process.

In the meantime, the ion exchange membrane process began to emerge in the middle of the 1970s and was undergoing significant technological improvement. In the second half of the 1970s, the ion exchange membrane process was initially installed at chlor-alkali plants by the first movers who had themselves developed the technologies. Although at that time the technological performance of the ion exchange membrane process was not favourable compared with the diaphragm process, they learned by actually using their own technologies for industrial production and utilized these practical experiences for future developments. As further progress had been achieved in technological performance, other chlor-alkali producers gradually started to introduce the ion exchange membrane process in the early 1980s, replacing the mercury process and later the diaphragm process as well. Most of the introductions of the ion exchange membrane process subsequently took place just a few years before the extended deadline. The last chlor-alkali plant based on the mercury process was finally converted at the end of June in 1986, 13 years after the government's initial decision to eliminate the mercury process in the Japanese chlor-alkali industry. When the mercury process was completely abolished, the installed capacity of the ion exchange membrane process accounted for little more than half of the total production capacity. Since then, the share of the ion exchange membrane process has increased steadily, reaching more than 95% in 1999.

On the other hand, Figure 4 shows that the diaphragm-process share has decreased steadily since the early 1980s, and the once-dominant process currently accounts for less than 5% of the total production capacities in Japan. This suggests that the mercury-based plants that had been converted to the diaphragm process were soon converted again to the ion exchange membrane process. We thus examined how long the chlor-alkali plants that had introduced the diaphragm process were operational. Figure 7.5 shows the operating period of the chlor-alkali plants that had adopted the diaphragm process in Japan. The figure indicates that all of the chlor-alkali plants that had been converted to the diaphragm process following the phase-out regulation were subsequently converted to the ion exchange membrane process. As a result, the operating period of these diaphragm plants was very short, an average of only 10 years, which is far shorter than the normal, approximately 40-year period of plant operation in the case of chemical industry (Society of Chemical Engineers of Japan 1998).

Process conversions on this scale require a significant amount of investment in the industry. Significant resources were allocated in order to replace the mercury process with the diaphragm process or the ion exchange membrane process. The process conversions undertaken from 1973 to 1988 cost the Japanese chlor-alkali industry 334 billion yen as a whole. Of the total cost of 287.3 billion yen invested in converting the existing mercury-based plants to the diaphragm or ion exchange membrane

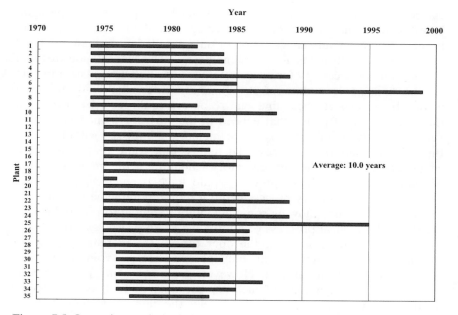

Figure 7.5 Operating period of chlor-alkali plants adopting the diaphragm process in Japan

process, 231.8 billion yen was spent during the first phase of the process conversion programme implemented from 1973 to 1977 (Japanese Ministry of International Trade and Industry 1989). That means that approximately 80% of the total investment for converting mercury-based plants was made at the initial stage of the process conversion programme. During this period, 41 plants introduced the diaphragm process whereas only three adopted the ion exchange membrane process. Assuming that the investment cost for the construction of a plant was equal between that of the diaphragm process and the ion exchange membrane process, more than 90% of the 231.8 billion yen investment spent during the first phase of the conversion programme was used to introduce the diaphragm process, which was quickly scrapped.

This demand on financial resources constituted a considerable burden to the chlor-alkali industry, which had already been severely hit by the rise in energy prices due to the oil crisis during the same period. The sum of the industry's annual turnovers during the first phase of the conversion programme – that is, from 1973 to 1977 – was 630.9 billion yen (Japanese Ministry of International Trade and Industry 1985). The financial resources devoted to converting mercury-based plants to diaphragm-based plants, which were then converted again to the ion exchange membrane process in a very short period of time, totalled more than one-third of the industry's turnover for the same period. This clearly indicates that the investment necessary for process conversions had a significant impact on the financial condition of the Japanese chlor-alkali industry as a whole. In retrospect, these financial resources could have been saved if the mercury-based plants that existed in the early 1970s had been converted directly to the ion exchange membrane process, without going through the diaphragm process. To realize that route of technological change, however, a different regulatory schedule for the implementation of abolishing the mercury process would have been necessary. If the phase out of the mercury process had not required implementation within a few short years, allowing some flexibility in timing to test and evaluate the technological progress of alternative clean processes carefully, it would have been possible for the operators of the mercury process to switch directly to the ion exchange membrane process, avoiding this considerable waste in investment. However, given the acute public health and environmental impact of mercury contamination it was necessary for the government to step in and minimize the damage through the best available means at the time.

Conclusion

There have been intensive opposing debates with regard to the effects of environmental regulation on industrial competitiveness. On the one hand, concerns have been raised about the negative effects of increasingly stringent regulations on industries. That is, stringent environmental regulations will force firms to invest a considerable amount of financial resources for compliance, and consequently their competitiveness will be lost against those firms in countries with lax environmental regulations. Environmental regulations can impose significant costs and hamper productivity, and thereby hinder the ability of companies to compete in international markets by requiring firms to spend additional resources for pollution abatement and control without increasing the output of primary products. On the other hand, the Porter hypothesis claims that stringent environmental regulations will actually enhance the competitive position of firms by encouraging them to undertake more R&D activities and consequently to produce better innovations in the long run. We could consider two versions of the Porter hypothesis. First, the necessity to comply with increasingly stringent environmental regulations will prompt companies to re-examine their products and production processes carefully and will ultimately lead to an increase in resource productivity by avoiding unnecessary wastes (Mark I). Second, innovative companies that go beyond mere compliance could succeed in creating radically new technologies that they can then make available to other companies faced with regulatory constraints (Mark II).

Our analysis suggests that end-of-pipe technology will only increase the total cost of manufacturing in the first instance. Thus, the argument that environmental regulations decrease industrial competitiveness would basically be applicable to the case of the end-of-pipe technology. In contrast, structural change such as that experienced by the chlor-alkali industry eliminates the formation of pollution from within the production process by altering chemical reactions. As clean technology is a radical innovation involving the whole production process, the capital investment for installation is normally larger than end-of-pipe technology. Adoption of cleaner production techniques thus adds to production costs, at least initially. It is possible that production costs for the clean technology will eventually decrease. At the same time, there is usually more than one potentially appropriate cleaner production technology, making for a considerable degree of uncertainty in environmental policymaking and business decision making.

Increasing public concern about mercury contamination forced the Japanese government to introduce policy that completely eliminated the mercury process in Japan. The stringent regulation created a large, secured demand for mercury-free, cleaner production type technologies, instead of end-of-pipe technologies. As the regulatory schedule for the conversion of the mercury process was initially set with a rigid, short-term deadline, most of the chlor-alkali manufacturers had no choice other than to adopt the diaphragm process, which had been long established at the level of industrial applications. With the limited amount of time available to conduct research and development, technologies for the diaphragm process had to be mainly introduced from abroad. While chlor-alkali plants based on the mercury process were converted to the diaphragm process, the disadvantage of the diaphragm process in terms of the production cost, combined with soaring energy prices following the oil crisis and the poor quality of the final product from the diaphragm process, led to innovation in policymaking to facilitate a successful transition from a polluting technology (the mercury process) to a cleaner technology (the ion exchange membrane process).

The stringent policy of abolishing the mercury process provided strong incentives to work on radically new, clean technologies. Companies with earlier experiences in developing ion exchange membranes from other industries were able to seize this opportunity created by binding regulation to innovate with regard to the infant ion exchange membrane process for chlor-alkali production. Through the technical assessment of the ion exchange membrane process by the expert committee the government, acting in an interactive and deliberative manner, modified the original schedule for process conversion and postponed the deadline for the complete elimination of the mercury process. This adjustment to the regulatory schedule allowed more time for the innovative companies to intensify R&D activities on the ion exchange membrane process and to gain learning experiences through their own operation of chlor-alkali plants, promoting further progress in the promising technology. The ion exchange membrane process advanced to become the best technology. Currently the vast majority of chlor-alkali plants in Japan use the ion exchange membrane process while the technology is increasingly being adopted by chlor-alkali producers in other countries.

Subsequent incremental improvements to the ion exchange membrane process technology have improved energy efficiency and made it economical even compared to the mercury process. One could argue that stringent environmental regulation produced the appropriate impetus for innovation in the chlor-alkali industry, as suggested in the Mark I analysis of the Porter hypothesis. In addition, the developed ion exchange membrane process has been exported to other chlor-alkali producers in countries such as Taiwan, where there are similar regulations on the use of the mercury process. This new competitive advantage to the innovative companies through stringent regulation is consistent with the Mark II analysis of the Porter hypothesis.

The mercury-based plants that had been converted to the diaphragm process immediately following the policy of mercury elimination, were later converted again to the ion exchange membrane process. The operating period of these plants, based on the diaphragm process, turned out to be significantly shorter than that of plants operated under normal conditions, and the substantial amount of capital invested to introduce the diaphragm process was not utilized to the full extent until the end of the plant lifetime and thus effectively ended up wasted. Although the rigid regulatory schedule was subsequently modified, the technological transition turned out to be costly. In this sense, the stringent policy of immediately abandoning the existing mercury process produced a significantly negative effect on the competitive position of those companies that had to undertake two successive technological conversions. This suggests that the effects of environmental regulation on competitiveness are rather complex, requiring careful examination of conditions surrounding the industry, companies and technologies.

There are important policy implications from this case study of the Japanese chlor-alkali industry. Environmental regulations should be designed to encourage innovation in clean technologies, which have the possibility of achieving economic and environmental objectives at the same time. Improving an existing process by developing end-of-pipe technologies is likely to lead only to additional production costs. Stringent regulations ought to be implemented in a long-term framework to allow sufficient time for experience and experimentation with alternative clean technologies. To do this, it is necessary that regulations accommodate a certain degree of flexibility to take advantage of the most up-to-date information. Institutional mechanisms need to be established to accumulate, assess and diffuse knowledge on clean technologies. This is particularly important for cleaner technologies that involve a much larger level of uncertainty than end-of-pipe technologies, particularly in cases where the speed of technological change is rapid and the uncertainty about future progress is considerable.

Since it is normally difficult for policymakers to closely keep up with the rapidly changing state of technological development in industry, direct support for R&D activities focusing on specific clean technologies would not be sufficient. It is necessary to focus on creating new demands for clean technologies through regulatory incentives. When resourceful companies are convinced that there will be large and stable demands for clean technologies, they are encouraged to make innovative efforts with these technologies, as the companies did in Japan, even without receiving any direct support for their R&D activities. Consistent with Kemp's argument in this volume, it is important to maintain the diversity of options for clean technologies and attempt to steer, through policy, various desirable technological trajectories.

In acquiring accurate and delicate information and making a proper assessment of evolving technologies, the way in which communication and information exchange are practiced among policymakers and experts in industry and academia are particularly important. The recent emergence of voluntary agreements between industry and government in industrialized countries provides the potential for collaborative arrangements among industrial firms and between the government and industry. At the same time, it is also important to maintain objectivity and transparency in setting the targets and monitoring the results through independent actors so as to avoid the hazard of regulatory capture. As each country has its own peculiarity in the relationship between government, industry and academia, institutional mechanisms in which information on technological development is acquired and assessed would be different. Accordingly, the appropriate mode of information acquisition and assessment to encourage innovation in clean technologies could be diverse, depending on the locally specific institutional structure. This further underlines the centrality of deliberative policymaking in taking account of context specificities.

REFERENCES

Asahi Chemical Industry (1998) "Chlor-Alkali Plant Capacity Employing Asahi Chemical Bipolar Process", Asahi Chemical Industry, January.

Asahi Glass (1999) "AZEC Electrolyzer Supply Record", Asahi Glass, August.

Asahi Shinbun (1973a) "Ariake-kai ni 'Daisan Minamata-byo' " ('The Third Minamata Disease' in the Ariake Sea), 22 May.

Asahi Shinbun (1973b) "Tokuyama-wan Engan, Jumin ni Minamata-byo no Utagai" (An Allegation of the Minamata Disease in the Tokuyama Bay area), 11 June.

Chlorine Engineers Corp (1999a) "CME Supply Record", Tokyo, Japan.

—— (1999b) "Diaphragm Cell Supply Record", Tokyo, Japan.

—— (1999c) "MBC Supply Record", Tokyo, Japan.

—— (2000) "Supply Record of CEC's IEM Electrolyzer", Tokyo, Japan.

Council for the Promotion of Countermeasures against Mercury Pollution (1973) "Dai 3-kai Suigin-to Osen Taisaku Suishin Kaigi Giji Yoshi" (Abstract of the note of the third meeting of the Council for the Promotion of Countermeasures against Mercury Pollution), 10 November.

—— (1977) "Dai 4-kai Suigin-to Osen Taisaku Suishin Kaigi Kettei", (Decisions of the fourth meeting of the Council for the Promotion of Countermeasures against Mercury Pollution), 25 May.

—— (1979) "Dai 5-kai Suigin-to Osen Taisaku Suishin Kaigi Kettei", (Decisions of the fifth meeting of the Council for the Promotion of Countermeasures against Mercury Pollution), 17 September.

—— (1980) "Dai 6-kai Suigin-to Osen Taisaku Suishin Kaigi Kettei", (Decisions of the sixth meeting of the Council for the Promotion of Countermeasures against Mercury Pollution), 22 September.

—— (1981) "Dai 7-kai Suigin-to Osen Taisaku Suishin Kaigi ni tsuite" (On the seventh Meeting of the Council for the Promotion of Countermeasures against Mercury Pollution), 18 December.

—— (1982) "Dai 8-kai Suigin-to Osen Taisaku Suishin Kaigi ni tsuite" (On the eighth meeting of the Council for the Promotion of Countermeasures against Mercury Pollution), 26 November.

European Chemical News (1974) "Electrolytic Chlor-Alkali Plants in Japan Licensed by Hooker".

Expert Committee for Technical Evaluation of the Ion Exchange Membrane Process (1977) "Ion Kokanmaku-ho Gijutsu Hyoka Kekka" (Results of Technical Evaluation of the Ion Exchange Membrane Process), Committee for the Promotion of Process Conversions in the Soda Industry, 25 October.

—— (1979) "Ion Kokanmaku-ho Gijutsu Hyoka Kekka" (Results of the Technical Evaluation of the Ion Exchange Membrane Process), Committee for the Promotion of Process Conversions in the Soda Industry, 13 June.

Irukayama, Katsuro (1977) "Countermeasures and Unresolved Problems", in Tadao Tsubaki and Katsuro Irukayama, eds., Minamata Disease: Methylmercury Poisoning in Minamata and Niigata, Japan, Tokyo: Kodansha.

Jaffe, Adam B., S. R. Peterson, P. R. Portney and R. N. Stavins (1995) "Environmental Regulation and the Competitiveness of U.S. Manufacturing: What Does the Evidence Tell Us?" Journal of Economic Literature 33: 132–163.

Japan Soda Industry Association (1973a) "Denkai Soda Kogyo no Jitsujo" (Real situation of the electrolytic soda industry), statement, 27 June.

—————— (1973b) Request to the Minister of the Environmental Agency Regarding the Real Situation of the Soda Industry, 11 July.

—————— (1974) "Seiho Tenkan ni kansuru Sho-Mondai ni tsuite" (Various issues on the process conversion), Soda to Enso 2: 1–13.

—————— (1975) Soda Handobukku (Soda Handbook), Tokyo: Japan Soda Industry Association.

—————— (1976) "Tokkyo kara mita Shokuen Denkai ni okeru Kinzoku Yokyoku/ Ion Kokanmaku-ho Kanren Gijutsu no Genjo, Bessatsu 2: Tokkyo Gaiyo Ichiran-hyo" (Current situation of technologies related to the metal electrode and the ion exchange membrane process for brine electrolysisin terms of patents, supplement volume 2: lists of patent abstracts), Technology Examination Document, December.

—————— (1977) "Shokuen Denkai ni okeru Kinzoku Yokyoku/Ion Kokanmaku-ho Kanren Tokkyo no Genjo, Tsuiroku-ban I: Showa 57.7–12 Kokoku/Kokai-bun" (Current situation of patents related to the metal electrode and the ion exchange membrane process for brine electrolysis, sequel edition I: publications from July 1976 to December 1976), Technology Examination Document, September.

—————— (1978a) "Shokuen Denkai ni okeru Ion Kokanmaku-ho narabini Kakumaku-ho Kanren Tokkyo no Genjo, Tsuiroku-ban III: Showa 52.1–12 Kokoku, Kokai-bun" (Current situation of patents related to the ion exchange membrane process and the diaphragm process for brine electrolysis, sequel edition III: publications from January 1977 to December 1977), Technology Examination Document, December.

—————— (1978b) "Shokuen Denkai ni okeru Kakumaku-ho Kanren Tokkyo no Genjo, Tsuiroku-ban II: Showa 30–51 nen Kokoku/Kokai-bun" (Current situation of patents related to the diaphragm process for brine electrolysis, sequel edition II: publications from 1955 to 1976), Technology Examination Document, April.

—————— (1979a) "Dai-2-ki Seiho Tenkan Shisaku ni taisuru Yobo" (Request regarding policies for the second phase of the process conversion), Letter to the Committee on Commerce and Industry, Policy Research Council, Liberal Democratic Party, 14 June.

—————— (1979b) "Shokuen Denkai ni okeru Ion Kokanmaku-ho narabini Kakumaku-ho Kanren Tokkyo no Genjo, Tsuiroku-ban V: Showa 53.1–12 Kokoku, Kokai-bun" (Current situation of patents related to the ion exchange membrane process and the diaphragm process for brine electrolysis, sequel edition V: publications from January 1978 to December 1978), Technology Examination Document, December.

—————— (1980a) "Dai-2-ki Seiho Tenkan Mondai no Shuhen" (Around the issue of the second phase of the process conversion), Soda to Enso 8: 17–29.

—————— (1980b) "Dai-2-ki Seiho Tenkan ni kansuru Yobosho" (Request regarding the second phase of the process conversion), Letter to the Basic Industry Bureau, Ministry of International Trade and Industry, 14 September.

——— (1982) Nihon Soda Kogyo Hyakunen-shi (Centennial History of the Japanese Soda Industry), Tokyo: Japan Soda Industry Association.

——— (1985) "Soda Kogyo Kankei no Kinyu oyobi Zeisei Sochi ni tsuite" (On the financial and tax measures related to the soda industry), Soda to Enso 1: 20–25.

——— (1988) "Denryoku" (Electric Power), Soda to Enso 5: 46–55.

——— (1991a) "Shokuen Denkai ni okeru Ion Kokanmaku-ho Kanren Tokkyo no Genjo, Tsuiroku-ban VI: Showa 54–63 nen Kokoku/Kokai-bun, Dai 1 Bunsatsu: Denkai Hoho oyobi Kanren Gijutsu, C-1 Sotai Kozo" (Current situation of patents related to the ion exchange membrane process for brine electrolysis, sequel edition VI: publications from 1979 to 1988, vol. 1: electrolytic methods and related technologies, C-1 cell structure), Technology Examination Document, July.

——— (1991b) "Shokuen Denkai ni okeru Ion Kokanmaku-ho Kanren Tokkyo no Genjo, Tsuiroku-ban VI: Showa 54–63 nen Kokoku/Kokai-bun, Dai 2 Bunsatsu: Denkai Hoho oyobi Kanren Gijutsu, C-2 Denkai Hoho, C-3 Sonota" (Current situation of patents related to the ion exchange membrane process for brine electrolysis, sequel edition VI: publications from 1979 to 1988, vol. 2: electrolytic methods and related technologies, C-2 electrolytic methods, C-3 other), Technology Examination Document, July.

——— (1992a) "Shokuen Denkai ni okeru Ion Kokanmaku-ho Kanren Tokkyo no Genjo, Tsuiroku-ban VI: Showa 54–63 nen Kokoku/Kokai-bun, Dai 3 Bunsatsu: Ion Kokanmaku, M" (Current situation of patents related to the ion exchange membrane process for brine electrolysis, sequel edition VI: publications from 1979 to 1988, vol. 3: ion exchange membranes, M), Technology Examination Document, July.

——— (1992b) "Shokuen Denkai ni okeru Ion Kokanmaku-ho Kanren Tokkyo no Genjo, Tsuiroku-ban VI: Showa 54–63 nen Kokoku/Kokai-bun, Dai 4 Bunsatsu: Denkyoku (E), Ensui Seisei (B), Sono-ta (T) oyobi Kakumaku (D)" (Current situation of patents related to the ion exchange membrane process for brine electrolysis, sequel edition VI: publications from 1979 to 1988, vol. 4: electrodes (E), brine purification (B), other (T) and diaphragms (D)), Technology Examination Document, July.

——— (1998) "Denryoku" (Electric Power), Soda to Enso 12: 42–48.

Japanese Ministry of International Trade and Industry (1973) "Soda Kogyo ni okeru Suigin-ho kara Kakumaku-ho eno Tenkan Kijun" (Criteria for the conversion from the mercury process to the diaphragm process in the soda industry), 19 November.

——— (1975) "Kasei Soda Yuzu Jisshi Yoko" (Outline for the implementation of barter trades of caustic soda), Division of Basic Chemicals, Bureau of Basic Industries, 9 June.

——— (1979) "Kasei Soda Kogyo Seiho Tenkan Kankei Shiryo" (Documents on process conversions in the caustic soda industry), Division of Basic Chemicals, Bureau of Basic Industries, May.

―――― (1985) "Kasei Soda Kogyo no Genjo" (Current situation of the caustic soda industry), Division of Basic Chemicals, Bureau of Basic Industries, November.

―――― (1989) "Soda Kogyo no Genjo to Kadai" (Current situation and problems in the soda industry), Division of Basic Chemicals, Bureau of Basic Industries, August.

Kanto Denka Kogyo (1998) Kanto Denka Kogyo Rokuju-Nenshi (Sixty-Year History of Kanto Denka Kogyo), Tokyo.

Katsumura, Tatsuo (1979) "Soda Seiho Tenkan o Isoguna" (Do not rush into process conversions for soda production), Asahi Shinbun, 30 July.

Nikkei Sangyo Shinbun (1975a) "Shoden Kawasaki Kojo no Kakumaku-ho niyoru Kasei Soda Seizo Setsubi Kansei – Jisha Gijutsu de Seisan Kaishi" (Showa Denko completes construction of caustic soda production facilities with diaphragm process: Start of production with own technology), 19 June.

―――― (1975b) "Tsurumi Soda, Soda Setsubi wo Isshin, Noryoku 20% Appu" (Tsurumi Soda Renews Soda Facilities, 20% Increase in Capacity), 2 December.

Palmer, Karen, Wallace E. Oates and Paul R. Portney (1995) "Tightening Environmental Standards: The Benefit-Cost of the No-Cost Paradigm?" Journal of Economic Perspectives 9(4): 119–132.

Porter, Michael and Claas van der Linde (1995a) "Green and Competitive: Ending the Stalemate", Harvard Business Review, September–October: 120–134.

―――― (1995b) "Toward a New Conception of the Environment-Competitiveness Relationship", Journal of Economic Perspectives 9(4): 97–118.

Shibata, Hiroshi, Y. Kokubu and I. Okazaki (1977) "The Nobel Diaphragm Cell: A Flexible Design for High Currents and Its Performance Characteristics at 330 kA", Symposium on Diaphragm Cells for Chlorine Production, London: Society of Chemical Industry.

Showa Chemical (2001) "Nenpu" (Chronology).

Society of Chemical Engineers of Japan (1998) Kagaku Purosesu: Kiso kara Gijutsu Kaihatsu made (Chemical Processes: From Fundamentals to Technological Development), Tokyo: Tokyo Kagaku Dojin.

Takeshita, Tetsuo (1990) "Showa Denko Diaphragm Chlor-Alkali Technology", Thirty-third Chlorine Plant Operations Seminar and Workshop Sessions, Washington, D.C.: Chlorine Institute.

Tokuyama (2002) "Research and Development Themes and Electrolytic Plants at Tokuyama", Tokyo.

Tsubaki, Tadao and Katsuro Irukayama, eds. (1977) Minamata Disease: Methylmercury poisoning in Minamata and Niigata, Japan, Tokyo: Kodansha.

Tsurumi Soda (2001) "Kaisha Enkaku" (Corporate Chronology).

Yarime, Masaru (2003) "From End-of-Pipe Technology to Clean Technology: Effects of Environmental Regulation on Technological Change in the Chlor-Alkali Industry in Japan and Western Europe", Ph.D. dissertation, University of Maastricht, the Netherlands, 8 May.

8

Reconfiguring environmental regulation: Next-generation policy instruments

Neil Gunningham

The environmental impact of industry, especially pollution, has been subject to regulation for at least three decades, under an approach that is somewhat unfairly called "command and control" regulation.[1] This approach typically specifies standards, and sometimes technologies, with which the regulated must comply (the "command") or be penalized (the "control"). It commonly requires polluters to apply the best feasible techniques to minimize the environmental harm caused by their activities. Command and control has achieved some considerable successes, especially in terms of reducing air and water pollution. However, this "first generation" of environmental regulation has been widely criticized by economists for inhibiting innovation and for its high costs, inflexibility and diminishing returns.

The problems of command and control can be overstated and its considerable achievements too easily dismissed. At the same time, its limitations have led policymakers and regulators to recognize that it provides only a part of the policy solution, particularly in a rapidly changing, increasingly complex and interdependent world. However, regulatory reform must take place in an environment of shrinking regulatory resources, making it necessary in some contexts to design strategies capable of achieving results even in the absence of a credible enforcement regime (as when dealing with small and medium-sized enterprises), and in almost all circumstances to extract the "biggest bang" from a much diminished "regulatory buck".

This paper is about how to design regulation and alternatives to regulation in this economic and political context, in a manner that facilitates innovation and is both effective in protecting the environment and efficient in that it does so at the least cost to regulators and regulated enterprises. It takes as its starting point the proposition that command and control regulation has indeed made a substantial contribution in many areas of environmental policy, particularly in relation to laggards, and will continue to do so in the future. However, it is also clear that the low-hanging fruit has largely been picked, and that in an increasingly complex, diverse and interdependent society, "first generation regulation", in the form of command and control, is a blunt tool that is not well-suited to meet many of the challenges which lie ahead.

The intention is not to rehearse the conventional arguments about the strengths and weaknesses of command and control, but rather to examine the next generation of regulation and regulatory tools developed to curb the environmental excesses of business.

The crucial question is: where should one go next in terms of regulatory policy? The challenge is to find ways to overcome the inefficiencies of traditional regulation, to devise better ways of encouraging innovation and of achieving environmental protection at an acceptable economic and social cost. This will involve the design of a "second phase" of regulation: one that still involves government intervention, but selectively and in combination with a range of market and non-market solutions, and of public and private regulatory orderings.

The following sections will examine the potential of the main "second generation" instruments, including self- and co-regulation, voluntarism, informational regulation, the shift from technology to performance and process-based standards and the role of regulatory flexibility. It will then review recent empirical work by the author and others on the pulp and paper industry to suggest that the model that evolved out of that research may be a useful way of contextualizing and evaluating second-generation instruments. The final section sketches out the value of these instruments in light of our findings in the pulp and paper industry to arrive at some broad conclusions about the link between environmental regulation and innovation.

Next-generation environmental regulation and policy options

In designing innovative regulation, it is crucial to remember that "one size does not fit all". Different sized organizations experience different challenges in complying with regulations, and very different regulatory strategies will be needed to address them (contrast the issues in regulating transnational corporations with those of regulating small and medium-sized enterprises). So, too, it is necessary to design different strategies for different industry sectors: what is appropriate for the chemical industry may be entirely inappropriate for regulating agriculture (Gunningham and Grabosky 1998).

It is equally important to recognize that different organizations will be differently motivated. Enterprises will range from those that aspire to be environmental leaders to the recalcitrant or incompetent who, in the absence of effective regulation, will lag far behind minimum standards. While a traditional deterrence approach may be appropriate for rational actors, in practice there are many problems with simple deterrence theory, not least because social actors do not necessarily behave as economic models predict. Recent research increasingly demonstrates the importance of bounded (rather than full) rationality, and the related importance of a range of non-traditional strategies including negative publicity, informal sanctions and shame; the significance of maintaining legitimacy; and of cooperation and trust in defining organizational behaviour.

Parker (OECD 2000a: 73) sums up these developments as follows: "The picture of the organisation as an amoral calculator moved by appropriate deterrence to 'do the right thing' must be supplemented by the facts that organisations can sometimes be persuaded to do the right thing, that some influential actors within organisations will be highly motivated to be legal or socially responsible for its own sake, that the existence of deterrence threats will not necessarily be a feature of daily decision making, that many organisations will behave in ways that they feel maintain their legitimacy in the eyes of industry peers, customers or governments irrespective of individual cost and efficiency calculations, and that even where formal sanctions are applied, it is their informal ramifications (shame and negative publicity) that are more effective motivators".

In essence, achieving efficient and effective regulation and encouraging innovation is a far more complex activity than mainstream neo-classical economists believe(d) it to be, requiring a much broader range of strategies, tailored to a much broader range of motivations and harnessing a much wider range of social actors. Recognizing this, many recent theorists and practitioners of regulatory design have moved beyond command and control strategies to a more holistic approach that examines the effectiveness of mixes of regulatory strategies that will utilize the complexity and variety of motivations underlying compliance. Adopting such an approach implies the need to develop a sophisticated view of the target population of regulation, including: the characteristics of the marketplace; how individual organizations are structured and make decisions; what incentives are likely to motivate people to comply with regulation; and obstacles to their compliance (OECD 2000a).

The following section identifies a number of crucial ways in which regulatory design has moved beyond the "first generation" of command and control regulation, and a number of individual policy instruments.

Broadly speaking, policy instruments can be located on a continuum from the least to the most interventionist. For example, the paradigm case of the latter is command and control regulation in the American mould: highly prescriptive and enforced coercively. At the other extreme are instruments such as pure voluntarism, education and some information-based approaches. In between (in escalating degrees of intervention) lie mechanisms such as self-regulation and economic instruments.[2]

Self-regulation

Self-regulation is not a precise concept, but for present purposes it may be defined as a process whereby an organized group regulates the behaviour of its members (OECD 1994: 7). Most commonly it involves an industry-level organization (as opposed to the government or individual firms) setting rules and standards (codes of practice) relating to the conduct of firms in the industry.

Because standard-setting and identification of breaches are the responsibility of practitioners, with detailed knowledge of the industry, this will arguably lead to more practicable standards, more effectively policed. There is also the potential for utilizing peer pressure and for successfully internalizing responsibility for compliance. Moreover, because self-regulation contemplates ethical standards of conduct that extend beyond the letter of the law, it may significantly raise standards of behaviour and lead to a greater integration of environmental issues into the management process. Finally, and crucially, in some circumstances and forms, self-regulation holds out the possibility of encouraging dissemination of information about new technologies and of thereby facilitating their more rapid introduction.

Yet in practice, self-regulation often fails to fulfil its theoretical promise. The evidence suggests that self-regulation is rarely effective in achieving compliance (i.e., obedience by the target population/s with regulation/s) – at least if it is used as a "stand alone" strategy without sanctions. This is because self-regulatory standards are often weak, enforcement is commonly (although not invariably[3]) ineffective, and punishment is secret and mild. Moreover, self-regulation commonly lacks many of the virtues of typically conventional state regulation, "in terms of visibility, credibility, accountability, compulsory application to all, greater likelihood of rigorous standards being developed, cost spreading, and availability of a range of sanctions" (Webb and Morrison 1996).

Nevertheless, there is a growing number of increasingly sophisticated self-regulatory schemes in the sphere of environmental protection, which at least in some contexts and when they are underpinned by other instruments (see below), may yet make an important positive contribution to environmental protection. Best known examples include the chemical industry's Responsible Care programme, which applies in over 40 countries, safety-regulation of nuclear power plants by the Association of Nuclear Power Producers (INPO) in the United States, and the Canadian forest industry's Sustainable Forest Management Certification System.[4]

However, there is very limited empirical literature on environmental self-regulation, not least because such initiatives are relatively new and there is a paucity of quantitative data to facilitate evaluation of their compliance effectiveness.[5] Even such studies as do exist commonly ignore the potential "soft effects" (OECD 2000b: 3) of such initiatives. An exception is Rees's sophisticated analysis of Responsible Care, which demonstrates how the chemical industry has achieved behavioural change through two crucial *internal* processes. The first is its capacity to build an industry morality: a set of industrial principles and practices that defines right conduct and spells out the industry's public commitment to moral restraint and aspiration. The second is the extent to which it is capable of institutionalizing responsibility through the development of industry-wide policies and procedures to ensure a strong and effective commitment to the values or ideals the industry claims to uphold, the integration of accountability and transparency in corporate decision-making and the capacity to "moralize social control" (Rees 1997). Both of these characteristics are likely to nurture innovation within individual firms.

As with other instruments, self-regulation works better in some circumstances than in others, and not all industries lend themselves to self-regulation through industry associations. Rees uses the term "community of shared fate" to refer to circumstances in which poor performance on the part of one member reflects adversely upon, and indeed, may jeopardize the interests of the entire industry (Rees 1994). These circumstances facilitate the mobilization of peer pressure and self-regulation to ensure that no one member "lets the side down".

Self-regulation is most likely to work when certain conditions are present, such as relatively few industry players, high exit costs, a history of cooperation, availability of expertise and resources for regulation in the industry, mechanism for punishing non-compliant behaviour, consumer pressure for compliance, fair dispute resolution mechanisms and the presence of a significant degree of public participation or oversight

(Priest 1997: 233). From the above list it will be apparent that a major concern is to curb the incidence of free-riding, whereby rogue firms seek to claim the public relations and other benefits of scheme membership while avoiding the obligations it entails. Unfortunately, free-riding is often an almost insurmountable problem, because the criteria identified above, or any approximation to them, are only likely to be met in a small number of circumstances.

The paucity of success stories in the empirical literature (OECD 1999)[6] should make one extremely reticent about relying on unilateral programmes as a basis for providing any form of regulatory relief or other concessions from government, notwithstanding industry suggestions that it should do so. Indeed, the history of the Institute of Nuclear Power Operators (INPO), which is arguably the most successful of such initiatives, suggests that an underpinning of government regulation and enforcement will almost invariably be crucial to maintain credibility and effectiveness (Rees 1994).

Voluntary agreements

At a general level this category embraces agreements between governments and individual businesses or industry sectors, taking the form of "non-mandatory contracts between equal partners, one of which is government, in which incentives for action arise from mutual interests rather than from sanctions" (OECD 1994: 7). However, the variety of such agreements makes precise classification difficult (OECD 1999). The most common categories are (a) public voluntary agreements such as "challenge" programmes and (b) negotiated voluntary agreements between governments and industry. There is very little evidence to suggest the former has a positive impact on innovation and for present purposes we focus on the latter (OECD 1999: 132).

Negotiated agreements involve specific commitments to environmental protection elaborated through bargaining between industry and a public authority. In Europe they are usually entered into by an industry association and government against a backdrop of threatened legislation: the tacit bargain being that if the industry will commit to reach given environmental outcomes through its own initiatives, government will hold off on legislation it would otherwise contemplate enacting to address the problem. The vast majority of these agreements have been reached at a collective level and are not binding on individual corporations, with potential sanctions also being confined to the collective level. They are quite distinct from the sorts of legally binding agreements made between individual enterprises and a government agency in the United States of America, whereby the government offers regulatory flexibility in exchange for "beyond compliance" environmental performance, and whereby the individual enterprise would risk individual liability or eviction from the agreement for breach.[7]

From a public policy perspective, the attractions of negotiated agreements include the promised capacity to achieve better environmental outcomes at less cost to both government (which may avoid or reduce the costs of standard development and monitoring) and business (which can flexibly use its expertise to develop its own solutions to environmental problems). It is assumed that business will have knowledge far superior to government as to how to achieve any given outcome at the least cost (including through innovation) and that it should be facilitated to do so. However, the crucial question is whether industry will be motivated to do so under a voluntary agreement, or whether better outcomes could be achieved with very much the same flexibility via other means such as the imposition of performance standards or economic instruments.

Unfortunately, the empirical literature on negotiated agreements is very limited. Many existing agreements lack clear targets, and have inadequate reporting requirements and deadlines, making evaluation of their success extremely difficult. Indeed, one of the few things upon which almost all analysts of voluntary agreements seem to agree is that far too little attention has so far been given to evaluating either their economic or environmental benefits (Beardsley 1996; Davies and Mazurek 1996; Harrison 2001; NRC 1997). However, preliminary assessments of the value of the early voluntary agreements are not encouraging (Harrison 2001). One general survey of voluntary agreements has also concluded that many of the first generation of negotiated agreements have not been markedly successful. Even the claim that negotiated agreements tend to reduce administrative burden is not confirmed by existing empirical evidence or analysis (OECD 1999: 131).

There may be a variety of reasons for the very modest success of many of the first generation of voluntary agreements, including: the central role of industry in the target-setting process, the scope for free-riding, the uncertainty over regulatory threats, non-enforceable commitments, poor monitoring and lack of transparency (OECD 1999). In turn, the manifest deficiencies in the design of first-generation instruments suggest a number of lessons about how to design such agreements better in the future. For example, the OECD has identified a number of "success" criteria that if followed may achieve more positive results (Covery and Leveque 2001; OECD 1999).

A number of particular issues emerge from the various empirical studies and analyses conducted to date.[8] First, voluntary agreements are often best used when an environmental problem is in its early stages and it is premature to regulate it directly. For example, it has been pointed out that *agreements* have been preferred over *regulation* in waste management because of the technological uncertainty that prevailed, and because public authorities needed close industry cooperation in order to define realistic objectives and to encourage innovation (OECD 1999). In the case of agreements on climate change, a main reason for their use lies in their greater acceptance by industries compared with environmental taxes. Governments use them as a lesser evil in terms of the distortion of competition in a context where no uniform means for the reduction of greenhouse gases have yet been defined on the international level (Borkey and Leveque 1998). As the OECD (1999: 134) has pointed out, "In this regard voluntary approaches can be regarded as a policy instrument with a transitional function, i.e., to work until time is ripe for other regulations to come into force. They are particularly suitable for this role, since they are likely to generate soft effects and learning, and hence can help improve the future design of more traditional instruments".

Second, as has been argued elsewhere (Gunningham and Grabosky 1998), the weaknesses of voluntarism can often be compensated, and its strengths enhanced by combining it with most, but not all, forms of command and control regulation. To do so may improve both the flexibility and cost effectiveness of overall environmental policy and achieve substantial savings in administrative costs. For example, voluntary programmes can be used to complement conventional regulation by encouraging the use of environmental management systems (EMS) or other management tools that facilitate meeting legal standards and achieving better environmental performance. Conversely, regulations set the boundaries and the parameters for the flexibility provided through voluntary measures (OECD 1999).

Such an underpinning of government regulation may be particularly important in curbing free-riding. Indeed, it is often highly desirable that such agreements should be combined with other policy instruments. Sometimes this will include direct regulation, sometimes the threat of regulation – which will be triggered automatically if certain voluntary targets are not met and sometimes by combining voluntary agreements with economic instruments.[9]

Third, voluntary agreements do seem to generate major positive "soft effects" such as collective learning, generation and diffusion of information, learning by doing and demonstration effects, increased stakeholder participation and consensus building (OECD 1999: 131). Since many voluntary agreements aim at increasing environmental awareness of the industry rather than short-term environmental impacts, these effects should not be lightly dismissed and can be anticipated to have considerable implications for innovation.

Finally, the evaluation of negotiated agreements requires a dynamic analysis: the second generation of such agreements are somewhat different from the first, and considerably more likely to provide public interest benefits. Targets now tend to be set by government rather than by industry; government negotiators are much more sensitive to the risks of setting targets that merely reflect improvements that would happen anyway; and there is a movement toward linking negotiated agreements with other policy instruments – such as taxes – or to complement rather than replace existing regulations. Greater efforts are also being made in terms of transparency and third-party input. Whether these developments will justify the faith of advocates of the voluntary approach, and whether the additional transaction costs of building in essential checks and balances will render such instruments too costly, remains to be seen.

Economic instruments

In the 1980s, the OECD recognized the potential application of economic instruments, and began to give the concept wider circulation amongst policymakers. This, combined with the increasing awareness of the limits of traditional regulatory enforcement, has led to the growing acceptance and use of economic instruments in western industrial states (Eckersley 1995; Rehbinder 1993). The value of such instruments in the environmental context has been comprehensively examined in a number of OECD publications. For this reason, they will not be further explored here.

Informational regulation and civic environmentalism

An increasingly important alternative or supplement to conventional regulation is what is becoming known as "informational regulation" (Sabel, Fung and Karkkainen 2000). As the OECD (1994: 8) puts it: "People and businesses often care deeply about contributing responsibly to the public good (businesses also care about 'reputation'), and governments can use information, communication, encouragement, peer pressure, and education strategies to convince the public of the need for change. In contrast to command and control, informational regulation involves the state encouraging (as in corporate environmental reporting) or requiring (as with community right to know) information about environmental impacts but without directly requiring a change in those practices. Rather, this approach relies upon economic markets and public opinion as the mechanisms to bring about improved performance.

Informational regulation is targeted almost exclusively at large enterprises, and in particular at public companies (which are vulnerable to share price and investor perceptions) and those who are reputation sensitive, because is it essentially these types of enterprise which are most capable of being rewarded or punished by consumers, investors, communities, financial institutions and insurers on the basis of their environmental performance. The overall strategy is to empower these groups to use their community and/or market power in the environmental interest by providing them with a sufficient quality and quantity of information as to enable them to evaluate an enterprise's environmental performance. Such a strategy becomes even more effective as companies recognize the importance of protecting their "social license" and the need to improve their environmental performance in order to do so. There have been a number of experiments with the use of informational regulation that have demonstrated its potency even in circumstances where conventional regulation is weak.

Informational regulation is growing rapidly, partly because of the success of some of the early initiatives, partly because it offers a cost effective and less interventionist alternative to command and control in a period of contracting regulatory resources, partly because of its capacity to empower communities and NGOs, and partly because changes in technology make the use of such strategies increasingly viable and cost-effective.

Probably the most successful and best known form of information regulation is the use of community right to know (CRTK) and pollution inventories. The basis of these policy instruments is to require individual companies to estimate their emissions of specified hazardous substances. This information is then used to compile a publicly available inventory, which can then be interrogated by communities, the media, individuals and environmental groups and other NGOs who can ascertain, for example, the total emission load in a particular geographical area, or the total emissions of particular companies. The latter information in particular enables comparison of different enterprises' emissions and can be used to compile a "league table" which identifies both leaders and laggards in terms of toxic emissions. Such benchmarking exercises, facilitated by easy access to the relevant information, enable the shaming of the worst and rewarding of the best companies. The evidence suggests that well-informed communities use this information both to ensure tight enforcement of regulations and to pressure enterprises to improve their performance even in the absence of regulations, thereby providing considerable incentives for innovation. The foremost example of this approach is the United States Toxic Release Inventory (TRI).

Recognizing the potential value of this approach, a number of countries have followed the United States example and have introduced laws compelling disclosure of pollution and chemical hazard information. However, not all such inventories and similar instruments will be equally effective and much will depend upon their particular design features. While the large majority of assessments of the United States TRIs are strongly positive, the more recent Canadian scheme has yet to prove its worth, and there is only weak evidence that the latter has been effective in promoting voluntary emissions reductions. In Australia, the National Pollutant Inventory (NPI) was so severely weakened by industry-proposed amendments that environmental groups withdrew from the consultation process and the quality of available information under it remains extremely problematic.

Another example of informational regulation is provided by the PROPER PROKASIH in Indonesia. Under this programme, priority polluters are required to negotiate (legally unenforceable) pollution control agreements with teams comprising public agencies, environment groups and regional development groups. Regulators rank the performance of individual facilities using surveys, a pollution database of team reports and independent audits. An enterprise's pollution ranking is readily understood by the public, being based on a colour coding (gold and green for the best performers, black, blue, and red for those not in compliance). The programme has been very successful in improving the environmental performance of participating enterprises. A recent study that examines the programme over time suggests that community pressure and negative media attention, and increased likelihood of obtaining ISO 14001 certification, are the major stimuli for improved environmental performance (Afsah and Vincent 1997).

Space precludes a discussion of other forms of informational regulation such as the use of corporate reporting on environmental (and on ethical and social) performance, and product labeling and certification. Suffice it to say that informational regulation strategies work better in some circumstances than others. The evidence suggests that they work best with respect to large companies and environmentally aware communities. Community right to know, for example, relies heavily on the energies of local communities in using the information and pressuring enterprises to improve their environmental performance. Where an environmental hazard involves no immediate threat to human health, or where there is no identifiable local community or where we are dealing with non-point source pollution not readily measured and traced back to its origins, then this instrument has far less to offer. Similarly, corporate environmental reporting is dependent upon the willingness of public interest groups to follow through on its results and to shame both bad performers and praise good ones. Finally, eco-labelling relies upon the willingness of consumers to buy "green" products and upon their capacity to distinguish between these and other classes of product (especially in an area where there are many other labels to decode).

A related development is the growth of "civic regulation", whereby various manifestations of civil society act in a variety of ways to influence corporations, consumers and markets, often by-passing the state and rejecting political lobbying in favour of what they believe to be far more effective strategies.[10] Sometimes NGOs take direct action, usually targeted at large reputation-sensitive companies. Greenpeace's campaign against Shell's attempted deep-sea disposal of the Brent Spar oil rig is one example. Sometimes they boycott products or producers deemed to be environmentally harmful, as with the effective boycott of Norwegian fish products organized by Greenpeace in protest against that nation's resumption of whaling. Market campaigning focusing on highly visible branded retailers is a particularly favoured strategy.[11] Less so are campaigns that seek to provide a market premium for "environmentally preferred" produce, due largely to the unwillingness of consumers to support such a strategy. More recently, certification programmes such as the Forest Stewardship Council are "transforming traditional power relationships in the global arena. Linking together diverse and often antagonistic actors from the local, national and international levels ... to govern firm behaviour in a global space that has eluded the control of states and international organizations" (Gereffi et al. 2001).

However, the evolving role of civic regulation has not taken place entirely divorced from state intervention. On the contrary, either in response to pressure from the institutions of civil society or in recognition of the limits of state regulation, governments are gradually providing greater roles for communities, environmental NGOs and the public more generally. Thus a number of second-generation policy instruments are geared to empower various institutions of civil society to play a more effective role in shaping business behaviour, thus facilitating civic regulation. These include not only the sort of CRTK legislation described above, but also a variety of other mechanisms that seek to empower third parties, for example, by giving environmental NGOs or communities a "seat at the table" (and enabling them to influence directly planning or licensing conditions), by providing them with the standing to bring a legal action, or the information with which to threaten the reputation capital of large corporations.

Maximizing innovation: Specification, performance or process standards?

Performance standards instead of specification and technology rules

In designing environmental standards and securing compliance on the part of target groups, it is vitally important to determine what *types* of standards to adopt (Gunningham and Johnstone 1999). For example, what kinds of measures are most likely to achieve best policy outcomes? What techniques are most likely to influence organizational behaviour, to be flexible, encourage innovation, produce environmental benefits at an acceptable cost, provide practical guidance to employers and be easy to enforce? It has been pointed out that "in many circumstances the real problem facing policymakers is not to select the best strategy for achieving compliance but to decide what it is the regulated are to be asked to comply with" (Hopkins 1994). In this context, traditionally, two main types of standard were thought to be available: specification and performance standards.

A specification or technology standard is a standard that tells the firm precisely what measures to take and requires little interpretation on the firm's part. Such a standard is defined in terms of the specific types of methods that must be used in a specific situation and in terms of its emphasis on the design and construction of these safeguards. Because of definitional precision, specification/technology standards have the virtue of enabling employees and inspectors to ascertain readily whether the employer meets or breaches those standards. These standards thus offer administrative simplicity and ease of enforcement. Empirical evidence confirms the reluctance of inspectors to relinquish the detail of specification standards in favour of broader-based (and perhaps more ambiguous) performance standards (Carson et al. 1989).

There are, however, serious disadvantages in the use of specification standards across the board. Specification standards, to be effective, must usually be extremely detailed to cover all kinds of machines and plant layouts; a near impossible task. Such an approach tends to result in a mass of detailed legislation, difficult to comprehend or keep up to date. Moreover, because such standards are prescriptive they do not allow duty holders to seek least-cost solutions and accordingly are unlikely to be cost-effective in the majority of circumstances. Similarly, they inhibit innovation and do not encourage best practice (box 8.1).

In contrast, a performance standard is one that specifies the outcome of the environmental improvement but that leaves the concrete measures to achieve this end open for the employer to adapt to varying local

Box 8.1: The Yorktown Experiment

Recognizing the substantial limitations of command and control regulation in its traditional forms, a number of innovative approaches have been developed in recent years. A milestone in this respect was a joint enterprise in the United States between Amoco Corporation and the EPA, known as the Yorktown Project. This project began by documenting the numerous ways in which the conventional system of regulation curtails innovation. It went on to show that site-specific flexibility to achieve environmental objectives fosters innovation and leads to more cost-effective solutions in a manner which far surpasses the "one-size-fits-all" approach. A key conclusion of the project was that the objectives of environmental regulations can be achieved more cost-effectively if the regulated community is allowed to devise individualized plant-specific compliance plans. For example, the participants in the project unanimously selected the most effective pollution prevention options for a particular facility, that solution often being far removed from what the existing regulations prescribed. The United States EPA found that, for example, by applying outcome standards for benzene emissions to the whole of Amoco's Yorktown plant, rather than specific rules mandating certain technology in the smokestacks, Amoco would have been able to achieve greater emissions reductions at much lower cost. The project team concluded that by prioritizing projects in this manner, equivalent release reductions could have been achieved at 25% of the cost.

circumstances. That is, rather than specifying exactly *how* to achieve compliance, a performance standard sets a general goal and lets each employer decide how to meet it. A considerable attraction of performance standards is that because they focus on the outcomes to be achieved rather than on the precise hazards to be controlled or the means of controlling them, they can adapt to changes in technology and the creation of new hazards (unlike specification standards which commonly fail to keep pace with technological change). Performance standards also allow firms flexibility to select the least costly or least burdensome means of achieving compliance and encouraging innovation. On the other hand, because they are sometimes imprecise, performance standards are to that extent more difficult to enforce than specification standards, and inspectorates have commonly experienced considerable difficulties of adjustment.

Over the last few years most policy makers and commentators have swung heavily in favour of the use of performance rather than specification standards. Of particular influence has been Michael Porter and Claus van der Linde's argument that a well-designed regulatory system can foster innovation by concentrating on outcomes (i.e., performance standards) rather than on techniques (i.e., specification- or technology-based standards). This is because performance standards free up an enterprise to respond to a regulator's requirement in the way that it best thinks fit. In evidence, they cite the relative success of the Scandinavian and United States governments in achieving emissions reductions in the pulp and paper industry. The Scandinavian companies "developed innovative pulping and bleaching technologies that not only met emission requirements but also lowered operating costs" (Porter and van der Linde 1995: 129). American companies, in contrast, did not respond to regulation by innovating because United States specification- or technology-based regulations did not permit companies to "discover how to solve their own problems".[12]

However, as indicated above, performance standards offer less guidance to employers as to what is required of them and this presents particular problems for small and medium-sized enterprises. For these companies, effective compliance will be facilitated by the provision of more precise guidance as to how to identify and resolve problems. This could be provided through technical data sheets and other advisory material that could be issued not only by regulatory agencies but also by independent standard-setting bodies or even by industry itself. However, it may also be desirable, as under comparable occupational health and safety legislation, to insert a statutory provision making clear that compliance with the advisory material/code of practice will be deemed to be compliance with the performance standard (Gunningham and Johnstone 1999).

Process standards

Notwithstanding the considerable contribution that both specification and performance standards have made toward improving environmental compliance and performance, both approaches have a substantial limitation: namely they only require enterprises to achieve *minimum* standards and provide no incentives or encouragement to go beyond those minima. They do not encourage continuous improvement or industry best practice. Nor do they directly encourage enterprises to develop an environmental culture or to "build in" environmental considerations at every stage of the production process.

Certainly, for some enterprises, particularly those with little expertise, sophistication, or commitment to the environment (e.g., many small firms, those with high labour mobility), it may not be realistic, at least in the short term, to expect compliance with anything more than the legal minima, and even bringing them up to this standard may be a considerable achievement. Both performance and specification standards continue to make a substantial contribution in this regard.

However, there are many other enterprises that, potentially at least, could achieve far more than those minima. An important role of law is to encourage them to do so. For some enterprises, at least, the law could do far more by developing a different approach. For these enterprises, there is considerable potential in developing a new phase of standard design – process and management system standards that provide not only considerable flexibility and enable enterprises to devise their own least-cost solutions, but that give them direct incentives to go "beyond compliance" with minimum legal standards.

Process standards address *procedures* for achieving a desired result. These standards specify the processes to be followed in managing nominated hazards and have been most used in respect of hazards that do not lend themselves to measurement, or to address risk assessment more generally. They are based on a systematic approach to controlling and minimizing risks and, as we will see, are a precursor to EMS-based approaches. One example of this approach is the European Union's Control of Major Accident Hazards (COMAH) Directive (Seveso II), which requires the provision by the facility (and assessment by the government regulator) of comprehensive installation safety reports. Other examples include the safety case regime adopted by various nations for offshore oil platforms, and the requirements for suppliers of hazardous substances to provide Material Safety Data Sheets to users, for health monitoring in relation to highly hazardous substances, and for the management of major hazardous facilities.

Within the United States one of the most developed examples of this approach is Rule 112(r) of the 1990 Clean Air Act amendments, which requires regulated facilities to prepare and execute a risk management programme that contains the following elements: a hazard assessment to determine the consequences of a specified worst case scenario and other accidental release scenarios on public and environmental receptors and provide a summary of the facility's five-year history of accidental releases; an accidental release prevention programme designed to detect, prevent and minimize accidental releases; and an emergency response programme designed to deal with any accidental release in order to protect both human health and the environment.

Process-based approaches, however, represent only one aspect of a full-blown organizational and systems-based approach because they are largely confined to specific hazards or processes, and/or to the process of risk assessment and control. Even when these requirements are incorporated generally, they still concern only one aspect of a fully developed and comprehensive systems-based approach. As we will see, although process-based standards have something in common with a broader EMS-based approach, and can be integrated within it, it is only the latter that provides a coherent strategy for addressing the environment in an entire enterprise, or across an entire facility.

Environmental management systems and regulatory flexibility

An EMS is a management tool intended to assist an organization to achieve environmental and economic goals by focusing on systemic problems rather than individual deficiencies. That is, it involves the assessment and control of risks and the creation of an in-built system of maintenance and review. Its focus is on the organizational structure, responsibilities, practices, procedures and resources for implementing and maintaining environmental management. The basic elements of such a system include the creation of an environmental policy, setting objectives and targets, implementing a programme to achieve these objectives, monitoring and measuring its effectiveness, correcting problems and reviewing the system to improve overall environmental performance.

In principle, an EMS has the potential to deliver continuous improvement and embed cultural change on environmental issues within the organization. A particular attraction of an EMS is its capacity to move corporate thinking on environmental performance from the sort of compartmentalization that characterized the earlier generation of pollution control instruments (vertical standards addressing discrete areas of activity) to a horizontal standard that cuts across the functions of the organization, and integrates environmental considerations with other corporate functions and imperatives. An EMS can make costs, efficiency, productivity and environmental performance all part of the same decision-making process (Knight 1994).

The potential for an EMS to bring *some* enterprises beyond compliance and to encourage and reward innovation and continuous improvement was soon recognized by regulators.[13] But *how* could regulation be redesigned for this purpose? For some regulators, particularly in the United States of America, the answer lies in a two-track system of regulation whereby leading enterprises are offered regulatory flexibility in return for improved environmental performance. The incentives or rewards offered for participating in these initiatives include fast-tracking of licenses or permits, reduced fees, technical assistance, public recognition, penalty discounts under certain conditions, reduced burdens from routine inspections and greater flexibility in means permitted to achieve compliance. In return for the various incentives offered, industry is expected to go beyond compliance though an EMS-based approach to environmental protection (and in some instances to engage in stakeholder dialogue, to be more transparent and to take greater responsibility for the environmental behaviour of others in the supply chain).

However, there is a danger in this approach. An environmental management system should be used to complement rather than to replace other regulatory tools. While it is possible to envisage a scaled-back role for command and control regulation, particularly in relation to environmental leaders, it will still be necessary (at least in the short term) to maintain a variety of oversight and regulatory fall-back mechanisms (in particular, performance measures) to ensure that the system actually delivers the benefits of which it is capable in principle. For these reasons, many policy analysts argue that the new regulatory flexibility initiatives must be based on "ISO Plus" rather than merely on conformity with ISO 14001 itself. Unfortunately, this has not necessarily been the case in practice (Gunningham and Grabosky 1998).

Nevertheless, regulators are increasingly enthusiastic about a two-track approach incorporating regulatory flexibility. In the United States, state and federal regulators are now moving toward a more systematic approach, designed to provide rewards and incentives for improved compliance and high environmental performance. Under this approach, enterprises (or at least enterprises with certain environmental credentials) are offered a choice between a continuation of traditional forms of regulation on the one hand, and a more flexible approach (the central pillars of which are usually the adoption of an EMS, periodic internal environmental audits and community participation) on the other.

The ultimate test of the success or otherwise of regulatory flexibility initiatives such as the above is an empirical one. Despite their very considerable potential, the jury is still out on the strengths, weaknesses and ultimately the success of EMS-based regulatory flexibility initiatives more generally. It will be some time before we know whether and, if so, to what extent the benefits of the various initiatives outweigh the costs and whether they will indeed overcome many of the problems of traditional forms of regulation. Or whether the skeptics are correct in questioning why so many resources are being devoted to making the top 20% (or perhaps only the top 5%) even better, rather than concentrating on the most serious problems or on under-performers.

Motivating management to innovate

Governments have developed a variety of policy instruments intended to improve corporate environmental behaviour, and sometimes, but far from invariably, to encourage innovation. These range from traditional command and control approaches, through informational regulation (exemplified by the TRI) and market mechanisms, to regulatory flexibility initiatives intended to encourage, facilitate and reward environmental best practice. Increasingly too, voluntary initiatives complement direct government intervention.

The effectiveness or otherwise of such policy interventions depends crucially on what motivates corporations to improve their environmental performance. In seeking to understand environmental motivation, the economic, socio-legal and policy literature on regulatory administration has tacitly assumed that legal compliance with existing regulation by targeted groups is the key to meeting environmental objectives. And underlying that assumption is another: that regulated business corporations take costly measures to improve their performance *only* when they believe that legal non-compliance is likely to be detected and harshly penalized (OECD 2000a). From the viewpoint of traditional models of corporations as "amoral calculators" (Kagan and Sholz 1984), why would a profit-maximizing company want to comply if non-compliance was unlikely to be detected or punished? And furthermore, why would a company do more than the law requires since compliance is itself often expensive and over-compliance even more so?

Yet it is becoming apparent that there is considerable variation in how firms respond to regulatory pressures and, in at least some industries, considerable evidence of "beyond compliance" behaviour, much of it innovative in nature (Hoffman 1997; Prakash 2000; Smart 1992). Indeed, over the last decade a new body of literature has evolved on the "greening of industry". At its heart lies the unresolved question, "What are the determinants of greening?" Notwithstanding some valuable case studies (confined to environmental leaders) and some less-illuminating survey evidence, adequate empirical answers have not been forthcoming (Fuchs and Mazmanian 1998). We still know little about what motivates individual corporations (and indeed different facilities within the same corporation) to behave the way they do in the environmental context, or why some companies or facilities but not others choose to move beyond compliance or what social policy tools are likely to prove most effective in facilitating innovation and in achieving improved corporate environmental performance.

For example, although it is widely assumed that variations in regulation and regulatory enforcement account for differences in environmental performance by regulated businesses, it is far from clear that this is indeed the case. It is equally plausible (at least in economically advanced democracies) that differences among regulatory regimes have narrowed sharply, and that local social pressures, market incentives and corporate environmental management are now the chief determinants of variations in firm-level environmental performance, and of beyond-compliance behaviour in particular.

In summary, the degree of variation in, and the motivations for, corporate behaviour may be much broader than many researchers have imagined. This is of considerable practical importance: some existing regulatory strategies, in focusing on compliance, have failed to facilitate, reward or encourage beyond-compliance behaviour, or even inadvertently discouraged it. Others, such as the National Environmental Performance Track, are specifically designed to provide greater flexibility in regulatory response, and to reward beyond-compliance behaviour, but would benefit from a better understanding of what motivates such behaviour. Still others have argued that government-mandated self-regulation, or various forms of voluntarism are the key to progress, but again without a full understanding of how, to what extent, under what circumstances and why various corporations might be inclined to participate in such initiatives. In each case, corporate motivations are likely to have implications for their willingness or otherwise to seek out and implement innovative solutions, whether by technology or through incremental change. There is therefore a compelling case for studying "over-compliance" as well as compliance, and for developing a better understanding of the *reasons* for the variability in corporate motivation and environmental performance.

A recent study by Gunningham, Kagan and Thornton (2003)[14] of 14 pulp and paper manufacturing mills in Australia, New Zealand, British Columbia (Canada) and the states of Washington and Georgia in the United States demonstrates that regulation has been directly responsible for the large reductions in pulp mill pollution that stem from capital investments in very costly pollution control technologies. For example, the largest reductions in pulp mill discharge to water of harmful pollutants have stemmed from investments in expensive control technologies, particularly secondary wastewater treatment facilities and the substitution of chlorine dioxide for elemental chlorine as a bleaching agent (which often required construction of a chlorine dioxide plant).

Economic license constraints often affected the timing of those installations, as firms often successfully argued that they should coincide with periodic rebuilding or updating of primary production equipment. But sooner or later the regulatory license has trumped economic demands, partially through the implicit promise that all competitors would be obliged to make the same investment. And indeed, one of the most striking findings in our research has been the extent to which major investments in control technology have been made in response to pending or anticipated regulatory rules.[15] That is, the big jumps in wastewater environmental performance in pulp manufacturing were the products of "regulation-driven technological change": technology changes occurred in order to meet more stringent performance standards.[16] Less directly, regulatory rules (and corporate compliance or non-compliance with them) serve as a benchmark for groups other than regulatory officials who evaluate and influence corporate behaviour – financial analysts, environmental advocacy groups, politicians and corporate environmental managers.

Yet governmental regulation, as conventionally viewed, does not fully explain two clear and important findings. First, the pulp mills we studied did not merely comply with regulation but operated "beyond compliance" in significant ways, for example by reducing water pollution to levels well below the limits required by the companies' regulatory permits. Second, notwithstanding substantial convergence over time, the pulp mills differed significantly in the extent to which they had gone beyond legal compliance. That variation did not correlate closely with the demands of the firms' regulatory licenses. Nor did the purported greater prescriptiveness and deterrence threat of United States environmental regulation make pulp mills in the US better environmental performers on average than those in Canada, Australia or New Zealand. More broadly, there was more variation *within* than *across* regulatory jurisdictions.

Rather than regulation, social license pressures and the character of corporate environmental management appear to be the most powerful factors that prod some firms further beyond compliance than others. Conversely, in a highly competitive commodity market such as pulp manufacturing, economic pressures limit how far even the most environmentally committed firm can leap ahead of its competitors, at least in making non-incremental environmental gains through costly new technologies that are not clearly likely to pay for themselves in financial terms. Although the "environmental strategists" and "true believers" in our sample were able to make steady incremental progress through "win-win" measures such as better employee training and dedicated maintenance regimes, we found little evidence of a rich supply of major "win-win" investments that environmentally committed corporate managers could make, and hence little evidence that simply exhorting managers toward environmental excellence could substitute for regulation in overcoming tough economic constraints. Management does matter, but, to paraphrase Marx, while companies make their own history, they do so in circumstances not of their own choosing.

If the pulp industry is any guide, governments pay attention to economic constraints facing the industry as well. They rarely mandate the use of such costly new environmental technologies in the absence of the demonstrated economic viability of the technology or major public pressure, as in the case of the dramatic reaction to the discovery of dioxins in pulp mill effluent. Far from inflicting a technology-forcing, one-size-fits-all set of regulatory requirements on all regulated firms, as critics of regulation often suggest, a close examination of the permits of pulp mills reflects a governmental propensity, in all the jurisdictions we studied, to tailor requirements to the technological and economic constraints of particular regulated entities.

One lesson of this study, therefore, is that government regulation might be viewed less as a system of hierarchically-imposed, uniformly-enforced rules than as a coordinative mechanism, routinely interacting with other sources of pressure for socially responsible corporate behaviour such as markets, local and national environmental activists and the culture of corporate management. If regulation is less important than environmental management and social pressures in inspiring beyond-compliance corporate activity, a competent regulatory system spurs progress by reassuring corporate environmental leaders that their less-committed competitors also will be compelled to spend the money to achieve environmental outcomes that the leaders have demonstrated are technologically and economically feasible. Moreover, in the programmes we studied regulators issued permits that required firms to file their own plans for analysing and reducing designated emissions or environmental hazards; after review and perhaps renegotiation by regulators, the company plan became a binding regulatory obligation. By "delegating the details", regulated entities were prodded to undertake periodic, if not continuous efforts to keep up with or advance the state of the art in environmental protection.

Another central finding of our study was that social pressures (what we term the business firms' "social licenses") provide a particularly powerful point of leverage. Community and environmental advocacy groups in particular tend to act as effective watchdogs and de facto regulators, shaming and otherwise pressuring companies into beyond-compliance environmental performance. While they can sometimes play this role in the absence of any form of state intervention, their effectiveness, we have observed, is enhanced by various forms of facilitative government regulation. For example, information and monitoring requirements can empower social actors if environmental information about facilities is easily accessible and sufficient to allow for meaningful interpretation of the data. Rules that require facilities to inform the public of environmentally significant actions and monitoring redress some of the inherent information assymetries that occur between regulators, regulatees and the public, and allow social actors to most appropriately target their actions.[17]

Moreover, our research indicates that government actions that *procedurally* empower local communities can have significant effects. In New Zealand, mills reported having become much more responsive to community environmental concerns after communities were given the legal right to challenge the terms of each facility's "consent" (permit), and thereby gained the power to delay the introduction of new processes or technology. In an Australian jurisdiction, similar effects flowed from a new law that obligated firms to prepare and comply with an environmental improvement plan, including a commitment to consultation with local communities. In Canada and the United States, the permitting process has long been open to the public and allowed for public comment on permitting decisions. Such public access has been extended in the United States through programmes such as Project XL and the Environmental Leadership Programme, which make it a condition for providing greater regulatory flexibility, that participating companies provide information to, and consult with, local communities.[18]

From our research, we developed a broader model that we believe has considerable resonance for addressing a range of questions concerned specifically with what motivates innovation – whether in terms of the development of new technology or incremental improvement in production processes.

The license model

The "license model" views business enterprises as simultaneously motivated and constrained by a multi-faceted "license to operate", which includes not only the terms of their regulatory permits and legal obligations, but also an often-demanding "social license" and a constraining "economic license", which represent the demands of social and economic actors respectively. For example, local fishermen might want to ensure that they can catch bass in local rivers, national environmental groups might want to ensure the protection of an endangered species and institutional lenders might want a reasonable rate of return on their investments. These demands translate into specific requirements for the business enterprise: to ensure that the quality of their discharge does not threaten the bass population, to ensure that their facility's operation does not threaten an endangered species, and to meet market rates of return.

These regulatory, economic and social license requirements are monitored and enforced by the stakeholders who generate them, and who commonly seek leverage by exploiting a variety of license terms.[19] For example, environmental groups not only enforce the terms of the social license directly (e.g., through shaming and adverse publicity) but also seek to influence the terms of the economic license (e.g., generating consumer boycotts of environmentally damaging products) and of the regulatory license (e.g., through citizen suits or political pressure for regulatory initiatives). Thus the interaction between the different types of licenses often exceeds the effect of each one acting alone. The terms of some legal license provisions extend the reach and impact of the social license by directly empowering social activists or by giving them access to information or a role in the permit-granting process, which they can use to pressure target enterprises. Conversely, a company that fails to respond appropriately to social license obligations risks a tightening of its regulatory license, as frustrated community activists turn for help to politicians and regulators. However, the terms of each strand of the "license to operate" often are far from certain or immutable, and are therefore subject to interpretation. What might be considered a "reasonable" rate of return depends in part upon general market conditions and the particular investor. Different community groups can make conflicting demands. And different regulators can have different interpretations of the same set of environmental rules. Moreover, proactive corporate officials sometimes can reshape some license terms – by providing information to and negotiating with regulators or environmental activists, by engaging in community outreach and education and scanning for technologies and procedures that simultaneously cut costs and improve the firm's environmental performance. In effect, the influence of the regulatory, economic and social licenses on environmental performance depends on an "intervening variable" – managerial attitudes, or the combination of attitudes and executive action called "environmental management style". Management style is the perceptual filter through which management interprets its license to operate.

Management style not only filters management's perception of stakeholder demands, it is also, in turn, influenced by those demands, although not wholly determined by them. Corporate culture, history, network relationships and individual membership also play key roles in determining how a business enterprise interprets its environment in general, and environmental license requirements in particular. Figure 8.1 shows the license model of corporate environmental behaviour.

Theory and practice: What works?

Reviewing the "second generation" instruments described above against our empirical findings in the pulp and paper industry, the question arises, what works in practice? Our study of the pulp and paper industry suggests the following:

Self-regulation

There is little if any evidence to support a greater role for industry self-regulation. The normal vehicle for ensuring industry-level self-regulation is the industry association itself. But in the case of this industry the asso-

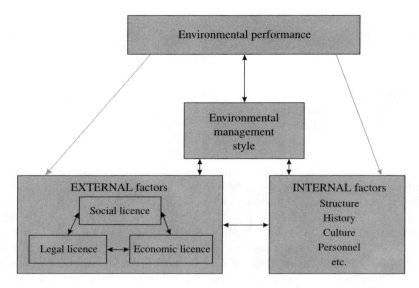

Figure 8.1 License model of corporate environmental behaviour

ciation has adopted a lowest common denominator approach, which has been seriously detrimental to innovation. Indeed, it has been characterized as producing a "crabs in the basket" effect, where if any one company seeks to generate changes ahead of its competitors it will be drawn back into line as a result of peer pressure or more direct economic pressure. For example, one pulp company that experimented with totally chlorine-free pulp found it had to abandon that experiment because its customers (other pulp companies in the United States of America) boycotted its pulp.

Voluntary agreements

There is little evidence to support a greater role for voluntary initiatives. As indicated above, the greatest changes in the environmental performance of the industry have been technological changes driven by regulation. Regulatory modelling seems to be a far greater influence than voluntary initiatives in getting firms up to a minimum standard of performance. Although pulp companies in Wisconsin have, through their industry association, focused more recently on voluntary improvements, the outcome of this initiative is not yet known.

Information and civil regulation

Many companies voluntarily choose to go beyond compliance. Their motives are mixed and some choose to go much further than others. Within this group lie the greatest prospects for innovation. Yet for some of these companies the aspiration is only to build in a "margin of safety" to ensure that they do not fall below compliance. Such firms are still essentially reactive and regulation driven. But others go much further. We found the greatest driver for them was the perceived terms of their "social license". Informational regulation (which enables communities and NGOs to monitor mills' environmental performance and to compare that of different mills) and civic regulation (especially procedural mechanisms that empower community groups and rights of standing that all allow them to take legal action) are particularly powerful levers to improved environmental performance and to greater innovation.

Regulatory flexibility

At the heart of regulatory flexibility initiatives lies the EMS and an assumption that by encouraging and rewarding companies to adopt such a system they will thereby build in continuous improvement and cultural change. Put more broadly, underlying such approaches is the belief that such flexibility will "harness the power of competition to stimulate profitable clean technology and other environmentally beneficial innovations" (Smith 1997). This assumption is largely untested. Our research suggests that "management" matters much more than "management systems". In other words, the companies in our sample that were most committed to environmental improvement and were the most innovative were those that had a particular culture and set of perceptions: in our terms they were either "environmental strategists" or "true believers" and were far more likely to scan for environmental opportunities, see openings for incremental technological innovation and believe that such innovations would result in "win-win" outcomes. But that leaves open the question of how policymakers might best shift corporate attitudes and motivation. It is by no means clear that mandating or encouraging them to adopt a management system is the best way to go (Coglianese and Nash 2001).

Technology, performance and process standards

In this industry at least, future technological change is likely to be driven by regulation (Ashford and Heaton 1983).[20] Yet governments are understandably reluctant to base performance standards on new technology that is unproven, for should the unproven technology fail other jurisdictions will not adopt the requirement, and local industry may be put at a competitive disadvantage. Nevertheless, even without specifying more stringent performance standards, regulatory agencies are able to influence the development of new technologies by specifying their long-term goals and engaging industry officials in a dialogue about pathways and timetables for achieving them. For example, the United States EPA notes in the preamble to its cluster rule that it "believes that the mill of the future will approach closed loop operations", and suggests an avenue by which this objective might be achieved.[21]

The implied government capacity to make such technologies, once developed by industry leaders, mandatory for all firms provides some incentive for the leaders to experiment and innovate, thereby obtaining first-mover advantages.[22] It also provides some incentive for laggards not to fall too far behind current industry practice and to avoid costly retrofits if new technology becomes required. Regulation can stimulate greener technological innovation and adoption of innovative technology by decreasing uncertainty. Thus regulation in general can be used to steer ("herd") industry toward excellence by setting a regulatory trajectory.[23] This effect is intensified because regulations, health and environmental concerns, and technological innovations in any jurisdiction commonly ripple through to other jurisdictions by virtue of the process of "regulatory modelling".[24]

The "herding process" can be facilitated by the provision of good information about the relative environmental performance of regulatory leaders and laggards. For the most part, regulatory systems' performance in this regard has been disappointing. In conducting this research, for example, we faced tremendous difficulties in obtaining accurate and accessible data that could usefully be compared over time and between facilities.[25] Good evaluations of government or corporate policy require accurate, *comparable* outcome data. Monitoring requirements can provide such data if they take into account more than the compliance of a particular facility at a particular point in time. Monitoring requirements could allow for evaluative research and policy analysis if care is taken to ensure that the data collection they require allows for comparison over time and between facilities, and if the manner in which the data is reported assures data quality and facilitates accessibility.

Conclusion

There are a variety of policy strategies available that might, subject to political and economic constraints, encourage environmental innovation. These include not only forms of "command and control" regulation, but also the much more flexible, imaginative and innovative forms of social control that bring together business firms, governments and third parties. But just as the causes of major environmental problems are many and various, so too are their solutions. Strategies to address environmental degradation are context-specific.[26] Which sorts of policies work will be highly dependent on the characteristics of the environmental issue under consideration and the context in which the issue is to be addressed. The empirical findings reported above are perhaps not generalizable beyond the commodity-based and reputation-sensitive "heavy" industries. At the very least, however, the license model developed in this paper does offer important insights into the interplay between environmental policy and environmental innovation. As such, it may contribute to a better understanding of what drives innovation, both technological and incremental, in a variety of different contexts and industries.

Notes

1. This paper is drawn from material published in N. Gunningham and D. Sinclair (2002) Leaders and Laggards: Next Generation Environmental Regulation, UK: Greenleaf Press. The author gratefully acknowledges the contribution of Darren Sinclair, who substantially conducted the case studies used in the book and referred to in this paper.
2. Of course, it is easier to weigh the relative merits of different instrument categories at the extremes of the interventionism continuum than those located close together in the middle.
3. For example, it should be noted that the American Forest and Paper Association had, by mid-2001, expelled 16 industry members and that contract-based enforcement was increasingly being viewed as a credible substitute for self-regulators' lack of criminal enforcement powers.
4. This code of practice was devised in response to European boycott initiatives and premised on industry awareness that national and international market forces demand independent, reliable certification systems. See further G. T. Rhone (1996) Canadian Standards Association Sustainable Forest Management Certification System, Ottawa, Canada: Industry Canada.
5. For a comprehensive survey see Priest (1997).
6. Particularly chapter 3 and references therein.
7. The Dutch environmental covenants, represent (in European terms) an unusual hybrid, since these agreements both address collective and sector-wide environmental issues and are legally binding on individual companies through the permit system, and are thus intimately linked to mainstream command and control. Rather than playing an ancillary or supporting role (as is the case with many European collective agreements), they are a key component of Dutch environmental policy. For all these reasons, they defy formal classification. They have nevertheless been very influential and represent an important and apparently successful model.
8. Of these the most influential include OECD (1999) and Covery and Leveque (2001).
9. The French and German agreements on packaging-waste recycling are backed by decrees, specifying the regulations that would be enforced if voluntary agreements fail.
10. Civil society is conventionally defined as involving "citizens acting collectively in a public sphere to express their interests, passions and ideas, exchange information, achieve mutual goals, make demands on the state and hold public officials accountable. Civil society is an intermediary entity, standing between the private sphere and the state" (Diamond 1996).
11. For example, a highly successful Greenpeace campaign has been largely responsible for sensitizing European consumers (particularly in Germany and the United Kingdom) to the clear-felling of old-growth forests. This has had a profound impact upon North American companies exporting to those markets, who are increasingly being pressured

by European buyers to provide evidence that the timber they supply has come from sustainably harvested sources.

12. Porter and van der Linde (1995). However, it should be noted that while the Porter and van der Linde view is in some respects (e.g., the extent to which it is rational for enterprises to pursue win-win solutions) a controversial one, the overall benefits of performance over specification standards in the large majority of situations is now widely recognized.

13. An increasing number of large enterprises now recognize their obligations to comply with environmental regulation and do so irrespective of the likelihood of detection or sanction, in contrast to an earlier generation, which frequently sought to evade it. Increasingly, such corporations are also developing environmental strategies that incorporate pollution prevention, internal compliance auditing and compliance assurance programmes. Some are also actively seeking out win-win outcomes.

14. See also Kagan, Gunningham and Thornton (2003).

15. Regulatory regimes do not evolve in isolation. On the contrary, jurisdictions commonly model their legislation on that of other jurisdictions. Indeed, Braithwaite and Drahos (2000: 291), in their study of global business regulation, found that "in all the countries we visited for this research, substantial parts of national environment protection laws were modelled from other nation's laws". And Harrison (2002), in a comparison of environmental standards setting in the United States, Canada and Sweden notes that "There has been considerable convergence in both regulatory standards and industry performance". Of course, there is often a time lag between one jurisdiction adopting a particular regulatory solution and it being taken up elsewhere, but in an industry like pulp and paper – with a high environmental profile, plus relatively standard processes of production and environmental technologies – it is hardly surprising that substantial inter-governmental modelling took place.

16. The academic literature on regulation draws a distinction between regulations that specify "performance standards" (e.g., maximum emissions for particular substances) and regulations that mandate the use of specific control technologies ("technology standards"). Michael Porter and Claas van der Linde (1995) have argued that performance standards can foster innovation because they free up an enterprise to respond to a regulator's requirement in the way it best thinks fit. In evidence, they cite the relative success of the Scandinavian and United States governments in achieving emissions reductions in the pulp and paper industry. The Scandinavian companies, under a performance based regime, "developed innovative pulping and bleaching technologies that not only met emission requirements but also lowered operating costs". American companies, in contrast, did not respond to regulation by innovating because the United States specification- or technology-based regulations did not permit companies to "discover how to solve their own problems" (Porter and van der Linde 1995: 129). However, in the Washington state permits we reviewed, we found that mills were not generally required to install particular technologies but were required to meet performance standards, although these in turn were based on certain model control technologies. This most often led to the installation of the model technology. In addition, where permits did require the installation of a specific technology, this requirement had usually been arrived at after negotiations between the regulator and regulatee, or only applied if certain conditions were met. Similarly, in all the jurisdictions in our study, pulp mills' environmental developments generally were driven by *performance* standards rather than by governmental mandates to use specific technologies. These findings are in keeping with a ten-country OECD study of the pulp and paper industry, which states: "The permitting processes followed impose release conditions, including limits. These are developed on the basis of existing technology capable of meeting the limits. Mills are permitted to choose what equipment to install to meet the limits. Flexibility is granted in

enabling them to do this in the most cost effective manner. Specific technologies are not mandated. In some cases, permit conditions include the installation of specified equipment. It is noted that this is attained through prior discussions between the permitter and permittee. The specification therefore reflects an agreement between the parties, and not the mandating of equipment" (OECD 2000: 15).

17. See for example, Clark (2001).
18. See further Gunningham and Sinclair (2002), chapter 8.
19. Economic stakeholders include shareholders, customers, clients, suppliers and institutional investors and lenders. Legal stakeholders include regulatory, judicial and legislative officials at all levels of government: municipal, state and federal. Social stakeholders include local community groups, national environmental groups and, on occasion, the general public.
20. For a discussion of the relationship of regulation and technology in a somewhat similar context see Ashford and Heaton (1983).
21. Sixty-three *Federal Register* 18535.
22. Note Porter and van der Linde's (1995) characterization of United States pulp and paper regulations in the 1970s, which they argue prevented American companies from realizing first mover advantages because it "ignored a critical principle of good environmental regulation: Create maximum opportunity for innovation by letting industries discover how to solve their own problems".
23. Finnish pulp mills have found that this dynamic incentive to reduce averages below limits in order to avoid accidental short-term exceedances has, however, been reduced by the fear expressed by many that discharges far below the permit limits are likely to result in tighter permits.
24. In an industry with as high an environmental profile as the pulp and paper industry, in which the processes of production are relatively standardized, substantial modelling apparently takes place. For example, a number of our respondents pointed to the close relationship between United States and Canadian environmental regulations particularly, but similar technology-related regulatory solutions could also be found in New Zealand and Australia. On the process of regulatory modelling generally, and its importance, see further Braithwaite and Drahos (2000), chapter 25.
25. For example, some facilities would report pollutant discharges in efficiency units (pounds per unit of production), others in concentration units (pounds of pollutant per litre of water) and others in impact units (pounds per day). However, the data required to make the conversions (production per day, discharge volume per day) between these units was often not provided. Even when production figures were given, frequent changes were made as to how production levels were reported, so that consistency over time and between facilities was difficult to maintain. Sometimes, although the same parameter was being monitored, the laboratory analytic techniques differed. Or different parameters were used to try and measure a similar environmental problem (chlorine discharges vs absorbable organic halides vs dioxin). While most jurisdictions required that data be collected relatively frequently, there was no consistency as to how often it was reported. Facilities were sometimes required to take daily measurements but only report annual averages. Data was also difficult to obtain, sometimes requiring a visit to the local regulatory agency and copying down the numbers on the company's report. Electronic data was available in some jurisdictions, but the data quality was not always as good as one would wish. For example, the United States EPA's Permit Compliance System contains discharge monitoring report data for all permitted facilities in their country. However, a value of 4.3 1,000 lbs/day is often entered into the database as 4.3 lbs/day instead of 4,300 lbs/day. Automated data quality routines ought to be able to identify such problems.
26. For a similar conclusion see Opschoor and Turner (1994).

REFERENCES

Afsah, Shakeb and Jeffrey A. Vincent (1997) Putting Pressure on Polluters: Indonesia's PROPER Programme, Harvard Institute for International Development, available from http://www.hiid.harvard.edu/pub).

Ashford, Nicholas A. and George R. Heaton (1983) "Regulation and technological innovation in the chemical industry", Law and Contemporary Problems 46(3): 109–157.

Beardsley, Daniel (1996) Incentives for Environmental Improvement: An Assessment of Selected Innovative Programs in the States and Europe, Washington, D.C.: Global Environmental Management Initiative.

Borkey, Peter and François Leveque (1998) "Voluntary Approaches for Environmental Protection in the European Union", OECD Working Paper.

Braithwaite, John and Peter Drahos (2000) Global Business Regulation, Cambridge: Cambridge University Press.

Carson, W. G., W. B. Creighton, C. Hennenberg and R. Johnstone (1989) "Victorian Occupational Health and Safety: An assessment of law in transition", La Trobe/Melbourne Occupational Health and Safety Project, Victoria, Australia: La Trobe University, Department of Legal Studies.

Clarke, D. P. (2001) "EPA in the Information Age", Environmental Forum 18(3): 22–34.

Coglianese, Cary and Jennifer Nash (2001) "Environmental Management Systems and the New Policy Agenda," in Cary Coglianese and Jennifer Nash, eds., Regulating from the Inside: Can Environmental Management Systems Achieve Policy Goals?, Washington, D.C.: Resources for the Future.

Covery, F. and François Leveque (2001) "Applying Voluntary Approaches: Some Insights from Research", CAVA (Concerned Action on Voluntary Approaches), International Policy Workshop on the Use of Voluntary Approaches, Brussels, 1 February 2001.

Davies, Terry and Jan Mazurek (1996) "Industry Incentives for Environmental Improvement: Evaluation of U.S. Federal Initiatives", Washington, D.C.: Global Environment Management Initiative.

Diamond, Larry (1994) "Toward Democratic Consolidation", Journal of Democracy 5: 4–17.

Eckersley, Robyn (1995) Markets, the State and the Environment, Melbourne, Australia: Macmillan Press.

Fuchs, Doris A. and Daniel A. Mazmanian (1998) "The Greening of Industry: Needs of the Field", Business Strategy and the Environment 7(4): 193–203.

Gereffi, Gary, J. Humphrey and T. Sturgeon (2001) "Introduction: Globalisation, Value Chains and Development", IDS Bulletin 32(3): 1–9.

Gunningham, Neil and Peter Grabosky (1998) Smart Regulation: Designing Environmental Policy, Oxford: Oxford University Press.

Gunningham, Neil and Richard Johnstone (1999) Regulating Workplace Safety, Oxford: Oxford University Press.

Gunningham, Neil, Robert Kagan and Dorothy Thornton (2003) Shades of Green: Business, Regulation and Environment, San Francisco: Stanford University Press.

Gunningham, Neil and Darren Sinclair (2004) "Curbing Non-Point Source Pollution: Lessons from the Swan-Canning", Environmental and Planning Law Journal 21: 181–199.

Harrison, Kathryn (2001) "Voluntarism and Environmental Governance", in E. Parson, ed., Governing the Environment, Toronto: University of Toronto Press.

——— (2002) "Ideas and Environmental Standard Setting: Environmental Regulation of the Pulp and Paper Industry in Canada, the United States, and Sweden", Governance 15: 65–96.

Hoffman, Andrew J. (1997) From Heresy to Dogma: An Institutional History of Corporate Environmentalism, San Francisco: New Lexington Press.

Hopkins, Andrew (1994) "Compliance With What? The fundamental regulatory question", British Journal of Criminology 34(4): 431–443.

Kagan, Robert, Neil Gunningham and Dorothy Thornton (2003) "Explaining Corporate Environmental Performance: How Does Regulation Matter?" Law and Society Review 37.

Kagan, Robert A. and John T. Sholz (1984) "The Criminology of the Corporation and Regulatory Enforcement Styles", in Keith Hawkins and John Thomas, eds., Enforcing Regulation, Boston, Mass.: Kluwer-Nijhoff.

Knight, Alan (1994) "International Standards for Environmental Management" 17(3), UNEP: Industry and Environment.

National Research Council (NRC) (1997) Fostering Industry-Initiated Environmental Protection Efforts, Washington, D.C.: National Academy Press.

Organization of Economic Cooperation and Development (OECD) (1994) "Meeting on Alternatives to Traditional Regulation", Paris: OECD.

——— (1999) Voluntary Approaches for Environmental Policy: An Assessment, Paris: OECD.

——— (2000a) "Reducing the Risk of Policy Failure: Challenges for Regulatory Compliance", OECD/PUMA Working Paper 77, Paris: OECD.

——— (2000b) "Private Initiatives for Corporate Responsibility: An Analysis", DAFFE/IME 21, Paris: OECD.

Opschoor, J. B. and R. K. Turner, eds. (1994) Economic Incentives and Environmental Policies: Principles and Practice, Dordrecht, the Netherlands: Kluwer Academic Publishers.

Porter, Michael E. and Claas van der Linde (1995) "Green and Competitive: Ending the Stalemate", Harvard Business Review, September–October: 120–134.

Prakash, Aseem (2000) Greening the Firm: The Politics of Corporate Environmentalism, Cambridge: Cambridge University Press.

Priest, Margot (1997) "The Privatization of Regulation: Five Models of Self-Regulation", Ottawa Law Review 29(2).

Rees, Joseph V. (1994) Hostages of Each Other: The transformation of nuclear safety since Three Mile Island, Chicago: University of Chicago Press.

——— (1997) "The Development of Communitarian Regulation in the Chemical Industry", Law and Policy 19(4).

Rehbinder, Eckhard (1993) "Environmental Regulation Through Fiscal and Economic Incentives in a Federalist System", Ecology Law Quarterly 20: 57–83.

Rhone, Gregory T. (1996) Canadian Standards Association Sustainable Forest Management Certification System, Ottawa: Industry Canada.

Sabel, Charles, Archon Fung and Bradley Karkkainen (2000) Beyond Backyard Environmentalism, Boston, Mass.: Beacon Press.

Smart, Bruce (1992) Beyond Compliance – A New Industry View of the Environment, Washington, D.C.: World Resources Institute.

Smith, Maureen (1997) The US Paper Industry and Sustainable Production, Cambridge, Mass.: MIT Press.

Webb, Kernaghan and Andrew Morrison (1996) "The Legal Aspects of Voluntary Codes", a draft paper presented to the Voluntary Codes Symposium, Office of Consumer Affairs, Industry Canada and Regulatory Affairs, Treasury Board, Ottawa.

9

Transitions and institutional change: The case of the Dutch waste subsystem

Saeed Parto, Derk Loorbach, Ad Lansink and René Kemp

About 150 years ago recycling was common practice in the Netherlands. Individual entrepreneurs collected such items as glass, metals, old fabrics and organic waste and sold them on for secondary use. The metals and fabrics were reused and the organic waste served as fertilizer for the land or feed for farm stock. This relatively effective and stable entrepreneurial system came under increasing pressure from the end of the nineteenth century by intensive industrialization, the subsequent economic boom, population increase and urbanization. A centralized, government-controlled system based on collection, incineration and landfilling was developed to deal with increasing amounts of waste and to minimize the health effects of untreated waste in urban centres. Until the late 1950s waste was perceived as something to get rid of and keep out of sight. This perception changed in the 1960s.

The next 40 years saw the development of a very differentiated waste-handling system in the Netherlands. Through regulation and later privatization, the Dutch government stimulated a series of developments that led to the emergence of an integrated waste subsystem.[1] Understanding the underlying reasons for these developments offers important insights for policymakers and political economists concerned with the interplay between societal change, policy development, innovation and the emergence of environmental technologies. For example, it is likely that because of the speed at which the industrial production system operated, the large amounts of waste generated could not be effectively managed at the desired speed by the individual entrepreneurs and the waste management technologies in use at the time. This may have led the industrial waste generators to dispose of wastes through the quickest means possible, i.e., by dumping or landfilling, and depriving the private entrepreneurs of the supply of wastes. At the same time, because of rising consumption levels the amounts of residential or post-consumer waste increased exponentially.

The rise in waste volumes forced the government to act and develop a waste-handling arena (subsystem), complete with its infrastructure, rules and regulations, and technologies. It is reasonable to suggest that since its formation the waste subsystem has undergone an evolutionary process characterized by significant ebbs and flows as a result of a coming together of a host of exogenous and endogenous factors. These factors include increased environmental awareness, particularly since the late 1960s and early 1970s, educational programmes, scientific discoveries and innovations within and outside the subsystem and insights into the relation between waste and health. Today around 90% of the total waste generated in the Netherlands is managed through recycling, reuse and incineration.

We need more than intuition along the above lines to provide an in-depth account of the evolution of the Dutch waste subsystem, however. To investigate the link between environmental regulation and environmental innovation we need to understand how the waste subsystem has evolved over time and as a result of what set of intervening factors. From a policymaking perspective we need to determine the conditions that are likely to induce significant change and lead to relative stability within the subsystem. Numerous studies of innovation dynamics have underlined the importance of the institutional context (Cooke and Morgan 1998; Gertler and Wolfe 2002; Lundvall et al. 2002; Nelson 1995). There remains, however, a significant gap between the extensive literature on institutions and the equally impressive body of literature on innovation systems. A major difficulty in bridging this gap arises from the multiplicity of meanings and interpretations associated with such phrases as "institution" (Neale 1987; Nelson and Sampat 2001), evolutionary change and innovation. There are in addition numerous systems, scales and levels at or through which institutions, innovation and evolutionary change may be studied. Innovation at the firm, sector, cluster or national scale occurs in a co-evolving institutional context – the institutional context shapes the innovation path and is in turn transformed by it. Thus from a policy perspective, analyses of transitions in the Dutch waste subsystem need to be integrated with the institutional dynamics that collectively facilitate or curtail advancement toward a different stable state.

To understand why such significant changes have occurred within the Dutch subsystem, we need to identify the institutions, significant events (including innovations), and the processes of institutionalization set in motion by these events. In this chapter our main goal is to establish that the Dutch waste subsystem has been undergoing transitions since before 1900 and that each transition may be identified through a set of institutions operating at and through different levels of interrelation, scales of governance and systems. Further, we argue that an institutionalization process set in motion by the occurrence of a specific event or a series of interconnected events preceded the emergence of each of these institutions. Adopting the concept of transitions (see Kemp, this volume) and drawing on the institutionalist literature, we examine the evolution of the Dutch waste subsystem to underline the institutional dynamics of environmental innovation. We pay particular attention to the regulatory aspects of this evolution. We view the transformation of the waste subsystem much in the same way as Kingdon (1984) viewed the structural change in the aviation industry in the United States: we thus set out to identify problems, policies and politics to explain when, how and why innovations[2] have occurred in the Dutch waste subsystem over time.[3]

Transitions in the Dutch waste subsystem

There appears to have been two transitions in the waste management subsystem since around 1900. The first transition was signalled with the government assuming direct control of municipal waste collection and disposal, effecting a move from unregulated handling of waste to centralized systems of disposal. The stabilization period for the first transition appears to have been between the 1920s and the 1960s. The second transition began in the 1970s and was to a large extent related to widespread concerns about the state of the environment.

The second transition, from centralized disposal to management of waste, was characterized by significant changes in production and consumption patterns. The stabilization period for transition two seems to have commenced in the late 1970s and ended by the mid 1990s. It may be suggested that a third transition, or a period of turbulence preceding a new transition, may have started in the late 1990s. The basis for this suggestion includes new European Union directives on waste management, a significant drop in the total volume of non-separated household waste from the peak 1995 level, liberalization of waste markets and the "entrepreneurial" initiative by some waste operators to take advantage of weakly regulated waste subsystems of the former Eastern bloc countries or the cheaper landfilling fees of other member states to export domestically generated waste.

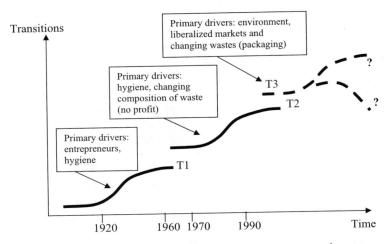

Figure 9.1 Transitions in the Dutch waste management subsystem

As we noted in the introduction to this chapter, recycling and reuse were common practice in the Netherlands prior to industrialization, and there existed a stable small-scale private sector in waste. Rapid industrialization and accompanying socio-economic changes associated with it undermined the stability of this sector. The growing population in the cities became more and more vulnerable to infection and disease due to the accumulation of untreated household and human waste. The first initiatives to systematically collect household waste, not surprisingly, were in the big cities where littering became a serious health and hygiene concern. The first permit to collect waste is said to have been issued in 1847 to a Dr. Sarphati who was authorized to collect household waste (Tellegen and Wolsink 1998). In addition, a new niche was emerging for innovation in the use of organic materials and human waste (feces) in fertilization processes. Recycling formally started in the Netherlands on 25 January 1920 with the establishment of the Algemeene Vereeniging voor de Lompen – en Metaalhandel (Federation of Lamp and Metal Handlers).

Transition 1: From unregulated handling to centralized systems of disposal

In the beginning of the twentieth century, a strong tendency toward living in urban areas necessitated the development of large-scale sewage systems and the installation of toilets in houses. The introduction of artificial fertilizer weakened the demand for organic fertilizer resulting in an enormous decrease in the use of organic (compost) waste. The collection of organic waste for economic gain became progressively less attractive. In parallel, the process of economic growth and the manufacturing of more and more consumable products created new waste streams resulting in a substantial increase in the total amount of waste generated. A direct outcome of these developments was the withdrawal by private entrepreneurs from collecting waste. The government was compelled to become involved in the business of waste collection, treatment and disposal. It may be suggested that these developments collectively represent a transition from a diversified, decentralized market for waste to a more centralized and uniform public waste-collection system.

Disposal of waste through landfilling seems to have been the method of choice for the government in the early stages of the transition from private to public waste management. The location of landfill sites was as contentious then as it is now. In the beginning of the twentieth century there were protests by local residents against landfilling the Naardermeer near Amsterdam (Wolsink 1996). These protests led to the formation of the Vereniging tot Behoud van Natuurmonumenten (Society for the Preservation of Nature) in 1905 and the designation of the Naardermeer as the first nature reserve in the Netherlands.

The combination of a shortage of landfilling space and the social pressure to handle waste differently led to an increase in the waste incinerated and drew attention to developing new technologies for more efficient incineration methods. In 1912, the first incineration plant was opened in Rotterdam, while Leiden and Amsterdam followed in 1914 and 1918, respectively. The small incinerator built in the Hague in 1918 was unique in generating electricity, a significant innovation in waste management. The shortage of landfilling space in the immediate areas where the waste was being generated led to the emergence of transportation operators such as the Vuilafvoer Maatschappij (Waste-removal association, VAM) whose role was to transport household wastes to other areas for use as fertilizer or disposal. For example, the VAM transported household waste to the province of Drenthe, where it was used to fertilize the land.

Trends suggest that the stabilization period of transition one in waste management commenced in the early 1920s. The stability continued well into the 1960s and was characterized by the continued operation of the incineration plants built between 1912 and 1918. This period also witnessed a slow but steady increase in landfilling and innovation in landfilling practices such as capturing and flaring landfill gases. The situation thus seemed relatively stable and there appeared to be no rationale for changing course.

Transition 2: From centralized waste disposal to waste management

In the 1960s economic progress led to an enormous increase in general production and consumption and therefore in the production of waste. The increase in waste was caused by an increase in the use of plastics, most notably in packaging materials, and the production of disposable products. The new waste types were not suitable for composting and the dominant practice in "managing" them was landfilling. By the beginning of the 1970s the environmental impacts of landfilling had become a matter of public interest. This interest was compounded by widespread concern about the negative impacts of consumerism, reflected in the Club of Rome report in 1972 and the oil crisis in 1973. Combined with growing dissatisfaction with waste and wasteful consumption, concerns were raised about how waste was being managed. These concurrent developments appear to have determined the evolution trajectory of the waste subsystem over the next 30 years.

During this period one of the major challenges for government agencies dealing with waste was the shortage of landfilling space and scarcity of sites to build incineration plants. The mounting volumes of waste created a niche for private companies to transport large amounts of waste to Belgium where landfilling space was still plentiful, and public opinion about waste was significantly less negative relative to the Netherlands. At the same time, the Dutch government introduced regulation to reduce waste volumes and, based on analysing the waste composition, took innovative steps to eliminate or reduce the volume of certain waste streams. A key outcome of these developments was the Waste Substances Act (1977, Stb. 455) (Afvalstoffenwet) that defined the structure and the procedures for the management of waste in the production and composition of products, the use of packaging materials, treatment and disposal of waste and the separated-waste collection system. In general, the government in the 1970s tried to both limit the total amount of waste produced and take innovative steps to go beyond landfilling in the management of waste.

Numerous innovations in the production process to eliminate waste took place as direct consequences of the Waste Substances Act. In addition, the restriction placed by the act on certain waste types and materials provided an incentive for product innovation based on use of unrestricted materials – the act forced producers and consumers to consider a fuller life cycle for products. Notable innovations during this period included small-scale recycling of glass and fabrics as well as the reuse of materials through second-hand stores. In the meantime, the government continued to search for innovative ways to better manage waste. One such innovation was "Lansink's Ladder", a hierarchically ordered list of methods to manage waste from prevention to landfilling.[4] The ladder was inspired by Lansink's earlier knowledge of reversible and irreversible thermodynamics, and his experience of being a key participant in discussions on waste incineration. Lansink's Ladder coincided with and was bolstered by the European Commission's Directive on Waste in 1975.

The motion on Lansink's Ladder was tabled and passed in the parliament in 1979, to become official policy in 1981 and a law in the Environmental Management Act (1989, 1994). The hierarchy of waste management according to Lansink's Ladder went from prevention, through reuse (of products), recycling (of materials), incineration (with energy production) and landfilling as the last option. The need for the prevention of waste was considered to be necessary as well as obvious.

Arguably, the evolution of Lansink's Ladder is intimately related to the societal desire to deal with waste appropriately and to prevent adverse environmental impacts. Pressed by the government and societal demand, by the end of the 1970s waste handlers reluctantly but increasingly had accepted the separated-waste collection system. The uncertainties associated with developing standards for recycling or separated-waste collection systems significantly weakened the willingness of businesses and organizations to start participation in managing waste. Government forced the waste operators to take an active interest in developing or adopting new practices.

The initial reluctance to adopt the separated-waste system came from the municipal waste-collection services that literally had to change their routines, standard practices and some of their old structures. Other actors, including environmental non-governmental organizations (ENGOs) and private businesses, promoted and performed new activities such as the collection of paper, glass and other recyclable materials. The systematic collection of the bulk of recyclable waste and organic materials would become institutionalized by the 1990s. In addition to the primarily endogenous factors that shaped the evolution of the waste subsystem, there were also quite significant exogenous factors. During the early 1980s there were serious concerns about the devastating effects of acid rain and deforestation.

Also evident in the 1980s was a shift of focus from welfare to well-being issues, including a healthy environment. The concern about environmental well-being was in part fuelled by revelations that old landfill sites such as Vogelmeerpolder near Amsterdam, one near Lekkerkerk and numerous others elsewhere in the country were leaking, causing pollution and environmental damage. The pollution was in part a product of landfilling practices during transition one (from the early 1900s to the 1960s), though the main damage seems to have taken place between 1960 and 1970 when thousands of barrels of toxic waste were illegally dumped on former waste sites. New building plans revealed very high toxicity levels in Lekkerkerk and there were many protests against the public health effects of building residential housing on former landfill sites. The government was pressured to initiate programmes for clean up, pollution prevention, reuse and recycling to more effectively manage waste.

A major consequence of the developments in the 1980s was the rise in the appeal of Lansink's Ladder as a "cognitive institution" among policymakers: incineration was actively being promoted by government agencies as the preferred option over landfilling. This led to an increase of investments in incineration plants and related technologies throughout the 1980s. Also in this period, interregional and international transportation of waste increased, stimulated by profit-seeking entrepreneurs and a lack of domestic landfill capacity. This led to the first European regulation on hazardous waste transportation in 1984.

Nevertheless, the total volume of household waste continued to rise from over 3 million kilograms in 1971 to over 4 million kilograms in 1980. Despite all the recycling initiatives the total amount of waste steadily increased, from 4 million to over 4.5 million kilograms between 1980 and 1990. However, the rate of increase was half the rate of increase during the 1970s when it seemed that the volume of waste was closely aligned with consumption and production as measured by GDP. In the 1980s a decoupling seems to have occurred between waste generation rates and production and consumption rates (figure 9.2). Also, despite a

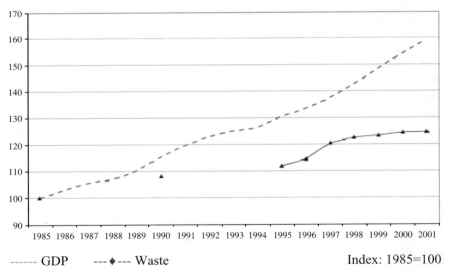

Figure 9.2 Decoupling of GDP and waste generation

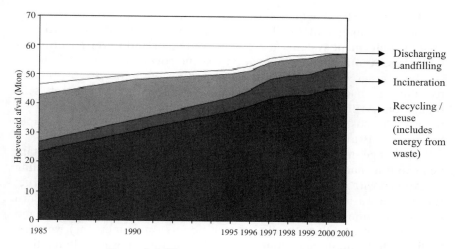

Figure 9.3 Waste generation levels since 1985

general increase in the total volume of waste generated, by 2001 the disposal of production wastes through effluent discharge had been effectively eliminated, the rate of growth for landfilled waste had slowed down, and incineration and reuse/recycling rates had increased (figure 9.3).

Regardless of the controversies surrounding the issue of incineration and the ever-increasing total volume of waste, figure 9.3 clearly demonstrates that policies to steer waste away from landfill sites have been highly successful. This outcome is in part attributable to a realization at the end of the 1980s that systematic management of waste required long-term, integrated and innovative policies. The change of perception among the policymakers underpins the development of NMP1, which formulated long-term (15-plus years) environmental targets. Other factors contributing to the institutionalization and the subsequent emergence of formal structures for waste management in the Netherlands include the dioxin scandal of Lickebaert, when dioxin residues (by-products of incineration) contaminated water sources resulting in serious illness among people and farm animals. By the 1980s the perception of incineration as an environmentally sound method of waste disposal had begun to change dramatically.

A closer look at these developments reveals intense innovative activity at all levels. For example, in response to the dioxin scandal the government devised ambitious plans, besides NMP1, on pollution prevention and reuse to minimize waste. "Producer responsibility" was introduced to minimize consumer-generated waste, and Afval Overleg Orgaan

(AOO: a specialized agency set up by VROM [the Ministry of Housing, Physical Planning and the Environment]) was founded to coordinate waste management systems and policies of higher and lower governmental bodies. Another policy innovation was the covenant on Verpakkingen (packaging agreement), which was devised by the national government to minimize packaging by suppliers of packaged goods through self-regulation. At the societal level, the Rio Summit in 1992 re-emphasized the need for sustainable development and thus provided additional impetus for the institutionalization of national environmental protection.

The change in perception of waste among individuals and the resultant behavioural change in terms of household waste separation and recycling co-evolved with changes in the practices of waste operators and the structure of the waste subsystem. By necessity, waste operators had to learn how to accommodate regulatory requirements regarding collection and handling of waste. Structurally, deposit depots (milieuperrons) were established to facilitate maximum citizen participation in waste elimination/ minimization efforts, and the so called VAM-vats (green boxes for organic waste) were distributed to every household. Regulatory and structural changes set in place in the 1980s were followed with further regulation and structural change in the early 1990s. Regulations on emissions and landfilling were accompanied by the establishment of new organizations such as VVAV (Vereniging van Afvalverwerkers, an organization of waste management companies, 1991) and the VAOP (Vereniging Aanbieders Oud Papier: organization of recyclable waste flows, 1992). A general law on environmental protection was passed in 1994 (wet milieubeheer). In this period the waste subsystem stabilized, with established institutions and a functioning market. Despite these developments, there are concerns that the new policy context of the European Union is likely to generate significant challenges for the Dutch waste subsystem.[5]

Transition 3: Managing waste for sustainability or a regress into past practices?

It is not yet clear whether the events since around 1995 will result in a more, or less, desirable transition in the waste subsystem. Less formal involvement by the national government in the waste subsystem could arguably undermine the significant progress made during the 1980s and 1990s. At the same time, given the learning that has occurred during the second transition, an argument could be made in favour of self-regulation, particularly in the private sector, in waste management. The basis for this argument is that waste management is now largely institutionalized within major corporations and numerous firms driven by new awareness of social obligations and cost savings.

The evolution of the Dutch waste subsystem can be described in terms of changes in the behaviour of agents and in the structure of the political economy of waste. One may also underline changes in perceptions of waste, emergence of mental models (cognitive institutions) and laws (regulative institutions) on how to deal with waste, changes in the behaviour of individuals and organizations to act more responsibly toward waste (behavioural and constitutive institutions, respectively), and the stratification of public and private actors through the formation of alliances and interest groups (associative institutions). Thus, researching transitions from an institutional perspective has to focus on discovering events, interrelations, phenomena or situations as they occur over time in a reasonably well-defined subsystem. In the next section we demonstrate how such a framework for analysing transitions may be applied.

Analysis: Institutions of the Dutch waste subsystem

Based on what has been described thus far, the evolution of the Dutch waste subsystem can be closely aligned with changes in the institutions that structure the subsystem. The grouping of institutions under behavioural, cognitive, associative, regulative and constitutive types (table 9.1) allows closer examination of how the subsystem has evolved over time. For example, Lansink's conceptualization in 1979 of a waste hierarchy first emerged as a mental model (a cognitive institution) in response to the problem of mounting volumes of waste coupled with a shortage of landfill space. An institutionalization process that followed had the following key characteristics: formal adoption through policy of the ladder, public information initiatives to increase awareness, financial incentives to encourage/coerce individuals and organizations to minimize waste generation, structural change to accommodate and treat separated wastes, and legislation to forbid irresponsible waste generation and management.

This process led to the transformation of the Lansink Memorandum into law in 1986 and to an elaborate business model (a regulative institution) widely adopted by industry in the 1980s. A similar point may be made about the European Eco-management and Audit Scheme (EMAS) and ISO 14001 environmental management system (cognitive institutions) which in time also became regulative institutions and widely adopted by private and public organizations (table 9.1).

Evidence of transitions can be found in the official government statistics, collected since 1985. It is important to note that until relatively recently official statistics were not collected for many of the subsystem's streams. Indeed, the policy to collect data may be viewed as an "event" that catalysed the institutionalization of data collection on waste. As

Table 9.1 Institutions of the Dutch waste management subsystem (1970–present)

Institution type	Example/catalytic event
Behavioural: Institutions as standardized (recognizable) social habits – manifested in activities of individuals and groups as reflections of social norms	Recycling and domestic and industrial waste separation by individuals or groups of individuals (1970s–present)
Cognitive: Institutions as mental models and constructs or definitions – manifested primarily in what society expects of individuals	Lansink's Memorandum (1972–79); liberalized markets (1980s); business models for environmental management, e.g., EMAS, ISO 14001, (late 1980s); formalized producer responsibility (1990s)
Associative: Institutions as mechanisms facilitating prescribed or privileged interaction among different private and public interests	Policy networks around air and water issues (1970s–present); citizens' and producers' networks to define waste management policy on packaging, collecting, separating, recycling, incineration and landfilling
Regulative: Institutions as prescriptions and proscriptions	Surface water and air pollution legislation (1970s); covenants (1980s, 1990s); Lansink's Ladder (1980s–present); incineration guidelines (1980s); environmental audits (1990s)
Constitutive: Institutions setting the bounds of social relations	Government environmental departments (1970s); organizational waste management divisions (1990s); NMP+ (1980s, 1990s, 2000); Liberalized waste markets (1990s); formalized producer responsibility (1999); National Waste Plan (2000)

Based on Parto (2005)

table 9.2 shows, in the 15 years between 1985 and 2000 an increase of 21.6% over the whole period can be noted. These increases correspond with increases in economic growth as measured by GDP and population.

Crucial to understanding why transitions occur is to identify the key institutions that come into existence, change in response to and/or reflect (and deflect) the impact of identifiable events such as landfill and energy shortages, groundwater contamination issues in the 1970s, significant changes in production and consumption patterns and the emergence of liberalized markets in the 1980s. These events, as well as others identified in table 9.1, have acted as triggers and/or catalysts for a series of innovations and institutionalization processes that have evolved over time into

Table 9.2   Increase in total waste produced, 1985–2000

Period	Increase (%)
1986–1990	7
1991–1995	3.6
1996–2000*	11
Total	21.6

Source: AOO, RIVM, CBS
*Total waste numbers in 2000 are comparable with those in 1999, 2001 and 2002

new structures that shape interrelations at different levels. To gain additional insight into the information provided through secondary data sources, interviews were held with key informants from the Dutch waste subsystem in late 2003 and early 2004, followed by a workshop in March 2004. The findings from the interviews and the workshop are reported in narrative form in the remainder of this section.

Innovation and institutional change in waste management

The waste subsystem's institutions have not all changed or changed equally. To illustrate, the official definition of waste (a cognitive institution) in the Netherlands has remained unchanged and simply describes waste as "that which is no longer wanted or needed". This is consistent with the definition provided in the 1975 EEC (European Economic Community) Directive on waste. However, the perception of waste has changed quite dramatically, resulting in the emergence of behavioural institutions at different levels of interrelation. The perception has changed from just "waste" being disposed of by individuals and organizations without much contemplation and handled primarily by municipalities, to an elaborate industrial sector that distinguishes between different waste streams and provides services and infrastructure to absorb the bulk (about 90%) of the generated waste. Almost instinctively, most individuals and organizations separate different types of waste. The internalization of formal procedures on waste disposal (a cognitive institution) has led to the emergence of routines (behavioural institutions) among individuals and organizations for handling waste. Another aspect of the changed perception is that waste management firms now view waste as a commodity as long as it can be reused, recycled, recovered or resold while many subscribers to Lansink's Ladder view waste as a potential energy source.

Regulations and formal guidelines have continually refined the typology of waste through successive prescriptions and proscriptions (regulative institutions) while new markets have emerged (constitutive institutions) in response to new regulations and guidelines on waste handling or innovations to extract further use from waste. Regulative and constitutive institutions have created new market niches and new needs that have in turn bolstered innovation within the subsystem. Also, there has been horizontal and vertical integration in the Dutch waste market in response to the restructuring of domestic and European markets (both constitutive institutions). There are now numerous multinational waste corporations that have taken over the previously Dutch-owned waste management firms, while some Dutch energy providers such as ESSENT have been taking over waste-to-energy operations (incinerators). A further reorganization of the market is likely because of a general move toward market liberalization within the EU. On the basis of the typology in table 9.1, we interpret the emergence of market liberalization as an idea (a cognitive institution) in the 1980s that acted as a catalyst to set in motion a process that led to a redefinition of the "bounds of social relations" in the market (constitutive institution) in the 1990s.

Institutional change in the Dutch waste subsystem led to a series of innovations including the introduction of the deposit system for product containers, post life-cycle disposal fees on appliances and vehicles, chain integration and design for disposal. The dioxin problems of the 1980s led to the emergence of a series of regulations which in turn catalysed the emergence of new technologies throughout the incineration process, from input separation and preparation techniques through to burning methods and the treatment of the outputs. The end results of these innovations were cleaner emissions from incineration and more effective fly ash collection and treatment systems. At the same time, technology was adopted from other sectors for waste treatment including the adaptation of pellet-making machines (used mainly in the production of animal feed) to produce pellets from plastic packaging materials. Some of the key informants interviewed expressed concerns about the "lock-in" effect of incinerators for requiring a steady or increasing supply of combustible wastes as fuel to generate energy, however.

When asked what had facilitated the transformation of the waste subsystem, the key informants identified a number of catalytic events (table 9.3). There appeared to be consensus among the key informants that there had been a major transformation in the waste subsystem and that a period of stability had set in. But there were also concerns about the liberalization of the waste market within the European Union and how it might destabilize the Dutch waste subsystem. For example,

Table 9.3 Dutch waste subsystem's catalytic events

Catalytic event	Endogenous	Exogenous
Landfill capacity shortages	✓	
Environmental problems (soil and groundwater contamination)	✓	
Increased environmental awareness	✓	✓
Public environmental awareness campaigns	✓	
Formalized environmental education in schools	✓	
Creation of VROM and AOO	✓	
Club of Rome Report		✓
1970s oil crisis		✓
Environmental regulations	✓	
Voluntary initiatives	✓	✓
Covenants	✓	
Financial incentives	✓	
EEC Directive on Waste (1975)		✓
Emergence and institutionalization of ENGOs	✓	
Availability of and access to information on environmental issues	✓	✓
Emergence of new technologies	✓	✓
Acceptance of key technologies such as incineration	✓	
Availability of suitable technologies in other sectors	✓	✓
Increased government funding for R&D on environmental issues	✓	

In the Netherlands things are contained and under control. But we need to raise the bar at the EU scale for waste management to the Dutch [high] standards. European Union policies need to be implemented and regulations properly and evenly enforced. The EU's packaging regulation leaves it to individual members to choose between regulation and covenant. This causes disparity in implementation and the playing field.[6]

Similarly,

The waste policy in the Netherlands is of quite high standards. Because of the wish by VROM to open the borders for waste, Dutch waste that could go to incinerators to generate energy is leaving the country to be landfilled somewhere else. Of course we want access to the European market but we don't want a dismantling of what has been built over so many years in the Netherlands. We have a level playing field. In the Netherlands we have a landfill ban on burnable waste and also we have the highest landfill tax in Europe (about eighty euros). When you open the borders then you see the movement by collectors who opt for the cheapest landfill tax possible, regardless of waste type or distance. In Germany there is no landfill tax. This threatens the structure of the waste system in the Netherlands. Somehow policy has to address this problem.[7]

And,

The liberalization of the market is very bad for the stability of waste management in the Netherlands. The controls are gradually being relaxed. With the single market in the European Union, transporters of waste will do whatever they want by looking for the cheapest way of getting rid of waste. There is definitely an advantage, in that markets for recycling, reuse and recovery are being expanded. But the point is [Dutch] regulation is being undermined.[8]

These comments seem consistent with our assessment of the current status of the Dutch waste subsystem as indicated in figure 9.1 (T3). That is, a period of instability which began to set in around 1995 is likely to continue and could be a new predevelopment-phase of the subsystem with the final outcome (next stable state) as yet undetermined. Given the unanimity of the comments on the current status and the main catalytic events responsible for the evolution of the subsystem, the key informants were asked "What issues or factors should be the focus of policy on waste?" This question generated a more differentiated set of views:

We need to change people's behaviour. We have to somehow reduce the amount people generally consume. We have to make households do more source separation. But this is very difficult. Waste in the Netherlands is a very prominent issue because of space. We can use this to our advantage by being more innovative in terms of policy, consuming habits and technological development.[9]

Or,

[We need to increase] public awareness on waste, especially with households. They consume the most.... We [should] make deals with industry on waste-to-energy co-arrangements. Industry is also the main source of our landfill waste [and] they are a fixed target. We [should] use economic instruments like landfill taxes and other incentives and disincentives, for example, one euro for a garbage bag. Waste management should be promoted as not only environmentally crucial but economically viable.... We should concentrate also on the supply side, like packaging, advertising.[10]

And,

We should anticipate and prevent the occurrence of chaos in the Dutch waste subsystem due to liberalization without control. All we need to do is to take a look at what happened to the railway network operations in England or look at our own experience with the liberalized energy market (2003) – nobody seems to want to invest in the sector anymore. We need a package of measures including financial incentives, regulations, covenants and market harmonization. Education is sufficient at the moment. We now need to apply these other measures.[11]

Moves toward more liberalized waste markets were not opposed by any of the key informants. However, as the last quote clearly illustrates, there are serious reservations about liberalization without constitutive institutions to set the "bounds of social relations" or regulative institutions to act as "prescriptions and proscriptions". Some, however, advocate controlled liberalization as a means to improve the performance of the subsystem:

> We have to watch out for the effects of the liberalized European Union market on the Dutch market since we don't know what the outcome will be. We should delegate more responsibility to the main actors like the private sector, the packaging industry and the car industry. We need to invest in education about the need to integrate waste by closing the loop. We should initiate more prevention drives.[12]

The key informants also unanimously agreed that the positive rate of increase in the total volume of waste could not be reduced to zero because it was driven by long-established and institutionalized consumption patterns. However, there were numerous ways of absorbing this waste by "using the tools we have imaginatively and thoughtfully" (key informant 6).

The modern Dutch waste subsystem is the product of numerous types of institution with varying degrees of importance and life span. If we assume that the gap between total waste generated and treated is indeed closing, we can conclude that the 1990s signify a period of stability in a long-term transition in the Dutch waste subsystem. This is evident in changed behaviour by individuals, organizations and large sections of the society. Change is also evident in the perception of waste by individual decision makers in private and public capacities. The change in the perception of waste is reflected in social and economic values, legislation, habits and the appearance of new institutional forms such as private and public lobby groups. Retrospectively, the period starting in the early 1970s and lasting to the early 1990s may be described as the combined "acceleration" and "take-off" stages as denoted in figure I.2. Arguably, the acceleration and take-off stages received a direct boost from the formal presentation of Lansink's Ladder (1979) to the policy makers. As the dates in table 9.1 show, this period also witnessed a proliferation of formal institutions. Today, around 90% of the total waste in the Netherlands is diverted from landfills through recycling, reuse and incineration.

Households and firms appear to have internalized certain behavioural traits at will, because of care for the environment, and/or by obligation because of an effective system of sanctions.

Conclusion

An examination of the Dutch waste subsystem since the late 1960s reveals that the significant events of the 1970s catalysed a series of institutionalization processes that significantly transformed the subsystem. The increase in the amounts of waste as well as the problems related to the disposal of waste led to regulatory and structural changes during the 1980s, especially the legal codification of Lansink's Ladder in the Environmental Management Act. This was followed by further regulation and structural change in the early 1990s. Regulations on emissions and land-filling were accompanied by the establishment of new organizations such as the VVAV, AOO and VAOP. Also, numerous regulations were devised ranging from general laws on environmental protection (wet milieubeheer, incorporating Chemical Wastes Act [1976] and the former Waste Substances Act [1977]) to the various Environmental Policy Plans (NMP). Despite these efforts it seems that although an increasingly larger part of the waste generated has been put to good use, the total amount of waste generated has steadily increased (figure 9.3).

The increasing volumes of waste have been attributed to the unsustainable production and consumption patterns that characterize all modern economies (Daly and Cobb 1989; Meadows et al. 1972) and the general growth of the population. In any case and as far as the policy and practice of waste management in the Netherlands are concerned, it is not at all clear how the current trajectory will evolve over the next few decades. The new institutional context created by the European Union brings new challenges and numerous opportunities for the waste subsystem in the Netherlands. The new context is increasingly multi-level in terms of public-private interrelations, multi-system in terms of the integrated social-economic-environmental policymaking frameworks, and multi-scale in terms of the governance of socioeconomic and environmental domains. The main challenge comes from pressures to rely on market forces to induce economic efficiency and long-term viability in waste management. The consequences of relinquishing government control could arguably undermine the significant progress made in the handling (though not elimination) of waste during the 1980s and 1990s. At the same time, given the learning that has occurred during the transitions identified in this paper, an argument could be made in favour of self-regulation, particularly in the private sector, in waste management.

Our intuition and the analysis of the empirical data in this paper suggest that there have, indeed, been significant changes amounting to at least two transitions in the Dutch waste subsystem. The analysis in this paper provides a first attempt at understanding the dynamics of these transitions through institutional change. In table 9.1 we illustrated that behavioural norms such as recycling have become instituted at the individual and organizational levels: a mental model such as recycling emerged and became widely routinized (behavioural institution) while another mental model, Lansink's Ladder, was adopted as the basis for policymaking to generate legislation, covenants and guidelines as regulative institutions. In addition, private and public networks became established as associative institutions through collaboration and mutual trust to assess and redesign the waste subsystem. Finally, government environmental departments and private sector waste management divisions were set up to become constitutive institutions setting the bounds for managing waste.

The evolution of the waste subsystem in the Netherlands makes a convincing case for vertical policy integration in bringing about societal change. The chapter on the Dutch waste subsystem is far from fully written however. The subsystem is likely to undergo further changes due to two relatively new (and potentially catalytic) events of "Europeanization" and market liberalization. Understanding the institutionalization processes that have been, and are likely to be, triggered by these two events is essential for deciding on future policymaking options in waste management.

Appendix

Chronology of major events in the Dutch waste management subsystem

1875: The general Nuisance Act (Hinderwet), originated from Napoleonic times. The intent was to control the danger, damage and nuisance caused by industry and increasingly also other installations (Lieffernik 1997: 211, cited in Haverland 1999: 105).

1975–1977: The Waste Substances Act (Afvalstoffenwet, Stb. 455), dealing mainly with municipal waste and underlining the responsibilities of the national, provincial and municipal levels of government. Under this act:

1. Municipalities specify the frequency of household waste collection (at least once a week);

2. Provinces are responsible for granting permits for landfills, waste in- cinerators and other waste processing facilities; generating statistics on generated waste and methods of processing; and drawing up waste plans, to be revised every five years; and,

3. National government oversees the implementation of the act.

1979–1985: Coming to force of all provisions of the Waste Substances Act, particularly Article 27 to enact regulations to reduce waste volumes.

1979: The Lansink Memorandum (Motie Lansink): The Memorandum proposed the "waste hierarchy" consisting of the following options: (1) prevention, (2) product recycling (reuse), (3) material recycling, (4) incineration with energy recovery, (5) incineration and (6) landfill/ controlled dumping.

1982: The environmental division of the Ministry of Public Health and Environmental Hygiene was incorporated into the newly established Ministry of Housing, Physical Planning and the Environment (VROM).

1983: Environmental Policy Integration Plan was issued. The plan inte- grated environmental problems across air, water and soil media.

1988: The Memorandum on the Prevention and Recycling of Waste Ma- terials: This Memorandum was prepared by VROM officials in consulta- tion with the experts from RIVM (*Rijksinstituut voor Volksgezondheld en Milieu* – National Institute for Public Health and the Environment) and issued by the government in reaction to a critical report by the Dutch En- vironmental Advisory Board (CMRH) and the subsequent discussions with parliamentary committees. The memorandum was one of the first such documents to promote the "closure of material cycles" as a means of preventing pollution and the generation of waste. This approach marked a new phase in waste management in the Netherlands. The mem- orandum also adopted the waste hierarchy as developed in the previous Lansink Memorandum of 1979. The targets were presented as govern- ment preferences, non-binding and intended for guiding consultations on waste reduction targets by the target groups. These consultations, re- ferred to as "strategic discussions", were to set specific targets and artic- ulate implementation plans to meet them. The "indicative" targets set by the government included waste reduction, reuse, recycling, incineration and disposal.

According to Koppen (1994, cited in Haverland 1999: 113), the Memo- randum on the Prevention of Waste Materials formalized the informal process through which waste had been managed in practice in the Neth- erlands. The government used the term "strategic discussion" to stan- dardize and formally adopt the negotiation procedures that had devel- oped during the consultations of the target groups. Strategic discussion became the official procedure for government to regulate waste manage- ment and formed the foundation for the various covenants that emerged in later years. The negotiation procedures that defined strategic discussions were also consistent with the Dutch tradition of consultation, proportional representation and consensus building. In waste management the intent appears to have been one of emphasizing partnerships so as to internalize "the problem".

1989: National Environmental Policy (Kiezen of Verliezen). The NMP took a "management approach" to environmental problems and identified waste disposal as one of eight environmental areas of concern. Targets were defined for waste processing, waste prevention, reuse and recycling programmes. Waste streams were associated with target groups whose activities directly affected the generation of particular wastes. The target groups included "industry" and "consumers and retail trade".

1994: Environmental Management Act (incorporating the Chemical Wastes Act and the Waste Substances Act).

Packaging waste was identified in the act as a primary area of concern. Elimination of certain packaging materials, separate collection of certain waste types, and the use of container deposits were legislated as means to minimize the amount of packaging waste generated (Koppen 1994: 153, cited in Haverland 1999: 105).

Concurrent with these developments, the national government also sought to achieve voluntary agreements with the private sector on matters of toxic waste elimination and solid waste reduction. "Institutional" barriers in the early stages of implementation included:

1. End-of-pipe orientation of available solutions;

2. Lack of experience of personnel in charge of policy implementation, e.g., issuing advice, licenses and permits to waste management operators;

3. Lack of cooperation between policy implementers and established civil servants;

4. Lack of appropriate resources, e.g., funding, personnel, to implement policy;

5. Disagreement by the sub-national policy implementers with the authoritarian approach of VoMill, which was also deemed to have more sympathy with the interests of those to be controlled than with the civil servants in the Hague;

6. Insufficiently developed or instituted accountability mechanisms at all levels; and,

7. Because of the above, implementers often tended to react rather than pursue an active and systematic approach to issuing permits/licenses

The first phase of the Dutch packaging waste policy started in the early 1970s and ended in the mid 1980s. During this phase the government proceeded in an ad hoc manner to deal with the packaging waste problem. During the same period there were also signs of commitment to waste reduction by the packaging chain members, in part in reaction to the pressure from environmental non-governmental organizations involved in awareness raising of consumers through boycotts and information campaigns. In 1973 a group of members of parliament put forward a proposal for legislation on packaging waste, which, while not successful, pointed to the fact that the issue of packaging waste had reach the realm of national politics.

The response by a group of packaging chain members was to establish the Foundation of Packaging and the Environment (Stichting Verpakking and Milieu – SVM) in 1971. The group members represented a broad spectrum of the packaging chain from manufacturers of packaging materials to retailers (Haverland 1999: 106). By the early 1990s, SVM represented some 60 to 80% of the packaging chain members (Haverland 1999: 107). It has been suggested that SVM's primary concern was to ensure that the demands by the public and the environmentalists did not undermine the interests of the packaging chain members (Peterse 1992: 202, cited in Haverland 1999: 107). Despite its reactive origins, the SVM evolved into a meditative body between the government, environmental groups and packaging-sector interests. The SVM actively sought to pursue and assist in the implementation of its environmental/packaging policies by the affiliates (Peterse 1992: 202–4, cited in Haverland 1999: 107).

A shift of paradigm from end-of-pipe to "waste hierarchy" is said to have occurred in 1979, marked by the issuance of the Lansink Memorandum (Motie Lansink). The waste hierarchy consists of the following options: (1) prevention, (2) product recycling (reuse), (3) material recycling, (4) incineration with energy recovery, (5) incineration and (6) landfill/ controlled dumping. The Lansink Memorandum on waste informed the 1989 National Environmental Policy Plan (NMP) and the waste chapter in the 1994 Environmental Management Act (Wet Milieubeheer WM 1994; Schuddeboom 1994: 100, cited in Haverland 1999). The memorandum promoted prevention of waste and stimulation of reuse. Since reuse would reduce the demand for primary packaging materials, and therefore adversely affect the manufacturers of primary packaging, the SVM mediated for an agreement among the sub-system actors on the recycled contents of packaging materials (Peterse 1992: 203, cited in Haverland 1999: 107).

1985: Joint Declaration and Code of Conduct on Drink Containers: The declaration anticipated the European Directive on liquid containers that came into effect in the same year and was to be implemented by 1987. The declaration and the directive shared the premise that implementation was to be based on voluntary agreements. The declaration was signed by VROM (VoMill's successor), the Ministry of Agriculture (LNV), the Ministry of Economic Affairs (EZ), statutory trade associations, SVM and the Foundation of Food Retailers (Stichting Centraal

Bureau Levensmiddelenhandel, SCBL) (Klok 1989: 170, cited in Haverland 1999: 108). The declaration did not reflect or incorporate the wishes of VROM that had argued for a return system and was thus biased toward the interests of the packaging industry.

1987: Code of Conduct on PET bottles: The Code of Conduct was signed in 1987 by VROM, LNV, EZ, the soft drinks trade association and SCBL to implement a deposit-on-return system. Fierce boycotting campaigns by environmentalists and producers of PET preceded the signing of the Code of Conduct. The resultant 10-cent deposit system was seen as too low by VROM, environmentalists and the government to generate commitment by consumers and retailers to recycling PET bottles. The lack of commitment was coupled with structural problems that affected the market for recycled PET. It may be argued that consumer and government pressure to limit the volume of PET waste and further advances in the technology of PET production led to the emergence of refillable PET bottles with a deposit of one guilder. The production of non-reusable PET bottles was gradually but completely phased out (Ingram 1997: 10 and Schuddeboom 1994: 106, cited in Haverland 1999: 110).

The Chernobyl disaster (1986) and the publication of *Our Common Future* (World Commission on Environment and Development, 1987) pushed concern for the environment to the top of political agenda in most OECD countries. The impacts of this renewed focus on the environment are said to have been felt more in the Netherlands, possibly for the same reasons as in the 1960s and 1970s. (These reasons included the inclusive Dutch political system of representation, small geographical size coupled with high population density and chronic environmental issues such as soil contamination). Forty-five per cent of the electorate viewed the environment as the most important issue, while 20% of Dutch adults were members or registered supporters of an environmental organization compared to Britain's 11% and a European average of 4.2%.

The emergence of "sustainable development" as an all-encompassing concept paved the way for a political convergence characterized by markedly less radical agendas of environmental groups, the popularization of "the environment" among ordinary citizens, increased membership of environmental organizations, and professionalization and institutionalization of environmental groups. A number of government and non-government committees included environmentalists as participating members of their proceedings (Bressers and Plettenburg 1997: 118, cited in Haverland 1999: 110). The publication of *Zorgen voor Morgen* in 1988 by RIVM was a turning point in the government's approach to environmental protection. The report expressed alarming concern about the state of the environment in the Netherlands, emphasized the importance of attending to the sources of pollution, and viewed environmental protection as a longer-term project requiring policies spanning decades rather than years. In terms of waste generation, the report identified industry and consumers as the key sources of the problem.

In 1987, the National Environmental Advisory Board urged government and industry to pay attention to waste prevention. The board attributed the urgency to the inherent limits imposed by the Netherlands' small size, geography and dense population. The potentially adverse implications of waste generation for societal well-being within these confines were used by the board to argue for a substantial decrease in waste generation. In 1988, after a lengthy meeting of the environmental committee of the Dutch parliament, the minister promised to formulate concrete plans for waste reduction.

Notes

1. "Subsystem" is used here to delimit a composite domain or arena with identifiable system components, e.g., social, economic, ecological, political and so forth. A subsystem is by definition a part of an interconnected, interdependent whole.
2. In our analysis we adopt a broad view of innovation to include novelty in policy-making approaches and the emergence of "mental constructs" such as recycling and waste separation.
3. See the appendix for a chronology of major events of the Dutch waste subsystem.
4. The hierarchy went from prevention, through reuse (of products), recycling (of materials) and incineration (with energy production), to landfilling as the last option.
5. This general concern is discussed further later in this paper.
6. Key informant 1 (private sector).
7. Key informant 2 (private sector association).
8. Key informant 5 (environmental NGO).
9. Key informant 3 (journalist – specialized trade magazine).
10. Key informant 4 (governmental organization).
11. Key informant 5 (environmental NGO).
12. Key informant 6 (government expert).

REFERENCES

Cooke, P. and K. Morgan (1998) The Associational Economy, New York: Oxford University Press.

Daly, H. E. and J. B. Cobb (1989) For the Common Good: Redirecting the Economy Toward Community, the Environment, and a Sustainable Future, Boston, Mass.: Beacon Press.

Gertler, M. S. and D. A. Wolfe, eds. (2002) Innovation and Social Learning: Institutional Adaptation in an Era of Technological Change, Basingstoke, England: Macmillan/Palgrave.

Haverland, M. (1999) National Autonomy, European Integration and the Politics of Packaging Waste, Amsterdam, Netherlands: Thelathesis.

Kingdon, J. (1984 [1995]) Agendas, Alternatives, and Public Policies, Boston, Mass.: Little, Brown.

Lundvall, B.-Å., Bjorn Johnson, Esben Sloth Andersen and Bent Dalum (2002) "National systems of production, innovation and competence building", Research Policy 31(2): 213–231.

Meadows, Donella H., Dennis L. Meadows, Jorgen Randers and William W. Behrens (1972) The Limits to Growth, New York: Universe Books.

Neale, W. C. (1987) "Institutions", Journal of Economic Issues 21(3): 1177–1206.

Nelson, R. R. (1995) "Co-evolution of Industry Structure, Technology and Supporting Institutions, and the Making of Comparative Advantage", International Journal of the Economics of Business 2(2): 171–84.

Nelson, R. R. and B. N. Sampat (2001) "Making Sense of Institutions as a Factor Shaping Economic Performance", Journal of Economic Behavior and Organization 44: 31–54.

Parto, S. (2005) "Economic Activity and Institutions: Taking Stock", Journal of Economic Issues 39(1): 21–52.

Tellegen, Egbert and Maarten Wolsink (1998) Society and its Environment: An Introduction, Reading, England: Gordon and Breach Science Publishers.

Wolsink, M. (1996) "Dutch Wind Power Policy", Energy Policy 24: 12, 1079–1088.

10

Integrating environmental and innovation policies

René Kemp

This chapter briefly examines the effects of innovation policies in bringing forth environmental innovations – innovations offering environmental gains relative to existing technologies.[1] It is found that innovation policy is insufficiently oriented toward green system innovations and badly coordinated with other areas of policy, especially environmental policy. Suggestions are given for integrating environment and innovation policies. One such suggestion is the use of programmes for system innovations offering sustainability benefits. Such programmes should be selected and implemented as part of long-term transition policies that are concerned with redirecting the trajectories of development. A model of transition management is outlined in the paper and applied to mobility. In the model, alternative trajectories are explored in a forward-looking yet adaptive manner. The model has been developed by the author together with Jan Rotmans and has been adopted by the Dutch government as a steering model for working toward sustainable energy, mobility and agriculture.

The structure of the chapter is as follows. The section immediately following this discusses the environmental effects of innovation policies and outlines a new perspective on environmental innovation policy. This is followed by a discussion centring on the innovation effects of environmental policy and makes a plea for the combination of policy instruments and programmes for system innovation. A description of the model for transition management, and the applications for transition management to sustainable mobility appear ahead of the summary and conclusions.

258

Environmental effects of innovation policies

All OECD countries have an innovation policy, superseding the science and research policies of the past. Such policies are aimed at helping private companies innovate and orient toward economic, not environmental, goals. But new technology can also bring environmental gains and thus may alleviate the trade-offs between environmental well-being and environmental quality (Jaffe and Stavins 1990: 1). Environmental benefits are often a gratis effect of new technology. Advanced technologies tend to be more resource-efficient while generic technologies in information and communication may be utilized to serve environmental purposes. For example, sensors aid waste management and help to limit pollution by providing crucial process information to operators. The environmental benefits from innovations may be accidental, in the sense that the original research leading to these innovations was not environmentally motivated or because the innovations are inherently more environmentally benign.[2]

The sensor example demonstrates that environmental technologies should not be privileged as the source for achieving environmental gains (Williams and Markusson 2002). There are other sources for obtaining environmental improvement as well, such as new processes that are more resource-efficient, a shift toward cleaner products and behavioural change. This suggests that it is better to talk about "innovation for the environment" which includes innovations that are not environmentally motivated (Berkhout 2002). There is also a second reason for not privileging environmental technologies, which is that they may lead to a transfer of environmental problems or add to the costs of the company. This holds true for end-of-pipe technologies that cause a waste problem unless the captured pollution and treated emissions are reused. Whether the captured or treated pollution is utilized depends on the existence of markets for waste and the economics of reuse vis-à-vis the costs of waste disposal. Fly ash is used in cement production and sewage sludge from communal wastewater treatment plants is burned in cement kilns.

Environmental technology can be supported through special innovation programmes. Examples are the Dutch "Milieu en Technologie" programme and the German BMBF research programme for environmental research and environmental technology. In the German programme a total of 1,402 projects were supported, receiving €646 million (Angerer 2002). The funds were distributed among various environmental fields. Most of the projects consisted of treatment technology, or cleaning technology, keeping in with the past orientation of environmental policy toward end-of-pipe solutions. Forty per cent of the projects were oriented to water pollution, 33% to waste management, 6% to air pollution and

15% to clean technologies and environmentally sound products (Angerer 2002). The share of 15% for clean technologies and environmentally sound products, in which pollution is prevented rather than dealt with, is very low. The lion's share of the money went to cleaning technologies.

From a policy evaluation perspective, it is important to establish the extent to which the two programmes encouraged firms to carry out research that would not have otherwise been undertaken. It is also important to ascertain whether the affected firms were encouraged to undertake environmental technology projects earlier or in a more elaborate way. These issues were investigated through an evaluation by ISI (Fraunhofer-Institut für Systemtechnik und Innovationsforschung), the results of which are described in Angerer et al. (1997). The results were quite positive. Thirty-six per cent of the projects would not have succeeded without this support and 38% of the projects were carried out with greater scope than initially planned. Only 5% of the projects were carried out in the same way as initially planned, despite the availability of additional funds, reflecting a free rider effect. However, the evaluators noted that the free rider effect was low compared to other programmes. The high behavioural influence (additionality) of the German programme is probably due to the fact that the subsidy was quite high (51% on average). A second explanation might be that many of the projects were end-of-pipe solutions for which the incentives for innovation were less favourable than for normal innovations.[3]

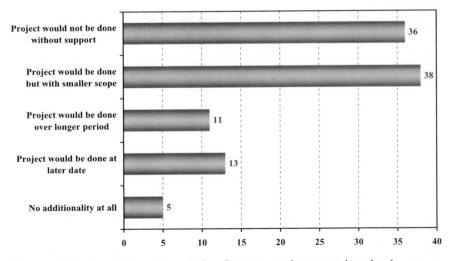

Figure 10.1 The additionality of the German environmental technology programme between 1980 and 1992

Additionality is one criterion to evaluate programmes. Another criterion is whether the innovations are used and the magnitude of the environmental benefit connected with their use. There is no information on the environmental impact and actual use of the innovations supported by the German programme, but the evaluation study by ISI found that 16% of the projects had a decisive influence on the design or implementation of environmental regulation. A further 20% were supportive but not decisive to policy changes (Angerer 2002).

The German BMBF programme was more successful than the Dutch Sustainable Technology Development Programme (DTO), an interdepartmental research programme for sustainable technologies that ran from 1993–1997. The additionality of DTO was very high but neither policymakers nor industry utilized the results. The goal of the programme was to identify and work toward technology options offering a factor 20 improvement in environmental efficiency while satisfying human needs in terms of nutrition, transport, housing and water supply and protection. Industry was an important actor in the programme. In the DTO programme, industrial opinion leaders were asked to think about long-term technological solutions offering magnitude environmental benefits. They were selected for their imagination and their position within industry because the programme wanted to influence the industrial research agenda. Many of the industry people were research directors. In total, 25 million guilders (€11.3 million) were spent under the programme by the Dutch government. The financial contribution from industry was low, about 10% of the costs of the illustration projects, in the form of money and time. The DTO programme led to the development and articulation of 14 illustration processes for sustainability.

The project was successful in tapping into the participants' imagination and led to ideas for system innovation and networks of collaboration but failed to influence industry's research agenda in a significant way for the simple reason that the technologies were not economical. Their use would require a change in the frame conditions, giving the sustainable technologies a competitive edge. A five-million-guilder (€2.3 million) programme of knowledge transfer called DTO-KOV followed the first programme but again did not address the root problem of unfavourable frame conditions. The absence of a pull mechanism frustrated the further development of these technologies and the creation of new systems.

A programme that was very successful in terms of the immediate utilization of the results is the Danish Clean Technology Development Programme, described in Georg, Røpke and Jørgensen (1992). Under the programme, industries and private and semi-governmental research institutions could apply for financial aid for developing and implementing clean technology. The programme was oriented toward stimulating preventive process solutions and cooperation among technology suppliers, research institutes, consultancy firms and users. The Danish Environmental Protection Agency played an active role in selecting environmentally beneficial projects and in finding the right partner with whom to cooperate. That is, the agency acted as a "matchmaker" to elicit environmentally innovative solutions, something that previous subsidy programmes had failed to do.[4] According to the authors, the Danish programme was a success. In almost all cases, appropriate technical solutions were found for the environment problems at hand. In more than half of the projects, substantial environmental improvements were achieved at low costs. Some projects led to net economic gains for the polluting firms.

Suggestions for a better innovation policy for the environment

The above examples show that the experiences of innovation policy in promoting innovation for the environment are mixed. Two key considerations for innovation policy are (behavioural) additionality of support and utilization of results. One way of making sure that the results will be utilized is by funding projects that are close to the market or by reducing the government share of support for projects that are economically less viable and environmentally less beneficial. Many countries have followed this road. But this disadvantages projects for which no market yet exists, as is often the case for environmental innovations.

The additionality of support for projects most likely to be economical may also be low. There is a conflict between achieving greater additionality of support and commerciality of the results. The former suggests the support of high-risk, high-reward projects that are unlikely to produce immediate results, the latter just the opposite. This suggests the use of programmes for both types of projects. Nowadays most developed countries have programmes for environmental technologies and sometimes clean technology. Few countries have programmes for "factor 10 innovations" (or even factor 20 solutions).[5] The Netherlands is an exception, although the programmes are very technology-oriented.[6] Support for radical innovations, clean technology and environmental technologies is probably best organized through separate programmes. It is hard to factor in environmental criteria in normal research programmes because it is hard for evaluators to assess the environmental merits ex ante.[7]

There is also a need for a more integrated innovation policy for the environment in order to increase the usefulness of innovation research and support policies. There are several ways to do this. First, innovation policy for the environment could be targeted to areas in which innovation is needed. Innovation support could also be informed by sustainability agendas and by transition agendas in which the sustainability goals are translated into specific policy goals.[8] Countries without transition agendas could set up task forces to this end.

Second, the experiences with the Dutch programme for sustainable technologies (DTO) suggest that there is a need for support programmes that go beyond the support of research. There really is a need for programmes for system innovation, such as integrated mobility or industrial ecology, to explore visions of sustainability through research and the real use of new technologies in society. Such support programmes should be time-limited and flexible to prevent the creation of "white elephants".[9] System innovation in the socio-technical realm involves changes in socio-technical systems beyond a change in (technical) components. It is associated with new linkages, new knowledge, different rules and roles, new guiding principles and a new logic of appropriateness, and sometimes new organizations. System innovation usually consists of a combination of new and old components and may even consist of a novel combination of old components, as in the case of industrial ecology – the closing of material streams through the use of waste output from one company by another.[10]

It is important to have programmes for system innovation because system innovation may provide factor 10 improvements in environmental impact compared to the factor 2 improvements associated with incremental changes or factor 5 improvements connected with partial system design (Weterings et al. 1997). System innovation is not style about environmental innovation but about system changes offering environmental benefits alongside other types of benefits – economic and social – although there may be trade-offs, especially in the early phases.

Third, more attention should be paid to the hazards and negative side effects of new technologies for the environment and society at large. Part of the budget for innovation support could be earmarked for environmental assessment or, more generally, technology assessment. The share does not have to be high; 1% could already suffice (Angerer 2002).[11]

Fourth, apart from the support for demonstration projects there should be programmes for technology experimentation. Sustainability requires experimentation. The primary goal of experiments should be to learn: about the product but also about the sustainability effects. Technology experimentation is an important element of programmes for system innovation. Such programmes should be more than demonstration cases and aim at increasing learning. Analysing eight experiments with sustainable transport, Hoogma et al. (2002) found that more could have been learned if the experiments had been set up with the objective of generating learning. Most of the learning was of a technical nature, the projects were largely self-contained, and hardly stimulated second-order learning. As a result, the experiments contributed little in facilitating co-evolutionary processes involving social change (Hoogma et al. 2002).[12] With one exception, they were not undertaken from a long-term sustainability vision, to be explored through a series of experiments.

Fifth, environmental policy should be more oriented to innovation. Environmental authorities (regulators and permitters) should take stock of innovation possibilities and provide incentives for the exploitation of such possibilities. Innovation research findings about possibilities to deal with environmental problems could be used for setting long-term emission limits – to create a market for new environmental solutions. Ashford (1994) has argued for a technology options analysis for environmental policy and technology-forcing standards. A challenging environmental policy can certainly promote innovation. The disadvantage is that such policies can be disruptive, compromise quality or result in additional economic costs. For example, the use of catalytic converters in response to regulation led to an increase in fuel consumption of as much as seven miles per gallon in 1981 (White 1982), whereas the converters themselves were ineffective at low temperatures, which meant that they were ineffective for short trips. The superiority of market-based instruments in pulling innovation still needs to be demonstrated – which is one reason why they should be used, apart from the efficiency gains associated with their use.

The innovation effects of environmental policy

There is much talk about the inadequacies of environmental policies. Past policies can be criticized for failing to realize environmental goals, being overly expensive for the private sector and failing to encourage innovation and dynamic efficiency. Kemp (1997) cites several examples of environmental policies that stimulated innovation, but the common technology response is that of focusing on end-of-pipe solutions and incremental process changes with limited environmental gains. Several harmful substances have been eliminated through product substitution but there are few examples of radical product or process change in response to environmental policy.

This raises the question: why did the policies fail to promote more radical innovation and dynamic efficiency? One explanation – well-recognized in economic literature – is the capture of government policies by special interests. Concretely, this means that firms influence the design and implementation of regulations to which they are subjected. A second, complementary, explanation is that regulations are often based on available solutions which may stifle innovation. Successful attempts to stimulate environmental innovation include programmes to phase out PCBs, eliminate the use of lead in gasoline and the removal of CFC through substitution by HCFCs and HFCs. There have also been innovations in end-of-pipe technology and in products such as ecologically benign detergents, paints and cars. However, on the whole, environmental policy has been too unchallenging to generate systemic innovative responses.

Also, new policy instruments such as innovation waivers and environmental covenants have failed to bring about innovative solutions (Kemp 2000). Probably more could have been achieved through better-designed instruments. Much will depend on the level of the economic incentive and the barriers to innovation (especially market barriers to outsiders). That incentive-based policies will bring forth innovative responses has been questioned (Burtraw 2000; Christensen 2001; Kemp 1997). One way to stimulate technological innovation is through R&D programmes for environmental technologies or more environmentally benign energy technologies. However, with R&D support there is always the danger that the programmes promote second-rate technologies and provide windfall gains to the recipients. For example, 64% of the projects funded under the German BMBF research programme for environmental research and environmental technology fall under this category. In the Netherlands, investment subsidies for environmental investments granted under the WIR (Wet Investeringsregeling) induced only 8% of the companies to undertake investments they would not have done otherwise (Kemp 1997: 25).

Another strategy is to specify strict environmental standards that require the development of new technologies. This should be done only in situations where the environmental risks are large and acute and when there is consensus about the most viable technological solution or trajectory. Otherwise there is a danger that technology-forcing standards lock industry into overly expensive and sub-optimal technical solutions. In such circumstances there is a need for further research and experimentation to learn about the technological possibilities and their advantages and disadvantages both in terms of economic and social benefits and environmental gains. When using direct regulation, policymakers should pay careful attention to the actual design of standards: their strictness, differentiation, timing, administration, flexibility and enforcement. The experience of the United States with innovation waivers and tradeable permits (described in Hahn 1989) illustrates that the ways in which instruments are designed and implemented are important determinants of the technological response from the industry. The American experience confirms the need for a balance between certainty, stringency and flexibility.

Technology compacts (covenants about innovation), described in Banks and Heaton (1995), appear useful for promoting technological innovation by setting an agenda of phased increments of technological change. But there is the danger of strategic behaviour on the part of industry that may claim that it is impossible to develop technology that is both environmentally superior and economically feasible.

To maximize the chances of success, policy instruments should be combined to generate synergistic effects (Blazejczak et al. 1999; Feitelson et al. 2001; Norberg-Böhm 1999; OECD 2000; Kemp 1997). A combination of standards with economic instruments is particularly useful as it combines effectiveness with efficiency. Automobile fuel economy standards in the United States set progressive fuel economy targets for automobile manufacturers in the 1979–1985 period, generating environmental effectiveness and economic efficiency (Greene 1990). Tradeable pollution permits also combine effectiveness with efficiency and should therefore be used more. Currently, a nationwide market exists for sulphur dioxide (SO_2) in the United States where utilities can trade SO_2 rights at the Chicago Board of Trade. According to one evaluation, the tradeable permits for sulphur dioxide emissions reduced the costs of the 1990 acid rain programme by 55% (Ellerman et al. 2000, cited in Cramton 2000) but few patentable innovations emerged from it (Burtraw 2000).

There is a need for government authorities to *explicitly* focus on technical change (rather than implicitly through a change in the economic frame conditions) and to be concerned with institutional arrangements beyond the choice of policy instruments. Government has to act as a change agent for innovation. This requires different roles for policymakers: that of a sponsor, planner, regulator, matchmaker, alignment actor and a "creative game regulator".

There is also a need for policy to be oriented toward system innovation involving structural change as well as the development and diffusion of environmental technologies. This should be done in a forward-looking, reflexive manner. Conventional planning and implementation approaches are inadequate because of inherent rigidities, in particular the inability to respond to changed conditions or unanticipated problems. In general, planners should be focused on dynamics in technology and markets, bottom-up initiatives on new technology and systems for achieving long-term change that go beyond exercises aimed at a pale greening of existing systems. Policies should be used to stimulate changes, both incremental and radical, aimed at managing transitions to a sustainable steady state. For this, the model of transition management can be used.

Transition management

Transition management is an attempt to alter socio-technical trajectories. The focus is on trajectories of production and use of functional goods and services (energy, mobility, food, health care), but it can also be applied more widely to public decision-making and economy-wide changes. Sustainability benefits may for instance be achieved through a resource-efficient economy. Transition management is a form of process management against a group of goals set by society. It is developed as a model for working toward sustainability benefits through system changes. Society's problem-solving capabilities are mobilized and translated into a transition programme, which is legitimized through the political process.

It is *not* an attempt to steer society toward a predetermined outcome. Transition management joins with ongoing dynamics and builds on bottom-up initiatives around problems and solutions. Developments are *modulated* into directions that are viewed more desirable, with the desirability being defined and assessed as part of an ongoing process. Alternative developments are explored *besides* possibilities to improve the system. Transition management is based on a two-pronged strategy. It is oriented toward both system improvement (improvement of an existing trajectory) and system innovation (representing a new trajectory of development or transformation).

Important aspects of transition management are long-term goals for functional systems and the visions for meeting these goals. The long-term goals for functional systems are chosen by society, but the systems to satisfy these goals are not collectively chosen. For the systems to be developed or to occur, one relies on the outcomes of processes of variation and selection. In terms of coordination, one relies on markets and collective decision-making in terms of goals and programmes for system innovation.

Policy is adaptive and opts for small steps. Transition management is oriented toward achieving structural change in a stepwise manner. It differs from existing policy in the following sense:

- Long-term thinking (at least 25 years) as a framework for short-term policy;
- Visioning followed by actions and strategies for learning about the visions;
- Thinking in terms of more than one domain (multi-domain) and different scale levels (multi-level); how developments in one domain (level) gel with developments in other domains (levels); trying to change the strategic orientation of regime actors;
- A focus on learning and the use of a special learning philosophy of "learning-by-doing";

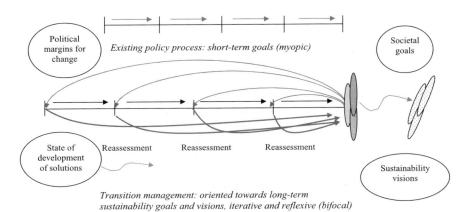

Figure 10.2 Current policy versus transition management

- Progammes for system innovation; and
- Learning about a variety of options (which requires a wide playing field). A simplified view of the difference between existing policy and transition management is given in figure 10.2.

Transition management does not constitute a total break. Many of the required elements for transition management already exist in some form. For instance, foresight activities are part of the policy-making process. What is new is that such activities are followed by coherent action by policymakers to learn about alternative futures on the basis of experiments and programmes for system innovation.

Transition management cycle

Transition management is a cyclical and iterative process. There are various cycles. One such cycle consists of four main activities: the establishment and further development of a transition arena for a specific transition theme; the development of long-term visions for sustainable development and of a common transition agenda; the initiation and execution of transition experiments; and the monitoring and evaluation of the transition process. These four activities are cyclically represented in figure 10.3.

A transition cycle takes about two to five years, depending on the practical context within which one has to operate. This transition management cycle will be described below in somewhat more detail.

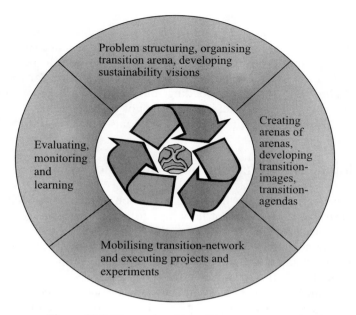

Figure 10.3 The cycle of transition management

Establishment, organization and development of a transition arena

A novel and important aspect of transition management is the establishment and organization of a transition arena in which innovators and visionaries meet. The transition arena is a place for imaginative thinking. It would operate besides (partly independent from) the normal policy-making networks dominated by incumbent actors having an interest in the status quo. The selection of participants for this transition arena is of vital importance. They should be open-minded visionaries and able to look beyond their own domain or working area. In addition, the participants must have the ability to convey the developed vision(s) and set it out within their own organization. The participants need to be willing to invest a substantial amount of time, energy and resources to play an active role in the transition arena process.

The government's task is to set up transition arenas and facilitate interactions within them both in terms of process and substance. A continuous process of feeding the participants in the arena with background information and detailed knowledge on a particular topic is necessary to catalyse and maintain a process of coproduction of knowledge among the participants. This is of vital importance, because arena experience shows that in most cases arena participants have insufficient resources to become fully immersed in the process. The arena is a novel institution for out-of-the-box thinking, with the results feeding into innovation decisions of organizations willing to innovate. The goal is not to strive for consensus but to discuss problem perceptions, long-term goals and transition paths.

Development of transition goals and visions

Transition management is based on transition goals about what is societally desirable and visions of how best to attain desirable goals. Functional systems provide useful entry points for beginning the process of transition management. Examples of possible entry points include energy as a reliable, cheap and clean commodity. The goal-setting process would be combined with the formulation of quality images, or visions of how the goals could be met. Quality images may be sector-specific or go beyond sectors. Decentralized energy production from renewable sources, clean coal and safe nuclear power are examples of the quality images for energy. An example of an economy-wide quality goal is eco-efficiency: less material use per unit of output resulting in less environmental impact. The quality image should be formulated in a stakeholder process. In outlining transitional pathways, transition visions must be appealing and imaginative so as to be supported by a broad range of actors. Inspiring final visions are useful for mobilizing social actors, although they should also be realistic about innovation levels and capabilities within the functional subsystem in question.

The goals and visions should be adapted in the course of time, reflecting new priorities, but may stay constant for a long time. New priorities may lead to different sustainability goals and visions and pathways to attain them. This is visualized in figure 10.4 in the form of a basket of quality images (goals), each of which is arrived at through a different path. In transition management each quality image is investigated while caution is taken not to allow one quality image to dominate the transition process. This approach maximizes system variation and leads to the selection of the most appropriate vision to attain goals based on the basket of quality images.

This evolutionary goal-seeking process represents a radical break from the current practices in environmental policymaking where quantitative standards are set on the basis of studies of social risk, and adjusted for

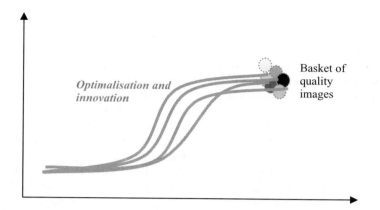

Figure 10.4 Transition as a goal-seeking process with multiple transition images and goals

political expediency. Risk-based target setting is doomed to fail when many issues are at stake and when the associated risks cannot easily be expressed as fixed, purely quantitative objectives. This holds true for climate change but also for sustainable transport.

Transition management thus differs from so-called "blueprint" thinking, which operates from a fixed notion of final goals and a dominant vision. Figure 10.4 shows the similarities and differences between current policymaking and transition management. In each case, interim objectives are used. However, in transition management these are derived from the long-term goals (through what is called "backcasting") and contain qualitative as well as semi-quantitative measures. Apart from content goals or objectives, transition management uses process objectives (speed and quality of the transition process) and learning objectives (what has been learned from the experiments carried out, what is blocking progress, identification of things we want to know). In transition management, learning is thus a policy objective in its own right.

Transition agenda

A transition agenda can be designed based on a shared problem and sustainability vision(s). A transition agenda contains common problem perceptions, goals, action points, projects and instruments. Of crucial importance is clarity on roles and responsibilities of the actors, including government and industry, where a significant portion of innovation activity takes place. The monitoring of this joint action programme is important to guarantee that the transition agenda is complied with. The transition agenda would be oriented to different trajectories reflecting actors' interests, competencies and beliefs about what is best or feasible.

An adequate transition agenda forms a binding element in the transition process. It coordinates action between mutually dependent actors. Coordination is thus achieved not only through markets but also through collective choice and new institutions. The transition agenda requires a balance between structure and flexibility. Structure is needed to position the scales and levels at which the issue in question is present, and to frame the issue in terms of themes and sub-themes. The coherence between the various sub-themes and scales/levels is a separate, important point on the transition agenda. Structuring the transition agenda is time-consuming but pays off in terms of increased quality in the transition management process (Dirven, Rotmans and Verkaik 2002). Flexibility is needed because by definition the transition agenda is dynamic and changes over time. The transition agenda helps to translate long-term thinking into short-term action. Agenda setting is an iterative and cyclical process that is a learning process in itself.

Use of transition experiments and programmes for system innovation

Programmes for system innovation are a key element of transition management. Here one should think of a programme for intermodal transport or decentralized electricity systems. The programmes should be time-limited and should be adapted in light of experience. Important elements of these programmes are transition experiments, strategic experiments based on system innovation and transition visions. The crucial point is to measure to what extent these experiments and projects contribute to the overall sustainability system goals, and to measure in what way a particular experiment reinforces another experiment. The aim is to create a portfolio of transition-experiments that reinforce each other and whose contribution to the sustainability objectives is significant and measurable.

Preferably these experiments need to link up with currently ongoing innovation projects and experiments in such a way that the existing energy put into these innovation experiments can be used as much as possible. Often, many experiments already exist, but these are not set up and executed in a systematic manner, as a result of which the required cohesion is lacking. Because transition experiments are often costly and time consuming, the current infrastructure for innovation experiments should be used as much as possible. This puts some constraints on the feasibility and running time of these experiments. The execution runs through the existing networks of the arena participants to ensure the direct involvement of these forerunners.

As noted before, the experiments are best undertaken as part of a portfolio approach. Because transition processes are beset with structural uncertainties, it is important to keep a number of options open and to explore the nature of these uncertainties through the transition experiments. Through experiments, useful lessons may be learned about technology, risks, user acceptance, distribution of costs and benefits and so on which will inform the next steps and lead to adjustments of the transition visions, images and goals. In this search and learning process scenarios play an important role, in particular explorative scenarios which attempt to explore future possibilities without too many decision-making constraints. Explorative scenarios allow for an exploration of which options and experiments are most promising and feasible, and which ones drop out. This leads to a necessary variation and selection of options, taking account of possible sustainable futures.

Monitoring and evaluation of the transition process

Transition management involves monitoring and evaluation as a regular and continuous activity. Two different processes should be monitored: the transition process itself and the cycle of transition management. The monitoring of the transition process itself consists of the monitoring of macro-developments in terms of the slow changes in stocks, of niche developments in terms of short-term fluctuations of streams, and of regime developments.

The monitoring of the transition management cycle consists of the monitoring of actors within (also "outside" the arena; just as important) the transition arena: their behaviour, networking activities, alliance forming and responsibilities with regard to activities, projects and instruments; the monitoring of the transition agenda: the actions, goals, projects and instruments agreed on; and the monitoring of the actions themselves: the barriers, prospects, points to be improved, etc.

The overall learning philosophy is that of "learning-by-doing". Monitoring learning processes, however, is easier said than done. The phenomenon of "learning" is for many still an abstract notion that cannot be easily translated into components for monitoring. It is therefore important to formulate explicit learning goals for transition experiments that can be monitored. It should also be recognized that the evaluation of the learning processes is in itself a learning process, and may lead to an adjustment of the developed transition vision(s), transition-agenda and the transition management process within the transition-arena. Failure to meet interim objectives is analysed to determine whether unexpected social developments or external factors not taken into account played a role, or whether the actors involved did not comply with the agreements. After the first cycle has ended, a new transition management cycle starts, which takes another few years. In the second round of this innovation network the proliferation of the required knowledge and insights is central, which requires a specific strategy for initiating a broad learning process.

Creating and maintaining public support

Because these transition management cycles take several years within a long-term context of 25 to 50 years, the creation and maintenance of public support is a continuous concern. When quick results do not materialize and setbacks are encountered, it is important to keep the transition process going and avoid a backlash. One way to achieve this is through participatory decision-making and the societal choice of goals. But societal support can also be created in a bottom-up manner, by engaging in experiences with technologies in areas in which there is local support. The experience may take away fears elsewhere and give proponents a weapon. With time, solutions may be found for the problems that limit wider application. Education too can allay fears, but real experience is probably a more effective strategy. Through the prudent learning on the use of new technologies in niches, societal opposition may be circumvented.

Case study: Transition management for sustainable mobility

This section applies the model of transition management to a sector for which the current development pattern is not sustainable: the individual use of gasoline and diesel cars. Problems related to car use consist of pollution, congestion, traffic accidents and noise. In the Netherlands, costs related to traffic accidents are estimated at 11.5 billion guilders (€5.2 billion). Pollution and traffic deaths have decreased but are still at levels viewed as too high. The societal costs of congestion increased by 70% during 1990–2000 and are estimated at 1.7 billion guilders (0.3% of GDP) (Ministry of Transport, Public Works and Water Management 1999). It proved extremely difficult to deal with these problems. Attempts to dissuade people from using cars failed. Automobility increased by 25% from 1986 to 1995 and is still growing. In the Netherlands, the government's attempt to introduce road pricing to use the infrastructure more efficiently failed because of social opposition. Recently an environmental advisory council (Vromraad) said that automobility should be accepted as a given. These problems are not unique – every country with high levels of car use suffers from the same problems, which may lead to the conclusions that there is no alternative. But things are not as hopeless as they may appear. It is certainly true that there are no immediate solutions and that we have to opt for a process of long-term change involving a multitude of innovations, technical ones and institutional ones, resulting in systems that offer attractive services for the users while limiting the social costs.

A real complication in this example is that there is no clear vision of sustainability. Every option has disadvantages. Instead of thinking of a single solution, one should think about a range of solutions that jointly create an attractive new transport concept, such as chain mobility. One needs to learn about alternative mobility, gain experience with it, and through this create a path that alters people's expectations and views, who may then commit themselves to support a new mode of transport. The articulation and assessment of visions of sustainability and transport should be done as part of a participatory integrated assessment process to evaluate the following (as well as other) options:

- *Customized mobility*: individualized public transport, the selective use of cars which are combined with other forms of transport (chain mobility);
- *Mobility management*: the management of traffic streams through road pricing, platooning (automatic vehicle management) information services, automatic zone access management using transponders to control access to city centres, parking policy, perhaps the use of tradeable kilometre credits where people get mobility rights that they can use or sell;
- *Cleaner cars*: low-emission internal combustion cars, electric vehicles (hybrid vehicles or full electric vehicles powered by batteries or fuel cells), urban cars, long-distance energy-efficient cars with gas turbines;
- *Underground transport*: this may take various forms including the radical option of vacuum pipes for transporting capsules;
- *Teleworking*: working from home or a local telecentre, using modern computer communication and teleconferencing, reducing the need for commuting but, as a rebound effect, possibly leading to increased travel outside work;
- *Spatial planning* limiting the need for transport: compact cities, the (re)location of office buildings close to (public) transport nodes; and
- *Regulation* that strongly favours and encourages customized mobility and discourages car use in specific zones.

The last four options have received much attention from public decision-makers. For sustainability, the first two options should receive more attention. I estimate the benefits from customized mobility roughly at a factor 5, compared to benefits of factor 2 and factor 2 to 4 associated with transport management and improved car-based forms of transport. Customized mobility involves many "innovations": in vehicle technology (such as urban cars and long-distance cars), changes in ownership, better public transport, mobility centres where individual users can change from one type of transport to another, and mobility agencies that supervise and manage fleets of cars, buses, and bicycles). In transition management, choice is not made among the available options. Rather, all options are explored simultaneously. This is particularly important as these options can reinforce and sustain one another: green vehicles can be used by car-sharing organizations and both high-speed trains and personalized forms of public transport promote chain mobility.

These ideas are not new and have appeared in numerous government publications. One of the main barriers to success is that policy is not oriented toward long-term visions but toward individual solutions.

How does a transition policy for sustainable mobility look? One important element is the choice of transition goals consistent with sustainability visions, such as customized mobility, mobility management and underground transport. The visions should be assessed and compared with each other. The public should be involved in such assessments because sustainable development is what people want as consumers and citizens for themselves and for later generations. The involvement of the public helps to legitimize programmes of structural change and circumvents destructive opposition (NIMBY ["not in my back yard"] problems). The involvement of the public in the setting of transition goals and discussions about future transport constitutes a big break with the past, when transport engineers decided about transport policy.

Secondly, given the uncertainty about what solutions are most sustainable, there should be experimentation with promising technologies and the creation of niches for promising technologies through strategic niche management. A key question of course is what technologies one should experiment with. According to the proponents of *Strategic Niche Management* (Hoogma et al. 2002; Kemp et al. 1998; Schot and Rip 1997), pathway technologies – technologies that help to bridge the gap between the current regime and a new (sustainable) one, and thus help to escape lock-in – should be supported. This is already well accepted in Dutch transport technology policy. The *Perspectievennota Verkeer en Vervoer*, outlining the government long-term transport strategy (Ministry of Transport, Public Works and Water Management 1999) in the Netherlands talks about "key technologies for system innovation"[13] and mentions electronic vehicle identification, automatic vehicle control, interoperability and a global positioning system as key technologies for system innovation. To these we would like to add: electric propulsion and transport information and booking and reservation systems. Both electric propulsion and transport telematics have great potential for achieving environmental sustainability benefits, especially in the long term when they are part of an integrated mobility system.

A short-term option is hybrid electric vehicles with batteries besides an internal combustion engine. A long-term electric option is fuel-cell vehicles. The fuel-cell vehicle is viewed as a magical environmental solution because it does not emit any pollutants, but it is expensive and there is also a safety issue with carrying substantial amounts of highly explosive hydrogen.

The experiments should be more than demonstration projects. They should be set up in such a way that both suppliers and users learn about new possibilities. Basic assumptions and existing expectations should be tested. Car manufacturers should be stimulated to rethink their assumptions about what a car should do while users should be stimulated to rethink their mobility needs and how to satisfy these. Of course there is always a chance that the supported technology turns out to be a no-go. Failures should be accepted and new options identified.

A third element of a transition policy for sustainable mobility is "programmes for system innovation". Candidate programmes are programmes for both chain mobility and electric mobility. Specific programmes are often met with criticism from, especially, economists, who say that the government cannot pick winners. The government programmes toward batteries for instance has been often criticized because it did not lead to the widespread use of battery vehicles. It contributed however to the use of hybrid vehicles, using batteries, and encouraged companies to investigate lightweight construction and aerodynamic designs. It did not lead to the development of a battery with a long range and low costs. Practicing transition management in this case means that attention should be refocused on hybrid vehicles and fuel-cell vehicles. But this does not mean the battery programmes were not valuable. The programmes should be based on promising options, they should be time-limited and the need for stimulation should be continuously assessed, and when the programme is not necessary or desirable it should be eliminated.

In innovation studies, it is well-recognized that in the early period of their development radical innovations need a lot of support: they hold promise but are still ill-developed in terms of user requirements. The user requirements and best configuration for meeting them may not yet be clear. This calls for the need to stimulate promise-requirement cycles and the attendant resource mobilization activities (Rip and Schot 1999), so as to build a forceful agenda (for development work in the technological niches) on which general interests appear in addition to (short-term) actors' interests. One should not rely altogether on the solutions favoured by established actors who are likely to be locked into old ways of thinking and have an interest in the status quo. The most innovative electric vehicles were developed outside the automobile industry (Hoogma et al. 2002).

A candidate programme is a programme for chain or customized mobility.[14] Chain mobility (or integrated mobility) makes positive contributions to all dimensions of sustainability. It reduces congestion and leads to lower emissions and fewer accidents by discouraging over-reliance on individual car use. At present there is a gap between individualized and collective transport, but various innovations may help to bridge the gap. These include:

- *Individual forms of collective transport.* These make public transport more flexible and more directly tied to the transport needs of the consumer. Examples are "dial-a-bus" and collective taxis (such as the Dutch "trein-taxis"), using information technology for route planning and vehicle tracking;
- *Collective use of private means of transport.* These include car sharing, bicycle sharing, ride-sharing (e.g., car-pooling), "stock-market" systems for sharing long-distance trips and voluntary schemes for transporting disabled or elderly people. The attractiveness of such systems increases with their size and the incorporation of other innovations such as smart cards for accessing cars and bicycles; and
- *Transit information systems and mobility information services.* Services to provide public information on how to combine different modes of transport. The existence of such information services may help different transport companies to better align their services and optimize the overall transport system.

The above innovations will help car drivers to move away from the single-vehicle-use paradigm and the individual use of cars. Integrated mobility requires new or modified infrastructure (transfer places), system reorganization (the creation of mobility agencies and cooperation between transport companies), technological change (in information and ticketing systems) and setting standards for interoperability.[15] Mobility is an area in which the Netherlands can achieve a great deal on its own because it is not dependent on foreign efforts to reduce their emissions under an international treaty and there are no competitive disadvantages involved because transport services are domestically provided by Dutch companies. Even the truck sector stands to benefit from it because chain mobility leads to a more efficient use of existing infrastructure.

Another vision of sustainability for transport that should be further explored is mobility management, the control of traffic streams. Road pricing is still controversial but differential pricing is widely in use in other areas, such as train fares and theatres, and accepted by the public. The recent experiment in London, England with imposing a surcharge on motorists travelling in the City's central zone should be observed closely for implications for other urban centres with traffic congestion problems.

The above actions should be pursued as part of transition agendas in which there are short-term learning goals and long-term transition goals and actions. The transition agenda for transport should not be dominated by transport engineers, individual car users, the automobile industry or public transport companies. There should be an orientation toward innovation and innovative actors. The agenda should be set through a consultative, discursive process and based on a commitment to change. This is probably best organized through the set up of a transition arena (Dirven, Rotmans and Verkaik 2002), a network of innovators willing to explore something new that could contribute to a transition, and the set up of a transition council with independent experts. The council should be forward-looking and safeguard the transition goals and transition process. It should be composed of policy actors (government, business, NGOs) and independent experts to oversee transition processes. The involvement of independent actors helps to prevent it from being dominated by vested interests. It is important to create a distance between the council and the government because the government is often a part of the problem and is ill-equipped to deal with innovation issues.

The transition endeavour should be institutionalized through transition agendas and the allocation of roles, tasks and responsibilities both for transition management in general and for customized mobility and mobility management. Local transport policy should be coordinated with national transport policy. National authorities should disseminate the lessons from experiences at the local level and make sure that there are many experiences. An important focus should be the introduction of mobility agencies and the cooperation between transport actors, in particular public transport companies, who could be asked to offer mobility services rather than a bus service or train service.

Transition management is not entirely concerned with consensus and does not rule out the use of control policies, such as standards and economic incentives. Both corrective- and push-policies are needed in managing transitions. The policies can be chosen and legitimized as part of the transition endeavour or independently from it. For example, the use of carbon dioxide taxes and other types of economic incentives can be legitimized by the economic principle of internalizing external costs.

Commitment to a transition may facilitate the introduction of such policies. Perhaps this is the reason for the Dutch government to adopt transition management as the steering model to work toward sustainability. Transition management can be used to achieve greater coherence in policy and in societal actions toward sustainability.

Conclusions

This chapter has looked at the experiences with innovation policy and environmental policy in bringing forth innovations for the environment, noting that current incentives for environmental innovations are weak.

Practical suggestions are offered both for innovation policy and for environmental policy to stimulate innovations for the environment. A case has been made for programmes for system innovation offering sustainability benefits, to complement existing programmes for environmental technology.[16] Programmes for system innovation offer environmental benefits alongside other types of benefits. Such programmes should be time-limited and flexible. Examples include programmes for novel protein foods as substitutes for meat, integrated mobility and industrial ecology.[17] Other possibilities include:

- Targeting innovation policy to areas in which innovation for the environment is needed;
- Conducting environmental assessment and broader system assessment;
- Supporting technology experiments for sustainability; and
- Embedding innovation policy in environmental policy.

This chapter has also described a policy model for managing the change process: transition management. The model has been developed by the author, Jan Rotmans and others and is being used in Dutch policymaking.[18] Transition management consists of a deliberate attempt to change socio-technical trajectories. It is aimed at utilizing and reorienting existing dynamics to attain transition goals as envisioned by society. The goals and policies to further the goals are constantly assessed and periodically adjusted in development rounds. Through its focus on the long term and its attention to system dynamics it aims to overcome the conflict between long-term necessities and short-term concerns.

The value of transition management is that it orients myopic actors to the future and to societal goals, creates societal support for a transition (resulting in a politically legitimized transition programme) and commits societal actors to change. Transition management provides a basis for coordination of public and private action. It does not fix a path but explores various options. It tries to modulate dynamics by exploring bottom-up initiatives in a strategic way. It adds a top-down element to bottom-up initiatives and is oriented toward learning and institutional change.

Transition management relies on social learning and on policy learning. The commitment to social learning is not a substitute for politics. Transition management starts from the premise that political disagreements over sustainability issues will remain for the foreseeable future. Rather than making a political argument for a specific solution, transition management promotes experimentation with available options to move in a societally determined direction to address a shared problem or set of problems. Managing transitions is certainly not something for government alone, society as a whole should be involved in the process in some way: as citizens choosing long-term goals, as consumers changing their habits, and as members of various social strata unified through a commitment to sustainability.

Reflexivity and learning are key elements since transition management is concerned with social trajectories in an open-ended manner – it is deliberative and adaptive, attaching great importance to learning and innovation. Blueprints are replaced with broad goals to be attained through linking ongoing dynamics and bottom-up initiatives. Transition management calls for taking advantage of ongoing developments to explore multiple visions and seek better choices. The model is being used for sustainable energy policies in the Netherlands but could also be used for managing the transition to sustainable mobility. Ways to do this are outlined in the chapter. It is believed that the model can also be used in other countries where a change in mobility patterns is needed.

Notes

1. The paper is based on "An Integrated Policy for Innovation for the Environment", presented at the six countries programme conference "Innovation Policy and Sustainable development: How can innovation policy incentives make a difference?", Brussels, 28 February and 1 March 2002. It is also based on joint work with Jan Rotmans and others for the Fourth Dutch National Environmental Policy plan (NMP-4). The paper benefited from discussions at the BLUEPRINT workshop environmental innovation systems on 23–24 January 2002, in Brussels. BLUEPRINT is a STRATA project funded by the European Commission analysing the possibilities for an integrated policy for environmental innovation. See http://www.blueprint-network.net.
2. It would be interesting to investigate the relative contribution of environmental technologies (technologies that are environmentally motivated) and normal technologies to environmental improvement for specific types of pollution. Energy saving in manufacturing has almost certainly more to do with energy prices than with energy covenants. Energy savings in consumer devices and housing owes probably more to energy efficiency regulations and subsidies coupled to energy labels. Greene (1990) tested the relative influence of energy prices and the CAFE fuel-economy standards on automobile fuel efficiency and found that the regulations were twice as important as energy prices.
3. The weak incentive for developing technologies with greater environmental efficiencies has to do with the fact that most regulations are based on existing technologies. Such

regulations provide no incentive to go beyond existing control efficiencies, they only provide an incentive to develop solutions that are less expensive than those in use.

4. The project was more than a subsidy programme. The programme brought together firms with an environmental problem and firms and research institutes that could provides solutions to these problems.

5. Factor 10 refers to a tenfold decrease in overall environmental impact. Factor X is more a concept which expresses an ambition than a quantitative measure because in reality it practically impossible to aggregate all environmental impacts into one measure.

6. A programme for sustainable technology that is less technology oriented is NIDO (Nationaal Initiatief Duurzame Ontwikkeling). NIDO is a programme that supports "jump projects", initiatives that offer sustainability benefits. It is less technology focused than DTO and EET and more oriented toward practical implementation. The NIDO budget for 2001 was €3.9 million. The private contribution to these projects was €1.6 million. Apart from supporting the programmes financially, NIDO helps participating parties with obtaining additional funds and the dissemination of knowledge. The small size of the projects and short period of support (two years) meant that for some projects (such as the shift to low-emission energy system or a different type of transport system), the support from NIDO was too little to have much of an impact.

7. This was noted by Ken Guy at the 6CP Conference, "Innovation Policy and Sustainable Development", held in Brussels on 28 February–1 March 2002.

8. Transition agendas are an element of transition management for sustainability, a concept explained later in this paper.

9. A related distinction is that between sustaining innovations and disrupting innovations (Christensen 1997).

10. Three other examples, described in Ashford et al. (2001) are: biomass-based chemistry, multiple sustainable land use (the integration of the agricultural function with other functions in rural areas) and flexible, modular manufactured construction.

11. This suggestion is made by Angerer in his paper for the BLUEPRINT workshop on environmental innovation systems. The paper can be downloaded from http://www.blueprint-network.net.

12. Co-evolution refers to processes that exercise mutual influence on each other by being part of each other's selection environment. The influence may be positive (mutualistic relationship) or negative (when two options compete or when one development's growth limits the growth of another).

13. Sleuteltechnologieën voor systeemvernieuwing.

14. The two things are strongly related. Chain mobility is an example of customized mobility that in the short term will consist of a different use of cars (which remain the dominant type of transport for a considerable time), not the use of integrated transport services. As chain mobility requires greater institutional change and changes in infrastructure than customized mobility, we suggest a programme for chain mobility rather than for customized mobility but the first could be pursued under the name of the latter.

15. As an aside, it is strange that in the Netherlands, the Perspectievennota Verkeer en Vervoer and the new national plan for traffic and transport (NVVP) do not make this a central topic for the whole of transport but merely mention it when talking about public transport.

16. Butter (2002) makes a similar plea for policies for system innovation, to be undertaken alongside policies for singular sustainable innovations and policies for enhancing the innovation climate.

17. The ultimate goal of industrial ecology is to close the loops in the system of production and eliminate waste.

18. See http://www.vrom.nl/pagina.html?id=10949 for details.

REFERENCES

Angerer, Gerhard (2002) "Orienting research policy to sustainability goals", paper for BLUEPRINT workshop "Environmental Innovation Systems", Brussels, Belgium, 23–24 January, available from http://www.blueprint-network.net.

Angerer, Gerhard, et al. (1997) Umwelttechnologie am Standort Deutschland. Der Ökologische un ökonomische Nutzen der Projektforderung des BMBF, Evaluation of Fraunhofer ISI. Heidelberg: Physica-Verlag.

Ashford, Nicholas A. (1994) "An Innovation-Based Strategy for the Environment", in Adam M. Finkel and Dominic Golding, eds., Worst Things First: The Debate over Risk-Based National Environmental Policies, Washington D.C.: Resources for the Future, 275–314.

———— (2001) "Government and Environmental Innovation in Europe and North American", paper presented at the "Towards Environmental Innovation Systems" conference, Garmisch Partenkirchen, Germany, 27–29 September.

———— (2002) "Environmental Transformation, Governance and Globalization", American Behavioral Scientist 45: 1417–1434.

Ashford, Nicholas A., Christine Ayers and Robert F. Stone (1985) "Using Regulation to Change the Market for Innovation", Harvard Environmental Law Review 9: 419–466.

Ashford, Nicholas A. and C. C. Caldart (2001) Pathways to Sustainable Industrial Transformation: Cooptimising Competitiveness, Employment and Environment, Cambridge, Mass.: Ashford Associates.

Ayres, R. U. and U. E. Simonis, eds. (1994) Industrial Metabolism, Tokyo: United Nations University Press.

Banks, D. R. and G. R. Heaton, Jr. (1995) "An Innovation-Driven Environmental Policy", Issues in Science and Technology, Fall.

Berkhout, Frans (2002) Response to William's paper for BLUEPRINT workshop "Environmental Innovation Systems", Brussels, Belgium, 23–24 January.

Blazejczak, J., D. Edler, J. Hemmelskamp and M. Jänicke (1999) "Environmental Policy and Innovation: An International Comparison of Policy Frameworks and Innovation Effects", in P. Klemmer, ed., Innovation Effects of Environmental Policy Instruments, Berlin: Analytica.

Burtraw, Dallas (2000) "Innovation under the Tradeable Sulphur Dioxide Emission Permits Programme in the US Electricity Sector", in OECD proceedings Innovation and the Environment, Paris: OECD, 63–84.

Butter, Maurits (2002) "A Three Layer Policy Approach for System Innovations", paper for BLUEPRINT workshop "Environmental Innovation Systems", Brussels, Belgium, 23–24 January.

Christensen, Clayton M. (1997) The Innovator's Dilemma: When New Technologies Cause Great Firms to Fail, Boston, Mass.: Harvard Business School Press.

Cramton, Peter (2000) "A Review of Markets for Clean Air: The US Acid Rain Programme by A. D. Ellerman, et al.", Journal of Economic Literature 38: 627–633.

Dirven, Jan, Jan Rotmans and Arie-Pieter Verkaik (2002) Society in transition: A new perspective, the Hague: InnovatieNetwerk Groene Ruimte en Agrocluster.

Feitelson, Eran, Ilan Salomon and Galit Cohen (2001) "From Policy Measures to Policy Packages: A Spatially, Temporally and Institutionally Differentiated Approach", in Eran Feitelson and Erik T. Verhoef, eds., Transport and the Environment: In Search of Sustainable Solutions, Cheltenham, England: Edward Elgar, 34–53.

Georg, S., I. Røpke and U. Jørgensen (1992) "Clean Technology-Innovation and Environmental Regulation", Environmental and Resource Economics 2(6): 533–550.

Greene, David L. (1990) "CAFE OR PRICE: An Analysis of Effects of Federal Fuel Economy Regulations and Gasoline Price on New Car MPG, 1978–89", Energy Journal 11(3): 37–57.

Hahn, R. W. (1989) "Economic Prescriptions for Environmental Problems: How the Patient Followed the Doctor's Orders", Journal of Economic Perspectives 3(2): 95–114.

Hoogma, Remco, R. Kemp, J. Schot and B. Truffer (2002) Experimenting for Sustainable Transport Futures. The Approach of Strategic Niche Management, London: EF&N Spon.

Jaffe, Adam B. and Robert N. Stavins (1990), "Evaluating the Relative Effectiveness of Economic Incentives and Direct Regulation for Environmental Protection: Impacts on the Diffusion of Technology", Paper for the WRI/OECD-Symposium Toward 2000: Environment, Technology and the New Century, 13–15 June, Annapolis, Maryland.

Kemp, R. (1997) Environmental Policy and Technical Change: A Comparison of the Technological Impact of Policy Instruments, Cheltenham: Edward Elgar.

——— (2000) "Technology and Environmental Policy: Innovation effects of past policies and suggestions for improvement", OECD proceedings Innovation and the Environment, Paris: OECD, 35–61.

Ministry of Transport, Public Works and Water Management (1999) "New national plan for traffic and transport (NVVP)", the Hague.

Norberg-Böhm, Vicki (1999) "Stimulating 'Green' Technological Innovation: An Analysis of Alternative Policy Mechanisms", Policy Sciences 32: 13–38.

OECD (2000) Innovation and the Environment, Paris: OECD.

Rip, A. and J. Schot (1999) "Anticipation on Contextualization: Loci for Influencing the Dynamics of Technological Development", in D. Sauer, and C. Lang (eds.) Paradoxien der Innovation: Perspektiven sozialwissenschaftlicher Innovationsforschung, Frankfurt/New York: Campus Verlag, 129–146.

Weterings, R., J. Kuijper and E. Smeets (1997) "Eighty-one possibilities of technology for sustainable develoment", final report of an environmental technology assessment commissioned by the Ministry of Housing, Physical Planning and the Environment (the Netherlands).

White, Lawrence J. (1982) "US Mobile Source Emissions Regulation: The Problems of Implementation", Policy Studies Journal 11: 77–88.

Williams, Robin and Nils Markusson (2002) "Knowledge and Environmental Innovation", paper for BLUEPRINT workshop "Environmental Innovation Systems", Brussels, Belgium, 23–24 January, available from http://www.blueprint-network.net.

11

Conclusion

Brent Herbert-Copley and Saeed Parto

The chapters in this book have approached the interplay between environmental regulation and innovation at the firm and policymaking levels from different perspectives, in different contexts and at different scales of analysis. Yap et al.'s study of environmental policymaking in Taiwan finds that public policy has played a key role in facilitating the move by many firms to cleaner production. The government used the "win-win" arguments *a la* Porter (1996) and adopted a carrot-and-stick approach, or what Yap et al. call "balancing the *yin* and *yang* forces", to motivate and steer firms toward meeting higher environmental protection standards. Over the course of its industrialization, Taiwan has managed to create the "right" types of formal institutions through which to effect change in firm behaviour. Furthermore, the government has demonstrated a capacity to be adaptive and take corrective structural measures to minimize environmental impacts of industrial activity. One such measure is the provision of technically trained civil servants who in turn train personnel from industrial firms in pollution-prevention techniques. A direct result of these efforts has been a relatively high degree of trust between the regulators and the regulated.

Yap et al.'s study of the evolution of environmental policymaking in Taiwan also underlines some important remaining challenges. For example, policymakers need to remain attuned to the fact that once the "low-hanging fruits" have been picked in moving toward cleaner production, firms will require additional incentives to incur costs aimed at further reducing their environmental impacts. Thus, innovation in environmental policymaking must be viewed as intimately linked with, and a key driver of, environmental innovation at the firm level. Much of the impetus for environmental innovation at the firm level will need to be provided through interactive policymaking and thoughtful structural adjustment aimed at closing the loop, in an industrial ecology sense (Graedel and Allenby 1995), in industrial production. While fully closing all the loops in any system of production remains but an ideal state to strive for, the systemic perspective offered by industrial ecology provides important clues as to where to look for the next batch of low-hanging fruits.

Based on a different level of analysis, Barton et al.'s sectoral study of the iron and steel industry in a multi-country setting finds that the adoption of new, less polluting process technologies has been due to seeking economic efficiency rather than being caused by environmental regulation. This sector is also characterized by its focus on reducing pollution through end-of-pipe solutions to minimize landfilling costs. In contrast to Yap et al.'s conclusions, Barton et al.'s findings raise an interesting question about the effectiveness of other policy tools besides regulations in promoting cleaner production. If economic disincentives such as higher dumping fees at landfill sites are consciously introduced through policy to discourage waste generation, one likely response by the industry is to innovate for waste minimization. Such innovation could occur at the end of the pipe, in the throughput processes, or in the input mix. Regardless of where the innovation occurs, there appears to be a relationship between rises in external costs of production (for example, higher landfilling fees, more expensive energy and water), the quest for economic efficiency and reduced pollution. Many external costs of production can be regulated through policy, providing policy makers with a range of incentives and disincentives to steer industrial activity toward cleaner production. But, as the authors demonstrate, the process does not end here.

Another important finding by Barton et al. is the export of pollution by pollution-intensive industries. The three sectors appear to have moved their most polluting segments from industrialized European countries to the less industrialized or transition countries where environmental policy, environmental regulations and regulatory enforcement are often less geared toward effective management of industrial pollution. Exporting pollution is a negative innovative response to internalizing environmental costs while raising consumer awareness so as to charge a higher premium for products with lower environmental impacts is a positive strategic innovation. In a sense, environmental regulation in industrialized European countries has resulted in market differentiation through emphasis on quality, a strategy pursued by the leather-tanning and the iron and steel industries to minimize competition from lower cost, foreign sources.

Responses to environmental regulation vary depending on the sector.

Barton et al. report that the powerful iron and steel interests in Europe have thus far managed to dissuade the European governments from imposing carbon or energy taxes so as to avoid higher production costs. In contrast, the tanning industry is fragmented and has only managed to exert influence at a national level in Italy where the sector is most organized. On a more positive note, Barton et al. report that there is also some encouraging evidence of environmental protection outside industrialized European countries. Some steel makers in Brazil and South Korea have been introducing equipment that incorporates the latest environmental technologies, making operations cleaner than their northern counterparts. This has been possible in part because it is more economical to incorporate environmental protection technologies in steel mills when they are being built than retrofitting the existing, often very old steel mills usually found in the industrialized north.

Based on their analysis, Barton et al. question the wisdom of the Porter (1991, 1996) "win-win" argument. Instead, what they find is that environmental regulation can cause significant shifts in sectoral distribution which has uncertain outcomes for competitiveness and environmental protection. Whether or not this shift leads to increased environmental protection very much depends on the industry, the country of operation and the power relationship between industry and government. Most importantly, these findings underline the importance of the scale, i.e., firm, sector or country, of analysis for win-win arguments.

Chudnovsky and Lopez find that both endogenous and exogenous factors contributed to improved environmental performance by the Argentinean firms. A process of fundamental restructuring in the late 1980s and early 1990s to liberalize the economy forced local firms to modernize in order to compete with the inflow of goods and services into Argentina. One outcome of this process was improvement in environmental management, an indicator for which is the increase in the number of firms certified to ISO 14001 from 9 in 1997 to around 350 in 2004. Another indicator is the increase in environmental expenditures that rose from approximately US$160 million in 1994 to US$480 million in 2000. Chudnovsky and Lopez suggest that in addition to domestic environmental regulation, Argentinean industry had to respond to exogenous pressures of the more tightly regulated markets in developed countries in order to compete. The formalization of environmental management through such measures as adopting ISO 14001 not only served as a marketing tool but also facilitated easier access to funds from foreign financial institutions.

The economic situation in Argentina has changed quite dramatically since the financial crisis in 2001. The projected trends based on pre-crisis data on environmental performance improvement and increased environmental innovation need to be adjusted for the new reconfigured economic environment. Nevertheless, the analysis by Chudnovsky and Lopez illustrates that innovation in pollution prevention is more diffused among large firms, particularly those with higher export sales and/or a higher foreign ownership component. This study shows that endogenous environmental innovation has been a by-product of cost-saving exercises. Environmental innovation has also been generally "simpler" among Argentinean firms compared to the more sophisticated pollution-prevention innovation evident in industrially more developed countries. This simplicity in innovation decreases with an increase in the firm size, however. As well, a direct relationship is established between more modern organizational management systems, a characteristic of larger and more established firms, and environmental innovation. The firms with established production control and quality management systems appear to have been the most innovative in developing and adopting pollution prevention technologies.

Chudnovsky and Lopez underline the importance of structural change in economy-wide environmental management. Undertaking structural change is at best difficult, and an incremental process even when backed by national policy and appropriately designed regulations and incentives. However, economies that are in a process of recovering from a period of turbulence have a significant advantage compared to other countries: the new economic structures can be designed and developed to incorporate many of the available pollution-prevention technologies with relative ease, paving the path to an ecologically modernized economy and moving closer to close the loop in the industrial production system consistent with the ideal of industrial ecology.

Herbert-Copley examined the response by the Canadian pulp and paper industry to new stringent environmental regulations introduced in the 1990s. The two-pronged approach employed by Herbert-Copley underlines the importance of adopting a systemic perspective on innovation to capture secondary process innovation in contrast to approaches that focus only on "new" product or process technologies developed largely endogenously by the firm. A key contribution of this perspective is the illumination on the role of institutional factors such as overlapping jurisdictional arrangements between the federal and provincial governments which collectively may have acted as deterrents to endogenous environmental innovation by firms.

The evidence provided in this analysis illustrates that there has been at least a partial transition (see Kemp and Parto et al., this volume) in the Canadian pulp and paper industry, despite the constraints of overlapping and often confusing jurisdictional arrangements on regulating the industry. Key events include the widespread media attention in 1987 and 1988 in response to the discovery of significant concentrations of dioxins in effluents from some paper mills in Ontario, and structural factors including the outmoded state of the sector have also contributed to this partial transition. One interesting characteristic of the partial transition is the difference in mix of adoption of the two main technologies in the pulp whitening process by the European and North American pulp and paper firms. During the 1990s the European pulp and paper industry largely opted for the totally chlorine-free (TCF) technology while the North American counterparts widely adopted elemental chlorine-free (ECF). The Europeans' environmentally superior technological transition may be attributed to the institutional dynamics that underpin the pulp and paper sector in Europe. An important characteristic of these dynamics is the central role played by associative institutions, e.g., environment and non-governmental organizations and industrial associations, in influencing the perception of key actors about the desirability of certain technologies. In Europe there was a stronger consumer influence forcing the adoption of the "cleaner" technology, i.e., TCF, whereas in Canada consumer influence was weaker and the influence of the sector's vested interests were stronger in shaping policy on eliminating dioxins and furans in effluent discharges from pulp and paper mills. These dynamics resulted in a higher proportion of ECF among the Canadian firms as the chosen technology than their European counterparts that mainly opted for TCF.

In his investigation of the dynamics, Herbert-Copley points out that there are relatively lower numbers of patents and employees in the Canadian sector compared to their counterparts in the United States and Scandinavia. He identifies low levels of intramural R&D spending and a weak domestic equipment manufacturing sector as potential constraints in the Canadian pulp and paper sector innovation system. Despite the existence of leading Canadian consulting companies specializing in design and engineering of pulp and paper mills, the tendency of the Canadian pulp and paper sector has been toward a continued application of imported abatement and control technologies coupled with incremental improvements in the efficiency of existing operations. The analysis of the secondary and primary data in this chapter suggests that regardless of numerous constraints, environmental regulations in Canada have spurred a significant wave of investment by the pulp and paper sector, albeit with a bias toward end-of-pipe technologies. A significant number of firms have also implemented in-plant changes to improve efficiency and, perhaps unintentionally, environmental management.

The picture that emerges from this analysis suggests that environmental regulations have not resulted in the development of innovative new solutions by Canadian pulp and paper mills or domestic equipment suppliers but have spurred the diffusion of proven technologies. While this diffusion is a necessary condition for a full transition comparable to one that has already occurred in the European pulp and paper sector, radical innovation is unlikely to occur in response to "better" policy measures because of the weakness of the pulp equipment manufacturing base. One possible solution suggested by Herbert-Copley is to shift the focus in policymaking from environmental regulations as a catalyst to environmental innovation, to innovation policy that facilitates adaptive R&D investments by the industry.

Gallagher's study of the Mexican economy underlines the role of structural change in determining the overall environmental impact of industrial activity. Since 1985, numerous industries from different countries have moved operations to Mexico to take advantage of abundant labour at low cost. Industrial assembly plants are best suited for the Mexican labour market because these plants rely heavily on a steady supply of unskilled labour at low cost. The adverse environmental impact of labour-intensive industrial assembly is significantly lower than capital-intensive operations such as steel or cement making. In addition, labour-intensive operations are cheaper to relocate than capital-intensive operations.

Gallagher points out that the restructuring of the Mexican economy and the increase in industrial output has not been matched proportionately with higher environmental impact, although environmental pollution has increased drastically since 1985. This mismatch is due to the contraction of capital-intensive sectors since 1985 while labour-intensive operations have expanded. Gallagher identifies a number of explanations for increased environmental deterioration. First, in contrast to Taiwan, Mexico did not put into place proper environmental management mechanisms including competence building, incentives and disincentives, knowledge diffusion and effective regulatory enforcement structures. There was, and remains, a significant implementation gap between formal policy and actual environmental protection at the firm level. To top this all and paradoxically, the federal budget for environmental protection of a few million dollars is literally dwarfed by the estimated US$36 billion cost to fix the environmental degradation that resulted from years of policy and budgetary neglect.

There have been innovative moves by the Mexican authorities to attend to the problem of industrial pollution. A recent development is the introduction of an incentive programme (FIPREV) to encourage firms to be audited for environmental management. The audit findings would then serve as the first step in a collaborative programme between the government and the audited firm to work out how best to address the firm's specific environmental problems and needs. Gallagher views such arrangements as key to resolving the paradox of industrialization and pollution prevention since the case of Mexico shows that technological change and environmental improvements will not automatically come with or follow economic integration. Building on the FIPREV initiative, Mexico could begin to build the necessary competence and systems of incentives, knowledge dissemination and regulatory enforcement.

Mexico is endowed with certain necessary prerequisites for successful environmental and innovation policy-making. The prerequisites include well-defined environmental regulations (though poorly enforced) based closely on the American model. In addition, Mexico is in close proximity to the United States and Canada as two advanced industrial economies and trading partners through NAFTA. NAFTA's trade rules and protocols require meeting certain environmental standards as a precondition for NAFTA-wide market access.

Adeoti's analysis of environmental policy-making in Nigeria underlines a sharp contrast between Nigeria and Mexico. Adeoti points out the importance of a structural foundation and appropriate institutional context for policy formation and implementation in general and for environmental protection in particular. His main conclusion is that in developing countries where environmental regulations are relatively weak and poorly enforced, "third party" factors can and do provide additional influences on how firms manage environmental impacts. Third-party factors include community pressure, influence of public corporations affected by pollution from industrial activity in the policymaking arena, influence of ENGOs, availability of environmental technology through local suppliers and availability of technology and best management practices through transnational parent companies.

Adeoti's study focuses on two key sectors of the Nigerian economy, namely, food processing and textiles. The sectors use substantial amounts of water as production input and generate high levels of wastewater. As a result, the sectors are relatively highly regulated under Nigerian legislation. Adeoti also points out that third-party factors often find ways and means of working with a regulatory framework, regardless of whether or not environmental regulations are effectively enforced. However, third-party factors cannot act as catalysts of positive change in environmental performance or environmental innovation without the support of formal legislative measures. In developing countries such as Nigeria, with weak structural foundation and inadequate institutional context, innovation policymaking must recognize the potentially key role played by third-party sources and tap into the knowledge provided by them.

Yarime's analysis of the transition in the Japanese chlor-alkali industry from the diaphragm technology to ion membrane process technology underlines the role of uncertainty in environmental policymaking when faced with serious environmental problems. In contrast to Nigeria, Japan is endowed with well-developed institutions and a mature structural foundation. However, this endowment was not sufficient to yield a timely and adequate response to the disastrous mercury contamination problem in Minamata Bay in 1956. The Japanese policymakers and firms had to collectively experiment with alternative approaches and technologies before deciding on the most appropriate solution. Yarime's chapter examines the co-evolution of the Japanese chlor-alkali industry and its regulatory arena since the mid-1950s. The Japanese government introduced stringent environmental regulations in the 1970s to stop the mercury contamination traced to the chlor-alkali industry. In a top-down manner, a newly appointed Countermeasures Council demanded that the industry install a closed effluent system to contain mercury by the end of 1974.

Initially, the government demanded that all chlor-alkali production had to adopt the "diaphragm process", the only available alternative technology at the time. However, once adopted, the diaphragm process proved to be uneconomic and producing inferior-quality product. The government's objective of safeguarding public health and the industry's concern about costs and loss of market share were clearly not being resolved adequately. Further investigation and experimentation with other technologies needed to be undertaken. The alternative technology was identified as the ion exchange membrane. The idea of using ion exchange membranes in the chlor-alkali process was not new and had been the subject of extensive research and development since the 1950s. The government's decision to fully eliminate the mercury process in the 1970s provided the necessary impetus for more concentrated and collaborative R&D activities into alternatives to the mercury process. Given the problems with the diaphragm process, the government responded to these developments by taking the initiative to examine the viability of each of the potential alternative technologies. The main criteria for the final selection included economic viability, quality of the end product and the time required to fully develop the technology. The government committed that R&D into alternative technologies for the chlor-alkali industry needed to be observed for two years before a decision was made on how to proceed with choosing the appropriate technology to replace the diaphragm process.

The approach adopted by the Japanese government to address the serious mercury contamination problem had two distinct phases. Due to the severity of the mercury contamination problem, the first phase was very much one of command and control. In the second phase, and perhaps "learning" from experience, the government adopted an approach to policymaking best described as deliberative or interactive. The approach was also consistent with ideal type approaches in policymaking to serve sustainable development in that every attempt was made to integrate environmental, economic and social needs through policy. Another important feature of the second phase in the transition from the mercury process to the ion membrane process technology is the interplay between innovation in policymaking and innovation by firms in a positive feedback loop. The industry has now reached a new state of stability following the elimination of the mercury process completely by 1986 and adoption of the ion membrane process technology by 95% of the firms by 2000. The remaining 5% of the firms are in the process of moving from the diaphragm process to the ion membrane process technology.

Yarime's analysis demonstrates that the transition from the mercury process technology to the ion exchange membrane technology began with the emergence of an acute environmental and health problem. Deliberative policymaking was successful in making good the mistakes of the first reactive decision by the policy makers to eliminate the mercury process. Through learning from experience and collaboration, policymakers were able to eliminate the problem at a later stage and steer the industry to adopt a technology that later was to become a competitive advantage.

Firms have different capacities to meet regulatory requirements depending on size and industry type, among other factors. Firms are also diverse in how they are motivated to protect the environment – there are those that do it willingly and those that need to be coerced through regulation or other (dis)incentives to change behaviour. Because of these differences among firms, providing impetus for innovation is far more complex than generally thought in mainstream economics and in the majority of policymaking circles. In some cases, recognition of this complexity has resulted in the emergence of what Gunningham calls "second-generation regulation" whereby the mix of instruments for environmental protection is very much determined by the context in which firms operate. In second-generation regulation there is shared awareness of environmental problems and there is trust between the regulator and the regulated. When environmental problems are not shared or are continually contested and there is diminished trust among the main proponents, it may be more appropriate to resort to formal regulation and persistent enforcement.

Innovative policymaking as described by Gunningham relies on the use of a variety of instruments, including voluntary initiatives, depending on the target firms and the larger context of economic activity. Policymaking flexibility through the use of multiple instruments as suggested by Gunningham is more conducive to experimentation, adaptation and hence innovation in finding solutions. If the policy intent is to initiate the emergence of an environmental innovation system, regulatory measures (comprising a variety of instruments) have to be designed in such a way as to spur innovative activity among the target firms. The maintenance of the system would very much depend on how technical, procedural and other information is gathered, processed and diffused to strengthen the system and ensure that it persists over the long term.

Gunningham's systemic perspective is shared by Kemp in his study of sustainable mobility. In making his case for transition management Kemp calls for "system innovation" as an explicit objective in environmental policymaking. By definition, system innovation goes beyond changes in technical components, e.g., end-of-pipe technologies, to establish new linkages, generate new knowledge and institute new rules, roles and organizations as the breeding ground for innovation in general and environmental innovation in particular. Rather than being imposed from above, system innovation combines new and old components and methods to close the loop in industrial production and to strive toward an industrial ecology. Other elements of transition management include mechanisms for the assessment of all new and emerging technologies for their environmental impact, mechanisms for the assessment of environmental policies for their innovation content, and elaborate programmes for technology experimentation so as to generate learning.

Parto et al. also employ a transition perspective in their analysis of the policy and practice in waste management in the Netherlands. Focusing on the role of formal and informal institutions, Parto et al. identify two qualitatively different transitions, the first from a largely self-organizing arena to a government-controlled one and the second from centralized waste disposal to centralized waste management. The overview of the subsystem also reveals that a third transition may have started in the early 1990s. Major catalysing events responsible for the latest turbulence in the subsystem include new European Union directives on waste management, significant drops in the total volume of non-separated household waste from the peak 1995 level, liberalization of the national waste market and integration into the EU market, and the availability of landfill site space in the former Eastern bloc countries as cheap alternatives to highly regulated and expensive landfill sites in most EU15 member states.

The regulation and evolution of the waste subsystem led to a series of innovations and technology adoptions/adaptations. For example, incineration was and remains a major final stage in the official waste hierarchy. Structural reliance on incineration catalysed the emergence of new technologies throughout the incineration process, from input separation and preparation techniques through to burning methods and the treatment of outputs. Some of these changes to the incineration process were based on technologies borrowed from other sectors while some were specific to the incineration process. Cleaner emissions and effective fly ash collection systems were products of this innovation process. However, key to the evolution of the Dutch waste subsystem is not technology adoption per se but the policy environment and innovativeness in policymaking, which appear to have led to innovation at the operational (firm) level.

The basic components of transition management are: the establishment of a transition arena; development of transition goals and visions; transition agenda; transition experiments and programmes for system innovation; monitoring and evaluation mechanisms of the transition process; and creating and maintaining public support. In short, transition management as described by Parto et al. and Kemp is concerned with conscious and conscientious efforts to steer sociotechnical trajectories toward a more sustainable, though not predetermined, future by nurturing innovation. The means for intervention to steer trajectories are not predefined but emerge based on outcomes of processes of variation and selection. As such, the selection of the means to steer relies on markets and collective decision-making to ensure the desirability and viability of outcomes.

Kemp applies the transition management model to the case of transportation based on gasoline- and diesel-powered individual vehicles. He argues that the adoption of the model in policymaking could make significant strides toward more sustainable transportation systems since many of the ingredients of such a system already exist. These include customized mobility based on a change of behaviour by users, incentives aimed at steering user choice of transportation mode, cleaner technology in cars, new public transportation infrastructure – such as underground systems, virtual-office arrangements eliminating the need to travel to work, ecologically conscious urban planning and regulations. Kemp concludes that these options have not been pursued equally, as elaborated in transition management, and thus potential synergies may not have been fully realized.

The chapters in this book raise several key questions and provide some insights into the interplay between environmental regulation, innovation as a process and a policy objective and the implications for integrated policymaking to simultaneously protect the environment and improve economic performance through increased innovative activity. All these case studies clearly indicate that regardless of the structural and institutional context, governments need to play a key role as the largest and most organized formal institution to facilitate environmental innovation through legislation *and* the use of other incentives. The extent and nature of intervention depends on the quality of interrelations between the regulators and the regulated, the magnitude and urgency of the problem at hand, and the structural and institutional context in which problems exist.

Arguably, it is operationally easier for an industrializing country like Taiwan to take advantage of the best available environmental technologies in a process of structured modernization. It is much harder for industrialized countries with older industries to make significant or radical structural change as high costs of retrofitting or physical replacement of old production systems render these options in most cases unfeasible, at least in the short term. This does not mean that industrialized countries should stop the search for innovative ways of eliminating or minimizing the environmental impact of their industrial activities.

The difference between industrialized and industrializing countries in their ability to effect ecological modernization raises questions about the universal validity of Porter's win-win argument – the validity of the argument depends very much on the context. For many older industries it is not economically feasible to fully meet high environmental management standards without structural and financial assistance. In an era of uneven labour and environmental standards across countries, particularly between the north and the south, and with the emphasis on cost competitiveness, there is a constant temptation for larger and more polluting industries to migrate to the south. However, the tendency to migrate, driven by rent-seeking firms, provides unique opportunities for the spread of best practices and technologies in environmental management. A central and necessary ingredient for taking advantage of these opportunities is, of course, an institutional will and political commitment to prioritize environmental protection in all manners of activity, from policymaking at the firm level to discussions of ecological well-being and sustainable development in various international forums.

REFERENCES

Graedel, T. E., and B. R. Allenby, eds. (1995) Industrial ecology, New Jersey: Prentice Hall.

Porter, Michael E. (1991) The Competitive Advantage of Nations, New York: The Free Press.

Porter, Michael E. (1996) "What is Strategy?", Harvard Business Review 74(6): 61–78.

Index